DECISION SUPPORT SYSTEMS
Putting Theory into Practice

SECOND EDITION

edited by

Ralph H. Sprague, Jr.

THE UNIVERSITY OF HAWAII

Hugh J. Watson

THE UNIVERSITY OF GEORGIA

PRENTICE HALL, Englewood Cliffs, New Jersey 07632

Library of Congress Cataloging-in-Publication Data

Decision support systems : putting theory into practice / edited by
  Ralph H. Sprague, Jr., Hugh J. Watson. -- 2nd ed.
      p.   cm.
  Bibliography: p.
  Includes index.
  ISBN 0-13-199035-7
    1. Management--Data processing. 2. Decision support systems.
I. Sprague, Ralph H. II. Watson, Hugh J.
HD30.23.D43 1989
658.4'03'0285--dc20   89-3970
                                                        CIP

Editorial/production supervision and
    interior design by Anne Pietropinto
Cover by Wanda Lubelska Design
Manufacturing Buyer: Laura Crossland

Printed in the United States of America
10 9 8 7 6 5 4 3 2

ISBN   0-13-199035-7

Prentice-Hall International (UK) Limited, *London*
Prentice-Hall of Australia Pty. Limited. *Sydney*
Prentice-Hall Canada Inc., *Toronto*
Prentice-Hall Hispanoamericana S.A., *Mexico*
Prentice-Hall of India Private Limited, *New Delhi*
Prentice-Hall of Japan, Inc., *Tokyo*
Simon & Schuster Asia Pte. Ltd., *Singapore*
Editora Prentice-Hall do Brasil, Ltda., *Rio de Janeiro*

To Hawaii's beach-front benches

Contents

Preface

There have been significant developments in the field of decision support systems (DSS) during the past few years. The technology is changing rapidly, and the way companies are organizing to build and use DSS is also changing. Because of these rapid changes, there has been an abundance of news articles, conferences, seminars, and journal articles describing the advancement of DSS. Unfortunately for students and faculty, many of these resources are not readily available in the formal literature. News articles are brief and sketchy, conference proceedings are expensive and not widely circulated, seminars are seldom documented, and carefully prepared journal articles frequently require several years to come into print.

We have prepared this book specifically to deal with this problem. Articles from the trade literature and conference proceedings have been chosen and organized to characterize recent developments in DSS. We have specifically sought out readings that give life to the theory and concepts of DSS in order to enrich the understanding and learning of students.

In addition, we have provided several valuable resources. A listing of DSS software vendors that have special prices for educational institutions is provided. This listing also summarizes the features of the vendors' DSS products. The cross-referenced bibliography will help students and faculty who wish to pursue some areas of DSS in more depth.

THE USE OF THE BOOK

This book can be used in several ways:

As the main text in a DSS course. Many DSS courses include hands-on DSS building experiences with software products such as IFPS. The book of readings would be appropriate as the main text in a course that takes this approach. It would also be useful in those courses that are based on current literature alone.

As a supplementary text in a DSS course. The book of readings could be used with another DSS text to provide broader DSS perspective. The readings are especially complementary to Sprague and Carlson's *Building Effective Decision Support Systems* (Prentice Hall, 1982).

As a supplementary text in an MIS course. Many management information systems textbooks devote only a single chapter to DSS. This book of readings could be used to provide enhanced DSS coverage.

CHANGES TO THE SECOND EDITION

In this second edition we have continued the philosophy of drawing on the best literature to provide an up-to-date treatment of this dynamic field. The overall result is an expansion of readings from twenty to twenty-six, of which fifteen are new. We also paid particular attention to comprehensive coverage of the DSS field. In several cases, we have sought out the best authors in an important topic and commissioned a selection for this book. "Group Decision Support Systems" by Gray and Nunamaker and "Model Management Systems" by Blanning are examples. "Evolving Technology for Document-Based DSS" by Fedorowicz, and "A Comparison of Executive Information Systems, DSS, and Management Information Systems" by Turban and Schaeffer are two others.

In addition to comprehensive coverage, we have tried to provide a consistency of style and philosophy that is uncommon in readings books. In fact, more than half of the readings were authored, coauthored, or commissioned by us. This is not just bias on our part, but a desire to provide the consistency and coverage that allow the book to be used as a primary text on the subject.

We wish to draw special attention to the new Part 5, "The Evolving DSS Domain." It is clear that DSS is growing to encompass new areas such as group DSS, executive information systems, and expert systems. The six papers in this section indicate how we think this evolution is progressing.

ACKNOWLEDGMENTS

We would like to express our appreciation to the authors of the selections in this book, especially those who were gracious enough to accommodate our suggested changes, and to the publishers of the articles for allowing us to reprint them. Also, we would like to thank Pam Howell for secretarial assistance in the development of the book.

Ralph H. Sprague, Jr.
Hugh J. Watson

Introduction to Decision Support Systems: Putting Theory into Practice

It seems that new topics in information systems are introduced with grandiose promise, only to fall back to a limited and somewhat mundane role. The academics and visionaries develop a theoretical definition; the practitioners understand only pragmatic solutions. If the idea survives the overpromise and underdelivery backlash, it can usually make a valuable contribution to the field. Management information systems (MIS) originally promised to be the "electronic nervous system" for organizations; they actually became well-structured reporting systems. Office automation promised the paperless office; it actually became, first, word processing and, later, personal computers.

In a similar way, the promise of decision support systems (DSS) is contained in the following definition from Sprague and Carlson [1] that captures the key aspects of DSS. They define DSS as

- computer-based systems
- that help decision makers

- confront ill-structured problems
- through direct interaction
- with data and analysis models

This definition promises a set of rich and powerful systems to support decision making in a variety of areas. For a while, however, DSS to most practitioners meant a computer-based financial planning system. Fortunately, the promise of DSS is still understood and progress continues toward the richer promise.

At the same time, several major developments have influenced the direction and nature of DSS since they became popular in the mid-1970s. This book is intended to show how these developments have affected the way DSS theory has been put into practice in modern organizations.

THEORY INTO PRACTICE

One of the criticisms frequently leveled at an applied area of endeavor is that "there is no theory." Management information systems and decision support systems have each received this criticism. In the strict academic sense of the word, there is, of course, no "theory" of MIS or DSS. There are, however, conceptual frameworks or mental models that developers and practitioners use to organize their thinking and guide their activities. The absence of a true theory becomes a vacuous argument if usable, valuable systems are developed with the aid of a conceptual framework.

A popular conceptual framework for DSS evolved from the work of a group of people at the IBM Research Laboratory in San Jose, California, during the late 1970s. Articulated first in a journal article and later in a book, this framework became a popular way to look at DSS [1, 2]. Some of the key concepts from this framework include the following:

1. The technology for DSS must consist of three sets of capabilities in the areas of dialog, data, and modeling, what Sprague and Carlson call the DDM paradigm. They make the point that a good DSS should have *balance* among the three capabilities. It should be *easy to use* to support the interaction with nontechnical users, it should have access to a *wide variety of data,* and it should provide *analysis and modeling* in a variety of ways. Many systems claim to be DSS when they are strong in only one area and weak in the others.

2. Three *levels* of technology are useful in developing DSS. This concept illustrates the usefulness of configuring *DSS tools* into a *DSS generator* which can be used to develop a variety of *specific DSS* quickly and easily to aid decision makers.

3. DSS are not developed according to traditional approaches but require a form of *iterative development* that allows them to evolve and change as the situation changes.

4. Effective development of DSS requires an organizational strategy to build an *environment* within which such systems can originate and evolve. The environment includes a group of people with interacting roles, a set of hardware and software technology, and a set of data sources.

These concepts, along with others in the Sprague and Carlson framework, are explained more fully in the first reading and extended in the second. These two readings establish the conceptual base for the rest of the book.

RELATED DEVELOPMENTS

As DSS efforts were gaining strength in the late 1970s and early 1980s, several other trends evolved to have a major impact on DSS. These included the following:

1. The personal computer revolution; the hardware, the software, and the emphasis on ease-of-use through some common representations such as spreadsheets
2. The increasing capability and decreasing cost of telecommunications
3. The increasing availability of public databases and other sources of external data
4. The growth of artificial intelligence techniques such as expert systems and natural language processing
5. The rapid increase in end-user computing

Each of these trends is affecting the growth of DSS significantly; taken together, their effect is dramatic.

SHORT-RANGE TRENDS IN *DSS*

The intersection of the continued progress in DSS and the developments cited above has resulted in some important trends in DSS. We expect to see seven DSS trends in the near future:

1. Personal computer–based DSS will continue to grow. Spreadsheets will take on more and more functions, eventually encompassing some of the functions previously performed by DSS generators. Newer packages for "creativity support" will become more popular as extensions of analysis and decision making. These developments will further strengthen the use of the PC for these applications, but they will continue to be primarily for personal support for independent thinking and decision making rather than for institutional DSS such as budgeting and financial planning.
2. For the popular institutional DSS that support sequential, interdependent decision making, the trend is toward "distributed DSS"—close linkages between mainframe DSS languages and generators and the PC-based facilities. Vendors of both mainframe and PC products are now offering versions that run on, and link with, the other.
3. For pooled interdependent decision support, "group DSS" will become much more prevalent in the next few years. The growing availability of local area networks and group communication services, such as electronic mail, will make this type of DSS increasingly available.
4. Decision support system products will begin to incorporate, and eventually encompass, tools and techniques coming out of artificial intelligence work. The

self-contained, stand-alone products in artificial intelligence will prove to be like the stand-alone statistical and management science models of a decade ago—they will need to be embedded in a "delivery system" that facilitates their use. DSS will provide the system for the assimilation of expert systems, knowledge representation, natural language query, voice and pattern recognition, and so on. The result will be "intelligent DSS" that can "suggest," "learn," and "understand" in dealing with managerial tasks and problems.

5. Continued efforts to leverage the usefulness of DSS to gain benefit and value will result in focused versions targeted at specific sets of users or applications. The first strong thrust in this direction is executive information systems aimed at top managers, primarily for flexible reporting and status monitoring. EIS have enhanced graphics and other user-friendly capabilities, less modeling and analysis capability, and more support from systems professionals to customize the system to a specific executive.

6. DSS groups will become less like special project "commando teams" and more a part of the support team for a variety of other end-user support, perhaps as a part of an information center. The Mead case in Part 4 suggests how the broadening of the role of DSS groups might take place.

7. Cutting across all the trends given above is the continued development of user-friendly capabilities. This, more than any other feature, is what put DSS on the map and promises to put "a computer on every desk." The development of dialog support hardware, such as light pens, mouse devices, and touch screens, and high-resolution graphics will be further advanced by speech recognition and voice synthesis. Dialog support software such as menus, windows, and help functions will also continue to advance. The "virtual desktop" dialog pioneered by the Xerox Star, and currently used by Apple's Lisa and Macintosh computers, embodies many user-friendly features and has set the pace for other personal computers. Users appreciate the ability to quickly move the cursor (via a mouse), call up a menu, select an item on the menu, and get the results—all in two to three seconds. Selecting spreadsheet commands, storing files, initiating data communications— all can be handled in this manner. Features such as these will help support the growing use of DSS by both new and experienced users.

STRUCTURE OF THE BOOK

The readings have been selected to illustrate how the conceptual framework is being implemented in practice, recognizing the developments and trends cited above. They are organized into six major sections:

- Part 1 contains the two articles that define the conceptual framework.
- Part 2 deals with developing and using DSS. Specific topics include the process of iterative design, planning and organizing, and the several roles managers must play in encouraging the development and use of DSS.
- Part 3 treats the architecture of DSS, showing developments in each area of the dialog-data-model paradigm.
- Part 4 contains several readings that explore the evolving environment for DSS, with specific emphasis on the growth of personal computer usage in DSS.

- Part 5 contains six articles that present topics and systems that represent the expanding domain of the DSS field. Included are group DSS, executive information systems, and expert systems.
- Part 6 shows several specific applications of the DSS approach, not just in the popular area of finance but also in marketing, scheduling, and manufacturing.

Following Part 6 are some resources that we think will be valuable in pursuing the subject of DSS further. First is a listing of DSS software products that are available at reduced cost to educational institutions. Hands-on experience in DSS is quite valuable to students in learning and understanding how the systems can be used. Many vendors seem willing to make it possible for students to learn on their system. The bibliography, cross-referenced by topic, will help the reader who wants to pursue a specific DSS topic in more detail.

REFERENCES

1. SPRAGUE, RALPH H., AND ERIC D. CARLSON *Building Effective Decision Support Systems.* Englewood Cliffs, N.J.: Prentice-Hall, 1982.
2. SPRAGUE, RALPH H. "A Framework for the Development of Decision Support Systems," *MIS Quarterly,* 4, no. 4 (1980), 1–26.

PART 1

The Conceptual Foundation for DSS

In the late 1960s and early 1970s, the first decision support systems (DSS) began to appear. They were the result of a number of factors: emerging computer hardware and software technology; research efforts at leading universities; a growing awareness of how to support decision making; a desire for better information; an increasingly turbulent economic environment; and stronger competition pressures, especially from abroad. During the rest of the decade, there was a growing body of DSS research from the academic community, and an increasing number of organizations began to develop decision support systems. These experiences provided the conceptual foundation for DSS.

Ralph Sprague's article, "A Framework for the Development of Decision Support Systems" (Reading 1), played a major role in establishing DSS's conceptual foundation. It identifies the characteristics of a DSS, especially in contrast to the characteristics of electronic data processing (EDP) and management information systems (MIS). It also defines the various levels of DSS technology and the different organizational roles associated with DSS. The unique development approach for DSS is discussed. The DSS performance objectives from a user's perspective are stated. The technical capabilities from a builder's point of view are identified. The underlying DSS technology from the toolsmith's perspective is discussed. And in conclusion, the article considers issues associated with the future development of DSS.

A few years later, Sprague expanded the framework by arguing that the context of DSS and its applicability are often too narrowly viewed. His "DSS in Context" (Reading 2) argues that the boundaries of decision-making activities are difficult to define and that DSS are useful in supporting a wide range of activities that are goal-directed and process-independent—not defined in advance as a series of steps. Reading 2 also shows that the field of DSS lies at the convergence of evolutionary developments in EDP/MIS and management science.

1

A FRAMEWORK FOR THE DEVELOPMENT OF DECISION SUPPORT SYSTEMS

Ralph H. Sprague, Jr.

INTRODUCTION

We seem to be on the verge of another "era" in the relentless advancement of computer based information systems in organizations. Designated by the term Decision Support Systems (DSS), these systems are receiving reactions ranging from "a major breakthrough" to "just another 'buzz word'."

One view is that the natural evolutionary advancement of information technology and its use in the organizational context has led from EDP to MIS to the current DSS thrust. In this view, the DSS picks up where MIS leaves off. A contrary view portrays DSS as an important subset of what MIS has been and will continue to be. Still another view recognizes a type of system that has been developing for several years and "now we have a name for it." Meanwhile, the skeptics suspect that DSS is just another "buzz word" to justify the next round of visits from the vendors.

Reprinted by special permission of the *MIS Quarterly*, Volume 4, Number 4, December 1980. Copyright 1980 by the Society for Information Management and the Management Information Systems Research Center.

The purpose of this article is to briefly examine these alternative views of DSS, and present a framework that proves valuable in reconciling them. The framework articulates and integrates major concerns of several "stakeholders" in the development of DSS: executives and professionals who use them, the MIS managers who manage the process of developing and installing them, the information specialists who build and develop them, the system designers who create and assemble the technology on which they are based, and the researchers who study the DSS subject and process.

DEFINITION, EXAMPLES, CHARACTERISTICS

The concepts involved in DSS were first articulated in the early '70's by Michael S. Scott Morton under the term "management decision systems" [32]. A few firms and scholars began to develop and research DSS, which became characterized as *interactive* computer based systems, which *help* decision makers utilize *data* and *models* to solve *unstructured* problems. The unique contribution of DSS resulted from these key words. That definition proved restrictive enough that few actual systems completely satisfied it. Some authors recently extended the definition of DSS to include any system that makes some contribution to decision making; in this way the term can be applied to all but transaction processing. A serious definitional problem is that the words have a certain "intuitive validity"; any system that supports a decision, in any way, is a "Decision Support System."

Unfortunately, neither the restrictive nor the broad definition helps much, because they do not provide guidance for understanding the value, the technical requirements, or the approach for developing a DSS. A complicating factor is that people from different backgrounds and contexts view a DSS quite differently. A manager and computer scientist seldom see things in the same way.

Another way to get a feeling for a complex subject like a DSS is to consider examples. Several specific examples were discussed in The Society for Management Information Systems (SMIS) Workshop on DSS in 1979 [35]. Alter examined fifty-six systems which might have some claim to the DSS label, and used this sample to develop a set of abstractions describing their characteristics [1, 2]. More recently, Keen has designated about thirty examples of what he feels are DSS and compares their characteristics [26].

The "characteristics" approach seems to hold more promise than either definitions or collections of examples in understanding a DSS and its potential. More specifically, a DSS may be defined by its capabilities in several critical areas—capabilities which are required to accomplish the objectives which are pursued by the development and use of a DSS. Observed characteristics of a DSS which have evolved from the work of Alter, Keen, and others include:

- they tend to be aimed at the less well structured, underspecified problems that upper level managers typically face;
- they attempt to combine the use of models or analytic techniques with traditional data access and retrieval functions;

- they specifically focus on features which make them easy to use by noncomputer people in an interactive mode; and
- they emphasize flexibility and adaptability to accommodate changes in the environment and the decision making approach of the user.

A serious question remains. Are the definitions, examples, and characteristics of a DSS sufficiently different to justify the use of a new term and the inference of a new era in information systems for organizations, or are the skeptics right? Is it just another "buzz word" to replace the fading appeal of MIS?

DSS VERSUS MIS

Much of the difficulty and controversy with terms like "DSS" and "MIS" can be traced to the difference between an academic or theoretical definition and "connotational" definition. The former is carefully articulated by people who write textbooks and articles in journals. The latter evolves from what actually is developed and used in practice, and is heavily influenced by the personal experiences that the user of the term has had with the subject. It is this connotational definition of EDP/MIS/DSS that is used in justifying the assertion that a DSS is an evolutionary advancement beyond MIS.

This view can be expressed using Figure 1.1, a simple organizational chart, as a model of an organization. EDP was first applied to the lower operational levels of the organization to automate the paperwork. Its basic characteristics include:

- a focus on data, storage, processing, and flows at the operational level;
- efficient transaction processing;
- scheduled and optimized computer runs;

FIGURE 1.1 The Connotational View.

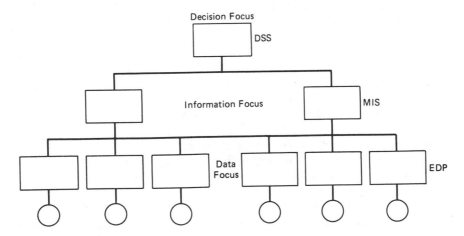

- integrated files for related jobs; and
- summary reports for management.

In recent years, the EDP level of activity in many firms has become a well-oiled and efficient production facility for transactions processing.

The MIS approach elevated the focus on information systems activities, with additional emphasis on integration and planning of the information systems function. In *practice,* the characteristics of MIS include:

- an information focus, aimed at the middle managers;
- structured information flow;
- an integration of EDP jobs by business function, such as production MIS, marketing MIS, personnel MIS, *etc.;* and
- inquiry and report generation, usually with a database.

The MIS era contributed a new level of information to serve management needs, but was still very much oriented to, and built upon, information flows and data files.

According to this connotational view, a DSS is focused still higher in the organization with an emphasis on the following characteristics:

- decision focused, aimed at top managers and executive decision makers;
- emphasis on flexibility, adaptability, and quick response;
- user initiated and controlled; and
- support for the personal decision making styles of individual managers.

This connotational and evolutionary view has some credence because it roughly corresponds to developments in practice over time. A recent study found MIS managers able to distinguish the level of advancement of their application systems using criteria similar to those above [27]. Many installations with MIS type applications planned to develop applications with DSS type characteristics. However, the "connotational" view has some serious deficiencies, and is definitely misleading in the further development of a DSS.

- It implies that *decision support* is needed only at the top levels. In fact, *decision support* is required at all levels of management in the organization.
- The decision making which occurs at several levels frequently must be coordinated. Therefore, an important dimension of *decision support* is the communication and coordination between decision makers across organizational levels, as well as at the same level.
- It implies that *decision support* is the only thing top managers need from the information system. In fact, decision making is only one of the activities of managers that benefits from information systems support.

There is also the problem that many information systems professionals, especially those in SMIS, are not willing to accept the narrow connotational view of the term "MIS."

To us, MIS refers to the entire set of systems and activities required to manage, process, and use information as a resource in the organization.

THE THEORETICAL VIEW

To consider the appropriate role of a DSS in this overall context of information systems, the broad charter and objectives of the information systems function in the organization are characterized:

> Dedicated to improving the performance of knowledge workers in organizations through the application of information technology.

■ Improving the performance is the ultimate objective of information systems—not the storage of data, the production of reports, or even "getting the right information to the right person at the right time." The ultimate objective must be viewed in terms of the ability of information systems to support the improved performance of people in organizations.

■ Knowledge workers are the clientele. This group includes managers, professionals, staff analysts, and clerical workers whose primary job responsibility is the handling of information in some form.

■ Organizations are the context. The focus is on information handling in goal seeking organizations of all kinds.

■ The application of information technology is the challenge and opportunity facing the information systems professional for the purposes and in the contexts given above.

A triangle was used by Robert Head in the late 1960s as a visual model to characterize MIS in this broad comprehensive sense [22]. It has become a classic way to view the dimensions of an information system. The vertical dimension represented the levels of management, and the horizontal dimension represented the main functional areas of the business organization. Later authors added transactional processing as a base on which the entire system rested. The result was a two dimensional model of an MIS in the broad sense—the total activities which comprise the information system in an organization. Figure 1.2 is a further extension of the basic triangle to help describe the concept of the potential role of a DSS. The depth dimension shows the major technology "subsystems" which provide support for the activities of knowledge workers.

Three major thrusts are shown here, but there could be more. The structured reporting system includes the reports required for the management and control of the organization, and for satisfying the information needs of external parties. It has been evolving from efforts in EDP and MIS, in the narrow sense, for several years. Systems to support the communication needs of the organization are evolving rapidly from advances in telecommmunications with a strong impetus from office automation and word processing. DSS seems to be evolving from the coalescence of information technology and operations research/management science approaches in the form of interactive modeling.

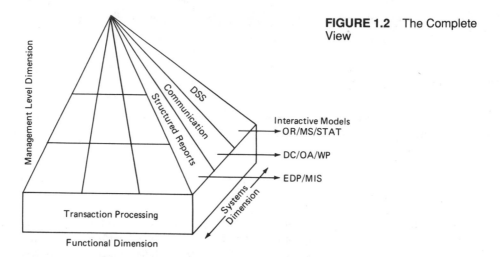

FIGURE 1.2   The Complete View

To summarize this introductory section, a DSS is not merely an evolutionary advancement of EDP and MIS, and it will certainly not replace either. Nor is it merely a type of information system aimed exclusively at top management, where other information systems seem to have failed. A DSS is a class of information system that draws on transaction processing systems and interacts with the other parts of the overall information system to support the decision making activities of managers and other knowledge workers in the organizations. However, there are some subtle but significant differences between a DSS and traditional EDP or so-called MIS approaches. Moreover, these systems require a new combination of information systems technology to satisfy a set of heretofore unmet needs. It is not yet clear exactly how these technologies fit together, or which important problems need to be solved. Indeed, that is a large part of the purpose of this article. It is apparent, however, that a DSS has the potential to become another powerful weapon in the arsenal of the information systems professional to help improve the effectiveness of the people in organizations.

THE FRAMEWORK

The remainder of this article is devoted to an exploration of the nature of this "thrust" in information systems called "DSS." The mechanism for this exploration is another of the often maligned but repeatedly used "frameworks."

A framework, in the absence of theory, is helpful in organizing a complex subject, identifying the relationships between the parts, and revealing the areas in which further developments will be required. The framework presented here has evolved over the past two years in discussions with many different groups of people.[1] It is organized in two major parts. The first part considers: (a) three levels of technology, all of which

[1]This article grew out of the workshop on DSS at the 1979 Annual Meeting of SMIS in Minneapolis [35]. Portions of the material were presented at two conferences in the summer [40, 41] and are included herein by permission.

have been designated as a DSS, with considerable confusion; (b) the developmental approach that is evolving for the creation of a DSS; and (c) the roles of several key types of people in the building and use of a DSS. The second part of the framework develops a descriptive model to assess the performance objectives and the capabilities of a DSS as viewed by three of the major stakeholders in their continued development and use.

THREE TECHNOLOGY LEVELS

It is helpful to identify three levels of hardware/software which have been included in the label "DSS." They are used by people with different levels of technical capability, and vary in the nature and scope of task to which they can be applied.

Specific DSS

The system which actually accomplishes the work might be called the *Specific DSS*. It is an information systems "application," but with characteristics that make it significantly different from a typical data processing application. It is the hardware/software that allows a specific decision maker or group of decision makers to deal with a specific set of related problems. An early example is the portfolio management system [20] also described in the first major DSS book by Keen and Scott Morton [23]. Another example is the police beat allocation system used on an experimental basis by the City of San Jose, California [9]. The latter system allowed a police officer to display a map outline and call up data by geographical zone, showing police calls for service, activity levels, service time, etc. The interactive graphic capability of the system enabled the officer to manipulate the maps, zones, and data to try a variety of police beat alternatives quickly and easily. In effect, the system provided tools to *amplify* a manager's judgment. Incidentally, a later experiment attempted to apply a traditional linear programming model to the problem. The solution was less satisfactory than the one designed by the police officer.

DSS Generator

The second technology level might be called a *DSS Generator*. This is a "package" of related hardware and software which provides a set of capabilities to quickly and easily build a Specific DSS. For example, the police beat system described above was built from the Geodata Analysis and Display System (GADS), an experimental system developed at the IBM Research Laboratory in San Jose [8]. By loading different maps, data, menu choices, and procedures or command strings, GADS was later used to build a Specific DSS to support the routing of IBM copier repairmen [42]. The development of this new "application" required less than one month.

Another example of a *DSS Generator* is the Executive Information System (EIS) marketed by Boeing Computer Services [6]. EIS is an integrated set of capabilities which includes report preparation, inquiry capability, a modeling language, graphic display commands, and a set of financial and statistical analysis subroutines. These capabilities have all been available individually for some time. The unique contribution of EIS is that these capabilities are available through a common language which acts on a common set of data. The result is that EIS can be used as a DSS Generator, especially for a Specific DSS to help in financial decision making situations.

Evolutionary growth toward DSS Generators has come from special purpose languages. In fact, most of the software systems that might be used as Generators are evolving from enhanced planning languages or modeling languages, perhaps with report preparation and graphic display capabilities added. The Interactive Financial Planning System (IFPS) marketed by Execucom Systems of Austin, Texas [18], and EXPRESS available from TYMSHARE [44], are good examples.

DSS Tools

The third and most fundamental level of technology applied to the development of a DSS might be called *DSS Tools*. These are hardware or software elements which facilitate the development of a specific DSS *or* a DSS Generator. This category of technology has seen the greatest amount of recent development, including new special purpose languages, improvements in operating systems to support conversational approaches, color graphics hardware and supporting software, etc. For example, the GADS system described above was written in FORTRAN using an experimental graphics subroutine package as the primary dialogue handling software, a laboratory enhanced rasterscan color monitor, and a powerful interactive data extraction/database management system.

Relationships

The relationships between these three levels of technology and types of DSS are illustrated by Figure 1.3. The DSS Tools can be used to develop a Specific DSS application directly as shown on the left half of the diagram. This is the same approach used to develop most traditional applications with tools such as a general purpose language, data access software, subroutine packages, etc. The difficulty with this approach for developing DSS applications is the constant change and flexibility which characterize them. A DSS changes character not only in response to changes in the environment, but to changes in the way managers want to approach the problem. Therefore, a serious complicating factor in the use of basic tools is the need to involve the user directly in the change and modification of the Specific DSS.

APL was heavily used in the development of Specific DSS because it proved to be cheap and easy for APL programmers, especially the APL enthusiasts, to produce "throw-away" code which could be easily revised or discarded as the nature of the application changed. However, except for the few users who became members of the APL fan club, that language *did not* help capture the involvement of users in the building and modification of the DSS. The development and use of DSS Generators promises to create a "platform" or staging area from which Specific DSS can be

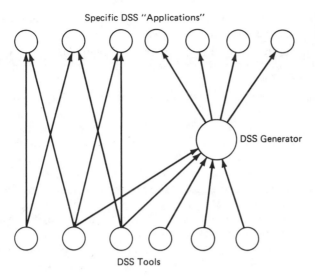

Specific DSS "Applications"

FIGURE 1.3 Three Levels of DSS Technology

DSS Generator

DSS Tools

constantly developed and modified with the cooperation of the user, and without heavy consumption of time and effort.

EVOLVING ROLES IN *DSS*

All three levels of technology will probably be used over time in the development and operation of a DSS. Some interesting developments are occurring, however, in the roles that managers and technicians will play.

Figure 1.4 repeats part of the earlier diagram with a spectrum of five roles spread across the three levels.

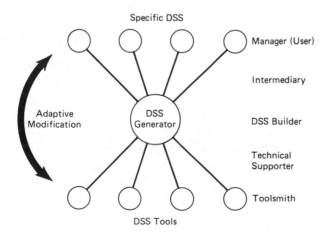

Specific DSS

Manager (User)

Intermediary

Adaptive
Modification

DSS
Generator

DSS Builder

Technical
Supporter

Toolsmith

DSS Tools

FIGURE 1.4 Three Levels of DSS with Five Associated Roles for Managers and Technicians

- The *manager or user* is the person faced with the problem or decision—the one that must take action and be responsible for the consequences.
- The *intermediary* is the person who helps the user, perhaps merely as a clerical assistant to push the buttons of the terminal, or perhaps as a more substantial "staff assistant" to interact and make suggestions.
- The *DSS builder* or facilitator assembles the necessary capabilities from the DSS Generator to "configure" the specific DSS with which the user/intermediary interacts directly. This person must have some familiarity with the problem area and also be comfortable with the information system technology components and capabilities.
- The *technical supporter* develops additional information system capabilities or components when they are needed as part of the Generator. New databases, new analysis models, and additional data display formats will be developed by the person filling this role. It requires a strong familiarity with technology, and a minor acquaintance with the problem or application area.
- The *toolsmith* develops new technology, new languages, new hardware and software, improves the efficiency of linkages between subsystems, etc.

Two observations about this spectrum of roles are appropriate. First, it is clear that they do not necessarily align with individuals on a one-to-one basis. One person may assume several roles, or more than one person may be required to fill a role. The appropriate role assignment will generally depend on:

- the nature of the problem, particularly how narrow or broad;
- the nature of the person, particularly how comfortable the individual is with the computer equipment, language, and concepts; and
- the strength of the technology, particularly how user oriented it is.

Some managers do not need or want an intermediary. There are even a few chief executives who take the terminal home on weekends to write programs, thereby assuming the upper three or four roles. In fact, a recent survey of the users of IFPS shows that more than one third of them are middle and top level managers [45]. Decisions which require group consensus or systems design (builder) teams are examples of multiple persons per role.

Secondly, these roles appear similar to those present in traditional systems development, but there are subtle differences. The top two are familiar even in name for the development of many interactive or online systems. It is common practice in some systems to combine them into one "virtual" user for convenience. The user of the DSS, however, will play a much more active and controlling role in the design and development of the system than has been true in the past. The builder/technical support dichotomy is relatively close to the information specialist/system designer dichotomy discussed in the ACM curriculum recommendations [3]. Increasingly, however, the DSS builder resides in the functional area and not in the MIS department. The toolsmith is similar to a systems programmer, software designer, or computer scientist, but is increasingly employed by a hardware or software vendor, and not by the user's organization. The net result is less direct involvement in the DSS process by the information systems professional in the EDP/MIS department. (Some implications of this trend are discussed later.) Moreover, the interplay between these roles is evolving into a unique development approach for a DSS.

THE DEVELOPMENT APPROACH FOR *DSS*

The very nature of a DSS requires a different design technique from traditional batch, or online, transaction processing systems. The traditional approaches for analysis and design have proven inadequate because there is no single comprehensive theory of decision making, and because of the rapidity of change in the conditions which decision makers face. Designers literally "cannot get to first base" because no one, least of all the decision maker or user, can define in advance what the functional requirements of the system should be. A DSS needs to be built with short, rapid feedback from users to ensure that development is proceeding correctly. It must be developed to permit change quickly and easily.

Iterative Design

The result is that the most important four steps in the typical systems development process—analysis, design, construction, implementation—are combined into a single step which is iteratively repeated. Several names are evolving to describe this process including breadboarding [31], L'Approache Evolutive [14], and "middle out" [30]. The essence of the approach is that the manager and builder agree on a small but significant subproblem, then design and develop an initial system to support the decision making which it requires. After a short period of use, for instance, a few weeks, the system is evaluated, modified, and incrementally expanded. This cycle is repeated three to six times over the course of a few months until a *relatively* stable system is evolved which supports decision making for a cluster of tasks. The word "relatively" is important, because although the frequency and extent of change will decrease, it will never be stable. The system will always be changing, not as a necessary evil in response to imposed environmental changes, but as a conscious strategy on the part of the user and builder. In terms of the three level model presented earlier, this process can be viewed as the iterative cycling between the DSS Generator and the Specific DSS as shown in Figure 1.4. With each cycle, capabilities are added to, or deleted from, the Specific DSS from those available in the DSS Generator. Keen depicts the expansion and growth of the system in terms of adding verbs which represent actions managers require [24]. Carlson adds more dimension by focusing on representations, operations, control, and memories as the elements of expansion and modification [11]. In another paper, Keen deals substantively with the interaction between the user, the builder, and the technology in this iterative, adaptive design process [25].

Note that this approach requires an unusual level of management involvement or management participation in the design. The manager is actually the iterative designer of the system; the systems analyst is merely the catalyst between the manager and the system, implementing the required changes and modifications.

Note also that this is different from the concept of "prototyping"; the initial system is real, live, and usable, not just a pilot test. The iterative process does not *merely* lead to a good understanding of the systems performance requirements, which are then frozen. The iterative changeability is actually *built into* the DSS as it is used over time. In fact, the development approach *becomes the system*. Rather than developing a system which is then "run" as a traditional EDP system, the DSS development approach results in the installation of an adaptive process in which a decision maker and a set of information system "capabilities" interact to confront problems while responding to changes from a variety of sources.

The Adaptive System

In the broad sense, the DSS is an adaptive system which consists of all three levels of technology in place and operating with the participants (roles), and the technology adapting to changes over time. Thus, the development of a DSS is actually the development and installation of this adaptive system. Simon describes such a system as one that adapts to changes of several kinds over three time horizons [34]. In the short run, the system allows a *search* for answers within a relatively narrow scope. In the intermediate time horizon, the system *learns* by modifying its capabilities and activities, i.e., the scope or domain changes. In the long run, the system *evolves* to accommodate much different behavior styles and capabilities.

The three level model of a DSS is analogous to Simon's adaptive system. The Specific DSS gives the manager the capabilities and flexibility to *search*, explore, and experiment with the problem area, within certain boundaries. Over time, as changes occur in a task, the environment, and the user's behavior, the Specific DSS must *learn* to accommodate these changes through the reconfiguration of the elements in the DSS generator, with the aid of the DSS builder. Over a longer period of time, the basic tools *evolve* to provide the technology for changing the capabilities of the Generators out of which the Specific DSS is constructed, through the efforts of the toolsmith.

The ideas expressed above are not particularly new. Rapid feedback between the systems analyst and the client has been pursued for years. In the long run, most computer systems *are* adaptive systems. They are changed and modified during the normal system life cycle, and they evolve through major enhancements and extensions as the life cycle is repeated. However, when the length of that life cycle is shortened from three to five months, or even weeks, there are significant implications. The resulting changes in the development approach and the traditional view of the systems life cycle promise to be one of the important impacts of the growing use of a DSS.

PERFORMANCE OBJECTIVES AND CAPABILITIES

Most of the foregoing discussion has dealt with some aspects of the technological and organizational contexts within which a DSS will be built and operated. The second part of the framework deals with what a DSS must accomplish, and what capabilities or characteristics it must have. The three levels of hardware/software technology and the corresponding three major "stakeholders" or interested parties in the development and use of a DSS can be used to identify the characteristics and attributes of a DSS.

At the top level are the *managers or users* who are primarily concerned with what the Specific DSS can do for them. Their focus is the problem solving or decision making task they face, and the organizational environment in which they operate. They will assess a DSS in terms of the assistance they receive in pursuing these tasks. At the level of the DSS Generator, the *builders* or designers must use the capabilities of the generator to configure a Specific DSS to meet the manager's needs. They will be concerned with the capabilities the Generator offers, and how these capabilities can be assembled to create the Specific DSS. At the DSS tool level, the *"toolsmiths"* are concerned with the development of basic technology components, and how they can be integrated to form a DSS Generator which has the necessary capabilities.

The attributes and characteristics of a DSS as viewed from each level must be examined. From the manager's view, six general performance objectives for the Specific DSS can be identified. They are not the only six that could be identified, but as a group they represent the overall performance of a DSS that seems to be expected and desirable from a managerial viewpoint. The characteristics of the DSS Generator from the viewpoint of the builder are described by a conceptual model which identifies performance characteristics in three categories: dialogue handling or the man-machine interface, database and database management capability, and modeling and analytic capability. The same three part model is used to depict the viewpoint of the "toolsmith," but from the aspect of the technology, tactics, and architecture required to produce those capabilities required by the builders.

Manager's View: Performance Objectives

The following performance requirements are phrased using the normative word "should." It is likely that no Specific DSS will be required to satisfy all six of the performance requirements given here. In fact, it is important to recall that the performance criteria for any Specific DSS will depend entirely on the task, the organizational environment, and the decision maker(s) involved. Nevertheless, the following objectives collectively represent a set of capabilities which characterize the full value of the DSS concept from the manager/user point of view. The first three pertain to the type of decision making task which managers and professionals face. The latter three relate to the type of support which is needed.

1. *A DSS should provide support for decision making, but with emphasis on semi-structured and unstructured decisions.* These are the types of decisions that have had little or no support from EDP, MIS, or management science/operations research (MS/OR) in the past. It might be better to refer to "hard" or under-specified problems, because the concept of "structure" in decision making is heavily dependent on the cognitive style and approach to problem solving of the decision maker. It is clear from their expressed concerns, however, that managers need additional support for certain kinds of problems.

2. *A DSS should provide decision making support for managers at all levels, assisting in integration between the levels whenever appropriate.* This requirement evolves

from the realization that managers at *all* organizational levels face "tough" problems as described in the first objective above. Moreover, a major need articulated by managers, is the integration and coordination of decision making by several managers dealing with related parts of a larger problem.

3. *A DSS should support decisions which are interdependent as well as those that are independent.* Much of the early DSS work inferred that a decision maker would sit at a terminal, use a system, and develop a decision *alone.* DSS development experience has shown that a DSS must accommodate decisions which are made by groups or made in part by several people in sequence. Keen and Hackathorn [24] explore three decision types as:

   Independent. A decision maker has full responsibility and authority to make a complete implementable decision.

   Sequential Interdependent. A decision maker makes part of a decision which is passed on to someone else.

   Pooled Interdependent. The decision must result from negotiation and interaction among decision makers.

   Different capabilities will be required to support each type of decision—personal support, organizational support, and group support, respectively.

4. *A DSS should support all phases of the decision making process.* A popular model of the decision making process is given in the work of Herbert Simon [33]. He characterized three main steps in the process as follows:

   Intelligence. Searching the environment for conditions calling for decisions. Raw data is obtained, processed, and examined for clues that may identify problems.

   Design. Inventing, developing, and analyzing possible courses of action. This involves processes to understand the problem, generate solutions, and test solutions for feasibility.

   Choice. Selecting a particular course of action from those available. A choice is made and implemented.

   Although the third phase includes implementation, many authors feel that it is significant enough to be shown separately. It has been added to Figure 1.5 to show the relationships between the steps. Simon's model also illustrates the contribution of MIS/EDP and MS/OR to decision making. From the definition of the three stages given above, it is clear that EDP and MIS, in the narrow sense, have made major contributions to the intelligence phase, while MIS/OR has been primarily useful at the choice phase. There has been no substantial support for the design phase, which seems to be one of the primary potential contributions of a DSS. There also has been very little support from traditional systems for the implementation phase, but some early experience has shown that a DSS can make a major contribution here also [42].

5. *A DSS should support a variety of decision making processes, but not be dependent on any one.* Simon's model, though widely accepted, is only one model of how decisions are actually made. In fact, there is no universally accepted model of the decision making process, and there is no promise of such a general theory in the foreseeable future. There are too many variables, too many different types of decisions, and too much variety in the characteristics of decision makers. Consequently, a very important characteristic of a DSS is that it provide the decision maker with a set of capabilities to apply in a sequence and form that fits each

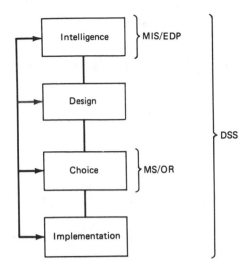

FIGURE 1.5   Phases of Decision Making

individual cognitive style. In short, a DSS should be process independent, and user driven or controlled.

6. *Finally, a DSS should be easy to use.* A variety of terms have been used to describe this characteristic including flexibility, user friendly, nonthreatening, etc. The importance of this characteristic is underscored by the discretionary latitude of a DSS's clientele. Although some systems which require heavy organizational support or group support may limit the discretion somewhat, the user of a DSS has much more latitude to ignore or circumvent the system than the user of a more traditional transaction system or required reporting system. Therefore, a DSS must "earn" its users' allegiance by being valuable and convenient.

THE BUILDER'S VIEW: TECHNICAL CAPABILITIES

The DSS Builder has the responsibility of drawing on computer based tools and techniques to provide the decision support required by the manager. DSS Tools can be used directly, but it is generally more efficient and effective to use a DSS Generator for this task. The Generator must have a set of capabilities which facilitate the quick and easy configuration of a Specific DSS and modification in response to changes in the manager's requirements, environment, tasks, and thinking approaches. A conceptual model can be used to organize these capabilities, both for the builders and for the "toolsmith" who will develop the technology to provide these capabilities.

The old "black box" approach is helpful here, starting with the view of the system as a black box, successively "opening" the boxes to understand the subsystems and how they are interconnected. Although the DSS is treated as the black box here, it is important to recall that the overall system is the decision *making* system, consisting of a manager/user who uses a DSS to confront a task in an organizational environment.

Opening the large DSS box reveals a database, a model base, and a complex software system for linking the user to each of them as shown in Figure 1.6. Opening

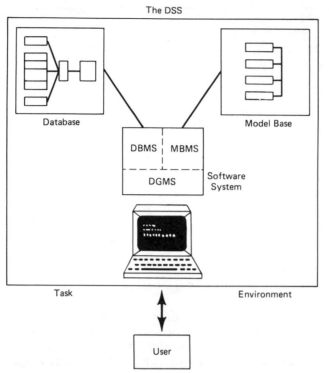

FIGURE 1.6 Components of the DSS

each of these boxes reveals that the database and model base have some interrelated components, and that the software system is comprised of three sets of capabilities: database management software (DBMS), model base management software (MBMS), and the software for managing the interface between the user and the system, which might be called the dialogue generation and management software (DGMS). These three major subsystems provide a convenient scheme for identifying the technical capability which a DSS must have. The key aspects in each category that are critical to a DSS from the Builder's point of view, and a list of capabilities which will be required in each category must now be considered.

THE DATA SUBSYSTEM

The data subsystem is thought to be a well understood set of capabilities because of the rapidly maturing technology related to databases and their management. The typical advantages of the database approach, and the powerful functions of the DBMS, are also important to the development and use of a DSS. There are, however, some significant differences between the Database/Data Communication approach for traditional systems, and those applicable for a DSS. Opening the Database box summarizes these key characteristics as shown in Figure 1.7.

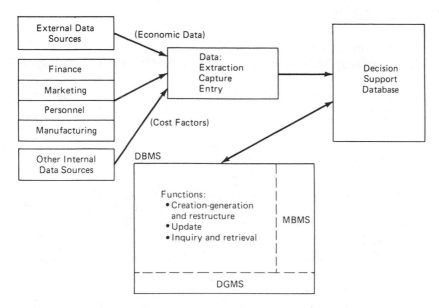

FIGURE 1.7 The Data Subsystem

First is the importance of a much richer set of data sources than are usually found in typical non-DSS applications. Data must come from external as well as internal sources, since decision making, especially in the upper management levels, is heavily dependent on external data sources. In addition, the typical accounting oriented transaction data must be supplemented with non-transactional, non-accounting data, some of which has not been computerized in the past.

Another significant difference is the importance of the data capture and extraction process from this wider set of data sources. The nature of a DSS requires that the extraction process, and the DBMS which manages it, be flexible enough to allow rapid additions and changes in response to unanticipated user requests. Finally, most successful DSS's have found it necessary to create a DSS database which is logically separate from other operational databases. A partial set of capabilities required in the database area can be summarized by the following:

- the ability to combine a variety of data sources through a data capture and extraction process;
- the ability to add and delete data sources quickly and easily;
- the ability to portray logical data structures in user terms so the user understands what is available and can specify needed additions and deletions;
- the ability to handle personal and unofficial data so the user can experiment with alternatives based on personal judgment; and
- the ability to manage this wide variety of data with a full range of data management functions.

THE MODEL SUBSYSTEM

A very promising aspect of a DSS is its ability to integrate data access and decision models. It does so by imbedding the decision models in an information system which uses the database as the integration and communication mechanism between models. This characteristic unifies the strength of data retrieval and reporting from the EDP field and the significant developments in management science in a way the manager can use and trust.

The misuse and disuse of models have been widely discussed [21, 28, 36, 39]. One major problem has been that model builders were frequently preoccupied with the structure of the model. The existence of the correct input data and the proper delivery of the output to the user was assumed. In addition to these heroic assumptions, models tended to suffer from inadequacy because of the difficulty of developing an integrated model to handle a realistic set of interrelated decisions. The solution was a collection of separate models, each of which dealt with a distinct part of the problem. Communication between these related models was left to the decision maker and intellectual process.

A more enlightened view of models suggests that they be imbedded in an information system with the database as the integration and communication mechanism between them. Figure 1.8 summarizes the components of the model base "box." The model creation process must be flexible, with a strong modeling language and a set of building blocks, much like subroutines, which can be assembled to assist the modeling process. In fact, there are a set of model management functions, very much analogous

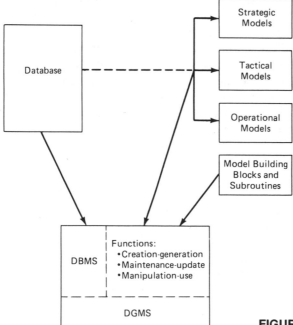

FIGURE 1.8   The Models Subsystem

to data management functions. The key capabilities for a DSS in the model subsystems include:

- the ability to create new models quickly and easily;
- the ability to catalog and maintain a wide range of models, supporting all levels of management;
- the ability to interrelate these models with appropriate linkages through the database;
- the ability to access and integrate model "building blocks;" and
- the ability to manage the model base with management functions analogous to database management (e.g., mechanisms for storing, cataloging, linking, and accessing models).

For a more detailed discussion of the model base and its management see [37, 38, 46].

The User System Interface

Much of the power, flexibility, and usability characteristics of a DSS are derived from capabilities in the user system interface. Bennett identifies the user, terminal, and software system as the components of the interface subsystem [5]. He then divides the dialogue or interface experience itself into three parts as shown in Figure 1.9:

1. *The action language*—what the user *can do* in communicating with the system. It includes such options as the availability of a regular keyboard, function keys, touch panels, joy stick, voice command, etc.

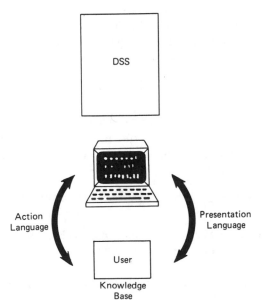

FIGURE 1.9   The User System Interface

2. *The display or presentation language*—what the user *sees*. The display language includes options such as character or line printer, display screen, graphics, color, plotters, audio output, etc.
3. *The knowledge base*—what the user *must know*. The knowledge base consists of what the user needs to bring to the session with the system in order to effectively use it. The knowledge may be in the user's head, on a reference card or instruction sheet, in a user's manual, in a series of "help" commands available upon request, etc.

The "richness" of the interface will depend on the strength of capabilities in each of these areas.

Another dimension of the user system interface is the concept of "dialogue style." Examples include the questions/answer approach, command languages, menus, and "fill in the blanks." Each style has pro's and con's depending on the type of user, task, and decision situation. For a more detailed discussion of dialogue styles see [13].

Although this just scratches the surface in this important area, a partial set of desirable capabilities for a DSS generator to support the user/system interface includes:

- the ability to handle a variety of dialogue styles, perhaps with the ability to shift among them at the user's choice;
- the ability to accommodate user actions in a variety of media;
- the ability to present data in a variety of formats and media; and
- the ability to provide flexible support for the users' knowledge base.

THE TOOLSMITH VIEW: THE UNDERLYING TECHNOLOGY

The toolsmith is concerned with the science involved in creating the information technology to support a DSS, and the architecture of combining the basic tools into a coherent system. The same three part model can be used to describe the toolsmith's concerns because the tools must be designed and combined to provide the three sets of capabilities.

Each of the three areas—dialogue, data handling, and model handling—has received a fair amount of attention from toolsmiths in the past. The topic of DSS and the requirements it imposes have put these efforts in a new perspective revealing how they can be interrelated to increase their collective effectiveness. Moreover, the DSS requirements have revealed some missing elements in existing efforts, indicating valuable potential areas for development.

Dialogue Management

There has been a great deal of theoretical and some empirical work on systems requirements for good man/machine interface. Many of these studies are based on watching users' behavior in using terminals, or surveying users or programmers to ascertain what they want in interactive systems [10, 16]. A recent study examines a series of interactive applications, many of which are DSS's, to assess the *type* of software capabilities required by the applications [43]. This study led directly to some creative work on the software architecture for dialogue generation and management systems (DGMS) as characterized in the model of the previous section [12]. This research uses a relation as the data structure for storing each picture or "frame" used in the system, and a decision table for storing the control mechanism for representing the potential users' option in branching from one frame to another.

Data Management

Most of the significant work in the database management area during the past several years is aimed at transaction processing against large databases. Large DBMS's generally have inquiry/retrieval and flexible report preparation capabilities, but their largest contribution has been in the reduction of program maintenance costs through the separation of application programs and data definitions. On the other hand, DBMS work has generally had a rather naive view of the user and the user's requirements. A DSS user will not be satisfied merely with the capability to issue a set of retrieval commands which select items from the database, or even to display those selected items in a report with the flexible definition of format and headings. A DSS user needs to interact repeatedly and creatively with a relatively small set of data. The user may only need 40–100 data variables, but they must be the *right ones;* and what is right may change from day to day and week to week. Required data will probably include time series data which are not handled comprehensively by typical DBMS's. Better ways are needed to handle and coordinate time series data as well as mechanisms for capturing, processing, and tagging judgmental and probabilistic data. Better ways are also needed for extracting data from existing files and capturing data from previously non-computerized sources. The critical area of data extraction with fast response, which allows additions and deletions to the DSS database from the large transaction database, was a major contribution of the GADS work [8, 29]. In short, the significant development in database technology needs to be focused and extended in some key areas in order to directly serve the needs of a DSS.

Model Management

The area of model creation and handling may have the greatest potential contribution to a DSS. So far, the analytic capability provided by systems has evolved from statistical or financial analysis subroutines which can be called from a common command language. More recently, modeling languages provide a way of formulating interrelationships between variables in a way that permits the creation of simulation or "what if" models. As we noted earlier, many of the currently viable DSS Generators have evolved from these efforts. Early forms of "model management" seem to be evolving from enhancements to some modeling languages, which permit a model of this type to be used for sensitivity testing or goal seeking by specifying target and flexibility variables.

The model management area also has the potential for bringing some of the contributions of artificial intelligence (AI) to bear on a DSS. MYCIN, a system to support medical diagnosis, is based on "production rules," in the AI sense, which play the role of models in performing analytic and decision guidance functions [15]. A more general characterization of "knowledge management" as a way of handling models and data has also been tentatively explored [7]. More recent work proposes the use of a version of semantic networks for model representation [17]. Though this latter work is promising, AI research has shown the semantic network approach to be relatively inefficient with today's technology. Usable capabilities in model management in the near future are more likely to evolve from modeling languages, expanded subroutine approaches, and in some cases, AI production rules.

ISSUES FOR THE FUTURE

At this stage in the development of the DSS area, issues, problems, and fruitful directions for further research/development are plentiful. At a "task force" meeting this summer, thirty researchers from twelve countries gathered to discuss the nature of DSS's and to identify issues for the future. Their list, developed in group discussions over several days, was quite long [19]. The issues given here, phrased as difficult questions, seem to be the ones that must be dealt with quickly, lest the promise and potential benefits of DSS's be diluted or seriously delayed.

What's a DSS?

Earlier it was noted that some skeptics regard DSS as "just another buzz word." This article has shown that there is a significant amount of content behind the label. The danger remains, however, that the bandwagon effect will outrun our ability to define and develop potential contributions of a DSS. The market imperatives of the multi-billion dollar information systems industry tend to generate pressures to create simple labels for intuitively good ideas. It happened in many cases, but not all, of course, with MIS. Some companies are still trying to live down the aftereffects of the overpromise/underdelivery/disenchantment sequence from the MIS bandwagon of the late '60's. Eventually, a set of minimal capabilities or characteristics which characterize a DSS should evolve. In the short range, a partial solution is education—supplying managers with intellectual ammunition they can use in dealing with vendors. Managers should and must ask sharp, critical questions about the capabilities of any purported DSS, matching them against what is really needed.

What Is Really Needed?

After nearly two decades of advancements in information technology, the real needs of managers from an information system are not well understood. The issue is further complicated by the realization that managers' needs and the needs of other "knowledge workers" with which they interact, are heavily interdependent. The DSS philosophy and approach has already shed some light on this issue by emphasizing "capabilities"—the ability for a manager to do things with an information system—rather than just "information needs" which too often infer data items and totals on a report.

Nevertheless, it is tempting to call for a hesitation in the development of DSS's until decision making and related managerial activities are fully understood. Though logically appealing, such a strategy is not practical. Neither the managers who face increasingly complex tasks, nor the information systems industry which has increasingly strong technology to offer, will be denied. They point out that a truly comprehensive theory of decision making has been pursued for years with minimum success.

A potential resolution of this problem is to develop and use a DSS in a way that reveals what managers can and should receive from an information system. For example, one of Scott Morton's early suggestions was that the system be designed to capture and track the steps taken by managers in the process of making key decisions, both as an aid to the analysis of the process, and as a potential training device for new managers.

The counterpart of the "needs" issue is the extent to which the system meets those needs, and the value of the performance increase that results. Evaluation of a DSS will be just as difficult, and important, as the evaluation of MIS has been. The direct and constant involvement of users, the ones in the best position to evaluate the systems, provides a glimmer of hope on this tough problem. Pursuit of these two tasks together may yield progress on both fronts with the kind of synergistic effect often sought from systems efforts. The iterative design approach and the three levels of technology afford the opportunity, if such a strategy is developed from the beginning.

Who Will Do It?

A series of organizational issues will revolve around the roles and organizational placement of the people who will take the principal responsibility for the development of DSS's. Initiative and guidance for DSS development efforts frequently come from the user area, not from the EDP/MIS area. Yet current technology still requires technical support from the information systems professional. The DSS builder may work for the vice president of finance, but the technical support role is still played by someone in the MIS department. To some extent, the demand for a DSS supports the more general trend to distribute systems development efforts out of the MIS department into the user department. The difference is that many DSS software systems, or generators, specifically attempt to directly reach the end user without involvement of the MIS group. The enlightened MIS administrator considers this a healthy trend, and willingly supplies the required technical support and coordination. Less enlightened DP administrators often see it as a threat. Some companies have set up a group specifically charged with developing DSS type applications. This strategy creates a team of "DSS Builders" who can develop the necessary skills in dealing with users, become familiar with the available technology, and define the steps in the developmental approach for DSS's.

How Should It Be Done?

One of the pillars on which the success of DSS rests, is the iterative development or adaptive design approach. The traditional five to seven stage system development process and the system life cycle concept have been the backbone of systems analysis for years. Most project management systems and approaches are based on it. The adaptive design approach, because it combines all the stages into one quick step which is repeated, will require a redefinition of system development milestones and a major modification of project management mechanisms. Since many traditional systems will not be susceptible to the iterative approach, a way is also needed for deciding when an application should be developed in the new way instead of the traditional way. The outline of the approach described earlier is conceptually straightforward for applications that require only personal support. It becomes more complicated for group or organizational support when there are multiple users. In short, DSS builders will need to develop a set of milestones, checkpoints, documentation strategies, and project management procedures for DSS applications, and recognize when they should be used.

How Much Can Be Done?

The final issue is a caveat dealing with the limitations of technical solutions to the complexity faced by managers and decision makers. As information systems professionals, we must be careful not to feel, or even allow others to feel, that we can develop or devise a technological solution to all the problems of management. Managers will always "deal with complexity in a state of perplexity"—it is the nature of the job. Information technology can, and is, making a major contribution to improving the effectiveness of people in this situation, but the solution will never be total. With traditional systems, we continually narrow the scope and definition of the system until we know it will do the job it is required to do. If the specification/design/construction/implementation process is done right, the system is a success, measured against its original objectives. With a DSS, the user and his systems capabilities are constantly pursuing the problem, but the underspecified nature of the problem insures that there will never be a complete solution. Systems analysts have always had a little trouble with humility, but the DSS process requires a healthy dose of modesty with respect to the ability of technology to solve all the problems of managers in organizations.

SUMMARY

The "Framework for Development" described above attempts to show the dimensions and scope of DSS in a way that will promote the further *development* of this highly promising type of information system.

1. The relationships between EDP, MIS and DSS show that DSS is only one of several important technology subsystems for improving organizational performance, and that DSS development efforts must carefully integrate with these other systems.

2. The three levels of technology and the interrelationships between people that use them provide a context for organizing the development effort.
3. The iterative design approach shows that the ultimate goal of the DSS development effort is the installation of an *adaptive system* consisting of all three levels of technology and their users operating and adapting to changes over time.
4. The performance objectives show the types of decision making to be served by, and the types of support which should be built into, a DSS as it is developed.
5. The three technical capabilities illustrate that development efforts must provide the DSS with capabilities in dialogue management, data management, and model management.
6. The issues discussed at the end of the article identify some potential roadblocks that must be recognized and confronted to permit the continued development of DSS.

In closing, it should now be clear that DSS is more than just a "buzz word," but caution must be used in announcing a new "era" in information systems. Perhaps the best term is a "DSS Movement" as user organizations, information systems vendors, and researchers become aware of the field, its potential, and the many unanswered questions. Events and mechanisms in the DSS Movement include systems development experience in organizations, hardware/software developments by vendors, publishing activities to report experience and research, and conferences to provide a forum for the exchange of ideas among interested parties.

It is clear that the momentum of the DSS Movement is building. With appropriate care and reasonable restraint, the coordinated efforts of managers, builders, toolsmiths, and researchers can converge in the development of a significant set of information systems to help improve the effectiveness of organizations and the people who work in them.

QUESTIONS

1. What characteristics of a DSS differentiate it from an EDP or an MIS?
2. Discuss the three levels of DSS technology. Give examples of each level.
3. Compare and contrast iterative design with the more traditional approaches (e.g., systems development life cycle).
4. Discuss the components of a DSS from a builder's perspective.

REFERENCES

1. ALTER, S. "A Taxonomy of Decision Support Systems," *Sloan Management Review,* 19, no. 1 (Fall 1977), 39–56.
2. ALTER, S. *Decision Support Systems: Current Practice and Continuing Challenges.* Reading, Mass.: Addison-Wesley, 1980.
3. ASHENHURST, R. L. "Curriculum Recommendations for Graduate Professional Programs in Information Systems," *ACM Communications,* 15, no. 5 (May 1972), 363–98.

4. BARBOSA, L. C., AND R. G. HIRKO   "Integration of Algorithmic Aids into Decision Support Systems," *MIS Quarterly,* 4, no. 1 (March 1980), 1–12.

5. BENNETT, J.   "User-Oriented Graphics, Systems for Decision Support in Unstructured Tasks, in *User-Oriented Design of Interactive Graphics Systems,* ed. S. Treu, 3–11. New York: Association for Computing Machinery, 1977.

6. BOEING COMPUTER SERVICES   c/o Mr. Park Thoreson, P.O. Box 24346, Seattle, Wash. 98124.

7. BONEZEK, H., C. W. HOSAPPLE, AND A. WHINSTON   "Evolving Roles of Models in Decision Support Systems," *Decision Sciences,* 11, no. 2 (April 1980), 337–56.

8. CARLSON, E. D., J. BENNETT, G. GIDDINGS, AND P. MANTEY   "The Design and Evaluation of an Interactive Geo-Data Analysis and Display System," *Information Processing—74.* Amsterdam: North Holland Publishing, 1974.

9. CARLSON, E. D., AND J. A. SUTTON   "A Case Study of Non-Programmer Interactive Problem Solving, *IBM Research Report RJ1382,* San Jose, Calif., 1974.

10. CARLSON, E. D., B. F. GRACE, AND J. A. SUTTON   "Case Studies of End User Requirements for Interactive Problem-Solving Systems," *MIS Quarterly,* 1, no. 1 (March 1977), 51–63.

11. CARLSON, E. D.   "An Approach for Designing Decision Support Systems," *Proceedings,* 11th Hawaii International Conference on Systems Sciences, Western Periodicals Co., North Hollywood, Calif., 1978, 76–96.

12. CARLSON, E. D., AND W. METZ   "Integrating Dialog Management and Data Management," *IBM Research Report RJ2738,* February 1, 1980, San Jose, Calif.

13. CARLSON, E. D.   "The User-Interface for Decision Support Systems," unpublished working paper, IBM Research Laboratory, San Jose, Calif.

14. COURBON, J., J. DRAGEOF, AND T. JOSE   "L'Approache Evolutive," *Information et Gestion No. 103,* Institute d'Administration des Enterprises, Grenoble, France, January–February 1979, 51–59.

15. DAVIS, R.   "A DSS for Diagnosis and Therapy," *DataBase,* 8, no. 3 (Winter 1977), 58–72.

16. DZIDA, W., S. HERDA, AND W. D. ITZFELDT   "User-Perceived Quality of Software Interactive Systems," *Proceedings,* Third Annual Conference on Engineering (IEEE) Computer Society, Long Beach, Calif., 1978, 188–95.

17. ELAM, J., J. HENDERSON, AND L. MILLER   "Model Management Systems: An Approach to Decision Support in Complex Organizations," *Proceedings,* Conference on Information Systems, Society for Management Information Systems, Philadelphia, December 1980.

18. EXECUCOM SYSTEMS CORPORATION   P.O. Box 9758, Austin, Tex. 78766.

19. FICK, G., AND R. H. SPRAGUE, JR., EDS.   *Decision Support Systems: Issues and Challenges.* Oxford, England: Pergamon Press, 1981.

20. GERRITY, T. P., JR.   "Design of Man-Machine Decision Systems: An Application to Portfolio Management," *Sloan Management Review,* 12, no. 2 (Winter 1971), 59–75.

21. HAYES, R. H., AND R. L. NOLAND   "What Kind of Corporate Modeling Functions Best?" *Harvard Business Review,* 52 (May–June 1974), 102–12.

22. HEAD, R.   "Management Information Systems: A Critical Appraisal," *Datamation,* 13, no. 5 (May 1967), 22–28.

23. KEEN, P. G. W., AND M. S. SCOTT MORTON   *Decision Support Systems: An Organizational Perspective.* Reading Mass.: Addison-Wesley, 1978.

24. KEEN, P. G. W., AND R. D. HACKATHORN   "Decision Support Systems and Personal Computing," Department of Decision Sciences, Wharton School, University of Pennsylvania, Working Paper 79-01-03, Philadelphia, April 3, 1979.

25. KEEN, P. G. W.   "Adaptive Design for DSS," *Database,* 12, nos. 1 and 2 (Fall 1980), 15–25.

26. KEEN, P. G. W.   "Decision Support Systems: A Research Perspective," in *Decision Support Systems: Issues and Challenges.* Oxford, England: Pergamon Press, 1981.

27. KROEBER, H. W., H. J. WATSON, AND R. H. SPRAGUE, JR.   "An Empirical Investigation and Analysis of the Current State of Information Systems Evolution," *Journal of Information and Management,* 3, no. 1 (February 1980), 35–43.

28. LITTLE, J. D. C.   "Models and Managers: The Concept of a Decision Calculus," *Management Science,* 16, no. 8 (April 1970), B466–85.

29. MANTEY, P. E., AND E. D. CARLSON   "Integrated Geographic Data Bases: The GADS Experience," IBM Research Division, *IBM Research Report RJ2702,* San Jose, Calif., December 3, 1979.

30. NESS, D. N.   "Decision Support Systems: Theories of Design," presented at the Wharton Office of Naval Research Conference on Decision Support Systems, Philadelphia, November 4–7, 1975.

31. SCOTT, J. H.   "The Management Science Opportunity: A Systems Development Management Viewpoint," *MIS Quarterly,* 2, no. 4 (December 1978), 59–61.

32. SCOTT MORTON, M. S.   *Management Decision Systems: Computer Based Support for Decision Making,* Division of Research, Harvard University, Cambridge, Mass., 1971.

33. SIMON, H.   *The New Science of Management Decision.* New York: Harper & Row, 1960.

34. SIMON, H.   "Cognitive Science: The Newest Science of the Artificial," *Cognitive Science,* 4 (1980), 33–46.

35. Society for Management Information Systems, *Proceedings of the Eleventh Annual Conference,* Chicago, September 10–13, 1979, 45–56.

36. SPRAGUE, R. H., AND H. J. WATSON   "MIS Concepts Part I," *Journal of Systems Management,* 26, no. 1 (January 1975), 34–37.

37. SPRAGUE, R. H., AND H. J. WATSON   "Model Management in MIS," *Proceedings, 7th National AIDS,* Cincinnati, November 5, 1975, 213–15.

38. SPRAGUE, R. H., AND H. J. WATSON   "A Decision Support System for Banks," *Omega—The International Journal of Management Science,* 4, no. 6 (1976), 657–71.

39. SPRAGUE, R. H., AND H. J. WATSON   "Bit by Bit: Toward Decision Support Systems," *California Management Review,* XXII, no. 1 (Fall 1979), 60–68.

40. SPRAGUE, R. H.   "Decision Support Systems—Implications for the Systems Analysts," *Systems Analysis and Design: A Foundation for the 1980's,* New York: Elsevier-North Holland, 1980.

41. SPRAGUE, R. H.   "A Framework for Research on Decision Support Systems," in *Decision Support Systems: Issues and Challenges,* ed. G. Fick and R. H. Sprague. Oxford, England: Pergamon Press, 1981.

42. SUTTON, J.   "Evaluation of a Decision Support System: A Case Study with the Office Products Division of IBM," San Jose, Calif.: *IBM Research Report FJ2214,* 1978.

43. SUTTON, J. A., AND R. H. SPRAGUE   "A Study of Display Generation and Management in Interactive Business Applications," San Jose, Calif.: *IBM Research Report No. RJ2392,* IBM Research Division, November 9, 1978.

44. TYMSHARE   20705 Valley Green Drive, Cupertino, Calif. 95014.

45. WAGNER, G. R.   "DSS: Hypotheses and Inferences," Internal Report, EXECUCOM Systems Corporation, Austin, Tex., 1980.

46. WILL, HART J.   "Model Management Systems," in *Information Systems and Organizational Structure,* ed. E. Grochia and H. Szyperski, 467–83. New York: Walter de Gruyter, 1975.

2

DSS IN CONTEXT

Ralph H. Sprague, Jr.

INTRODUCTION

The theme of the papers in this issue is to establish some perspective on the progress of DSS during the past 10 years. This paper contributes to that theme by considering DSS in a broad context—one that includes other efforts in information systems and management science. Over the past decade we have seen information systems evolve under a variety of names. Electronic Data Processing was augmented by management information systems, office automation, management reporting (or support) systems, executive information systems, and of course, decision support systems. Meanwhile, many of the analysis efforts established initially under titles such as management science, operations research, quantitative techniques and statistical analysis have been brought under the information systems function because so much analysis is now computer-based.

There have been a variety of models and paradigms to explain how these various systems and analysis efforts relate to each other. They usually include variables such

Sprague, Ralph H. Jr., "DSS in Context," *Decision Support Systems*, 3 (1987), pp. 197–202.

as the level of management served, the nature of the transaction, the type of data used, response times (batch or on-line) whether they are done by the data processing center or at the user's desk, whether they are based primarily on data or primarily on models etc. This paper proposes a characteristic which promises to be more helpful than these traditional measures for organizing the way information systems are built and used.

The initial section reexamines the overall objective or mission for information systems in organizations. The next section introduces the concept of Type I and Type II information handling activities which are to be supported or improved through the use of information systems. A third section contains a retrospective of some key developments during the past decade viewed in this new context. Finally, the paper suggests future developments we should expect, or pursue, to enhance the contribution of DSS to the overall mission.

THE OVERALL MISSION

In the frenetic, fast changing world of information systems, it is sometimes hard to keep perspective on the true objective or mission of information systems in organizations. New terms (buzz words?) are created, new systems proposed, and new products are developed with confusing rapidity. It sometimes seems that the true objective is to enlarge the power base of the IS department, or enhance the reputation of certain academics, or increase the market share of IS vendors. These may be somewhat legitimate outcomes, but they are by-products of a more important objective. I suggest that the ultimate mission of IS in an organization is *to improve the performance of information workers in organizations through the application of information technology.*

This mission is admittedly not very specific—with ambiguous words such as "improve" and "performance"—but there are two important implications nevertheless. First, it establishes people as the target of IS. Systems should be built to serve people. The kind of people—information workers—are those whose job is primarily handling information. The United States Bureau of Labor Statistics shows that more than 50 percent of the employees in the country are information workers. In some industries, such as banks, the percentage is above 90.

Second, information systems should increase performance. Merely producing reports, or supporting activities, or even "getting the right information to the right person at the right time" falls short unless the result is performance improvement. Certainly there will be problems defining "performance" and "improvement," but at least the general objective is clear.

SUPPORT FOR INFORMATION WORKERS

How can performance be improved? The generic word "support" has been used to infer the concept of using IS as a resource to leverage the activities of managers (Management Support Systems, Decision Support Systems). With information workers as the majority of employed people in the U.S. and most other advanced societies, it is clear that IS can be used in a multitude of ways to support a multitude of activities performed by information workers. In fact, some form of segmentation of information workers and their activities is required to better focus information system efforts to support them.

Type I and Type II Work

Several recent articles have explored an intuitive dichotomy labeled Type I and Type II information activity [1, 2]. The key characteristics of this dichotomy include:

1. Transactions: Type I work consists of a large volume of transactions with a relatively low value (or cost) connected with each. Type II work consists of fewer transactions, but each is more costly or valuable.
2. Process: Type I work is based on well defined procedures, while Type II work is process-independent.
3. Output: The output from Type I work is more easily measured because it is defined by quantities of procedural iteration. The focus is on performing the necessary process or procedure quickly, efficiently, and usually many times. Type II output is not easily measured because it consists of problem solving and goal attainment. You can assign a Type I task to an information worker by explaining the sequence of steps required to accomplish it. With a Type II task, you must specify the desired outcome. Figuring out the necessary steps in the sequence is part of the job, and may be significantly different for different people.
4. Data: Type I work uses data in relatively well structured form, whereas Type II work deals primarily with concepts which are represented in less well structured form, usually with a great deal of ambiguity.

At first glance this dichotomy looks similar to the "clerical" versus "managerial-professional" breakdown that has been used for many years. Upon closer examination, however, it is clear that clerical personnel, especially secretaries, frequently have process-independent tasks defined only by their outcome. Likewise, most managers and professionals have a certain proportion of their work which is process defined.

It can be argued that the nature of the task, according to this two-way classification, is the most important characteristic in determining what kind of support is required from information systems. It should be clear that most uses of information systems in the past have been for supporting Type I tasks. It is easiest and most natural to use a process engine (computer) to support process driven tasks. It is also clear that the challenge of the future is to use information systems to support Type II tasks. The nature of the tasks is different, the mentality required to do it is different, and so the information support must be different from the traditional Type I approaches.

Supporting Type II Work

There have been several attempts to support Type II work with information systems. In most cases, however, it has been done by providing Type II workers with better access to tools that have been used for Type I tasks.

For example, consider a typical breakdown of Type II functions.

1. Tracking, monitoring, alerting.
2. Problem-solving, analysis, design.
3. Communication.

Systems to support each one of these clusters of activities have evolved under the names Management Information Systems, Management Science (including Operations Research, statistics and mathematics), and Office Automation respectively. But they tend to be separate and diverse, poorly linked, and built on completely different structures. Note also that the Type II task we have called decision making, usually requires an intermixture of all three functions.

What is needed, then, is a system effort specifically focused on supporting Type II activities. To be specific, we should broaden our concept of DSS to include tracking-monitoring-alerting and communicating as well as the more traditional intelligence-design-choice view of decision making. This can be accomplished by merging the systems development in several areas into an amalgam of systems capabilities under the control of information workers performing Type II activities.

DSS AS INTEGRATOR

The DSS movement has become one of the most substantive on-going efforts to deal with support for Type II activities. Until recently, however, even this effort was based on using tools designed originally for Type I purposes. Traditional data base and modeling tools were integrated in a system with a facile interface to the user. The user contributed the mental capability to deal with the Type II task, while the system tools leveraged those mental skills.

A significant contribution of the DSS movement, however, was the merging and integration of previously separate tool sets into a unified whole more valuable than the sum of the parts. In fact, current DSS can be viewed as computer-based systems that lie at the intersection of two major evolutionary trends—*data processing* which has yielded a significant body of knowledge about managing data, and *management science* which is generating a significant body of knowledge about modeling. The confluence of these two trends forms the two major resources with which decision makers interact in the process of dealing with ill-structured tasks.

Data, models, and interaction support-(dialog) (the dialog-data-model paradigm) has become a popular way to categorize the sets of capabilities required in a DSS. (See Figure 2.1.) Let us consider how evolutionary developments in data processing and management science have led to the data base and model base capability of DSS [3].

The Data Processing Evolution

A helpful way to define the stages in the evolution of data processing is the following:

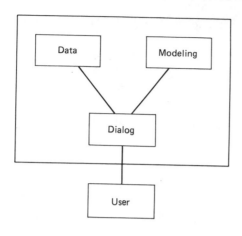

FIGURE 2.1   The DDM Paradigm

1. *Basic data processing*—characterized by stand-alone EDP jobs, mostly for transaction processing, with each program having its own files. Data handling was limited to such classic data processing functions as sorting, classifying, summarizing, etc.

2. *File management*—integrated EDP jobs for related functions, sometimes sharing files across several programs. This stage included attempts to develop common software for handling files (utilities), and prescribed ways to insure data security, integrity, backup, etc.

3. *Data base management*—a major capability of the MIS era, with particular emphasis on the software system for dealing with data separate from the programs that use it. The major impact of DBMS at this stage was the reduction of program maintenance, since data files could be modified without recompiling all the programs that used it. At this stage, DBMS software began to use data "models" to represent the way data were logically related.

4. *Query, report generation*—the addition of flexible report generators and "English-like" query languages to facilitate ad hoc requests and special reports. Emphasis here was on the direct access to data bases by non-technical people such as end users.

Figure 2.2 represents the steps in this evolution, from left to right. Note that each stage contributed a major capability that is still valuable in today's systems. In other words, we have not evolved beyond the need for the contribution of each stage, but have added capabilities to increase the value.

Throughout the EDP evolution, emphasis has been on manipulating data, initially in predefined ways to accomplish structured tasks, and later in flexible ways to accommodate ad hoc requests and preferences by individual users. Sophisticated ways of manipulating data (models) were embedded in the data processing system for some well-structured problems, for example inventory management, but modeling was generally considered a separate type of application. Users dealt with less well-structured problems by querying the data base, getting special reports, and then using their judgment.

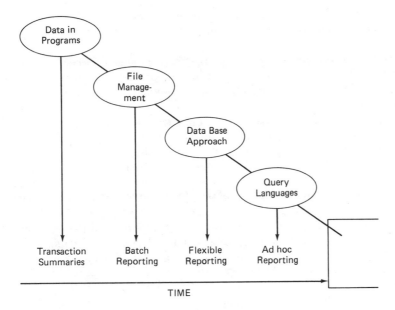

FIGURE 2.2 The Data Processing Evolution

In general, the data base approach evolving from the EDP tradition seemed to be characterized by the following objectives:

1. to effectively manage a large amount of data,
2. to establish independence between the data and the programs that used it,
3. to separate the physical and logical structures of data and deal with them separately,
4. to provide flexible, easy access to data by non-programmers.

The problems and limitations of this approach were related to its dominantly accounting-oriented historical data, and its focus on information flows and summaries. Unfortunately, for an important set of problems and decisions, getting "the right information to the right person" was necessary but not sufficient. That data often needed to be analyzed, interpreted, and extended with the use of some decision models being developed from Management Science/Operations Research efforts.

The Modeling Evolution

While data processing professionals were strengthening their ability to store and handle data, management scientists and operations researchers were increasing their ability to create "models" of a problem or situation and manipulate them to shed light on how to handle that problem. A similar sequence of evolutionary steps in the development of modeling might include the following:

1. *Symbolic models*—The early stages of modeling were characterized by heavy use of linear and nonlinear equations, sometimes in large sets of simultaneous equations.
2. *Computers as a computational engine*—The computer first became important to modeling as number crunchers to reduce large amounts of data to coefficient estimates for the equations, or as computational engines for solving sets of equations.
3. *Computer models*—Eventually, the computer took on a subtly different role. Rather than a device to compute a mathematical model, the computer program *became* the model. Computer variables became the symbols which were manipulated by the computer program instead of by mathematical operations. This approach led to a popular class of models that were not "solved" but rather "run" over time to observe the behavior of the model and thus shed light on the modeled situation.
4. *Modeling systems*—The computer became so important to modeling efforts that software systems were developed to handle classes of models. The software generally provided common data input formats, similar report formats, and integrated documentation. Modeling systems for statistical programs (for example SPSS) and mathematical programming (for example MPSX) are good examples.
5. *Interactive modeling*—As computers became more available in "time sharing" mode, interactive modeling became more feasible. Mini-computers and mainframes dedicated to on-line usage generally had libraries of models which could be called to do a variety of analyses. Unfortunately, it was common for the models to be stand-alone programs with different data requirements and formats and little if any linkage between the models.

Figure 2.3 graphically represents the stages in this modeling evolution, from right to left. Again, as before, each stage yielded knowledge or capability that contribute to be a valuable part of the tools available for dealing with problem solving decision making. Also, as before, the evolution led to the modeling capabilities utilized in DSS to help decision makers deal with Type II problems.

In summary, modeling evolution led to an increasingly close relationship between the models and computers, but continued to be separate from the data which they used. This seemed to reflect model builders' preoccupation with the model as the focus of attention and their hesitance to get intimately involved with data sources and structures. In general, the modeling efforts needed major contributions from the data base efforts of systems professionals.

Evolutions Converge

Figure 2.4 (on page 44) represents the convergence of these two trends into the data and modeling components of DSS. This figure can also be used to represent the range of systems that have been called DSS. Alter discussed "data oriented" versus "model oriented" DSS as those which depended more on data query or interactive modeling respectively [4]. Those DSS with a "balance" of capabilities occupy the center of the figure.

Each of the two development tracks—in data base and in modeling—were useful in their own right. They were each significantly lacking, however, in helping informa-

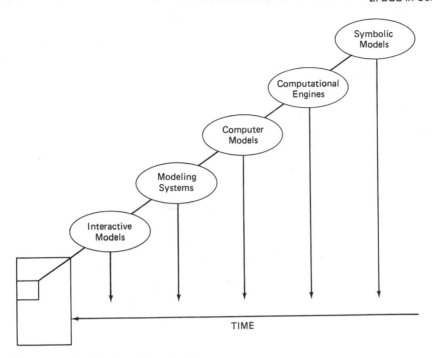

FIGURE 2.3 The Modeling Evolution

tion workers deal with Type II tasks. Developments in Decision Support Systems allowed each set of capabilities to realize their potential in this area. DSS extended and combined both the data base technology and the modeling technology, and gave non-technical users access to them. The data and models were intimately linked, and both were linked with the user.

Conversely, DSS makes demands on the data base and the modeling capability that were not necessary before. Specifically, DSS makes model management capabilities necessary. Without the integration requirements of DSS, modeling systems or libraries of interactive models would probably suffice. So as the need for model management capabilities became apparent, it was the DSS builders and researchers who began working on its development.

THE FUTURE

We are now positioned to continue this development track into the future. Viewing DSS in the broad context of supporting Type II information work will guide these developments to better integrate mechanisms to support monitoring-tracking-alerting as well as better integration of communication support systems. New developments from artificial intelligence will make major contributions to all three of the DSS capability sets. Data base management will benefit from infusion of library science as well as AI to create better ways to organize and manage text-based data. Developments in model

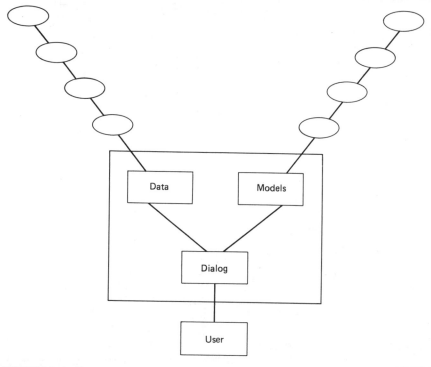

FIGURE 2.4 Evolutions Converge

management are leading to better ways of defining and manipulating models. Dialog will profit significantly from the inclusion of natural language processing techniques and voice recognition.

In summary, with a broad view of DSS's role in the overall mission of information systems in organization, the future is exceedingly bright. The DSS "movement" has made a major contribution during the past decade. The evolving DSS "discipline" promises to be even more significant in the next decade.

QUESTIONS

1. What is the difference between Type I and Type II information work?
2. Why is the distinction important to the design and use of DSS?
3. Trace the stages of the data processing and MIS evolution. What is likely to be the next stage?
4. Trace the stages of the management science evolution. What is likely to be the next stage?
5. Explain how parts of each of these evolutions have converged in DSS. What is likely to be the next stage in DSS?

REFERENCES

1. PANKO, R., AND R. H. SPRAGUE   DP Needs New Approach to Office Automation, *Data Management* (1984).

2. PANKO, R., AND R. H. SPRAGUE   Towards a New Framework for Office Support, ACM Conference on Office Automation Systems (Philadelphia, PA, 1982).

3. An earlier version of this section is included in: KONSYNSKI, B., AND SPRAGUE, R. H.   Future Research Directions in Model Management, *Decision Support Systems* 2, no. 1 (1986).

4. ALTER S.   A TAXONOMY OF DECISION SUPPORT SYSTEMS. *Sloan Management Review* 19, no. 1, 39–56.

PART 2

Developing and Using DSS

A number of activities are required before a DSS is available to support decision making. The organization must plan and organize both computer and human resources. Decisions must be made as to what hardware and software are required and where these resources will come from. Decisions must be made as to what roles will be assumed by various organizational personnel: Who will build the DSS? Who will support the DSS? While the answers to these and other questions are likely to evolve over time, it is important that they be carefully thought out. As with most organizational endeavors, thoughtful planning and organizing is an important key to success.

Once the planning and organizing for DSS has been accomplished, the development of specific decision support systems can begin. As was suggested in the first part of the book, the development approach for DSS differs from most other types of computer applications. It is important that these differences be clearly understood if DSS efforts are to be successful.

Once the DSS has been created, it can be put into use. This is when the payoff from the DSS is received. It should support all phases of the decision-making process and enhance the decision maker(s)' effectiveness.

This section contains four articles. Each article should make a contribution to your understanding of how decision support systems are developed and used.

Management becomes involved with a DSS in a variety of ways: as approver and administrator, developer, operator, and user of output. A number of issues related to these responsibilities are explored by Jack Hogue in "A Framework for the Examination of Management Involvement in Decision Support Systems" (Reading 3). The findings from a study of eighteen organizations with DSS help answer such questions as: What methods are used in evaluating the desirability of creating a DSS? How are managers involved in developing a DSS? Who are the hands-on users of a DSS? Are all phases of the decision-making process supported by a DSS?

A DSS can involve a substantial commitment of organizational resources. Peter Keen, in "Value Analysis: Justifying Decision Support Systems" (Reading 4), explores how a proposed DSS should be evaluated. He argues that typical methods such as cost-benefit and return on investment analysis are inappropriate for DSS. For the typical DSS, the costs and especially the benefits are difficult or impossible to quantify. As a method of analysis, Keen recommends "value analysis." This approach is consistent with the less formal approaches most managers seem to use in assessing technical innovations.

It is widely believed that decision support systems require a unique development approach. The names *iterative, evolutionary,* and *adaptive design* are all used to describe this approach in which requirements analysis, design, development, and implementation are all combined into a single phase which is reiterated in a short period of time. Maryam Alavi and Al Napier's article, "An Experiment in Applying the Adaptive Design Approach to DSS Development" (Reading 5), discusses and illustrates this development approach for DSS.

Jack Hogue and Hugh Watson in "Current Practices in the Development of Decision Support Systems" (Reading 5) provide additional insights into how decision support systems are being developed. Once again drawing upon data collected from eighteen organizations, they describe the nature of the development approach, user involvement in system development, the time required for system development, the incorporation of the decision maker's style into the system, the role of information systems and operations research/management science personnel in the development effort, and specific procedures and techniques used in system development. The factors that appear to affect system development are also discussed.

Conventional wisdom is that decision support systems are useful in assisting the intelligence, design, and choice phases of decision making. Brian Mittman and Jeffrey Moore in "Senior Management Computer Use: Implications for DSS Designs and Goals" (Reading 6) explore how senior executives are actually using decision support systems. Their study findings suggest that decision support systems support broader aspects of decision making than is frequently assumed.

3

A FRAMEWORK
FOR THE EXAMINATION
OF MANAGEMENT
INVOLVEMENT
IN DECISION SUPPORT
SYSTEMS

Jack T. Hogue

INTRODUCTION

The evolution of computer-based information system (CBIS) applications in organizations has been noted and studied in the literature [15]. Applications that have evolved are often organized into one of the categories of transaction processing system (TPS), management information system (MIS), or decision support system (DSS) [13, 22, 25]. Both TPS and MIS are directed toward structured information flows in support of lower and middle organizational processes.

    Decision support systems have a very specific purpose—the assistance of middle or upper level management decision makers with decisions of significant importance. Mann and Watson [17, p. 27] provide the following definition of a DSS:

> A decision support system is an interactive system that provides the user with easy access to decision models and data in order to support semi-structured and unstructured decision-making tasks.

Reprinted from the *Journal of Management Information Systems,* Vol. 4, No. 1, 1987, pp. 96–110. By permission of M.E.Sharpe, Inc., Armonk, NY.

A particularly significant difference between the TPS and MIS, on one hand, and DSS on the other, is that a variety of information supporting a specific decision is available in a variety of formats with a DSS. With the TPS and MIS, the available information is quite inflexible.

In order to evaluate the necessary levels and types of management involvement in DSS, a framework for such an investigation will be proposed. This framework is derived both from a logical, intuitive categorization of processes and from the existing literature. First, a framework for the examination of management involvement in DSS will be proposed and related to specific speculations/research in the literature. Then, results from a field study of 18 DSS will be used to examine and reinforce the framework.

FRAMEWORK FOR INVESTIGATION

Based upon and extending beyond existing research and speculation in the literature, this work proposes that the involvement of management in DSS separates logically into four areas. The manager, in relation to the DSS, serves as a(an):

  I. approver and administrator
 II. developer
III. operator
IV. user of output

It is with this fourfold conceptual taxonomy of roles that the involvement of management is to be examined. The basic fourfold taxonomy is proposed as a logical segmentation of management task with regard to DSS.[1] These four roles would appear to apply also to other categories of information systems (i.e., TPS and MIS); however, no such extension is being proposed in this research. Much of the subclassification of issues for the "developer" role and the "user of output" role is derived from the work of Sprague [22]. In the following sections, issues relevant to management's involvement in DSS with regard to the approver, developer, operator, and user roles will be presented, along with any supporting evidence from the literature. These specific issues will then be related directly to findings of a study of specific DSS.

Approver and Administrator

As an approver, the manager is functioning in a way quite consistent with other planning activities. It is generally the responsibility of management to judge the relative merits of alternative organizational investments and to accept these investments when it is to the benefit of the organization. In addition, DSS become an additional organizational entity requiring a position within the organization's structure and requiring relationships to other interacting organizational units.

With regard to the approver role, there are three basic issues to be investigated. First, how and by whom are DSS policy issues determined within the organization? The question of who sets policy has not been previously examined.

- DSS planning should be incorporated into corporate planning processes—Sprague and Carlson [23].
- In planning for implementation of the DSS into the organization, the political impact on power should be examined—Ahn and Grudnitski [1].

Second, how does management evaluate the DSS in terms of their benefit/cost to the organization?

- Financial evaluation of DSS is difficult and infrequent—Alter [2], Keen [12], McCosh and Scott Morton [18].
- DSS evaluation should be based upon both value-addition—Keen [12]—and cost-reduction—Meador and Keen [19].
- A "portfolio" approach should be utilized which considers risk and reward— Gremillion and Pyburn [8].

Third, how are DSS related to other organizational functions, specifically the more traditional CBIS functions?

- Some DSS resources are shared, and some are separate from other CBIS resources and controlled by user management—Blumenthal [5], Locander, Napier and Scamell [16], Sprague [22].

Developer

Once a DSS has been approved it must be brought into being; that is, it must be developed. Given that the function of the DSS is to support the manager's decision-making responsibilities, and given that decision making is a difficult task to specify or structure, it should not seem illogical that the manager would need to play a substantial role in the DSS development process.

There are four subconcerns relevant to the manager's role as DSS developer. First, at what points in the DSS development process is management involvement required?

- Management involvement should be heavy throughout development—Alter [3], Bahl and Hunt [4], Ginzberg [7], McCosh and Scott Morton [18], Sprague [22].
- Management should provide leadership in DSS development—Keen and Scott Morton [13], Keen and Wagner [14], Locander, Napier, and Scamell [16].
- DSS development is often promoted and fostered by the advocacy of an "organizational champion"—Curley and Gremillion [6], Hayes and Nolan [9], Sprague and Olson [24].

- DSS development should include a fostering of cooperation and coordination between user/managers and technical designers—Ahn and Grudnitski [1].
- User-led development approaches often lead to improved DSS performance—Kasper [11].

Second, how much time is required of management in developing the DSS? While no one has addressed this issue specifically, length of the total development effort has been examined.

- Total development time is short (1 day to 20 weeks)—Keen [12].

Third, how are the personal needs and style of the manager/decision maker incorporated into the DSS?

- The DSS should be developed to include the personal decision-making style of the manager—Keen [12], McCosh and Scott Morton [18].

Finally, what technology is used (or not used) by managers in developing the DSS? Very little research has been performed in this area.

- The nominal level of available DSS technology has a significant impact on the extent of user and manager involvement—Mann and Watson [17].

Operator

The actual operation of the DSS requires skills perhaps most dissimilar to those typically required of managers. There are differing "levels" of technical sophistication in DSS which require differing amounts of ability for use. It is expected that some amount of operational ability and actual operation of the DSS may be desired by managers.

Of managerial interest with regard to system operation are two general subissues. First, how much will management operate the DSS? There has been no prior examination of the frequency of management operation.

- Managers prefer to turn operation of the DSS over to their staff—Wagner [26].
- There is a "significant" number of upper managers sitting at terminals—Keen and Wagner [14].

Second, how is a manager's personal decision-making style maintained during operation of the DSS, if by other than the manager (e.g., an intermediary)? This issue has not been previously examined.

User of Output

In making decisions, managers typically make use of a variety of sources of information. Depending on the manager's own personal style (e.g., Simon's intuitive-rational dichotomy [21]), the emphasis placed on different information will, of course, vary.

The entire purpose of the DSS is to support the manager in his decision-making process by attempting to supply information the manager requests. In the final analysis it is with the outputs of the DSS that management is most interested.

The last of the four roles, user of output, contains four subconcerns. First, how is DSS output utilized by management vertically throughout the organization?

- The DSS should be used in support of managerial decision making at all levels of the organization—Keen and Scott Morton [13], McCosh and Scott Morton [18], Sprague [22].

Second, is DSS output used for decision making at the discretion of the user manager? This issue has not been examined. Third, does the DSS support managers in both individual and group decision making?

- The DSS should support both individual and group ("sequential interdependent" and "pooled interdependent") decision making—Keen and Scott Morton [13], Sanders and Courtney [20], Sprague [22], Huber [10].

Fourth, how does the DSS support management in the different phases of decision making (i.e., intelligence, design, choice)?

- The DSS should be able to assist the manager with all phases of the decision process—Keen and Scott Morton [13], McCosh and Scott Morton [18], Sprague [22].

THE STUDY

Study Methodology

The objective of this study is to investigate a large number of issues, many of which have been examined only to a limited degree (e.g., single case situations). Questionnaire study offers limited viability when examining a relatively new discipline such as DSS. The primary difficulty is in developing unambiguous questions. For these reasons, the in-depth personal field interview method was chosen. This permits individual explanations and clarifications when required and the ability to probe to varying levels of detail as issues of interest present themselves. Alter [2] has conducted a study with a similar approach; however, many of Alter's cases would not be considered DSS by today's standards.

Sample Selection

In order to facilitate the location of a sufficient number of DSS, the Dallas-Fort Worth-Atlanta areas were chosen as the study site. This was due to two factors. First, these areas host a high percentage of high-level corporate policy-making organizations.

This was desirable since DSS applications are most relevant for upper level policy decision making. Second, these areas provided a necessary convenience sample.

Selection of companies (see Table 3.1) was accomplished via telephone interviews with corporate personnel involved at high levels of both the CBIS function and other corporate areas (e.g., finance, marketing, planning). These initial conversations served to locate other corporate personnel involved with DSS applications. Of 109 total companies contacted, a sample of 18 separate companies was selected. These 18 were the only companies which had DSS which satisfied all of the essential criteria and most of the additional criteria (derived from Keen and Scott Morton [13] and Sprague [22]) listed below.

ESSENTIAL CRITERIA FOR A *DSS*

- Supports but does not replace decision making.
- Directed toward semistructured and/or unstructured decision-making tasks.
- Data and models organized around the decision(s).
- Easy to use software interface.

ADDITIONAL CRITERIA FOR A *DSS*

- Interactive processing.
- DSS use and control is determined by the user.
- Flexible and adaptable to changes in the environment and decision maker's style.
- Quick *ad hoc* DSS building capacity.

Conduct of the Interview

For each of the 18 companies in the sample, a 2- to 3-hour interview was conducted with the individual in the company who had the highest level of interaction with the development and use of the DSS. In all cases the interviewee was either a high ranking management decision maker (president or vice president) or a high ranking assistant to the decision maker (senior financial analyst or middle manager).

STUDY FINDINGS

This study examines numerous issues related to the involvement and role of management in decision support systems. Space does not permit an exhaustive presentation and discussion of all results. For this reason, study findings are first provided through a list of generalizations believed to be most relevant. These generalizations are intended to be brief and to the point. Each statement is accompanied by the percentage of total cases (n = 18) which was found to be in evidence for the generalization. These statements are hardly intended to be considered as fact, but rather as evidence to be evaluated in seeking to shed light on the issues. These generalizations are then

TABLE 3.1 Companies Studied for Decision Support Systems

COMPANY NAME	DECISION SUPPORT SYSTEM AREA	INDUSTRY	SCOPE OF BUSINESS	SALES ($)
American Airlines	Price and route selection	Transportation	International	3.5 million
American Petrofina	Corporate planning and forecasting	Oil & mining	National	2.1 billion
Central and Southwest Corporation	Corporate planning and forecasting	Utility	Regional	1.7 billion
Champlin Petroleum	Corporate planning and forecasting	Oil & mining	National	2.5 billion
First United Bancorporation	Investment evaluation	Financial	State	190 million
Frito-Lay, Inc.	Pricing, advertising, and promotion	Manufacturer	International	6 billion
General Dynamics	Price evaluation	Manufacturer	International	4.74 billion
Gifford-Hill & Company	Corporate planning and forecasting	Construction	International	560 million
Lear Petroleum	Evaluation of potential drilling sites	Oil & mining	National	90 million
Mercantile Texas Corporation	Corporate planning and forecasting	Financial	State	520 million
National Gypsum	Corporate planning and forecasting	Manufacturer	International	840 million
Southern Railway	Train dispatching and routing	Transportation	Regional	1.5 billion
Texas-New Mexico Power	Corporate planning and forecasting	Utility	Regional	216 million
Texas Oil & Gas Corp.	Evaluation of potential drilling sites	Oil & mining	National	1.6 billion
Texas Utilities Company	Corporate planning and forecasting	Utility	State	278 million
The LTV Corporation	Terms of real estate	Diversified	International	8 billion
The Western Company	Corporate planning and forecasting	Oil services	International	500 million
Zale Corporation	Evaluation of potential store sites	Retail	International	830 million

condensed and examined in relation to the framework recommended. This is done in the examination-of-findings section of the paper.

Approval and Administration of the DSS

1. Administration of the DSS is localized to specific individuals within the company/department (73%).
2. Administration of the DSS usually is at the departmental level (73%), but occasionally company-wide steering committees are utilized (27%).
3. Administration of the DSS is by middle and/or upper management (100%).
4. Administrative policy for the DSS is usually informal (72%).
5. DSS master plans rarely exist from either the organizational or departmental level (0%).
6. Evaluation of DSS benefit is either nonexistent (39%) or based upon intuitive value of qualitative benefits (45%).
7. Quantification of costs varies considerably with no analysis (50%), complete analysis of all factors (28%), or partial analysis of factors (22%).
8. Resource support for the DSS varies as to source, but usually:
   a. Hardware is provided by the data processing department or vendor (78%).
   b. System software is provided by data processing or vendor (72%).
   c. Communications linkage is provided by data processing or vendor (78%).
   d. Data are prepared and input by DSS user/operators (100%—one case shared responsibility with data processing).
   e. Logic is determined by DSS user/managers (94%—two cases shared responsibility with data processing).
   f. Development personnel are from the DSS user department managers and staff (94%) and frequently data processing or vendor (60%).

Development of the DSS

9. Involvement at some point in DSS development is very likely for both middle (83%) and upper (89%) management. See Table 3.2 for more specific points and levels of involvement.
10. Lower management is rarely involved with DSS development (22%).
11. Middle management is usually involved with all phases/stages of DSS development (72%).
12. Upper management is involved with DSS development primarily for idea generation, stating needs, and approval (72%).
13. DSS development is often accompanied by a strong organizational advocate for the DSS (44%).
14. Formal management approval is usually required at one or more points during development (72%).
15. Development time for the DSS varies considerably (near a uniform distribution from 1 week to 4 years).

TABLE 3.2   Management Involvement in the Development of the Decision Support System

STAGES*	Management Level			
	LOWER (%)	MIDDLE (%)	TOP (%)	ALL** (%)
Idea	0	61	61	100
Information requirements	0	78	61	100
Building	11	72	6	78
Testing	11	72	6	83
Demonstration	11	78	28	89
Acceptance	0	72	67	100

*Traditional stage labels were easy for respondents to relate to. With few exceptions, development evolved several times through the stages.
**Combines management involvement from all three managerial levels.

16. Management time required during DSS development averages 38% (for upper and middle management), but with considerable variation (from 0% to 100% of time).
17. Personal user style is usually provided for by including capabilities into the DSS to interact with multiple approaches of different users (100%).
18. Management utilization of tools for development (33%) is slightly less than utilization of generators for development (45%). See Table 3.3.

Operation of the Physical Components of the DSS

19. Operation of the DSS is usually performed by both management (72%) and staff (89%) from the user area.

TABLE 3.3   Personnel Involved with the Different Decision Support Systems Levels of Technology

TYPE OF EMPLOYEE	SPECIFIC DSS, PERCENTAGE OF COMPANIES	DSS GENERATOR, PERCENTAGE OF COMPANIES	DSS TOOLS, PERCENTAGE OF COMPANIES
Management			
Lower	17	6	6
Middle	56	33	22
Upper	22	6	6
Intermediary	83	37	39
Staff (decision maker)	6	0	0
Staff (builder)*	0	22	72

*A staff builder is, in all cases, a technician who appears in none of the other categories; this individual builds only for others to use.

20. Operation of the DSS by all personnel (management and staff) is rarely less than once per week (11%); however, management often uses the DSS less than once per week (56%).
21. Decision maker style/approach is maintained by the intermediary (when inter-mediatries are used—95% of managers at least occasionally use intermediaries) through the following:
   a. Easy access of intermediary to decision maker (100%).
   b. Easy access of intermediary to DSS (83%).
   c. Fast turnaround time on DSS ouptut (89% less than 1 minute).

Use of Output Generated by the DSS

22. Decision-making support is provided by the DSS primarily for middle and/or upper management (100%). Use by others is only occasional (17%). See Table 3.4.
23. Decision makers are rarely compelled to rely upon output from the DSS (6%).
24. Independent decisions are rarely made by managers when utilizing DSS output (6%). See Table 3.5.
25. Both pooled interdependent (67%) and sequential interdependent decisions (33%) are supported by DSS. See Table 3.5.
26. The intelligence phase of the decision-making process is almost always supported by the DSS (100%). See Table 3.6.

TABLE 3.4 Users of the Decision Support System for Decision-making Purposes

DECISION MAKER	PERCENTAGE OF COMPANIES
Management	
Upper	89
Middle	67
Lower	11
Middle and/or upper	100
Staff	11

TABLE 3.5 Form of Interaction between Decision Makers involving Decision Support System Output

FORM OF INTERACTION	PERCENTAGE OF COMPANIES
None	6
Shared interpretation of output	94
Sequential interdependent	33
Pooled interdependent	67

TABLE 3.6   Phases of the Decision-making Process Supported by the Decision Support System

PHASE	PERCENTAGE OF COMPANIES
Intelligence	100
Design	
What-if	100
Goal-seeking	60
Choice	33

27. The design phase is supported via either a what-if capability (100%) or a goal-seeking capability (60%). See Table 3.6.
28. The choice phase of the decision-making process is often supported by the DSS (33%). See Table 3.6.

EXAMINATION OF FINDINGS

The fourfold framework presented in this article has provided a useful basis for examining and classifying issues relevant to management involvement in DSS. The framework has also provided a good means for examining the "conventional wisdom" in the existing DSS literature. In this section of the paper the conventional wisdom is compared with study findings in an attempt of draw generalizations, where the two verify each other, and to point to departures from the conventional wisdom, where the two do not coincide.

In relating the literature with these study findings, it is important to be able to demonstrate that the findings are derived from essentially successful DSS. This is particularly important given the relatively limited sample size. Several mechanisms for evaluation of MIS success have been suggested, however; Welsch [27] has utilized a set of measures, specifically for evaluation of DSS success. These measures focus on three major issues: satisfaction of users with the "final" product, acceptability of the DSS to users, and frequency of use (if use is voluntary).

In this study user satisfaction was measured on a seven-point scale. Respondents were asked to indicate their satisfaction/dissatisfaction with the DSS. Table 3.7 demonstrates the high level of perceived satisfaction with the DSS. Acceptability of the DSS to the user was evaluated through an open-ended question asking the respondent to comment on acceptance of the DSS. None of the systems was described in any way other than "highly acceptable" or, "after some initial skepticism the system is now quite acceptable."

Frequency of use has often been recommended as a measure of information system success, if use of the system is voluntary. For all but one of the 18 cases, use of the DSS is completely voluntary, and for this one case, use is only occasionally

TABLE 3.7   Satisfaction/Dissatisfaction of the User with the Decision Support System

RANKING	PERCENTAGE OF COMPANIES
1–3	0
4	11
5	22
6	50
7	17
	100

Note: Measurement was on a 7-point scale with 1 = very dissatisfied, 4 = indifferent, and 7 = very satisfied.

dictated to the user. Use of the DSS was found to be quite high. All but two DSS are used at least once per week, and the majority are used at least ten times per week.

Approver and Administrator

- DSS planning should be incorporated into corporate planning processes.

It appears that formal planning for DSS is not the rule. While DSS are occasionally administered by a corporate steering committee, no master plan exists and policies are usually informally set by middle and/or upper managers within the user group.

- Financial evaluation of DSS is difficult and infrequent, but should still be based upon value-addition and cost reduction.

In providing approval for DSS it is apparent that management is conducting relatively little formal evaluation of costs or benefits. The cost factors, which are typically easiest to measure, generally are only partially measured or not measured at all. While benefits are often examined, measurement is primarily intuitive.

- Resource support for DSS and for other information system activities is shared in some cases and separate in some cases.

There appears to be a distinct segmentation between "technical" resource support and the "application" itself. Most technical support resources to include hardware (usually mini or mainframe), operating system capabilities, and communication linkages are provided and administered by formal information system personnel. The actual application itself is administered by management in the using area(s). This includes data input, application logic, and application maintenance.

Development of the DSS

■ , Management involvement should be heavy throughout development and should be in the form of a leadership role for the project.

Both middle and upper management are heavily involved in the projects, with middle management providing a strong leadership role throughout the process. Initiation of the project, as well as maintenance of support, is often accomplished through a middle or upper management advocate. Involvement thus appears to be quite heavy.

■ The DSS should be developed to include the personal decision-making style of the manager.

None of the DSS in this study attempted to formally model the manager's decision-making process as a way of accommodating a personal approach to the decision. Decision style was accommodated (for multiple potential managers) by building the capability into the DSS to interact with a variety of approaches or styles (e.g., variation in detail of output, tabular and graphical display).

■ The type of available DSS technology will have an impact on the extent of user and manager involvement in DSS development.

Findings are quite inconclusive here. While there was more involvement from managers when a DSS generator was used/available (43% vs. 33%), this would not seem to have been significant in affecting management involvement.

Operation of the DSS

■ There is a "significant" number of upper managers operating the DSS, but many (most) prefer to turn operation over to their staff.

In contrast to the literature, this study finds that a fairly high percentage of user managers operate the DSS directly. In most of the cases the managers often turn operation over to an intermediary, but still operate the DSS on occasion. The manager's own approach is maintained by the operating intermediary through frequent and easy access of the intermediary to both the manager and the DSS.

User of Output

■ The DSS should be used in support of managerial decision making at all levels of the organization.

Findings indicate that the DSS do support all managerial levels; however, there are significant differences in frequency. While middle and upper management are almost always supported, lower management was only rarely supported. Support is found to be at the discretion of the manager in all but one of the 18 cases.

- The DSS should support both individual and group decision-making processes of managers.

The DSS were found to support individual decision making in but one case. All other DSS (and their supported decisions) appear to involve at least one other person in a negotiable process. These decisions may be made sequentially (one individual after another, which is nearly individual decision making) or in a group process.

- The DSS should be able to assist the manager with all phases of the decision process.

Both intelligence and design were found to be supported in almost all cases. Choice was supported in one-third of the cases. This is likely due to the need for manager interaction to enable a choice to be made, since decision processes were not modeled.

CONCLUSIONS

The framework presented in this writing has provided a useful model for examining existing research/speculation in the DSS literature relating to management's role in DSS. By comparing the existing literature with results of a study of 18 DSS, we have found it possible to shed light upon certain aspects of the conventional wisdom in the field. This framework may further serve as a reference for future studies of management role in DSS.

While much of the conventional wisdom has been further supported by comparison with the case studies presented herein, much has been contradicted. In particular, corporate planning and administration of the DSS may be viewed as desirable, but have a long way yet to go. Further, approval processes need to focus on more specific cost and benefit measurements.

It appears that few DSS are actual models of decision maker processes. This may be true, and necessary, since most DSS appear to support multiple decision makers. It is difficult to draw conclusions about the level of technology (generator or tools) most appropriate for management. There is much intuitive appeal to facilitating manager involvement with a user-friendly generator, but this study did not bear this out. It could well be that a needed DSS will be built with whatever technology is made available (as in the study), but that significant improvements could be realized with a generator. This is a subject for further research.

Managers do operate the DSS, but less frequently than their intermediaries. This suggests the need for multiple interface "levels." This is needed to accommodate the infrequent, novice user and the frequent, expert user. Shared decisions appear to be the rule rather than the exception. There has been recent interest in "group decision support systems" for support of group decision making [22]. The study presented here would tend to indicate that specialized DSS for groups may not be essential, given a "conventional" DSS.

Management involvement in DSS is extensive in both breadth and depth. Management's role cuts across each of the areas of approval and administration, developer, operator, and user. This involvement must be expected and planned for. To date the most neglected aspect of DSS activity is planning for its approval and administration in the organization. Much additional research is needed in this area.

QUESTIONS

1. Briefly summarize how DSS are approved and administered.
2. Briefly describe how DSS are developed.
3. Briefly discuss how DSS are operated.
4. Briefly describe how the output from a DSS is used.

REFERENCES

1. AHN, T., AND GRUDNITSKI, G.   Conceptual perspectives on key factors in DSS development: A systems approach. *Journal of Management Information Systems,* 2, 1 (Summer 1985), 18–32.

2. ALTER, S.   A study of computer aided decision making in organizations. Unpublished Ph.D. dissertation, Cambridge, Mass., Massachusetts Institute of Technology, 1975.

3. ALTER, S.   Development patterns for decision support systems. *MIS Quarterly* (September 1978), 33–42.

4. BAHL, H. C., AND HUNT, R. G.   Problem solving strategies for DSS design. *Information and Management,* 8, 2 (February 1985), 81–88.

5. BLUMENTHAL, M.   Rift cited between MIS, decision support. *Computerworld,* 15, 6 (February 9, 1981), 28.

6. CURLEY, K., AND GREMILLION, L.   The role of the champion in DSS implementation. *Information and Management,* 6, 4 (1983), 203–209.

7. GINZBERG, M.   Redesign of managerial tasks: A requisite for successful decision support systems. *MIS Quarterly,* 2, 1 (March 1978), 38–52.

8. GREMILLION, L., AND PYBURN, P.   Justifying decision support and office automation systems. *Journal of Management Information Systems,* 2, 1 (Summer 1985) 5–17.

9. HAYES, R., AND NOLAN, R.   What kind of corporate modeling functions best. *Harvard Business Review,* 52, 3 (May–June 1974), 102–112.

10. HUBER, G.   Issues in the design of group decision support systems. *MIS Quarterly,* 8, 3 (September 1984), 195–204.

The author is indebted to Hugh Watson at the University of Georgia for his insights into the role of management in DSS.

11. KASPER, G. The effect of user-developed DSS applications on forecasting decision-making performance in an experimental setting. *Journal of Management Information Systems,* 2, 2 (Fall 1985), 26–39.

12. KEEN, P. Decision support systems: Translating analytic techniques into useful tools. *Sloan Management Review,* 22, 3 (Spring 1980), 33–44.

13. KEEN, P., AND SCOTT MORTON, M. *Decision Support Systems: An Organizational Perspective.* Reading, Mass.: Addison-Wesley, 1978.

14. KEEN, P., AND WAGNER, G. DSS: An executive mind-support system. *Datamation,* 25, 11 (November 11, 1979), 117–122.

15. KROEBER, D.; WATSON, H.; AND SPRAGUE, R. An empirical investigation and analysis of the current state of information systems evolution. *Information and Management,* 3 (1980), 35–43.

16. LOCANDER, W.; NAPIER, A.; AND SCAMELL, R. A team approach to managing the development of a decision support system. *MIS Quarterly,* 3, 1 (March 1979), 53–63.

17. MANN, R., AND WATSON, H. A contingency model for user involvement in DSS development. *MIS Quarterly,* 8, 1 (March 1984), 27–38.

18. MCCOSH, A., AND SCOTT MORTON, M. *Management Decision Support Systems.* New York: John Wiley and Sons, 1978.

19. MEADOR, M. J., AND KEEN, P. G. Setting priorities for DSS development. *MIS Quarterly,* 8, 2 (June 1984), 117–129.

20. SANDERS, G. L., AND COURTNEY, J. F. A field study of organizational factors influencing DSS success. *MIS Quarterly,* 9, 1 (March 1985), 77–93.

21. SIMON, H. *The New Science of Management Decision.* New York: Harper & Row, 1960.

22. SPRAGUE, R. A framework for the development of decision support systems. *MIS Quarterly,* 4, 4 (December 1980), 1–26.

23. SPRAGUE, R., AND CARLSON, E. *Building Effective Decision Support Systems.* Englewood Cliffs, N.J.: Prentice-Hall, 1982.

24. SPRAGUE, R., AND OLSON, R. The financial planning system at Louisiana National Bank. *MIS Quarterly,* 3, 3 (September 1979), 35–46.

25. SPRAGUE, R., AND WATSON H. MIS concepts: Part II. *Journal of Systems Management,* 26, 2 (February 1975), 25–30.

26. WAGNER, G. Optimizing decision support systems. *Datamation,* 26, 5 (May 1980), 209–214.

27. WELSCH, G. M. Successful implementation of decision support systems: Preinstallation factors, service characteristics, and the role of the information transfer, specialist. Unpublished Ph.D. dissertation, Northwestern University, Evanston, Illinois, 1980.

4

VALUE ANALYSIS: JUSTIFYING DECISION SUPPORT SYSTEMS

Peter G. W. Keen

INTRODUCTION

Decision Support Systems (DSS) are designed to help improve the effectiveness and productivity of managers and professionals. They are interactive systems frequently used by individuals with little experience in computers and analytic methods. They support, rather than replace, judgment in that they do not automate the decision process nor impose a sequence of analysis on the user. A DSS is in effect a staff assistant to whom the manager delegates activities involving retrieval, computation, and reporting. The manager evaluates the results and selects the next step in the process. Table 4.1 lists typical DSS applications.[1]

Traditional cost-benefit analysis is not well-suited to DSS. The benefits they provide are often qualitative; examples cited by users of DSS include the ability to examine more alternatives, stimulation of new ideas, and improved communication of

Reprinted by special permission of the *MIS Quarterly,* Volume 5, Number 1, March 1981. Copyright 1981 by the Society for Information Management and the Management Information Systems Research Center.

TABLE 4.1   Examples of DSS Applications

DSS	*APPLICATIONS*	*BENEFITS*
GADS Geodata Analysis Display System	Geographical resource allocation and analysis; applications include sales force territories, police beat redesign, designing school boundaries	Ability to look at more alternatives, improved teamwork, can use the screen to get ideas across, improved confidence in the decision
PMS Portfolio Management System	Portfolio investment management	Better customer relations, ability to convey logic of a decision, value of graphics for identifying problem areas
IRIS Industrial Relations Information	*Ad hoc* access to employee data for analysis of productivity and resource allocation	*Ad hoc* analysis, better use of "neglected and wasted" existing data resource, ability to handle unexpected short term problems
PROJECTOR	Strategic financial planning	Insight into the dynamics of the business, broader understanding of key variables
IFPS Interactive Financial Planning System	Financial modeling, including mergers and acquisitions, new product analysis, facilities planning and pricing analysis	Better and faster decisions, saving analysts' time, better understanding of business factors, leveraging managing skills
ISSPA—Interactive Support System for Policy Analysts	Policy analysis in state government; simulations, reporting, and *ad hoc* modeling	*Ad hoc* analysis, broader scope, communication to/with legislators, fast reaction to new situations
BRANDAID	Marketing planning, setting prices and budgets for advertising, sales force, promotion, etc.	Answering "what-if?" questions, fine-tuning plans, problem finding
IMS Interactive Marketing System	Media analysis of large consumer database, plan strategies for advertising	Helps build and explain to clients the rationale for media campaigns, *ad hoc* and easy access to information

[1]Detailed descriptions of each DSS shown in Table 4.1 can be found in the following references:

GADS:Keen and Scott Morton [12], Carlson and Sutton [6]

PMS:Keen and Scott Morton [12], Andreoli and Steadman [2]

IRIS:Berger and Edelman [3]

PROJECTOR:Keen and Scott Morton [12]

IFPS:Wagner [19]

ISSPA:Keen and Gambino [11]

BRANDAID:Keen and Scott Morton [12], Little [14]

IMS:Alter [1]

Other DSS referred to in this article are:

AAIMS:Klaas [13], Alter [1]

CAUSE:Alter [1]

GPLAN:Haseman [9]

analysis. It is extraordinarily difficult to place a value on these. In addition, most DSS evolve. There is no "final" system; an initial version is built and new facilities are added in response to the users' experience and learning. Because of this, the costs of the DSS are not easy to identify.

The decision to build a DSS seems to be based on value, rather than cost. The system represents an investment for future effectiveness. A useful analogue is management education. A company will sponsor a five day course on strategic planning, organizational development, or management control systems on the basis of perceived need or long term value. There is no attempt to look at payback period or ROI, nor does management expect a direct improvement in earnings per share.

This article examines how DSS are justified and recommends Value Analysis (VA), an overall methodology for planning and evaluating DSS proposals. The next section illustrates applications of DSS. Key points are:

1. a reliance on prototypes,
2. the absence of cost-benefit analysis,
3. the evolutionary nature of DSS development, and
4. the nature of the perceived benefits.

The section on the Dynamics of Innovation relates DSS to other types of innovation. It seems clear that innovation in general is driven by "demand-pull"—response to visible, concrete needs—and not "technology push."

The Methodologies for Evaluating Proposals section briefly examines alternative approaches to evaluation: cost-benefit analysis, scoring techniques, and feasibility studies. They all require fairly precise estimates of, and tradeoffs between costs and benefits and often do not handle the qualitative issues central to DSS development and innovation in general. The final part of the article defines Value Analysis.

The overall issue this article addresses is a managerial one:

1. What does one need to know to decide if it is worthwhile to build a DSS?
2. How can an executive encourage innovation while making sure money is well spent?
3. How can one put some sort of figure on the value of effectiveness, learning, or creativity?

It would be foolish to sell a strategic planning course for executives on the basis of cost displacement and ROI. Similarly, any effort to exploit the substantial opportunity DSS provide to help managers do a better job must be couched in terms meaningful to them. This requires a focus on value and a recognition that qualitative benefits are of central relevance. At the same time, systematic assessment is essential. The initial expense of a DSS may be only in the $10,000 range, but this still represents a significant commitment of funds and scarce programming resources. The methodology proposed here is based on a detailed analysis of the implementation of over twenty DSS. It is consistent with the less formal approaches most managers seem to use in assessing technical innovations. Value analysis involves a two stage process:

1. *Version 0:* This is an initial, small scale system which is complete in itself, but may include limited functional capability. The decision to build Version 0 is based on:

   a. An assessment of benefits, not necessarily quantified;

   b. A cost threshold—is it worth risking this amount of money to get these benefits?

   In general, only a few benefits will be assessed. The cost threshold must be kept low, so that this decision can be viewed as a low risk research and development venture, and not a capital investment.

2. *Base System:* This is the full system, which will be assessed if the trial Version 0 has successfully established the value of the proposed concept. The decision to develop it is based on:

   a. Cost analysis: What are the costs of building this larger system?

   b. Value threshold: What level of benefits is needed to justify the cost? What is the likelihood of this level being attained?

A major practical advantage of this two stage strategy is that it reduces the risks involved in development. More importantly, it simplifies the tradeoff between costs and benefits, without making the analysis simplistic. It is also a more natural approach than traditional cost-benefit analysis; until value is established, *any* cost is disproportionate.

DECISION SUPPORT SYSTEMS

The DSS applications shown in Table 4.1 cover a range of functional areas and types of tasks. They have many features in common:

1. They are *non-routine* and involve frequent *ad hoc* analysis, fast access to data, and generation of non-standard reports.
2. They often address "what-if?" questions; for example, "What if the interest rate is X%?" or "What if sales are 10% below the forecast?"
3. They have no obvious correct answers; the manager has to make qualitative tradeoffs and take into account situational factors.

The following examples illustrate the above points:

1. **GADS.** In designing school boundaries, parents and school officials worked together to resolve a highly charged political problem. A proposal might be rejected because it meant closing a particular school, having children cross a busy highway, or breaking up neighborhood groups. In a previous effort involving redistricting, only one solution has been generated, as opposed to six with GADS over a four day period. The interactive problem solving brought out a large number of previously unrecognized constraints such as transportation patterns and walking times, and parent's feelings.

2. **BRANDAID.** A brand manager heard a rumor that his advertising budget would be cut in half. By 5:00 p.m. he had a complete analysis of what he felt the effect would be on this year's and next year's sales.

3. **IFPS.** A model had been built to assess a potential acquisition. A decision was needed by 9:00 a.m. The results of the model suggested the acquisition be made. The senior executive involved felt uneasy. Within one hour, the model had been modified and "what if" issues assessed that led to rejection of the proposal.

4. **ISSPA and IRIS.** Data which had always been available, but not accessible, were used to answer *ad hoc,* simple questions. Previously, no one bothered to ask them.

These characteristics of problems for which DSS are best suited impose design criteria. The system must be:

1. *Flexible* to handle varied situations.
2. *Easy to use* so it can be meshed into the manager's decision process simply and quickly.
3. *Responsive* because it must not impose a structure on the user and must give speedy service.
4. *Communicative* because the quality of the user-DSS dialogue and of the system outputs are key determinants of effective uses especially in tasks involving communication or negotiation. Managers will use computer systems that mesh with their natural mode of operation. The analogy of the DSS as a staff assistant is a useful one.

Many DSS rely on prototypes. Since the task the system supports is by definition non-routine, it is hard for the user to articulate the criteria for the DSS and for the designer to build functional specifications. An increasingly popular strategy is thus to use a flexible DSS "tool" such as APL, or a DSS "Generator" [15]. These allow an initial version of a "Specific DSS" to be delivered quickly and cheaply. It provides a concrete example that the user can react to and learn from. It can be easily expanded or modified. The initial system, Version 0, clarifies the design criteria and specifications for the full DSS. Examples of this two phase strategy include:

1. **ISSPA**—built in APL. Version 0 took seventy hours to build and contained nineteen commands. The design process began by sketching out the user-system dialogue. New user commands were added as APL functions. Ten of the forty-eight commands were requested by users, and several of the most complex ones were entirely defined by users.

2. **AAIMS**—an APL-based "personal information system" for analysis of 150,000 time series. The development was not based on a survey or user requirements, nor on any formal plan. New routines are tested and "proven" by a small user group.

3. **IRIS**—a prototype was built in five months and evolved over a one year period. An "Executive language" interface was defined as the base for the DSS and a philosophy was adopted of "build and evaluate as you go."

4. **CAUSE**—There were four evolutionary versions. A phased development was used to build credibility. The number of routines was expanded from 26 to 200.

TABLE 4.2   IFPS Development Process

	DATA PROCESSING	STAFF ANALYST	MIDDLE MANAGEMENT	TOP MANAGEMENT
Who requested the application	0	4	30	66
Who built it	3	53	22	22
Who uses the terminal	0	70	21	9
Who uses the output	0	6	42	52

There have been several detailed studies of the time and the cost needed to build a DSS in APL. A usable prototype takes about three weeks to deliver. A full system requires another twelve to sixteen weeks.[2]

End-user languages similarly allow fast development. One such DSS "generator" is Execucom's IFPS (Interactive Financial Planning System), a simple, English-like language for building strategic planning models. The discussion below is based on a survey of 300 IFPS applications in 42 companies.[3] The models included long range planning, budgeting, project analysis, evolution of mergers, and acquisitions.

The average IFPS model took five days to build and contained 360 lines (the median was 200). Documented specifications were developed for only 16%. In 66% of the cases, an analyst simply responded to a manager's request and got something up and running quickly. Cost-benefit analysis was done for 13%, and only 30% have any objective evidence of "hard" benefits. 74% of the applications replace manual procedures. Given that most of the responding companies are in the Fortune 100, this indicates the limited degree to which managers in the planning functions make direct use of computers.

Most DSS are built outside data processing, generally by individuals who are knowledgeable about the application area. Table 4.2 gives figures on where requests for IFPS applications came from and how they are built.

The IFPS users were asked to identify the features of the language that contributed most to the success of the DSS. In order of importance, these are:

1. speed of response,
2. ease of use,
3. package features (curve-fitting, risk analysis, what-if?),
4. sensitivity analysis, and
5. time savings.

---

[2]See Grajew and Tolovi [8] for a substantiation of these figures. They built a number of DSS in a manufacturing firm to test the "evolutive approach" to development.

[3]IFPS is a proprietary product of Execucom, Inc., in Austin, Texas. The survey of IFPS users is described in Wagner [19].

TABLE 4.3   Relative Use of DSS Operators (PMS)

	Percentage of Use by Each Manager						PERCENTAGE OF USE
OPERATOR	A	B	C	D	E	F	BY ALL USERS
Table	22	22	38	22	76	57	47
Summary	40	10	30	8	0	38	17
Scan	0	26	5	24	0	0	4
Graph	14	4	13	30	5	0	8
Directory	2	0	0	0	1	4	1
Others	22	38	14	16	18	1	23

The evolutionary nature of DSS development follows from the reliance on prototypes and fast development. There is no "final" system. In most instances, the system evolves in response to user learning. A major difficulty in designing DSS is that many of the most effective uses are unanticipated and even unpredictable. Examples are:

1. **PMS**—the intended use was to facilitate a portfolio based rather than security based approach to investment. This did not occur, but the DSS was invaluable in communicating with customers.
2. **GPLAN**—the DSS forced the users (engineers) to change their roles from analysts to decision makers.
3. **PROJECTOR**—the intended use was to analyze financial data in order to answer preplanned questions and the actual use was as an educational vehicle to alert managers to new issues.

Usage is also very personalized, since the managers differ in their modes of analysis and the DSS is under their own control. For example, six users of PMS studied over a six month period differed strongly in their choice of operators (see Table 4.3).[4]

The benefits of DSS vary; this is to be expected given the complex situational nature of the tasks they support and their personalized uses. The following list shows those frequently cited in DSS cases studies, together with representative examples.[5] Table 4.4 summarizes the list.

1. INCREASE IN THE NUMBER OF ALTERNATIVES EXAMINED

- Sensitivity analysis takes 10% of the time needed previously.
- Eight detailed solutions generated versus one in previous study.
- Previously took weeks to evaluate a plan; now takes minutes, so much broader analysis.

---

[4]See Andreoli and Steadman [2] for a detailed analysis of PMS usage.

[5]This list is taken verbatim from Keen, "Decision Support Systems and Managerial Productivity Analysis" [10].

TABLE 4.4 DSS Benefits

	EASY TO MEASURE?	*BENEFIT CAN BE QUANTIFIED IN A "BOTTOM LINE" FIGURE?*
1. Increase in number of alternatives examined	N	N
2. Better understanding of the business	N	N
3. Fast response to unexpected situations	Y	N
4. Ability to carry out *ad hoc* analysis	Y	N
5. New insights and learning	N	N
6. Improved communication	N	N
7. Control	N	N
8. Cost savings	Y	Y
9. Better decisions	N	N
10. More effective teamwork	N	N
11. Time savings	Y	Y
12. Making better use of data resource	Y	N

- Users could imagine solutions and use DSS to test out hypotheses.
- "No one had bothered to try price/profit options before."

2. BETTER UNDERSTANDING OF THE BUSINESS

- President made major changes in company's overall plan, after using DSS to analyze single acquisition proposal.
- DSS alerted managers that an apparently successful marketing venture would be in trouble in six months' time.
- DSS is used to train managers; gives them a clear overall picture.
- "Now able to see relationships among variables."

3. FAST RESPONSE TO UNEXPECTED SITUATIONS

- A marketing manager faced with an unexpected budget cut used the DSS to show that this would have a severe impact later.
- Helped develop legal case to remove tariff on petroleum in New England states.
- Model revised in twenty minutes, adding risk analysis; led to reversal of major decision made one hour earlier.

4. ABILITY TO CARRY OUT *AD HOC* ANALYSIS

- 50% increase in planning group's throughput in three years.
- The governor's bill was published at noon "and by 5 pm I had it fully costed out."
- "I can now do QAD's—quick-and-dirties."
- System successfully used to challenge legislator's statements within a few hours.

5. NEW INSIGHTS AND LEARNING

- Quickened management's awareness of branch bank problems.
- Gives a much better sense of true costs.
- Identified underutilized resources already at analysts' disposal.
- Allows a more elegant breakdown of data into categories heretofore impractical.
- Stimulated new approaches to evaluating investment proposals.

6. IMPROVED COMMUNICATION

- Used in "switch presentations" by advertising agencies to reveal short-comings in customer's present agency.
- Can explain rationale for decision to investment clients.
- Improved customer relations.
- "Analysis was easier to understand and explain. Management had confidence in the results."
- "It makes it a lot easier to sell (customers) on an idea."

7. CONTROL

- Permits better tracking of cases.
- Plans are more consistent and management can spot discrepancies.
- Can "get a fix on the overall expense picture."
- Standardized calculation procedures.
- Improved frequency and quality of annual account reviews.
- Better monitoring of trends in airline's fuel consumption.

8. COST SAVINGS

- Reduced clerical work.
- Eliminated overtime.
- Stay of patients shortened.
- Reduced turnover of underwriters.

9. BETTER DECISIONS

- "He was forced to think about issues he would not have considered otherwise."
- Analysis of personnel data allowed management to identify for the first time where productivity gains could be obtained by investing in office automation.
- Increased depth and sophistication of analysis.
- Analysts became decision makers instead of form preparers.

10. MORE EFFECTIVE TEAM WORK

- Allowed parents and school administrators to work together exploring ideas.
- Reduced conflict—managers could quickly look at proposal without prior argument.

11. TIME SAVINGS

- Planning cycle reduced from six man-days spread over twenty elapsed days to one half day spread over two days.
- "Substantial reduction in manhours" for planning studies.
- "(My) time-effectiveness improved by a factor of 20."

12. MAKING BETTER USE OF DATA RESOURCE

- Experimental engineers more ready to collect data since they knew it would be entered into a usable system.
- "More cost-effective than any other system (we) implemented in capitalizing on the neglected and wasted resource of data."
- Allows quick browsing.
- "Puts a tremendous amount of data at manager's disposal in form and combinations never possible at this speed."

Table 4.4 adds up to a definition of managerial productivity. All the benefits are valuable but few of them are quantifiable in ROI or payback terms.

In few of the DSS case studies is there any evidence of formal cost-benefit analysis. In most instances, the system was built in response to a concern about timeliness or scope of analysis, the need to upgrade management skills, or the potential opportunity a computer data resource or modeling capability provides. Since there is little *a priori* definition of costs and benefits, there is little *a posteriori* assessment of gains. A number of DSS failed in their aims, but where they are successful, there is rarely any formal analysis of the returns. Many of the benefits are not proven. In managerial tasks there is rarely a clear link between decisions and outcomes, and a DSS can be expected to *contribute* to better financial performance, but not directly cause it. In general, managers describe a successful DSS as "indispensable" without trying to place an economic value on it.

THE DYNAMICS OF INNOVATION

DSS are a form of innovation. They represent:

1. a relatively new concept of the role of computers in the decision process;
2. an explicit effort to make computers helpful to managers who on the whole have not found them relevant to their own job, even if they are useful to the organization as a whole;
3. a decentralization of systems development and operation, and often a bypassing of the data processing department; and
4. the use of computers for "value added" applications rather than cost displacement.

There is much literature on the dynamics of technical innovations in organizations.[6] Its conclusions are fairly uniform and heavily backed by empirical data.

---

[6]See Tornatzky *et al.* [16].

Surveys of the use of computer planning models support these conclusions. In nine cases studied[7] the decision to adopt planning models was based on:

1. comparison with an ongoing system which involves examining either a manual or partially computerized system and deciding that some change is desirable;
2. comparison with a related system, such as a successful planning model in another functional area;
3. initiation of a low cost project; and
4. comparison with competitors' behavior resulting in the use of a "reference model" which reduces the need to estimate the impact of a model not yet constructed on improved decisions and performance.

Even in traditional data processing applications, the emphasis on value rather than cost is common. A survey of all the proposals for new systems accepted for development in a large multinational company found that even though cost-benefit analysis was formally required, it was used infrequently.[8] The two main reasons for implementing systems were:

1. mandated requirements, such as regulatory reports, and
2. identification of one or two benefits, rarely quantified.

Traditional cost-benefit analysis is effective for many computer-based systems. It seems clear, however, that it is not used in innovation. This may partly be because innovations involve R&D; they cannot be predefined and clear specifications provided. There is some evidence that there is a conflict in organizations between groups concerned with performance and those focused on cost. In several DSS case studies, the initiators of the system stress to their superiors that the project is an investment in R&D, not in a predefined product.

Surveys of product innovations consistently find that they come from customers and users rather than centralized technical or research staff. Well over three-quarters of new products are initiated by someone with a clear problem looking for a solution.[9] Industrial salesmen play a key role as "gatekeepers" bringing these needs to the attention of technical specialists. Even in the microprocessor industry, the majority of products are stimulated in this way by "demand-pull," not by technology-push."[10]

Case studies indicate that DSS development reflects the same dynamics of innovation as in other technical fields. Table 4.5 states the same dynamics of innovation as in other technical fields.

Methodologies for Evaluating Proposals

There are three basic techniques used to evaluate proposals for computer systems in most organizations:

---

[7]See Blanning, "How Managers Decide to Use Planning Models [4], *Long Range Planning,* Vol. 13, April 1980.
[8]See Ginzberg [7].
[9]See Utterback [17].
[10]See von Hippel [18].

TABLE 4.5   Dynamics of DSS Innovation

Innovations are value-driven	Main motivation for DSS is "better" planning, timely information, *ad hoc* capability, etc.
Early adopters differ from late adopters	DSS are often initiated by line managers in their own budgets; once the system is proven other departments may pick it up.
Informal processes are central	DSS development usually involves a small team; key role of intermediaries knowledgeable about the users and the technology for the DSS; data processing rarely involved; frequently DSS are "bootleg" projects.
Cost is a secondary issue	Costs are rarely tracked in detail; DSS budget is often based on staff rather than dollars; little change out of systems (this may reflect item below).
Uncertainty reduced by trial-ability, ease of understanding, clear performance value	Use of prototypes, emphasis on ease of use.

1. cost-benefit analysis and related ROI approaches—this views the decision as a *capital investment,*
2. scoring evaluation—this views it in terms of *weighted scores,* and
3. feasibility study—this views it as *engineering.*

Each of these is well-suited to situations that involve hard costs and benefits, and that permit clear performance criteria. They do not seem to be useful—or at least used—for evaluating innovations of DSS.

Cost-benefit analysis is highly sensitive to assumptions such as discount rates and residual value. It needs artificial and often arbitrary modifications to handle qualitative factors such as the value of improved communication and improved job satisfaction. Managers seem to be more comfortable thinking in terms of perceived value and then asking if the cost is reasonable. For example, expensive investments on training are made with no effort at quantification. The major benefits of DSS listed in Table 4.4 are mainly qualitative and uncertain. It is difficult to see how cost-benefit analysis of them can be reliable and convincing in this context.

Scoring methods are a popular technique for evaluating large-scale technical projects, such as the choice of a telecommunications package, especially when there are multiple proposals with varying prices and capabilities. Scoring techniques focus on a list of desired performance characteristics. Weights are assigned to them and each alternative rated. For example:

CHARACTERISTIC	WEIGHT	ALTERNATIVE	WEIGHTED SCORE
response time	.30	15	4.5
ease of use	.20	20	4.0
user manual	.10	17	1.7

Composite scores may be generated in several ways: mean rating, pass-fail, or elimination of any alternative that does not meet a mandatory performance requirement. Cost is considered only after all alternatives are scored. There is no obvious way of deciding if alternative A, with a cost of $80,000 and a composite score of 67, is better than B, with a cost of $95,000 and a score of 79.

Feasibility studies involve an investment to identify likely costs and benefits. They tend to be expensive and to focus on defining specifications for a complete system. They rarely give much insight into *how* to build it, and assume that the details of the system can be laid out in advance. DSS prototypes are a form of feasibility study in themselves. They are a first cut at a system. Some designers of DSS point out that Version "0" can be literally thrown away. Its major value is to clarify design criteria and establish feasibility, usefulness, and usability. The differences between a prototype and a feasibility study are important:

1. The prototype moves the project forward, in that a basic system is available for use and the logic and structure of the DSS already implemented.
2. The prototype is often cheaper, if the application is suited to APL or an end-user language.
3. The feasibility study is an abstraction and the prototype is concrete. Since DSS uses are often personalized and unanticipated, direct use of the DSS may be essential to establishing design criteria.

There is no evidence that any of these methods are used in evaluating DSS, except occasionally as a rationale or a ritual. More importantly, almost every survey of the dynamics of innovation indicates that they do not facilitate innovation and often impede it.

VALUE ANALYSIS

The dilemma managers face in assessing DSS proposals is that the issue of qualitative benefits is central, but they must find some way of deciding if the cost is justified. What is needed is a systematic methodology that focuses on:

1. value first, cost second;
2. simplicity and robustness—decision makers cannot, and should not have to, provide precise estimates of uncertain, qualitative future variables;
3. reducing uncertainty and risk; and
4. innovation, rather than routinization.

The methodology recommended here addresses all these issues. It relies on prototyping which:

1. factors risk, by reducing the initial investment, delay between approval of the project, and delivery of a tangible product; and
2. separates cost and benefit, by keeping the initial investment within a relatively small, predictable range.

If an innovation involves a large investment, the risk is high. Since estimates of costs and benefits are at best approximate, the decision maker has no way of making a sensible judgment. Risk is factored by reducing scope. An initial system is built at a cost below the capital investment level; the project is then an R&D effort. It can be written off if it fails. By using the DSS one identifies benefits and establishes value. The designer is also likely to learn something new about how to design the full system. The prototype accomplishes the same things as a feasibility study, but goes further in that a real system is built.

The benefit of a DSS is the incentive for going ahead. The complex calculations of cost-benefit analysis are replaced in value analysis by simple questions that most managers naturally ask and handle with ease:

1. What exactly will I get from the system?
   - it solves a business problem;
   - it can help improve planning, communication, and control; and
   - it saves time.
2. If the prototype costs $X, do I feel that the cost is acceptable?

Obviously the manager can try out several alternatives—"If the prototype only accomplishes two of my three operational objectives, at a lower cost of $Y, would I prefer that?" The key point is that value and cost are kept separate and not equated. This is sensible only if the cost is kept fairly low. From case studies of DSS, it appears that the cost must be below $20,000 in most organizations for value analysis to be applicable.

The first stage of value analysis is similar to the way in which effective decisions to adopt innovations are made. It corresponds to most managers' implicit strategy. The second stage is a recommendation; there is no evidence in the literature that it is widely used, but it seems a robust and simple extension of Version "0." Once the nature and value of the concept has been established the next step is to build the full DSS. The assessment of cost and value now needs to be reversed:

1. How much will the full system cost?
2. What threshold of values must be obtained to justify the cost? What is the likelihood they will occur?

If the expected values exceed the threshold, no further quantification is required. If they do not, then there must either be a scaling down of the system and a reduction in cost, or a more detailed exploration of benefits.

Value analysis follows a general principle of effective decision making—simplify the problem to make it manageable. A general weakness of the cost-benefit approach is that it requires knowledge, accuracy, and confidence about issues which for innovations are unknown, ill-defined, and uncertain. It therefore is more feasible to:

1. Establish value first, then test if the expected cost is acceptable.
2. For the full system, establish cost first, then test if the expected benefits are acceptable.

Instead of comparing benefits against cost, value analysis merely identifies relevant benefits and tests them against what is in effect a market price: "Would I be willing to pay $X to get this capability?" It is essential that the benefits be accurately identified and made operational. The key question is how would one know that better planning has occurred? The prototype is in effect an experiment in identifying and assessing it.

Figure 4.1 illustrates the logic and sequence of value analysis. The specific details of the method are less important than the overall assumptions, which have important implications for anyone trying to justify a DSS whether as a designer or

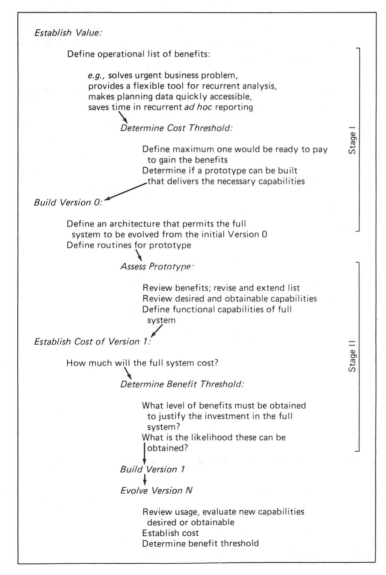

FIGURE 4.1
Value Analysis

user. Marketing a DSS requires building a convincing case. Figure 4.1 can be restated in these terms:

1. Establish value—the selling point for a DSS is the specific benefits it provides for busy managers in complex jobs.
2. Establish cost threshold—"trialability" is possible only if the DSS is relatively cheap and installed quickly. If it costs, say, $200,000, it is a capital investment, and must be evaluated as such. This removes the project from the realm of R&D and benefits as the focus of attention to ROI and tangible costs and inhibits innovation.
3. Build Version "0"—from a marketing perspective this is equivalent to "strike while the iron is hot." Doing so is possible only with tools that allow speedy development, modification, and extension.
4. Assess the prototype—for the marketer this means working closely with the user and providing response service.

Two analogies for DSS have been mentioned in this article: the staff assistant and management education. The strategy used to justify DSS depends upon the extent to which one views such systems as service innovations and investments in future effectiveness as opposed to products, routinization, and investment in cost displacement and efficiency. The evidence seems clear—DSS are a potentially important innovation. Value is the issue, and any exploitation of the DSS approach rests on a systematic strategy for identifying benefits, however qualitative, and encouraging R&D and experimentation.

QUESTIONS

1. What are the possible benefits from a DSS? Are these benefits easy to measure? Can these benefits be quantified in a "bottom line" figure?
2. Discuss the ways in which a DSS represents an innovation.
3. Describe how value analysis can be used to evaluate a proposed DSS.

REFERENCES

1. ALTER, S. *Decision Support Systems: Current Practice and Continuing Challenges.* Reading, Mass.: Addison-Wesley, 1980.
2. ANDREOLI, P., AND J. STEADMAN "Management Decision Support Systems: Impact on the Decision Process," Master's thesis, Sloan School of Management, Massachusetts Institute of Technology, 1975.
3. BERGER, P., AND F. EDELMAN "IRIS: A Transaction Based DSS for Human Resources Management," in "Proceedings of a Conference on Decision Support Systems," ed. E. D. Carlson, *Data Base*, 8, no. 3 (Winter 1977), 22–29.
4. BLANNING, R. "How Managers Decide to Use Planning Models," *Long Range Planning*, vol. 13, April 1980.

5. CARLSON, E. D., ed "Proceedings of a Conference on Decision Support Systems," *Data Base,* 8, no. 3 (Winter 1977).

6. CARLSON, E. D., AND J. A. SUTTON "A Case Study of Non-programmer Interactive Problem Solving," IBM Research Report, RJ13H2, San Jose, Calif., 1974.

7. GINZBERG, M. J. "A Process Approach to Management Science Implementation," Ph.D. dissertation, Sloan School of Management, Massachusetts Institute of Technology, 1975.

8. GRAJEW, J., AND J. TOLOVI, JR "Conception et Mise en Oeuvre des Systems Interactifs d'aide a la Decision: l'approche Evolutive," Doctoral dissertation, Université des Sciences Sociales de Grenoble, Institut d'Administration des Entreprises, France, 1978.

9. HASEMAN, W. D. "GPLAN: An Operational DSS," in "Proceedings of a Conference on Decision Support Systems," ed. E. D. Carlson, *Data Base,* 8, no. 3 (Winter 1977), 73–78.

10. KEEN, P.G.W. "Decision Support Systems and Managerial Productivity Analysis," paper presented at the American Productivity Council Conference on Productivity Research, Houston, Tex., April 1980.

11. KEEN, P.G.W., AND T. GAMBINO "The Mythical Man-Month Revisited: Building a Decision Support System in APL," paper presented at the APL Users Meeting, Toronto, Canada, September 1980.

12. KEEN, P.G.W., AND M. S. SCOTT MORTON *Decision Support Systems: An Organizational Perspective.* Reading, Mass.: Addison-Wesley, 1978.

13. KLAAS, R. L. "A DSS for Airline Management," in "Proceedings of a Conference on Decision Support Systems," ed. E. D. Carlson, *Data Base,* 8, no. 3 (Winter 1977), 3–8.

14. LITTLE, J.D.C. "BRANDAID," *Operations Research,* 23, no. 4 (May 1975), 628–73.

15. SPRAGUE, R. H., JR "A Framework for the Development of Decision Support Systems," *MIS Quarterly,* 4, no. 4 (December 1980), 1–26.

16. TORNATZKY, L. G., *et al.* "Innovation Processes and Their Management: A Conceptual, Empirical, and Policy Review of Innovation Process Research," National Science Foundation Working Draft, October 19, 1979.

17. UTTERBACK, J. M. "Innovation in Industry and the Diffusion of Technology," *Science,* vol. 183, February 1974.

18. VON HIPPEL, E. "The Dominant Role of Users in the Scientific Instrument Innovation Process," *Research Policy,* July 1976.

19. WAGNER, G. R. "Realizing DSS Benefits with the IFPS Planning Language," paper presented at the Hawaii International Conference on System Sciences, Honolulu, January 1980.

5

AN EXPERIMENT IN APPLYING THE ADAPTIVE DESIGN APPROACH TO *DSS* DEVELOPMENT

Maryam Alavi,
H. Albert Napier

INTRODUCTION

Decision Support Systems (DSS) are computer based systems designed to enhance the effectiveness of decision makers in performing semistructured tasks. With such tasks, the decision maker is uncertain about the nature of the problem/opportunity, the alternative solutions and/or the criteria or value for making a choice. Hence, the primary role of a DSS is to aid the judgment processes as the decision maker contends with poorly defined problems.

The way of designing a DSS is different from that of a transaction processing system. A fundamental assumption in the traditional "life cycle" approach is that the requirements can be determined prior to the start of the design and development process. However, Sprague [14] stated that DSS designers literally "cannot get to first

Maryam Alavi and H. Albert Napier, "An Experiment in Applying the Adaptive Design Approach to DSS Development," *Information & Management,* Vol. 7, No. 1, 1984.

base" because the decision maker or user cannot define the functional requirements of the DSS in advance. Also, as an inherent part of the DSS design and implementation process, the user and designer will "learn" about the decision task and environment, thereby identifying new and unanticipated functional requirements.

Generally, DSS designers have recognized that this circumstance calls for a departure from tradition: we suggest adaptive design. This is an emerging concept, and published empirical work in this area is very limited.

This article focuses on the adaptive design approach. First, conceptual issues of adaptive design are explored and discussed. Then a case study is presented. The empirical findings of this provide some insight into the application and the effectiveness of the approach. Some areas for future research are also identified.

THE ADAPTIVE DESIGN PROCESS

In an adaptive design approach, the four traditional system development activities (requirements analysis, design, development, and implementation) are combined into a single phase, which is iteratively repeated in a relatively short time [14]. The process is described in the context of the framework of Keen [9]. According to this framework, the major components of adaptive design include the builder, the user, and the technical system (DSS). During the design process, these elements interact with ("influence") each other. Hence, three adaptive links are established in this framework: the user-system, the user-builder and the builder-system.

In this framework, the user is either the manager or individual faced with a problem or opportunity. The user is responsible for taking action and its consequences. In some cases, the user may not directly interact with the technical system. Then, an intermediary provides the interface between the user and the system. The intermediary may play a clerical role (interact with the terminal to obtain user specified outputs) or play the role of a "staff assistant" (interact with the user and make suggestions) [14].

The DSS builder is the individual who develops the specific DSS with which the user or intermediary interacts. The builder should be knowledgeable about information systems technology and capabilities, and become familiar with the task for which the DSS is being designed. In some cases the builder may also play the role of user intermediary.

In the adaptive design framework, the technical system is the hardware/software provided to the user. A technical system is "configured" from DSS generator and/or DSS tools. A generator is a "package" which provides a set of capabilities to build a specific DSS quickly and easily [14]. An example of a DSS generator is the Executive Information System (EIS) marketed by Boeing Computer Services [4]. EIS capabilities include report generation, graphics, inquiry, and modeling languages which are available through a common command language. DSS tools are hardware and software elements applied to the development of a specific DSS or a DSS generator. Examples of DSS tools include general purpose programming languages, database management systems and financial planning languages. Many early DSS were developed by direct application of DSS tools.

User-System Interactions

The user-system link deals with the effect of a user's characteristics on the system utilization. Research by Dickson, Chervany and Senn [6] established that some individual characteristics, such as problem solving style, experience, background and skills, influence the quality and quantity of system utilization. Alavi and Henderson [1] showed that individuals with an "analytical problem solving" style are more willing and inclined to use DSS than "intuitive" individuals.

This link reflects user learning as a result of using the system. It is argued that through interaction with the DSS, the user's understanding and perception of the decision task and potential solutions are enhanced. Case studies [9] have shown this.

The builder-system link occurs as the builder adds new capabilities and functions to the system. System evaluation and change is feasible only if system architecture is flexible; i.e., new capabilities can be added with little expenditure of time and resources. The system-builder link concerns the demand placed on the builder for system evolution resulting from user and builder learning and changes in the decision environment.

User-Builder Interactions

User-builder interactions involve communication and collaboration between the user and builder during the DSS development process. Through these interactions, the user learns about the capabilities and possibilities for decision support and the designer learns about user requirements and builds credibility. Effective communication and collaboration between user and builder are key aspects of adaptive design.

A CASE STUDY

Background

The system discussed here has been implemented in a southwestern U.S. real estate development and management firm which had revenues of about 50 million dollars in 1982. Prior to development and implementation of the system, the firm had some experience related to computers, but none with DSS. The firm had an in-house IBM System 34 computer that was used primarily for transaction processing applications. The company purchased this computer in 1979.

Elements of Adaptive Design   The elements of adaptive design: The user, builder, and DSS in the case are depicted in Figure 5.1.

THE USERS.   The primary users of the decision support system, a corporate cash flow analysis and projection system, are the chief executive officer (CEO), the controller, the administrative vice president and the manager of operations. The CEO uses the system through an intermediary (the controller). Summary cash flow projection reports and sensitivity analysis results are used by the CEO for support of financial decisions,

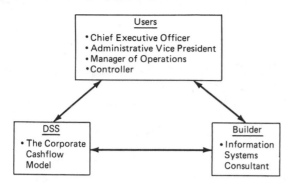

FIGURE 5.1 The Elements of Adaptive Design in the Case

such as: identifying times when cash is needed and when surpluses are available, making "hold" or "sell" decisions for existing properties, and in making investment decisions for new real estate development projects. The controller is a "hands-on" user; the system outputs and its "what-if" capability is used to assist in activities such as the determination of the timing of construction draws and major cash payment and tax planning. The administrative vice president and the manager of operations use the system in budgeting activities for individual projects. Clerical staff personnel perform the role of intermediary for the vice president and the manager. Some demographic characteristics of these users are summarized in Table 5.1. Prior to the implementation of the DSS, the users had no familiarity with decision support systems.

THE BUILDER. The DSS builder was an information systems consultant. The builder configured a cash flow model (the specific DSS) from a DSS generator, the Interactive Financial Planning System (IFPS) marketed by Execucom systems Corporation [8]. In the early stages of the project, the builder also acted as an intermediary to the CEO and the controller.

TABLE 5.1 Parameters of the DSS Users

ORGANIZATIONAL TITLE	NUMBER OF YEARS IN THE CURRENT POSITION	EDUCATIONAL BACKGROUND	AGE	DSS UTILIZATION MODE
1. Chief Executive Officer	19	Engineering	45	Through an intermediary (the controller)
2. Administrative Vice President	4	Engineering	48	Through an intermediary (a clerk)
3. Manager of Operations	7	Mathematics	37	Through an intermediary (a clerk)
4. Controller	7	Accounting	32	"Hands-on"

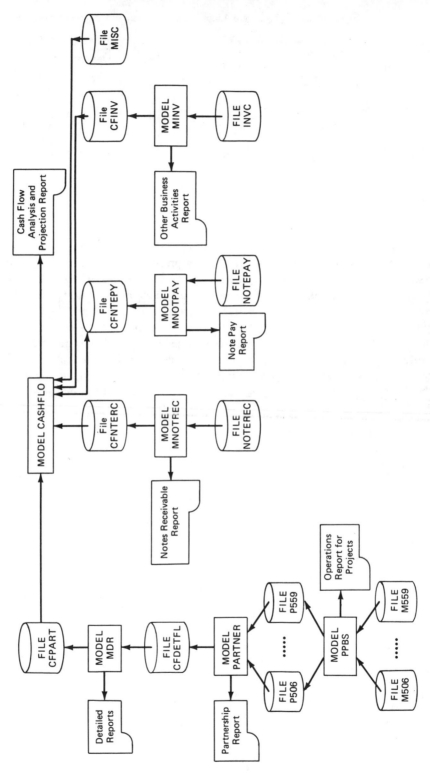

FIGURE 5.2 The DSS: Corporate Cash Flow System

THE *DSS:* THE CORPORATE CASH FLOW SYSTEM.   The corporate cash flow system consists of seven models and a set of datafiles, as illustrated in Figure 5.2. The DSS was developed using the IFPS modeling language and is processed on the Control Data Corporation (CDC) Cybernet timesharing system.

Model PPBS (Project Planning and Budgeting System) is used to project the cash flow operations for each real estate project. The datafiles for the model are prepared by the vice president of administration and the manager of operations. An intermediary, in this case a secretary, inputs the various datafiles and processes the Model PPBS using these files. Model Partner is processed for each property and a partnership report is printed. The datafiles for Model Partner are prepared by the controller. This requires the controller to obtain information from various operations personnel. After the datafiles are prepared, an intermediary, the controller's secretary, enters the data and processes Model Partner using the datafiles. The Model for Detailed Reports (MDR) generates detailed management reports and schedules for sources and uses of cash. The data for Model MDR is generated automatically by Model Partner. This model also generates the datafile CFPART, which is an input to the corporate cash flow model. Model Notes Receivable (MNOTREC) generates a note receivable report and a datafile (CFNTREC) of the totals by month for notes receivable. The input file to Model MNOTREC is the datafile NOTEREC. This input file is prepared by the accounting department and contains payment amounts for the notes receivable accounts. The controller's secretary enters this data and processes Model MNOTREC. The Model MNOTPAY generates a notes payable report. The accounting department prepares datafile (NOTEPAY), containing relevant payments to other organizations and individuals. The totals by month for notes payable are stored in file CFNTEPY which is used as input for the Corporate Cash flow model. The controller's secretary enters this data and processes Model NOTEPAY. Model Investment (MINV) produces a detailed report for other company financial activities. Totals by month for projected sales and projected costs and expenses are stored on datafile CFINV. The input file to Model MINV is datafile INVC which contains the projected revenues and expenses for the relevant business interests. The datafile is prepared by the accounting department. Again, the secretary of the controller acts as an intermediary by entering the datafile and processing Model MINV.

The Model Cash Flow (CASHFLO) provides a projection of cash flow and a report on sources and applications of cash. The cash flow model is developed with input files generated by the other 6 models contained in the system. In addition to these input files, the datafile MISC provides other necessary input to the cash flow model. The controller prepares and inputs the datafile MISC, and processes Model CASHFLO.

It should be noted that as the various models and datafiles were initially being developed, the DSS builder and user (the controller) did most of the data entry and all the model processing. After the system was well defined and procedures developed, more intermediaries were used by the controller. Furthermore, after each of the various key processing steps occurred (completion of Model PPBS for all projects, processing of Model Partner for all projects, etc.) the controller and personnel responsible for various operations reviewed the reports and data to make sure it was correct before going to the next step in processing the system.

The cash flow system is processed monthly. Additional cash flow reports are run, as necessary, to facilitate decision making using various parameters. These additional reports are processed using the "what-if" capability of IFPS. This decision support system evolved in an iterative fashion over a period of 2½ months.

Application of Adaptive Design Approach

Prior to development and implementation of the DSS, cash flow analysis and projections were performed manually. The process was time consuming, error prone, and did not provide opportunities for sensitivity analysis. The DSS development process was initiated by the CEO, who approached the builder and expressed the need for improving the effectiveness and timeliness of the cash flow projections. During an informal session with the builder that lasted about one hour, the CEO briefly described the dynamics of real estate financing, the characteristics of his business and his perceived need for timely, accurate information and the ability to perform sensitivity analysis.

Based on the chief executive officer's basic requirements, the builder developed a simple cash flow projection model. This model served two primary purposes:

- It demonstrated the potential for decision support and the essential features of a DSS.
- It enhanced the builder's understanding of the user's business and the environment.

Through the use of the simple cash flow model, with the builder acting as the intermediary, the chief executive officer quickly learned about the possible capabilities and features of the system. For example, the IFPS "What-If" and "Goal Seeking" commands were demonstrated by making various changes in model assumptions and parameters. After trying the initial system and entering some "What-If" commands, the chief executive officer perceived that a DSS could be built to assist in the projection and analysis of cash flow for his organization. The builder was then asked to develop and implement a cash flow system for the firm.

First Iteration   After the decision to build the cash flow system was made, but prior to initiating the development process, a 3-hour seminar providing an overview of financial planning and IFPS capabilities was conducted by the builder.

At the outset of the development process, the controller was somewhat hesitant about the attainment of the potential benefits and capabilities of the system. She also thought that the use of such a system might require more work than the manual system. To overcome this hesitancy, during the initial stage of the development process, the builder also assumed the role of educator. Specific examples of the potential capabilities and features of the system were provided to illustrate time savings and sensitivity analysis. The controller assumed a proactive role during the design process by providing information and input about the financial operations of the firm and the desired features of the system. Through this collaborative effort, with the builder providing the modeling expertise and the user (controller) providing the business expertise, the first version of the corporate cash flow system was created. The first version consisted of the following components:

1. The model CASHFLO, which generated the summary cash flow reports and projections for the CEO.
2. Models MNOTREC, MNOTPAY, MINV, and PARTNER and the associated datafiles.

The CEO was closely involved in the development of the first version of the cash flow system by monitoring the progress of the development effort and evaluating the system outputs. The first iteration of the cash flow model required 49 hours of the DSS builder's time, 25 hours of the controller's time and 10 hours of the chief executive officer's time. The first iteration of the system was completed in one month of elapsed time.

Second Iteration   All the users (the chief executive officer, the controller, the vice president of administration and manager of operations) actively participated in the second iteration of the system. This phase involved the development of Model PPBS and creation of the input files which contained detailed operational and financial data on individual properties. The level of effort spent in this phase was 31.5 hours of the DSS builder's time, 15 hours each of the vice president and the manager's time and 10 hours of the controller's time. The CEO spent 5 hours during the second iteration.

The CEO's role at this time involved monitoring the project activities and progress. The controller, vice president of administration, and manager of operations assisted in defining the output reports and the processing logic. They also developed the necessary input datafiles.

Third Iteration   At the completion of the second iteration, the functional requirements were all satisfied. However, operational use of the system indicated that the approach taken in the creation of the detailed reports (using model MDR) needed modification and refinement. A single model with a large matrix size was used to create the detail reports. If some of the detail reports had to be regenerated due to an error, the large model had to be reprocessed and all the detail reports regenerated. This was highly inefficient in terms of user time and computing resources. Hence, in the third iteration, the single large model was replaced by a set of 12 models that collectively generated the detailed report datafiles. These smaller models were more efficient. Furthermore, if one report had to be regenerated, only one small model had to be processed. "Command" files which automated the processing of the various processing segments were also developed to enhance the operation of the DSS.

The third iteration phase of the system was concluded by documenting the system and the operational procedures. The level of the effort spent at this iteration consisted of 60 hours of the builder's time and 20 hours of the controller's time.

Case Summary

The case involved the actual design and implementation of a decision support system for cash flow projections and analysis. The user group consisted of four decision makers: the CEO, the controller, the vice president of administration, and the manager of operations.

The design process can be best characterized as an iterative cycling between the DSS generator (IFPS) and the specific corporate cash flow system. With each cycle, the cash flow system was enhanced and new components were added. In each iteration, the typical systems development steps (analysis, design, construction and implementation) were united.

The user group was closely involved in the process of development and implementation. The total level of user effort was 90 person-hours. The cash flow system has been in operation for the past 1½ years. The system is operated solely by the users and is under their control.

The users are satisfied with the system and perceive it as a valuable and beneficial tool for use in cash flow decisions. Their perceived benefits of the system include: obtaining better control over the operations; ability to respond to environmental changes (e.g., in the interest rates) in a timely manner; and increased capability for decision analysis.

OBSERVATIONS ON THE CASE STUDY

During the development of the corporate cash flow decision support system, the following observations were made on the effectiveness and requirements of the adaptive design approach.

1. The adaptive design approach requires a high level of user participation and involvement. In this project, the users spent 90 person-hours in the development process compared to 140.5 person-hours spent by the builder. User involvement and cooperation seem to be a necessary condition for effective application of the approach. Hence, it may not be applicable to those design situations in which the user is unable or unwilling to participate actively in the design process.

2. During the early stages of the development process, there was rapid progress toward defining the user requirements and developing DSS capabilities to meet them. There were cycles of discussion, development, review of the output, and further development. Such rapid progress resulted in positive user attitudes. Furthermore, providing quick and tangible output in early stages established credibility for the DSS builder and helped in obtaining user cooperation.

3. Availability of a program generator and interactive computing resource were critical factors in the application of the approach. Capabilities provided by IFPS (self-documentation, ease of coding and making changes, data storage and retrieval, report generation, etc.) allowed rapid response to requirements and the iterative and modular development process used to develop the cash flow system.

4. Except for a 3-hour introductory seminar on financial planning languages and IFPS conducted at the outset, no other formal user training programs were needed. The interactions among the user, builder, and system, and the proactive role of the users in the design process decreased the requirements for formal user training.

5. The perceived need and usefulness of the system seemed to be the incentive for its adoption. No attempts at an explicit and formal cost/benefit analysis were made. Perceived value was established at the outset by using and evaluating a prototype cash flow system.

SUMMARY

The adaptive design approach seems to be useful and effective for DSS development. However, further experimentation and evaluation are required before suggesting it is universally applicable. The following are some areas in which research or investigation must be conducted to increase understanding of the approach and its applicability:

1. What are the advantages and disadvantages of the adaptive design approach relative to others?
2. What contextual variables (e.g., organizational and task) seem to impact the process of adaptive design? What variables enhance or constrain its application?
3. What is the impact of the adaptive design approach on the user? Is there user-related psychological satisfaction or dissatisfaction derived from this approach?
4. What is the impact of the adaptive design approach on the DSS builder?
5. What training and skills are required of the builder for successful application of the approach?
6. What technological tools and resources are required?

Adaptive design may only be effective given certain contingencies: it may work well in one environment but not in another. However, preliminary findings from this case study suggest that the approach has high potential for developing effective decision support systems.

QUESTIONS

1. What is it about DSS applications that requires an adaptive rather than a traditional development approach?
2. Describe the activities of the organizational personnel who were involved in the development of the corporate cash flow system. Discuss how the organizational roles of manager, intermediary, DSS builder, technical supporter, and toolsmith were filled.

3. Discuss the three iterations in the development of the corporate cash flow system.

REFERENCES

1. ALAVI, M., AND J. C. HENDERSON   "An Evolutionary Strategy for Implementing a Decision Support System," *Management Science,* 27, no. 11 (November 1981).

2. BALLY, L., J. BRITTAN, AND K. H. WAYNER   "A Prototype Approach to Information System Design and Development," *Information & Management,* 1 (1977), 21–26.

3. BERRISFORD, T., AND J. C. WETHERBE   "Heuristic Development: A Redesign of Systems Design," *MIS Quarterly,* March 1979, 11–19.

4. BOEING COMPUTER SERVICES   c/o Mr. Park Thoreson, P.O. Box 24346, Seattle, Wash. 98124.

5. BOLAND, R. J., JR.   "The Process and Product of System Design," *Management Science,* 24, no. 9 (1978), 887–98.

6. DICKSON, G. W., N. L. CHERVANY, AND J. A. SENN   "Research in Management Information Systems: The Minnesota Experiments," *Management Science,* 23, no. 9 (May 1977).

7. HAWGOOD, J., ED.   *Evolutionary Information Systems,* Proceedings of the IFIP TC 8 Working Conference on Evolutionary Information Systems, Budapest, Hungary, September 1–3, 1981 (Amsterdam: North Holland Publishing, 1982; ISBN: 0-444-86359-1).

8. IFPS USERS MANUAL, EXECUCOM SYSTEMS CORPORATION   P.O. Box 9758, Austin, Tex. 78766.

9. KEEN, P.G.W.   "Adaptive Design for DSS," *Database,* 12, nos. 1 and 2 (Fall 1980), 15–25.

10. KEEN, P.G.W.   "Value Analysis: Justifying Decision Support Systems," *MIS Quarterly,* March 1981, 1–15.

11. LIVARI, J.   "Taxonomy of the Experimental and Evolutionary Approaches to the Systemeering," in J. Hawgood, *Evolutionary Information Systems,* Proceedings of the IFIP TC 8 Working Conference on Evolutionary Information Systems, Budapest, Hungary, September 1–3, 1981 (Amsterdam: North Holland Publishing, 1982; ISBN 0-444-83539-1).

12. LUCAS, H. C.   "The Evolution of an Information System: From Key-Man to Every Person," *Sloan Management Review,* Winter 1978.

13. NAUMAN, J. G., AND M. A. JENKINS   "Prototyping: The New Paradigm for Systems Development," *MIS Quarterly,* 6, no. 3 (September 1982), 29–4.

14. SPRAGUE, R. H., JR.   "A Framework for the Development of Decision Support Systems," *MIS Quarterly,* December 1980, 1–26.

15. ZMUD, R. W.   "Individual Differences and MIS Success: A Review of the Empirical Literature," *Management Science,* 25, no. 10 (1979).

6

SENIOR MANAGEMENT COMPUTER USE: IMPLICATIONS FOR *DSS* DESIGNS AND GOALS

Brian S. Mittman,
Jeffrey H. Moore

INTRODUCTION

A review of the Decision Support System (DSS) literature suggests that "front-end" activities (hardware acquisition, software selection or development, modeling, data acquisition and analysis, training and education, etc.) constitute the major hurdles in DSS implementation. Numerous case studies of DSS development and implementation have been conducted (see, for example, Moore and Chang, 1983, and the cases in Keen and Scott Morton, 1978), but an extensive literature review has shown that published research on post-implementation routine use of DSS is rare (Scott Morton, 1983). In spite of their scarcity, however, surveys (e.g., Brightman, Harris and Thompson, 1981; Watson, Sprague and Kroeber, 1977) and interview studies of DSS use (Alter, 1980; Rockart and Treacy, 1982) have added considerably to our knowledge of DSS.

Brian Mittman and Jeffrey Moore, "Senior Management Computer Use: Implications for DSS Designs and Goals," *Transactions from the Fourth International Conference on Decision Support Systems, 1984.*

The study described here utilized both survey and interview methodologies in order to study the direct use of computers by senior executives. Our primary goal was to draw implications of this usage for research in decision support systems. Our belief is that "conventional-wisdom" of DSS, as expressed in the literature, is at odds with actual practice. Several authors have suggested this (e.g., Alter, 1977, and Moore and Chang, 1983), but empirical research remains sparse. The underlying motivation for the current study, then, is expressed by these questions:

- Are DSS's implemented primarily to support decision making?
- Which comes first: the decision situation or the DSS?
- Do the actual uses of a DSS differ from the intended ones?

METHODOLOGY AND DESCRIPTION OF THE SAMPLE

The research methodology was primarily empirical and exploratory, and consisted of two distinct phases. First, a telephone survey was conducted in order to (a) measure the extent of direct, hands-on computer use by senior management; and (b) identify potential subjects for the second phase of the study. The latter phase consisted of semi-structured interviews with 19 senior executives who make direct use of computers. The interviews were designed to determine how senior executives are actually using computers, with particular attention to decision support applications.

The telephone survey was conducted in April–June, 1983. A convenience sample of 120 Northern California firms was drawn from the 1982 edition of *Dun's Business Rankings,* and includes public and privately-held firms with annual sales between $10 million and $300 million. Of the original 120, thirteen firms were no longer in business or could not be contacted, yielding a net sample of 107 firms. Thirty-six of the firms are in electronics and computer-related industries, and the remaining 71 are in other industries.

The telephone survey consisted of 10-minute interviews with either a senior executive or member of an executive's staff, or a member of the financial or DP staffs who was knowledgeable about the executives' computer use. Respondents were asked if any of the firm's senior executives use computers; for executives who did, in fact, use computers, additional questions were asked concerning the types of hardware and software in use and the executives' computing experience. Executives who were reported to be using computers were then asked to participate in the personal interview phase of the study, and were sent a letter describing this phase in more detail.

Of the 107 phone-interview firms 55, or 51%, reported some direct use of computers by at least one senior executive. However, only 21 executives from 14 firms agreed to be interviewed. Of the 21 executives interviewed, two did not in fact directly use computers, leaving a sample size of 19 interviews. Of the 19 executives in the interview sample, 32% were Presidents or Chief Executive Officers, 53% were Vice-Presidents, and 15% were Chief Financial Officers or Corporate Controllers. Executives were considered to have "technical" backgrounds if they had acquired at least one college degree in a hard science or engineering discipline; 44% of the executives had

TABLE 6.1   A Profile of the Study Participants

	Firm			AVERAGE FIRM SALES REVENUE (MILLIONS)
	NUMBER	HIGH-TECH	NON-HIGH-TECH	
President/CEO	6	27%	38%	110
Vice-President	10	64%	38%	150
CFO/Controller	3	9%	24%	116
	19	100%	100%	

technical backgrounds. The firms they work for were considered "high-tech" if they were in electronics or computer-related industries; 58% of the executives were employed by high-tech firms. A further breakdown of the sample is given in Table 6.1.

Personal interviews were conducted in the executives' offices by either one or two interviewers. The interview outline contained both closed and open-ended items, and required 60 minutes. One half of the items dealt with the respondent's job activities and general computer systems used in the firm, and the remaining half focused on the executive's own computer use. The latter group of items included questions about the frequency and length of computer-use sessions, descriptions of inputs and outputs and their source of destination, respectively, and the nature of tasks for which computers were used. Questions concerning perceived reasons and beliefs about executive computer use were *not* included, because of uncertainties regarding the validity of responses to such questions in this context (Nisbett and Wilson, 1977). Data collection focused primarily on descriptions of the executives' actual computer use.

ANALYSIS AND RESULTS

Transcripts of the interview outlines were coded into 35 variables and reviewed by one of the interviewers for accuracy. One additional rating variable, "Extent of DSS Use," was developed by assigning a 0 to no DSS use and a 5 to 100% DSS use, with intermediate DSS use assigned in the 0–5 range. DSS use was operationally defined as the utilization of any or all of the following by the executives: "What If?" analysis, sensitivity analysis, or goal seeking analysis. Two raters independently rated all executives on the scale, based upon the interview transcripts. Inter-rater reliability was high, measuring .81 using the Spearman-Brown reliability statistic (Winer, 1971:286).

Small sample size precluded formal statistical hypothesis testing. Where given, statistics represent sample averages; in the case of real-valued variables sample standard deviations are also given.

Not unexpectedly, executives making direct use of computers are using personal computers. 79% use PC's directly, while only 42% utilize terminals on an interactive computer system. Four executives used both terminals and PC's. 74% of the executives use spreadsheets and the correlation between spreadsheet use and PC use was .86.

Database and word processing ranked next, and were used by 32% and 26% of the executives, respectively. Traditional high level programming languages were used by some of the executives: 21% reported using one or more in their computer work. With the exception of one executive who was utilizing a PC for 30 hours per week as part of a major development project, executives averaged 4.5 hours per week of computer use, with a standard deviation of 2.9 hours. Session lengths averaged 50 minutes with a standard deviation of 49 minutes, yielding an average 5.4 number of sessions per week per executive. A surprisingly high percentage of executives developed their own computer models: 84% of the executives wrote their own "programs," which usually meant developing spreadsheet templates. Of those using spreadsheets, 93% programmed their own. Furthermore, "consultants" or other intermediaries were rarely used by executives in the construction or use of computer models: only two executives utilized a custom model programmed by someone else, and 74% of the executives did all their own data entry.

84% of the executives utilized computer generated reports to facilitate communication of results to others. Destinations of reports were available for 13 of the 19 executives. Of these, 46%, 54%, and 31% went to staff, peers or superiors, and outsiders, respectively (multiple destinations occurred). Only one executive kept results entirely for his own use.

The above statistics clearly point to comparatively high use by these executives of computers for their managerial activities. However, it does not follow that these executives are necessarily employing this technology for decision support. The mean DSS Use rating averaged over the two raters is 1.6 on a scale of 0 (no DSS use) to 5 (exclusive DSS use). The median rating given by both raters was only 1 on the 0 to 5 scale, corresponding to "Slight DSS Use." Furthermore, an average of only 5.5 executives out of 19 were ranked above the mid-point of the DSS Use scale, and only 6 executives were rated above 1 on the scale by both raters. All 6 executives used decision support technology for "What If?" analysis. However, as measured by frequency of DSS use, only two executives did this on a regular basis—at least weekly. For the remaining 4 executives, the pattern is less clear; conservatively, 3 use DSS at least monthly, and one at least annually. Executives in the sample more frequently utilized computers for tabulating or consolidating historical data, formatting reports and preparing graphs for others, creating documents, keeping personal databases (To Do lists, etc.) and other maintenance or management control tasks. These uses related to communicating decisions or justifications directly or signaling indirectly to others much more often than they related to the decision making or decision evaluation activities normally ascribed to DSS.

DISCUSSION

The interview data were analyzed in terms of assumptions and propositions from the DSS literature, in line with our primary goal—to derive implications for DSS research. The resulting interpretations are but a few of the possibilities.

Discussion of the results is organized around three main points:

1. Senior executives are using computers directly *and* are programming their own models.
2. Computer use for implementation aspects of the decision process predominates over computer use for decision making aspects.
3. Analytical DSS use by senior executives is a small fraction of their general computer use.

Executive Computing

The telephone survey data show that, contrary to many expectations, senior executives *are* making direct use of computers. Furthermore, electronic messaging, mainframe data-base inquiry, and other MIS tasks are exceptional uses. Spreadsheet analysis and high-level programming are significantly more common uses of computers by these senior executives.

The interviews provided many details on the types of programming and spreadsheet analysis performed by the executives. Spreadsheet models designed and used by the executives were relatively simple, employing primarily simple arithmetic operations. Statistical analysis was limited to intuitive forms made possible by the occasional use of graphics. More significant from a DSS and OR/MS viewpoint, however, was the finding that few executives made hands-on use of spreadsheet models or other analytical tools programmed by staff or consultants. With two exceptions, analytical work performed by the executives themselves utilized self-programmed spreadsheets or programs only, rather than systems programmed by other parties.

Since relatively simple uses of decision support software were common in these executive offices, it is necessary to consider what implications such uses have for decision making and Decision Support Systems. The reluctance of managers to use models that they don't understand and the importance of insights and other benefits of performing an analysis or building a model (as opposed to merely using the results of the analysis or using a completed model) are popular ideas in the management science literature. The results of this study do not contradict these ideas. A spreadsheet model programmed by the executive who uses it is undoubtedly understood by the executive, and is more likely to be used than a model for which little end user effort was expended in model design and construction. While insights yielded by building relatively simple models are limited by this simplicity, learning to perform even simple analyses and the close inspection of data and routine reports necessary for spreadsheet modeling are valuable experiences nonetheless. Finally, although extreme simplicity may fail to yield useful insights into the working of a complex system, the other extreme—the sophistication of conventional OR/MS models—is not always necessary in order to obtain such insights (Geoffrion, 1976; Little, 1970).

Scott Morton notes the absence of discussions in the DSS literature of simple models and their benefits (1983:16). This absence is probably due in part to the lack of research involvement in the design of simple models. The fact that simple uses of decision support software are insufficiently documented in the literature should not be taken as an indicator of their unimportance, however. The models used by the managers in this study were transparent and constructed by the decision makers themselves. It is quite possible that simple decision support systems are having more of an impact on decision making than the more sophisticated systems documented in DSS case studies.

Perhaps most important for research in computer-aided decision making is the potential for direct managerial use of computers. Several authors have commented on this topic (e.g., Keen, 1976; Alter, 1977; Keen and Scott Morton, 1978:77; Sprague and Carlson, 1982:13–14), but rapid changes in computer hardware and software have been accompanied by changes in direct use patterns as well. The small amount of interview evidence relevant to this issue seems to indicate that executives tend either to perform most tasks necessary for use of a DSS, or else make no real use at all. DSS use through intermediaries was not a common alternative. When an executive is not directly involved in DSS use, the system may become secondary to the staff who use it: the staff become the DSS, and the system itself is irrelevant to the executive. Further research on long-term patterns of DSS use, in particular research utilizing a longitudinal design, will provide additional evidence relevant to this issue.

COMPUTER SUPPORT FOR DECISION IMPLEMENTATION

Conventional ideas about decision support systems view improved decision making as the primary purpose and use of DSS. In contrast, the interview results suggest that DSS benefits in other aspects of the decision process are frequently as important or more important than those in problem solving or decision making aspects.

Implicit in most DSS research is a model of decision making based upon the intelligence, design, and choice phases of decision making outlined by Simon (1977). The DSS model focuses on decision making aspects of the decision process—evaluating the problem, and identifying, analyzing, and selecting alternatives. Our interview data highlight another aspect of decision making in organizations, however: decision implementation. Decision making and decision implementation are not necessarily distinct phases of the decision process, nor is it the case that all managerial activities can be assigned solely to decision making or decision implementation categories. In fact, many activities can be seen as performing both roles. Nevertheless, a distinction between these two aspects of the decision process is useful in analyzing the role of DSS.

The interviews showed many instances of computer support in activities which can be interpreted both as decision making and decision implementation. It is difficult to maintain that the support is solely intended for one or the other role in such instances. However, activities which clearly belong only to one of the two categories were also seen; respondents reported numerous uses of decision support software in conjunction with activities which are difficult to interpret as decision making activities, but instead are decision implementation activities. These activities include decision communication, explanation, and justification.

The benefits of DSS use in communication among managers have been noted elsewhere (e.g., Keen, 1979). The communication emphasized in these previous discussions is not that required for decision implementation, however, but that needed for more effective decision making. Communication and explanation are necessary when complex decisions are explored and analyzed by more than one manager, and DSS use in facilitating such communication is an accepted benefit of DSS.

Many DSS uses in our interviews are difficult to interpret as decision making related communication, however. The noticeable lack of "what-if" analysis and explicit mentions of DSS use in communicating or justifying decisions are all indications not of DSS use in decision making, but rather in decision implementation. Hard copy containing decision results was frequently sent to parties both internal and external to the firm. The senior manager's peers and subordinates, the board of directors, bankers and financial analysts, customers and clients, suppliers, and others from whom cooperation and coordination are needed are all parties which received copies of computer output or other evidence of computer use by the executives in our sample.

Benefits of implementation uses of decision support software are due in part to the vividness and detail of the analysis and resulting output. For example, one CEO gives subordinates and external parties not only the aggregate financial goals and cash needs of his firm for the near term, but includes the calculations, intermediate results, and statistics used in determining the aggregate figures. In addition to communicating the financial goals unambiguously, the CEO signals other messages. Subordinates know that he has thought through the assumptions behind the financial goals and is serious about their importance and attainability. Bankers and directors are aware that he was personally involved in analyzing cash needs, and is aware of and responsible for the implications of the financing requests prepared by his finance department. Each of these messages improves decision implementation in some way.

Decisions requiring authorization by directors and/or external parties were also seen to be important candidates for computer support of implementation. Expansion, acquisition, and other major capital expenditure requests were among the examples seen in our interview sample. Again, both results of the analysis and the signaling benefits of merely demonstrating that computer-based analysis had been performed were perceived as major benefits of decision support software use by the executives.

The evidence discussed above indicates that these senior managers are using computers primarily in support of the implementation aspects of the decision process— explaining, justifying and communicating decisions. Numerous indications of the DSS role in decision implementation appear in the literature, as the following examples illustrate:

> In most of the instances where interactive problem solving was mentioned, the purpose was that of developing a report which would look good to someone else rather than of trying to find an answer which the user would act upon. (Alter, 1977:100)
>
> While the orthodox (academic) faith views DSS as tools for individual decision makers, users regard the concept as more relevant to systems that support organizational processes. They also feel they do not really use DSS for *decision making*. (Keen, 1980)

Stabell (1983) also notes the overwhelming emphasis in past DSS work on *support* rather than on *decision,* where the support has not been primarily that of the decision, and has not served effectively to improve decision making. Stabell cites examples of DSS use in support of other phases of the decision process, including decision implementation, evaluation and control. While past treatments of decision implementation uses of DSS have stressed their dysfunctional aspects, the following section discusses ways in which non-decision making applications of DSS may be useful.

Analytical Uses of Decision Support Software and Models of Decision Making

The interview data indicate that prescribed analytical uses of DSS—"what-if" analysis testing assumptions about uncertain values, the application of quantitative techniques in support of judgment, and the ability to analyze decision problems quickly—characterize few of the executives' computer uses. True DSS use coded from the data occurred very rarely, even among the executives who had significant amounts of computing experience, access to large amounts of internal and external data, and who used spreadsheet packages regularly for control and communication purposes. In spite of recent changes which have led to increases in managerial computer use (e.g., improvements in hardware and software and increasing managerial exposure to computers and modeling), DSS use by these managers is a relatively insignificant fraction of their general computer use.

Several explanations of this finding are possible, all of which focus on managerial decision making and the notions of analysis and decision making which are implicit in the DSS concept. The first explanation concerns the observed emphasis on DSS use for decision implementation discussed above, and the consequent rarity of analytical use of DSS. The image of senior managers spending significant amounts of time using computers to create justification and other aids for the explanation of decisions already made is inconsistent with the model of rational decision making implicit in much DSS research. If, in contrast, decisions are viewed from an "action perspective" (Brunsson, 1982), the behavior noted in our interviews is understandable. This perspective sees the implementation or "action phase" of decisions as more crucial to their success than the decision phase. The choice of an alternative is unimportant relative to its successful implementation. An action perspective is sensible only if attempts to discern the true values of alternatives relevant to most strategic and other high-level decisions are unlikely to be successful. A large number of studies suggest that success rates of attempts to analyze and make choices out of the type for which decision support is intended *are* low, with or without the assistance of computer-based or other types of forecasting and planning techniques (Hogarth and Makridakis, 1981). In this light, the usefulness of an action perspective becomes clear. If elaborate choice procedures are unlikely to yield better results than simple procedures, then relatively brief amounts of time and effort should be invested in their use. Once completed, however, communicating, justifying and explaining a decision is important to its success. In this view, decision communication and implementation are more important roles of senior managers than decision making roles, and are therefore natural areas for support. In fact, the interviews reported above suggest that many executives are indeed using decision support software for implementation support to a much greater extent than decision support.

Other views of decision making in organizations are also useful in making sense of the interview findings and considering their implications. The decision making model implicit in DSS work assumes the existence and knowledge of goals and preferences, assumptions about the future, and the operation of cause-effect relationships. All of these inputs are necessary for the proper identification and evaluation of alternatives, and eventual selection of a single course of action. The number of decision situations for which these inputs exist may be quite limited, however. Many decision situations, in particular those found at senior management levels, are characterized by ambiguities in preferences (March, 1978), non-existence of assumptions or complete uncertainty concerning the future, and incomplete knowledge of cause-effect relationships. March has suggested that in situations of this sort models requiring the inputs listed above are of questionable utility, and forms of intelligence utilizing these inputs in producing rational decisions are no longer appropriate. Instead, alternative forms of intelligence are necessary, forms in which answers are clearer than the premises from which a rational choice process might derive those answers (March, 1978:604). This view predicts a brief and inconsequential problem solving phase, followed by a comparatively significant emphasis on decision implementation.

Numerous additional perspectives on organizational decision making have been presented in the literature. Mintzberg, Raisinghani and Theoret (1976), Keen and Scott Morton (1978), and March (1981) discuss many of these perspectives. The majority of the alternative perspectives—alternatives to the rational model—suggest reasons for expecting DSS use to be different in several ways from DSS prescriptions. An adequate understanding of research results such as those reported in this paper, as well as the results of case studies and other DSS implementations, depends upon adequate understanding of organizational decision making. A more modest view of decision making in the context of other aspects of organizational activity, rather than as a focus of such activity, may lead to a better understanding of decision making (March, 1981) and DSS use alike. In general, viewing DSS in a larger context and using alternative decision making perspectives such as those discussed above provide several means of coming to a better understanding of DSS use.

SUMMARY

The study described here has shown several differences between the goals and intended benefits of DSS on the one hand, and the ways in which senior managers are using computers for decision-related tasks on the other. It is quite possible that the managers and firms studied would benefit from some of the prescriptions of DSS. More important for the present paper, however, are the potential benefits to the DSS field from the respondents' experiences with computers and decision support software, benefits derived from a better understanding of DSS use.

The interviews strongly suggest that DSS generators and tools are more useful to senior managers than a custom DSS. The range of decision situations faced by senior management is wide and decision situations for which DSS is useful occur infrequently.

Secondly, an exclusive focus on the decision making role of managers gives an inaccurate picture of managerial activity. DSS use occurs in the context of numerous other roles and activities, all of which must be considered in order to understand the role of computers in decision making.

Finally, our results support the notion of DSS as improving managerial effectiveness, broadly defined. Indeed, the executives interviewed displayed a wide variety of uses of decision support software, utilizing computers in activities as varied as decision making, decision implementing, and management control.

Further research will add to our understanding of existing and potential roles of computers in these activities.

QUESTIONS

1. Describe how executives are making direct use of computers.
2. What are the advantages of simple models in a DSS? The disadvantages?
3. Discuss the impact that a DSS has on the implementation of a decision.

REFERENCES

ALTER, STEVEN L. "Why Is Man-Computer Interaction Important for Decision Support Systems?" *Interfaces,* 7 (February 1977), 109–115.

ALTER, STEVEN L. *Decision Support Systems: Current Practice and Continuing Challenges.* Reading, Mass.: Addison-Wesley, 1980.

BRIGHTMAN, HARVEY J., SYDNEY C. HARRIS, AND WILLIAM J. THOMPSON "Empirical Study of Computer Based Financial Modeling Systems: Implications for Decision Support Systems," *DSS-81, Transactions,* June 1981.

BRUNSSON, NILS "The Irrationality of Action and Action Rationality: Decisions, Ideologies and Organizational Actions," *Journal of Management Studies,* 19 (January 1982), 29–44.

GEOFFRION, ARTHUR M. "The Purpose of Mathematical Programming Is Insight, Not Numbers," *Interfaces,* 7 (November 1976), 81–92.

HOGARTH, ROBIN, M., AND SPYROS MAKRIDAKIS "Forecasting and Planning: An Evaluation," *Management Science,* 27 (February 1981), 115–38.

KEEN, PETER G. W. "Computer Systems for Top Managers: A Modest Proposal," *Sloan Management Review,* 18 (Fall 1976), 1–17.

KEEN, PETER G. W. "Decision Support Systems and the Marginal Economics of Effort," Center for Information Systems Research Working Paper No. 48, Sloan School of Management, Massachusetts Institute of Technology, 1979.

KEEN, PETER G. W. "Decision Support Systems: A Research Perspective," Center for Information Systems Research Working Paper No. 54, Sloan School of Management, Massachusetts Institute of Technology, March 1980.

KEEN, PETER G. W., AND MICHAEL S. SCOTT MORTON *Decision Support Systems: An Organizational Perspective.* Reading, Mass.: Addison-Wesley, 1978.

LITTLE, JOHN D. C. "Models and Managers: The Concept of a Decision Calculus," *Management Science,* 16 (April 1970), B466–85.

MARCH, JAMES G. "Bounded Rationality, Ambiguity, and the Engineering of Choice," *Bell Journal of Economics,* 9 (Autumn 1978), 587–608.

MARCH, JAMES G. "Decisions in Organizations and Theories of Choice," in *Perspectives on Organization Design and Behavior,* ed. Andrew H. Van de Ven and William F. Joyce. New York: John Wiley, 1981.

MINTZBERG, HENRY, DURU RAISINGHANI, AND ANDRE THEORET "The Structure of 'Unstructured' Decision Processes," *Administrative Science Quarterly,* 21 (June 1976), 246–75.

MOORE, JEFFREY H., AND MICHAEL G. CHANG "Meta Design Considerations in Building DSS," in *Building Decision Support Systems,* ed. John L. Bennett. Reading, Mass.: Addison-Wesley, 1983.

NISBETT, RICHARD E., AND TIMOTHY D. WILSON "Telling More Than We Can Know: Verbal Reports on Mental Processes," *Psychological Review,* 84 (May 1977), 231–59.

ROCKART, JOHN F., AND MICHAEL E. TREACY "The CEO Goes On Line," *Harvard Business Review,* 60 (January–February 1982), 82–88.

SCOTT MORTON, MICHAEL S. "State of the Art of Research in Management Support Systems," Center for Information Systems Research Working Paper No. 107, Sloan School of Management, Massachusetts Institute of Technology, July 1983.

SIMON, HERBERT A. *The New Science of Management Decision* (rev. ed.). Englewood Cliffs, N.J.: Prentice-Hall, 1977.

SPRAGUE, RALPH H., JR., AND ERIC D. CARLSON *Building Effective Decision Support Systems.* Englewood Cliffs, N.J.: Prentice-Hall, 1982.

STABELL, CHARLES B. "A Decision-Oriented Approach to Building DSS," in *Building Decision Support Systems,* ed. John L. Bennett. Reading, Mass.: Addison-Wesley, 1983.

WATSON, H. J., R. H. SPRAGUE, AND D. W. KROEBER "An Empirical Study of Information Systems Evolution," *Proceedings, Tenth Hawaii International Conference on Systems Sciences,* Western Periodicals, North Hollywood, Calif., 1977.

WINER, B. J. *Statistical Principles in Experimental Design* (2nd ed.). New York: McGraw-Hill, 1971.

PART 3

The Architecture for DSS

Even though decision support systems can differ significantly, there are similarities. There is a software interface through which the user directs the actions and receives the output from the DSS. This is frequently referred to as the dialog between the user and the system. Then there is the database component which serves such functions as providing information in response to queries from the user; supplying data for the building, updating, and running of models; and storing intermediate and final results from analyses that are made. And finally there is the model base component. This component includes permanent models as well as modeling capabilities for building and updating models.

The software interface, database, and model base can be thought of as the architecture for a DSS. This section of the book provides one or more selections for each of these three components.

The first selection (Reading 7), by the editors of this book, deals with the data-dialog-modeling components of the DSS architecture in more detail. People differ in how they perceive and process data. It seems logical, then, that the dialog component of a DSS should be designed in such a way that it accommodates the needs and preferences of a particular user. Increasingly, this can be done through the flexibility available in emerging computer hardware and software technology. Bob Mann, Hugh Watson, Paul Cheney, and Chuck Gallagher, in "Accommodating Cognitive Style through DSS Hardware and Software" (Reading 8), discuss the current thinking in this area and illustrate how one DSS software product, IFPS/Personal, can provide this flexibility.

Decision support systems can be categorized as being ad hoc or institutional, depending on a number of characteristics, including whether they are used infrequently or on a repetitive basis. Carleen Garnto and Hugh Watson, in "An Investigation of Database Requirements for Institutional and Ad Hoc DSS" (Reading 9), describe the database component of two institutional and ad hoc DSS and suggest database differences that seem to exist between these two types of decision support systems. An understanding of these differences can facilitate the design of a DSS database.

An important new aspect of the database/data management component is the growing use of document data. It is easy to see how the data and information contained in documents, reports, memos, and even phone messages can be an extremely important resource for DSS. New technologies are now evolving that will make it possible to manage this data resource better, as explained by Jane Fedorowicz in Reading 10.

The modeling component is explained in Reading 11 by Robert Blanning, one of the most extensively published authors on this subject. Finally, we return to the dialog component in Reading 12, by John Carlson and Efraim Turban, to examine some new visually oriented capabilities for dialog, and how they can assist decision making.

7

THE COMPONENTS OF AN ARCHITECTURE FOR *DSS*

Hugh J. Watson,
Ralph H. Sprague, Jr.

INTRODUCTION

A useful way of thinking about the component parts of a decision support system (DSS) and the relationships among the parts is to use the dialog, data, and models (D,D,M) paradigm [8, 9, 10, 11]. In this conceptualization, there is the *dialog* (D) between the user and the system, the *data* (D) that support the system, and the *models* (M) that provide the analysis capabilities. While the components differ somewhat from application to application, they always exist in some form. Figure 7.1 provides a pictorial representation of the component parts of a DSS.

For users and DSS builders, it is important to understand how each component can be designed. For users, it creates an awareness of what can be requested in a DSS. For DSS builders, it suggests what can be delivered.

New technology continues to affect the dialog, data, and models components. For example, icon-based, touchscreen systems provide new options for directing the system. Relational database technology is influencing how data are stored, updated, and retrieved. Drawing from artificial intelligence advances, there is the potential for representing and using models in new ways.

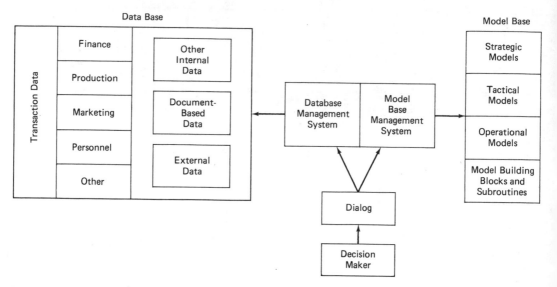

FIGURE 7.1 The Components of a DSS

Our purpose is to explore the component parts of a DSS. We will attempt to describe the richness of what is currently possible. Undoubtedly, emerging technology will continue to expand this domain.

THE DIALOG COMPONENT

An appreciation of the importance of the dialog component is gained by recognizing that from the user's perspective, the dialog is the system. What the user has *to know in order to use the system,* the options for *directing the system's actions,* and the alternative *presentations of the system's responses* are what is important. Bennett [1] refers to these dialog components as the *knowledge base,* the *action language,* and the *presentation language,* respectively. Unless they affect the dialog, the user typically has little interest in such considerations as the hardware and software used, how data are stored in memory, and the algorithms employed by the models. Such factors are often transparent to the user; that is, they are neither seen nor recognized.

General Considerations

When designing the DSS dialog, it is important to recognize who the potential users are. In some instances, there is a single user; more typically, the DSS has multiple users [4]. While much of the writing on DSS emphasizes its usefulness for supporting the poorly structured decision-making tasks of top management [10], the reality is that middle management and especially professional staff (e.g., financial planners, marketing researchers) are the hands-on users of DSS [4]. This does not mean that DSS is not used by top management. Rather, what often happens is that senior executives request information from a staff assistant who uses a DSS to obtain the information. Operating this way, the assistant is an extension of the DSS. As will be seen, this arrangement has important implications for dialog design.

It should be recognized that a dialog involves *simplicity* versus *flexibility* trade-offs. Dialogs that are simple to use typically offer less flexibility. For example, the old *question-answer* approach requires the user to respond to questions. While this approach is simple and is often appropriate for novice users performing well-structured tasks, it does not provide flexibility beyond what was planned by the system's designers. In this situation, the system is largely in control. *Menu*-oriented systems impose the same kind of structure on the user even though they provide a different dialog approach. By way of contrast, *command languages* place the user more in control but require additional knowledge to use the system. Command languages normally employ a verb-noun syntax (e.g., RUN SIMULATION, PRINT REPORT). Most DSS generators use variations of the command language approach. While DSS generators simplify the development and operation of a DSS, they require training and a frequency of use sufficient to remember their syntax. It is for these reasons that most top managers are not hands-on DSS users. They are unwilling or unable to take the time to be trained properly and have job responsibilities that do not allow frequent use.

When a DSS supports several uses, multiple dialog options can be designed for the system. This is sometimes referred to as a *tiered* dialog approach because there are several levels of dialog options. Novice users can employ the system in one way and more experienced ones can use it in another way. The availability of multiple dialog options also supports differences in cognitive style among users [7]. A person's *cognitive style* refers to the systematic and pervasive way that data are perceived and analyzed. For example, a *systematic* person processes data in a structured, step-by-step process, whereas an *intuitive* person may jump from one analysis process to another. A systematic person may feel comfortable with a menu-oriented dialog, but an intuitive person may want the flexibility offered by a command language.

Another dialog consideration is whether the DSS will be operated by the decision maker or an intermediary (sometimes call the *chauffeur*) [6]. With chauffeur-driven systems, the emphasis can be on the power and flexibility of the dialog. Ease-of-use features that might be critical to nonspecialists can be omitted, resulting in systems with less software "overhead."

The Knowledge Base

The knowledge base includes what the user knows about the decision and about how to use the DSS.

The user's knowledge of the problem is largely learned external to the DSS. The DSS allows the user to understand better the decision, but much about the problem must already be known. A notable exception is when a DSS is used to train new decision makers. In this case, the DSS is an educational vehicle.

Users can be trained in the use of a DSS in multiple ways [11]. The *one-on-one tutorial* is commonly employed with senior executives. *Classes* and *lectures* are efficient when many users require training. *Programmed* and *computer-aided instruction* are economical approaches when the DSS is expected to have a long life span and serve many users. A *resident expert* can respond to specific requests for help.

The DSS can include features that make it easier to use. Instruction manuals can be made available online. Any time during a session, a user can receive help by pressing a single key. The help can be made *context sensitive;* that is, depending on where the decision maker is in the use of the DSS, the system provides help that is customized for the situation.

Command or *sequence files* are useful to novice or infrequent users. These files contain preprogrammed instructions that are activated by a few simple keystrokes. Consequently, a user does not have to know any of the underlying commands, only how to execute the command file. As an example of a command file, at the end of each month, a senior manager may want to compare projected versus actual cash flow. Such an analysis is common with many financial DSS but often requires the user to enter a series of commands. In order to make it easy for the manager to obtain the analysis, the required commands might be put into a command file.

Comprehensive DSS generators usually support the creation and use of command files. Some have a "capture" feature, which functions by recording and saving all commands entered. The user issues a command to evoke the capture feature, enters the commands to be saved, and provides an appropriate filename.

The Action Language

The actions that the user can take to control the DSS can be described in a variety of ways, depending on the system's design. Question-answer, menu-oriented, and command language approaches have already been discussed. Other options exist, and additional attractive alternatives continue to appear.

Some DSS use an input-output form approach. The user is provided an input form and enters the required data. After all the data are input, the DSS performs the analysis and presents the results.

The visual-oriented interfaces developed by Apple for the Macintosh are growing in popularity. These interfaces use "icons," or pictorial symbols to represent familiar objects, such as a document, file folder, outbasket, or trash bin. The action language is usually implemented by using a mouse to move icons or to perform actions on them by selecting choices from a menu.

Voice input is the ultimate in ease of use. While important advances in voice input are being made, currently it is not a popular option for DSS. Existing technology supports only a limited vocabulary, must be typically calibrated to the user's voice, and offers discrete rather than continuous speech recognition. These limitations tend to make voice input only appropriate for individual DSS that are used in a highly structured manner. As the technology improves, however, more voice-oriented systems can be expected.

The physical actions required to direct a DSS have also undergone change. Keyboard input is no longer the only choice. Touchscreen and especially mouse-driven systems are common. These are attractive alternatives for executives who do not want to type.

The Presentation Language

The PC used on a stand-alone basis or as an intelligent terminal connected to a mainframe has significantly expanded and enhanced how output from a DSS is presented. Printed reports are no longer the only output option. In fact, in many instances there is no hard copy output. Instead, the output is presented on the screen, internalized by the decision maker, and discarded. The DSS can be rerun if the user needs to see the output again.

One of the greatest contributions of the PC is its superior *graphics* capabilities. Used with graphics software, a variety of graphs, in three dimensions and in color, are easily created. The current research on chip technology promises to improve graphics quality even more, providing nearly perfect resolution. Even though research has not clearly established the superiority of graphics over tabular output [5], its popularity speaks for its perceived usefulness.

Animation is beginning to be used for DSS output, especially for applications that involve the simulation of physical systems. Consider, for example, a DSS developed to support the design of a bank's drive-in teller facilities. With animation, it is possible to actually see the arrival of customers, the length of the queues, and the utilization of the servers under various conditions and different drive-in teller designs.

Voice output is also a possibility, even though it is not currently being used for DSS. As an example of its potential, consider a financial DSS where not only exception reports are provided, but a voice overlay describes or explains the exceptions.

Dialog Styles

Combinations or sets of options for implementing the knowledge base, the action language, and the presentation language, taken together, can be called a "dialog style." For example, one dialog style results in a system that requires users to keep a reference card (knowledge base) and to remember which commands to enter with a keyboard (action language) in order to obtain a printed report (presentation language). Quite another dialog style results from using a mouse to access pull-down menus and move icons on a color screen to get a graphical presentation of analysis results. The latter dialog style, popularized by the Apple Macintosh, is revolutionizing the dialog component in recent years.

Much of its popularity results from basing all the elements of the dialog around a familiar metaphor—the virtual desktop. The display screen represents a desktop, icons represent familiar objects on a desk (documents, file folders, etc.), and the mouse is used to move things around, open and close files and documents, and choose actions from the menu. The success of this dialog style suggests that most systems for DSS will eventually have a dialog component with a similar design.

THE DATA COMPONENT

Data play an important role in a DSS. Data are either accessed directly by the user or are an input to the models for processing. Care must be taken to ensure their availability.

Data Sources

Data for a DSS cannot be taken for granted. Some data can be obtained from the organization's *transaction processing* systems. But even then, some preparatory processing is often required.

Few DSS need data at the transaction level. Summarized data are more typically required and can be obtained in several ways. One way is to have the database management system (DBMS) for the transaction processing system extract the transaction data, summarize them, and make the data available to the DSS. Another option is to extract the data but have the processing done external to the DBMS. While this is ideally a computerized process, some DSS rely on manual processing. This may be appropriate when the processing requires little effort or when the DSS is needed quickly and a more "elegant" solution cannot be implemented in a timely manner.

Some organizations only give end users access to *extract files*. These are files maintained externally to the DBMS and are created specifically to meet the data needs of end users. Extract files are used for security, ease of access, and data integrity reasons. In organizations with extract files, the DSS obtains data from these files.

The previous comments suggest that the database for a DSS may be separate from the transaction processing database, and, for several reasons, this indeed is the case in most organizations. The same line of thinking that leads to extract files also supports the idea of a separate DSS database. Many people believe that it is best to not intermix the rather different worlds of end-user and information systems computing. Also, most DBMS for handling transaction data (e.g., IBM's IMS) were created for information systems specialists rather than end users and require considerable training. Also end users expect fast response times, and this may be a problem when they are competing with transaction processing applications for machine cycles. Because of the need for fast response times, organizations often dedicate a specific machine for end-user applications.

In addition to transaction data, *other internal data* may be needed. For example, subjective estimates from managers and engineering-related data may be needed. These kinds of data are seldom available from normal data processing activities. In order to have other internal data available, they must be collected, entered, and maintained. The collection effort may be difficult and time consuming because it requires a special initiative. If the data must be available on an ongoing basis, specific methods and procedures must be developed for keeping the data up to date. A good DBMS is required to support the entering, maintenance, and extraction of data.

External data may also be needed, especially for decision support at the upper managerial levels. Examples of external data include national and regional economic data, industry data, and competitive data. Like internal data, making external data available requires special efforts. Unlike internal data, external data may be purchased.

For example, marketing data can be purchased from firms such as A. C. Nielson, Market Research Corporation of America, and Brand Rating Index Corporation. The data are extracted from the commercial database, communicated to the user's organization, and entered into the organization's database.

Researchers and organizations are exploring how to include yet another type of data in a DSS: *document-based data*. Organizations have a wealth of data contained in documents such as memos, letters, contracts, and organization charts. If the contents of these documents can be electronically stored (e.g., videodisc) and then retrieved by key characteristics (e.g., topic, date, location), a powerful new source of information for decision support can be supplied to decision makers.

Vendor Contributions

Vendors are providing products with better database capabilities. At the PC level, products like dBase III make it easier to create, maintain, and use a database. Other products support downloading corporate data to the PC. Mainframe DSS generators have improved their database capabilities. Nearly all of the major vendors have "pipeline" software that extracts data from a DBMS, reformats the data, and places the data in the DSS generator's database.

THE MODEL COMPONENT

Models provide the analysis capabilities for a DSS. Using a mathematical representation of the problem, algorithmic processes are employed to generate information to support decision making. For example, a linear programming model of a production blending problem might reveal the cheapest way to blend a product while meeting product specifications.

Types of Models

There are many different types of models and various ways that they can be categorized. Important distinctions can be made on the basis of their *purpose, treatment of randomness,* and *generality of application.*

The purpose of a model can be either optimization or description. An *optimization model* is one that seeks to identify points of maximization or minimization. For example, management often wants to know what actions will lead to a profit or a revenue maximization or a cost minimization. Optimization models provide this information. A *descriptive model* describes the behavior of a system. In a sense, any model is a descriptive model if it is a valid representation of reality. But a descriptive model *only* describes the system's behavior; it does not suggest optimizing conditions.

Regarding randomness, nearly all systems are probabilistic. That is, the behavior of the system cannot be predicted with certainty because a degree of randomness is present. A *probabilistic model* attempts to capture the probabilistic nature of the system by requiring probabilistic data inputs and by generating probabilistic outputs. Even though most systems are probabilistic, most mathematical models are *deterministic*. *Deterministic models* employ single-valued estimates for the variables in the model and generate single-valued outputs. Deterministic models are more popular than probabilistic ones because they are less expensive, less difficult, and less time consuming to build and use, and they often provide satisfactory information to support decision making.

In terms of generality of application, a model can be developed for use with only one system (a *custom-built* model) or a model may be applicable to many systems (*ready-built* models). In general, custom-built models describe a particular system and, consequently, provide a better description than a ready-built model. However, they are generally more expensive for the organization, because they have to be built "from the ground up."

Model Base

The models in a DSS can be thought of as a *model base*. As Figure 7.1 shows, a variety of models can be included: strategic, tactical, and operational models and model-building blocks and subroutines. Each type of model has unique characteristics.

The *strategic models* are used by top management to help determine the objectives of the organization, the resources needed to accomplish those objectives, and the policies to govern the acquisition, use, and disposition of these resources. They might be used for company objectives planning, plant location selection, environmental impact planning, or similar types of applications. Strategic models tend to be broad in scope with many variables expressed in compressed, aggregated form. Much of the data required to fuel the models are external and subjective. The time horizons for the models are often measured in years, as are top management's strategic planning responsibilities. The models are usually deterministic, descriptive, and custom-built for the particular organization.

The *tactical models* are commonly employed by middle management to assist in allocating and controlling the use of the organization's resources. Applications include financial planning, worker requirements planning, sales promotion planning, and plant layout determination. The models are usually only applicable to a subset of the organization, like production, and there is some aggregation of variables. Their time horizon varies from one month to less than two years. Some subjective and external data are needed, but the greatest requirements are for internal data. The models tend to be deterministic, and in comparison to strategic models are more likely to provide optimality information and to be ready-built.

The *operational models* are usually employed to support the short-term decisions (e.g., daily, weekly) commonly found at lower organizational levels. Potential applications include credit scoring, media selection, production scheduling, and inventory control. Operational models normally use internal data in their operation. They are typically deterministic, often ready-built, and provide optimization information.

In addition to strategic, tactical, and operational models, the model base contains *model-building blocks and subroutines*. They might include linear programming, time-series analysis, regression analysis, and Monte Carlo sampling procedures. In form and size, these tools might range from a FORTRAN subroutine for calculating an internal rate of return to a packaged set of programs for exploring a generic class of problems (e.g., IBM's MPSX for mathematical programming problems). The model-building blocks and subroutines can be used separately for ad hoc decision support, or together to construct and maintain more comprehensive models.

Problems with Traditional Modeling

From a historical perspective, organizations' experiences with models are mixed. While there are many successes, there are often many failures. With hindsight, it is possible to identify the problems that lead to failure:

- Difficulties in obtaining input data for the models.
- Difficulties in understanding how to apply the output from models.
- Difficulties in keeping the models up to date.
- Lack of confidence in the models by users; therefore, the models are not trusted.
- Little integration among models.
- Poor interaction between the models and users.
- Difficult for users to create their own models.
- The models' little explanation for their output.

The DSS Approach to Modeling

The DSS approach to modeling attempts to minimize the traditional modeling problems by emphasizing that a *system* (e.g., dialog, data, and models working together) to support decision making is required.

The database is important to solving many of the problems. It provides the data required to build, use, and maintain the models. The output from the models is placed in the database, thus making the output accessible to other models and providing integration among the models.

A well-designed dialog enhances the likelihood that users will be able to develop their own models, operate the system successfully, keep it up to date, and apply the output to decision-making tasks. These considerations, along with high levels of involvement during the system development process, lead to greater confidence in the models.

The models in a DSS are likely to be useful because they are adequately supported by the data and dialog components. An interesting new development in modeling is the inclusion of artificial intelligence capabilities through which the models explain the factors that led to the output. For example, it might be explained that a decrease in profits is due to the drop in market share in the western region.

The DSS approach to modeling requires a model base management system (MBMS) with capabilities analogous to a DBMS. The most important capabilities include

- A flexible mechanism for building models.
- Ease of use of the models to obtain needed decision support.
- Methods for saving models that will be used again.
- Procedures for updating models.
- Methods for making output from a model available to other models as input.

Unlike a DBMS, a MBMS is not commercially available as a stand-alone product. Rather, it exists as a component capability of DSS generators. Consider, IFPS as an example. It has an English-like syntax with built-in functions that facilitate the building and updating of models (e.g., VALUE = INFLOWS – OUTFLOWS). Specifications for directing model execution are easily understood (e.g., SOLVE, MONTE CARLO). Models can be saved for future use (e.g., SAVE).

Considerable research is being conducted in MBMS. One stream of research focuses on applying and extending the relational model for DBMS to MBMS [2]. Another approach is to apply artificial intelligence concepts to model management [3]. Even though these research efforts have not resulted in commercially available products, they offer great potential.

CONCLUSION

The dialog, data, and models paradigm provides a powerful conceptual model for understanding the components and relationships in a DSS. Each is critical if a DSS is to live up to its decision support potential. The D,D,M paradigm is useful in understanding and assessing the capabilities of DSS generators, and to some extent has influenced the evolution of these products. Current DSS research can also be understood in the context of the D,D,M model.

QUESTIONS

1. What is meant by "From the user's perspective, the dialog is the system"? Do you agree with this statement? Discuss.
2. What data sources may be required by a DSS? To what extent are the data machine-readable? Discuss.
3. Compare and contrast the traditional and DSS approaches to modeling.

REFERENCES

1. BENNETT, J.   "User-Oriented Graphics, Systems for Support in Unstructured Tasks," in *User Oriented Design of Interactive Graphics Systems*, S. Treu (ed.). New York: Association for Computing Machinery, 1977.

2. BLANNING, ROBERT W.   "A Relational Theory of Model Management," in *Decision Support Systems: Theory and Application,* Clyde W. Holsapple and Andrew Winston (eds.). Berlin: Springer-Verlag, 1987.

3. ELAM, JOYCE J., AND BENN KONSYNSKI   "Using Artificial Intelligence Techniques to Enhance the Capabilities of Model Management Systems," *Decision Sciences* (Summer 1987), 487–502.

4. HOGUE, JACK T.   "A Framework for the Examination of Management Involvement in Decision Support Systems," *Journal of Management Information Systems,* no. 1 (1987), 96–110.

5. JARVENPAA, SIRKA L., GARY W. DICKSON, AND GERARDINE DESANCTIS   "Methodological Issues in Experimental IS Research: Experiences and Recommendations," *MIS Quarterly* (June 1985), 141–56.

6. KEEN, PETER G. W.   "Interactive Computer Systems for Managers: A Modest Proposal," *Sloan Management Review* (Fall 1976), 1–17.

7. MCKENNY, JAMES L., AND PETER G. W. KEEN   "How Manager's Minds Work," *Harvard Business Review* (July–August 1974), 79–90.

8. SPRAGUE, RALPH H., AND HUGH J. WATSON   "MIS Concepts: Part I," *Journal of Systems Management* (January 1975), 34–37.

9. SPRAGUE, RALPH H., AND HUGH J. WATSON   "MIS Concepts: Part II," *Journal of Systems Management* (February 1975), 35–40.

10. SPRAGUE, RALPH H.   "A Framework for the Development of Decision Support Systems," *MIS Quarterly* (December 1980), 1–26.

11. SPRAGUE, RALPH H., AND ERIC D. CARLSON   *Building Effective Decision Support Systems* (Englewood Cliffs, N.J.: Prentice Hall, 1982.

8

ACCOMMODATING COGNITIVE STYLE THROUGH *DSS* HARDWARE AND SOFTWARE

Robert I. Mann, Hugh J. Watson,
Paul H. Cheney, and Charles A. Gallagher

INTRODUCTION

Not all people are alike. This can be seen by casual inspection: some are tall, some are short; some have brown hair, some have blond hair. People also differ in their cognitive style, that is, the systematic and persuasive way that they think. Consequently, some are detail oriented, some look for general relationships; some are influenced by personal feelings, some are more objective. These differences are seen in day-to-day observations and are borne out by research.

Several conceptualizations and operationalizations have been used to examine cognitive style. Each, however, relates to one or both of the following activities: (1) the perception of data and (2) the formulation of knowledge from the assimilated data. Bariff and Lusk [2], in reviewing the many cognitive style constructs and measures, identified four major categories, three of which are particularly useful for our purposes here.

Robert I. Mann, Hugh J. Watson, Paul H. Cheney, and Charles A. Gallagher, "Accommodating Cognitive Style through DSS Hardware and Software," *Proceedings from the 19th Hawaii International Conference on Systems Sciences,* 1986.

The first category, *cognitive complexity,* has been operationalized as possessing three distinct properties: (1) differentiation, or the number of elements an individual seeks and assimilates in the cognitive process; (2) discrimination, or the way in which a person assigns slightly varying stimuli to different categories; and (3) integration, or the number and completeness of the rules a decision maker uses in the cognitive process. The cognitive complexity dimension classifies individuals along a continuum from simple to complex.

The second category, *field independence-dependence,* classifies individuals according to their tendency to perceive patterns of data that are relatively independent of their context, or as discrete items embedded in their context.

The third category, *thinking mode,* refers to a person's tendency to search the data for causal relationships that promote an algorithmic solution and to utilize abstract models, or to base the search on experience and common sense using trial-and-error, ad hoc hypothesis testing. Individuals are classified as either systematic (the former) or heuristic (the latter).

Zmud [32] has identified cognitive complexity, field independence-dependence, and thinking mode as the dimensions of cognitive style receiving the most attention in the information systems literature. The feeling has been that if more is known about the various types of cognitive styles and if the users of a system can be correctly categorized, it should be possible to design information systems that are more frequently used, result in greater decision-making effectiveness, and are better accepted by users.

A variety of areas have been explored by cognitive style researchers. For example, people having different cognitive styles have been shown to prefer different amounts of data [9, 17]. Research has shown that a person's cognitive style affects his or her preference for aggregate versus raw data [2] as well as detailed versus summary information [18]. Cognitive style has been found to influence the preference for quantitative versus qualitative information [10, 17, 18], preference for analysis [13], and preference for social information [7]. Preference for tabular versus graphic presentation [2, 4, 19, 22] and for a semantic, symbolic, or behavioral presentation have also been related to cognitive style. And finally, the use of decision-making aids has been shown to vary with cognitive style [4, 26].

The impact of considering cognitive style in DSS design is most significant in regard to the design of the dialog between the user and the system. This dialog can be thought of in terms of an action language and a presentation language [3]. It is through the action language that the user directs the system, whereas in the presentation language, the system provides output to the user. By designing the appropriate capabilities in the action and presentation languages, the cognitive style of the user can be accommodated.

THE PROBLEMS WITH USING COGNITIVE STYLE

Even though the idea of designing a DSS to accommodate a user's cognitive style has an intuitive appeal, and there has been considerable research in the area, current thinking has cast doubts on the usefulness of testing users to determine their cognitive style and designing a system accordingly. Several reasons are put forward in support of this position.

The current cognitive style research has yielded few if any operational guidelines for designing a DSS [9, 16]. Study findings have been inconclusive or inconsistent [1, 5, 9, 11, 12, 13, 16, 22, 26]. Some researchers believe that little of a practical nature can be conveyed to DSS designers that would allow them to design applications better [9, 16]. Others note that developing an empirically based body of knowledge takes a long time. Therefore, it is likely that hardware and software advances will outpace and largely negate the value of cognitive style research [8, 19].

Many factors affect decision making, and cognitive style is just one of them. Decisions are made within an organizational context that includes considerations such as company policies and whether the decision is made by an individual or a group. Decisions are also affected by their own context, such as the time available to consider the decision and the amount of information available [9, 16, 25]. They are also affected by individual differences in the decision maker, of which cognitive style is just one [9, 16, 32]. Other differences include training, experience, and intelligence. When all of these other factors are considered, the impact of cognitive style on decision making is probably minimal.

To incorporate a person's cognitive style into a DSS, his or her cognitive style must first be measured. This can be done in a variety of ways, none of which is completely satisfactory. One way is to talk with the person about how decision-making tasks are handled and to observe the decision maker at work [12, 16, 22, 26]. These are typical elements in any systems analysis. The approach is also time consuming and imprecise. Another alternative is to use physiological tests where the person's physiological processes are monitored [30]. For example, this can be done using EEGs where the person's brain waves in each hemisphere are measured in order to provide an indicator of where information processing takes place. Psychological tests can also be used. For example, embedded figures tests where the person attempts to identify figures in a larger picture can be used to assess his or her ability to identify details in a large context [5, 22]. Another alternative is the self-description tests, such as the Myers Briggs Type Indicator [2, 13, 14, 15, 17, 19, 27, 28]. These tests have subjects provide answers that best describe themselves and are used to categorize the person along various cognitive dimensions. These testing methods involve several problems. One that was mentioned previously is accuracy. Another frequent problem is getting the person to submit to a testing program. This becomes an ever greater problem with higher-level managers who do not have the time or especially the inclination to be tested.

There is also evidence that a person's cognitive style does not remain constant across various decision-making tasks [9, 16]. Managers change their cognitive style depending on the task. Consequently, in order to be accurate, the user's decision-making style would have to be assessed in the context of the decision to be supported.

There is also the problem of what to do about cognitive style when there are multiple users of a DSS. Research indicates that multiple users are very common [9, 11, 16, 21]. While there may sometimes be homogeneity in cognitive style among multiple users, this cannot be counted on and, in fact, is probably seldom the case.

The discussion of the problems of accommodating a particular cognitive style in the design of a DSS leads to the conclusion that it is seldom wise to try to custom build the dialog for a particular decision maker based exclusively on cognitive style considerations. Fortunately, another option is evolving. Hardware and software advances are making it possible for a decision maker to select dialog options that are deemed appropriate for the decision-making task at hand. These options include question-answer dialog, command languages, menus, joysticks, mice, touchscreens, function keys, voice input/output, text, and graphic output. Increasingly, many of these options are available in a single piece of hardware and/or software. This approach assumes that the decision maker is able to select and use the technology that is most appropriate for the current decision-making task.

ACCOMMODATING COGNITIVE STYLE WITH *IFPS*/PERSONAL

To illustrate the ability of newly emerging computer hardware and software to accommodate cognitive style differences, IFPS/Personal will be discussed. This product was developed and is marketed by Execucom Systems Corporation. It is a DSS generator which is used in a distributed DSS environment, runs on a PC with 512K of memory, and sells for $895. It is a high-level application development language that is easy to use and allows user interaction through a variety of dialog styles utilizing English-like terminology.

The heart of the system is a modeling language with built-in financial, mathematical, and statistical functions that gives users the ability to describe business relationships in business terms. Figures 8.2a, b, and c illustrate the base solution for the sample model shown in Figure 8.1. Notice the variety of display windows available. The decision maker can focus on any portion of the model together with the solution for that portion.

The modeling language includes what-if, goal seeking, and analyze capabilities. These features provide a better understanding of the relationship between the components of the model and allow the user to interrogate the model and data to test the sensitivity of selected variables. Figure 8.3 shows a what-if solution of the same model answering the question, "What will our solution look like if we set the price at $25 for the entire year?"

Suppose the decision maker wants to know what price to set for the product in order to achieve revenues of $15,000 in January, with a growth rate of 5 percent in subsequent months. The goal seek solution shown in Figure 8.4 provides that answer simply and quickly.

IFPS/Personal's integrated color business graphics capabilities allow the user to produce a variety of business graphics quickly and easily in a multitude of formats. Some of these formats are illustrated in Figures 8.5, 8.6, and 8.9.

The data manipulation system includes a full screen spreadsheet style data editor for easy entering and editing of data and for creating new data files. Powerful consolidation techniques allow the user to consolidate new data files from existing

```
COLUMNS JAN THRU DEC, 1985
\\
\\ SALES DATA
\\
REVENUES = PRICE * UNITS SOLD
UNITS SOLD = 700,750,775,800,800,825,850,850,850,800,800,800
PRICE = 21 FOR 3, 22 FOR 6, 24 FOR 3
\\
\\ CASH RECEIPTS
\\
CASH COLLECTIONS = 60% * REVENUES
RECEIVABLES = 5000, 40% * PREVIOUS REVENUES
TOTAL RECEIPTS = CASH COLLECTIONS + RECEIVABLES
\\
\\ CASH DISBURSEMENTS
\\
RAW MATERIALS = 4000 FOR 3, 4600 FOR 3, 5200
SALARIES = 4100,3800,4200,5700,5700,6100,6800,7000,7200,6500,6400,6400
FIXED EXPENSES = 2300 FOR 6, 2800
TAX PAYMENTS = 0,0,0,20700,0
INTEREST = DEBT * INTEREST RATE
TOTAL DISBURSEMENTS = SUM(RAW MATERIALS THRU INTEREST)
\\
\\ CASH FLOW RECONCILIATION
\\
BEGINNING CASH = 1000, PREVIOUS ENDING CASH + PREVIOUS DEBT
ENDING CASH = BEGINNING CASH + TOTAL RECEIPTS - TOTAL DISBURSEMENTS
\\
\\ DEBT CALCULATION
\\
DESIRED CASH = 22000 FOR 3, 24000 FOR 3, 27000
DEBT = IF    ENDING CASH < DESIRED CASH '
       THEN  DESIRED CASH - ENDING CASH '
       ELSE  0
INTEREST RATE = 1.33%
\\
\\ ANNUAL TOTALS
\\
REDEFINE 1985 = SUM([JAN] THRU [DEC])
REDEFINE 1985 FOR PRICE = REVENUES[1985]/UNITS SOLD[1985]
REDEFINE 1985 FOR BEGINNING CASH = BEGINNING CASH [JAN]
REDEFINE 1985 FOR ENDING CASH = ENDING CASH [DEC]
```

FIGURE 8.1   Cash Flow Model

FIGURE 8.2a   Base Solution with Default Windows

	JAN	FEB	MAR	APR	MAY	JUN
REVENUES	14700.00	15750.00	16275.00	17600.00	17600.00	18150.00
UNITS SOLD	700.00	750.00	775.00	800.00	800.00	825.00
PRICE	21.00	21.00	21.00	22.00	22.00	22.00
CASH COLLECTIONS	8820.00	9450.00	9765.00	10560.00	10560.00	10890.00
RECEIVABLES	5000.00	5880.00	6300.00	6510.00	7040.00	7040.00
TOTAL RECEIPTS	13820.00	15330.00	16065.00	17070.00	17600.00	17930.00
RAW MATERIALS	4000.00	4000.00	4000.00	4600.00	4600.00	4600.00
SALARIES	4100.00	3800.00	4200.00	5700.00	5700.00	6100.00
FIXED EXPENSES	2300.00	2300.00	2300.00	2300.00	2300.00	2300.00
TAX PAYMENTS	0.00	0.00	0.00	20700.00	0.00	0.00

```
REVENUES = PRICE * UNITS SOLD
UNITS SOLD = 700,750,775,800,800,825,850,850,850,800,800,800
PRICE = 21 FOR 3, 22 FOR 6, 24 FOR 3
CASH COLLECTIONS = 60% * REVENUES
RECEIVABLES = 5000, 40% * PREVIOUS REVENUES
TOTAL RECEIPTS = CASH COLLECTIONS + RECEIVABLES
RAW MATERIALS = 4000 FOR 3, 4600 FOR 3, 5200
SALARIES = 4100,3800,4200,5700,5700,6100,6800,7000,7200,6500,6400,6400
FIXED EXPENSES = 2300 FOR 6, 2800
```

```
  Base Solution                      VIEW MODE        Model CASHFLOW.MOD
View:   What_if    wIndows     Variables    Columns
        Set        Format      Analyze
```

	JAN	FEB	MAR	APR	MAY	JUN
REVENUES	14700.00	15750.00	16275.00	17600.00	17600.00	18150.00
UNITS SOLD	700.00	750.00	775.00	800.00	800.00	825.00
PRICE	21.00	21.00	21.00	22.00	22.00	22.00
CASH COLLECTIONS	8820.00	9450.00	9765.00	10560.00	10560.00	10890.00

	JUL	AUG	SEP	OCT	NOV	DEC
REVENUES	18700.00	18700.00	18700.00	19200.00	19200.00	19200.00
UNITS SOLD	850.00	850.00	850.00	800.00	800.00	800.00
PRICE	22.00	22.00	22.00	24.00	24.00	24.00
CASH COLLECTIONS	11220.00	11220.00	11220.00	11520.00	11520.00	11520.00

```
REVENUES = PRICE * UNITS SOLD
UNITS SOLD = 700,750,775,800,800,825,850,850,850,800,800,800
PRICE = 21 FOR 3, 22 FOR 6, 24 FOR 3
CASH COLLECTIONS = 60% * REVENUES
RECEIVABLES = 5000, 40% * PREVIOUS REVENUES
TOTAL RECEIPTS = CASH COLLECTIONS + RECEIVABLES
RAW MATERIALS = 4000 FOR 3, 4600 FOR 3, 5200
SALARIES = 4100,3800,4200,5700,5700,6100,6800,7000,7200,6500,6400,6400
FIXED EXPENSES = 2300 FOR 6, 2800
  Base Solution                      VIEW MODE          Model CASHFLOW.MOD
View:   What_if      wIndows     Variables    Columns
        Set          Format      Analyze
```

FIGURE 8.2b Base Solution with Solution Window Split Horizontally

information. The organization of data separate from the models simplifies model maintenance, since only the underlying business relationships need be contained in the model. Uncluttered by data, these relationships stand out clearly and allow modifications to be made easily. In addition, different users can develop and share independent models and data files. One model may be used by different organizational subunits with different data, or one set of data may be analyzed using different models.

Among its other capabilities, IFPS/Personal includes an extensive report generator for creating customized, presentation quality reports (Figure 8.7) and a command language for automating applications. The plot shown in Figure 8.9 was produced by the command file shown in Figure 8.8.

FIGURE 8.2c Base Solution with Solution Window Split Vertically

	JAN	FEB	MAR	APR	1985
REVENUES	14700.00	15750.00	16275.00	17600.00	213775.00
UNITS SOLD	700.00	750.00	775.00	800.00	9600.00
PRICE	21.00	21.00	21.00	22.00	22.27
CASH COLLECTIONS	8820.00	9450.00	9765.00	10560.00	128265.00
RECEIVABLES	5000.00	5880.00	6300.00	6510.00	82830.00
TOTAL RECEIPTS	13820.00	15330.00	16065.00	17070.00	211095.00
RAW MATERIALS	4000.00	4000.00	4000.00	4600.00	57000.00
SALARIES	4100.00	3800.00	4200.00	5700.00	69900.00
FIXED EXPENSES	2300.00	2300.00	2300.00	2300.00	30600.00
TAX PAYMENTS	0.00	0.00	0.00	20700.00	20700.00

```
REVENUES = PRICE * UNITS SOLD
UNITS SOLD = 700,750,775,800,800,825,850,850,850,800,800,800
PRICE = 21 FOR 3, 22 FOR 6, 24 FOR 3
CASH COLLECTIONS = 60% * REVENUES
RECEIVABLES = 5000, 40% * PREVIOUS REVENUES
TOTAL RECEIPTS = CASH COLLECTIONS + RECEIVABLES
RAW MATERIALS = 4000 FOR 3, 4600 FOR 3, 5200
SALARIES = 4100,3800,4200,5700,5700,6100,6800,7000,7200,6500,6400,6400
FIXED EXPENSES = 2300 FOR 6, 2800
  Base Solution                      VIEW MODE          Model CASHFLOW.MOD
View:   What_if      wIndows     Variables    Columns
        Set          Format      Analyze
```

	JAN	FEB	MAR	APR	MAY	JUN
REVENUES	17500.00	18750.00	19375.00	20000.00	20000.00	20625.00
UNITS SOLD	700.00	750.00	775.00	800.00	800.00	825.00
PRICE	25.00	25.00	25.00	25.00	25.00	25.00
CASH COLLECTIONS	10500.00	11250.00	11625.00	12000.00	12000.00	12375.00

	JUL	AUG	SEP	OCT	NOV	DEC
REVENUES	21250.00	21250.00	21250.00	20000.00	20000.00	20000.00
UNITS SOLD	850.00	850.00	850.00	800.00	800.00	800.00
PRICE	25.00	25.00	25.00	25.00	25.00	25.00
CASH COLLECTIONS	12750.00	12750.00	12750.00	12000.00	12000.00	12000.00

```
REVENUES = PRICE * UNITS SOLD
UNITS SOLD = 700,750,775,800,800,825,850,850,850,800,800,800
PRICE = 21 FOR 3, 22 FOR 6, 24 FOR 3
CASH COLLECTIONS = 60% * REVENUES
RECEIVABLES = 5000, 40% * PREVIOUS REVENUES
 Case
PRICE = 25


  What If Solution                        VIEW MODE        Model CASHFLOW.MOD
What_if:  Base       Get         Name      Save
          solVe      gOal_seek   Edit_case Update
```

FIGURE 8.3   What-If Solution

	JAN	FEB	MAR	APR	MAY	JUN
REVENUES	15000.00	15750.00	16537.50	17364.38	18232.59	19144.22
UNITS SOLD	700.00	750.00	775.00	800.00	800.00	825.00
PRICE	21.43	21.00	21.34	21.71	22.79	23.21
CASH COLLECTIONS	9000.00	9450.00	9922.50	10418.63	10939.56	11486.53

	JAN	FEB	MAR	APR	MAY	JUN
REVENUES	15000.00	15750.00	16537.50	17364.38	18232.59	19144.22
UNITS SOLD	700.00	750.00	775.00	800.00	800.00	825.00
PRICE	21.43	21.00	21.34	21.71	22.79	23.21
CASH COLLECTIONS	9000.00	9450.00	9922.50	10418.63	10939.56	11486.53

```
REVENUES = PRICE * UNITS SOLD
UNITS SOLD = 700,750,775,800,800,825,850,850,850,800,800,800
PRICE = 21 FOR 3, 22 FOR 6, 24 FOR 3
CASH COLLECTIONS = 60% * REVENUES
RECEIVABLES = 5000, 40% * PREVIOUS REVENUES
TOTAL RECEIPTS = CASH COLLECTIONS + RECEIVABLES
RAW MATERIALS = 4000 FOR 3, 4600 FOR 3, 5200
SALARIES = 4100,3800,4200,5700,5700,6100,6800,7000,7200,6500,6400,6400
FIXED EXPENSES = 2300 FOR 6, 2800
  Goal Seek Solution                     VIEW MODE        Model CASHFLOW.MOD
View:  What_if    wIndows     Variables   Columns
       Set        Format      Analyze
```

FIGURE 8.4   Goal Seek Solution

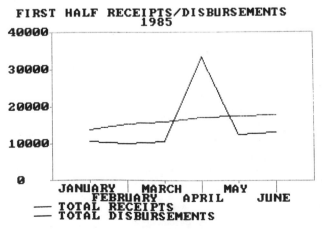

FIGURE 8.5   Sample Line Plot

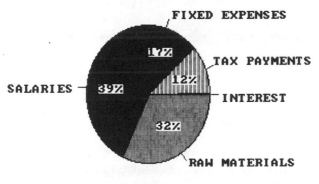

FIGURE 8.6 Sample Pie Chart

Although the command file appears complex, it was created by the IFPS/Personal LEARN facility. The LEARN facility simply creates a command file by capturing the key strokes of the user as the user processes the menu selections. Other IFPS/Personal features include mainframe communications, external program execution from within the system, and instant on-line help.

FIGURE 8.7 Sample Report

FIRST QUARTER CASH BUDGET
1985

	JANUARY	FEBRUARY	MARCH
CASH RECEIPTS:			
CASH COLLECTIONS	$8,820.00	$9,450.00	$9,765.00
RECEIVABLES	5,000.00	5,880.00	6,300.00
TOTAL RECEIPTS	$13,820.00	$15,330.00	$16,065.00
CASH DISBURSEMENTS:			
RAW MATERIALS	$4,000.00	$4,000.00	$4,000.00
SALARIES	4,100.00	3,800.00	4,200.00
FIXED EXPENSES	2,300.00	2,300.00	2,300.00
TAX PAYMENTS	0.00	0.00	0.00
INTEREST	236.97	0.00	0.00
TOTAL DISBURSEMENTS	$10,636.97	$10,100.00	$10,500.00
CASH FLOW:			
BEGINNING CASH	$1,000.00	$22,000.00	$27,230.00
ENDING CASH	$4,183.03	$27,230.00	$32,795.00

```
ƏXM1ƏX
ƏA5/MODEL
/GET
CASHFLOW
/PLOT
/VARIABLES
CASH COLLECTIONS THRU TOTAL RECEIPTS
/COLUMNS
APR THRU JUN
/OPTIONS
/TITLES
/1ST_LINE
CASH RECEIPTS
/2ND_LINE
SECOND QUARTER 1985
ƏESƏES/SHOW
ƏA5/LOG
/SAVE
```

FIGURE 8.8 Sample Command File Produced with the LEARN Capability

To illustrate how a variety of dialog styles are supported by IFPS/Personal, we will use the dimensions of cognitive complexity, field-independence, and thinking mode identified earlier. The following results from empirical studies were reported by Zmud [32]:

COGNITIVE COMPLEXITY

1. Complex subjects have been found to search for and use more information, to prefer aggregate rather than raw data, and to use more rules when integrating information.
2. Complex subjects used more complex, but less simple, information.
3. Complex subjects have been found to generate more decision alternatives, resulting in greater flexibility, but less confidence and more decision time.

FIELD-INDEPENDENCE/FIELD-DEPENDENCE

1. Field independent (high-analytic) subjects have been found to seek more information, to prefer detailed, aggregate, quantitative reports, and to require more decision time.

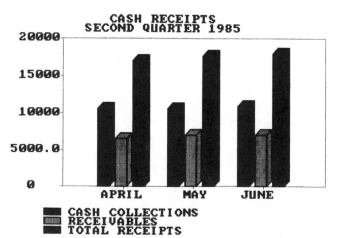

FIGURE 8.9 Sample 3d Bar Chart

THINKING MODE

1. Systematics have been seen to consistently prefer more quantitative information and require more decision time than heuristics.
2. However, systematics have been found in different studies to prefer both more and less information, and to prefer both aggregated and raw data when compared with heuristics.
3. This apparent contradiction is partially explained by the finding that systematics with access to decision aids requested less information than heuristics, while systematics without decision aids requested more information than heuristics; and heuristics with low task knowledge requested the most information.

User interaction with IFPS/Personal, and the process through which the user organizes and changes the information during the decision-making process, involves movement among a series of command levels called modes. The various modes allow the user to perform model creation, solution and integration, reporting, file manipulation, directing files to and retrieving files from the mainframe, and graphing.

Each mode or command level contains a command menu that allows the user to access another mode, activate a submenu, or perform some other operation. For example, the top level allows the user to access the editor, establish communications with the mainframe, or activate the model or data file mode.

The model mode allows the user to manipulate the current model using one of four different modes: data storage, plot, report, and view. The data manipulation, communications, plotting, and reporting capabilities of IFPS/Personal were described earlier. The view mode allows the user to display selected parts of a model solution and to interrogate the model through the what-if, goal seeking, and analyze capabilities.

The modes are structured in a clearly defined hierarchy, but movement between the modes is simple and quick, satisfying the heuristic's need to search data by trial-and-error, ad hoc hypothesis testing. Heuristics with access to IFPS/Personal would make more or less use of the data file system and communications, depending on their task knowledge. They would most likely make heavy use of graphics and the what-if capability in order to support their data search.

Systematics, however, would be expected to make less use of the data file system, communications, graphics, and consolidation techniques, but very heavy use of the analyze capability and the built-in mathematical, statistical, and financial functions and subroutines in order to analyze a limited amount of quantitative data thoroughly.

Complex subjects, to satisfy their need for complex, aggregate data, would be expected to heavily utilize the IFPS/Personal data file system, the data consolidation feature, the report writer, and integrated color business graphics. They would make extensive use of the built-in financial, mathematical, and statistical functions and subroutines and especially the what-if, goal seeking, and analyze capabilities. They, like the heuristics, would tend to move quickly through modes in order to generate multiple decision alternatives.

Simple subjects, on the other hand, would probably make less use of data consolidation and graphics, opting instead for raw data in tabular form. In their search for more data, they might make heavy use of the data file system and communications to download files from the mainframe. They would likely make less use of the built-in functions and subroutines, and use goal seeking only to find a "satisficing" solution.

Field independent subjects, to satisfy their need for a large amount of detailed, aggregate, quantitative reports, would be expected to heavily use the data file system, communications, data consolidation, and the report writer. They would make extensive use of the built-in functions, the what-if, goal seeking, and analyze capabilities, but little use of graphics.

Field dependent subjects would make less use of the report writer and more use of graphics in order to view the data embedded in their context. They would find less use for the what-if and analyze capabilities, the data file system, and communications.

SUMMARY

Even though there is an intuitive appeal to designing the dialog component of a DSS to accommodate the user's cognitive style, there are problems with this approach: cognitive style measurement problems, variations in a person's cognitive style over decision-making tasks, and the heterogeneity of cognitive style among multiple users. Fortunately, hardware and software advances are making it increasingly easy for a user to select from a number of dialog options depending on his or her preferences. The multipurpose capabilities of IFPS/Personal, coupled with the user's ability to move quickly and easily through the available modes consistent with his or her dialog style choices, illustrate the growing ability of emerging computer hardware and software to accommodate cognitive style differences.

QUESTIONS

1. What is meant by cognitive style?
2. Discuss the dimensions along which there are differences in cognitive style.
3. What are the problems in testing a person's cognitive style and designing a dialog for that person based on the cognitive style assessment?
4. Give examples of how different cognitive styles can be accommodated by IFPS/Personal.

REFERENCES

1. ALAVI, M., AND J. C. HENDERSON "An Evolutionary Strategy for Implementing a Decision Support System," *Management Science,* 27, no. 11 (1981), 1309–23.
2. BARIFF, M. L., AND E. J. LUSK "Cognitive and Personality Tests for the Design of Management Information Systems," *Management Science,* 23, no. 8 (1977), 820–29.
3. BARRETT, G. V., C. L. THORNTON, AND P. A. CABE "Human Factors Evaluation of a Computer-based Information Storage and Retrieval System," *Human Factors,* 10, no. 1 (1968), 431–36.
4. BENBASAT, I., AND R. G. SCHROEDER "An Experimental Investigation of Some MIS Design Variables," *MIS Quarterly,* 1, no. 1 (1977), 37–49.

5. BENBASAT, I., AND A. S. DEXTER "Individual Differences in the Use of Decision Support Aids," *Journal of Accounting Research,* 20, no. 1 (1982), 1–11.

6. BENBASAT, I., AND R. N. TAYLOR "The Impact of Cognitive Styles on Information Systems Design," *MIS Quarterly,* 2, no. 2 (1978), 43–54.

7. BLAYLOCK, B. K., AND L. P. REES "Cognitive Style and the Usefulness of Information," *Decision Sciences,* 15, no. 1 (1984), 74–91.

8. BRIGHTMAN, H. J., AND S. E. HARRIS "The Planning and Modeling Language Revolution: A Managerial Perspective," *Business,* 32, no. 1 (1982), 15–21.

9. DICKSON, G. W., J. A. SENN, AND N. L. CHERVANY "Research in Management Information Systems: The Minnesota Experiments," *Management Science,* 23, no. 9 (1977), 913–23.

10. EASON, K. D. "Understanding the Naive Computer User," *Computer Journal,* 19, no. 9 (1976), 3–7.

11. FERGUSON, R. L., AND C. H. JONES "A Computer Aided Decision System," *Management Science,* 15, no. 10 (1969), B550–61.

12. HELLRIEGEL, D., AND J. W. SLOCUM, JR. "Managerial Problem-Solving Styles," *Business Horizons,* 18, no. 6 (1975), 29–37.

13. HENDERSON, J. C., AND P. C. NUTT "The Influence of Decision Style on Decision Making Behavior," *Management Science,* 26, no. 4 (1980), 371–86.

14. HOY, F., AND W. R. BOULTON "Problem-Solving Styles of Students: Are Educators Producing What Business Needs?" *Collegiate News and Views,* 36, no. 3 (1983), 15–21.

15. HOY, F., AND D. HELLRIEGEL "The Kilmann and Herden Model of Organizational Effectiveness Criteria for Small Business Managers," *Academy of Management Journal,* 25, no. 2 (1982), 308–22.

16. HUBER, G. P. "Cognitive Style as a Basis for MIS and DSS Designs: Much Ado about Nothing?" *Management Science,* 29, no. 5 (1983), 567–79.

17. KERIN, R. A., AND J. W. SLOCUM, JR. "Decision-Making Style and Acquisition of Information: Further Exploration of the Myers-Briggs Type Indicator," *Psychological Reports,* 49, no. 1 (1981), 132–34.

18. KILMANN, R. H., AND I. I. MITROFF "Qualitative versus Quantitative Analysis for Management Science: Different Forms for Different Psychological Types," *Interfaces,* 6, no. 2 (1976), 17–27.

19. LUCAS, H. C., JR., AND N. R. NIELSON "The Impact of Mode of Information Presentation on Learning and Performance," *Management Science,* 26, no. 10 (1980), 982–93.

20. LUCAS, H. C., JR. *Why Information Systems Fail.* New York: Columbia University Press, 1975.

21. LUCAS, H. C., JR. *The Implementation of Computer-based Models.* New York: National Association of Accountants, 1976.

22. LUSK, E. J., AND M. KERSNICK "The Effects of Cognitive Style Report Format on Task Performance: The MIS Design Consequences," *Management Science,* 25, no. 8 (1979), 787–98.

23. LUTHANS, F., AND R. KOESTER "The Impact of Computer Generated Information on the Choice Activity of Decision Makers," *Academy of Management Journal,* 19, no. 2 (1976), 328–32.

24. MAISH, A. M. "A User's Behavior Toward His MIS," *MIS Quarterly,* 3, no. 1 (1979), 39–52.

25. MASON, R. O., AND I. I. MITROFF "A Program for Research on Management Information Systems," *Management Science,* 19, no. 5 (1973), 475–87.

26. MCKENNY, J. L., AND P. G. W. KEEN "How Managers' Minds Work," *Harvard Business Review,* 52, no. 3 (1974), 79–90.

27. MYERS, I. B. *Introduction to Type.* Palo Alto, Calif.: Consulting Psychologists Press, 1980.

28. MYERS, I. B.   *The Myers-Briggs Type Indicator*. Palo Alto, Calif.: Consulting Psychologists Press, 1962.

29. MYERS, I. B.   *Supplementary Manual: The Myers-Briggs Type Indicator*. Palo Alto, Calif.: Consulting Psychologists Press, 1962.

30. ROBEY, D., AND W. TAGGART   "Human Information Processing in Information and Decision Support Systems," *MIS Quarterly,* 6, no. 2 (1982), 61–73.

31. WRIGHT, W. F.   "Cognitive Information Processing Biases: Implications for Producers and Users of Financial Information," *Decision Sciences,* 11, no. 2 (1980), 284–89.

32. ZMUD, R. W.   "Individual Differences and MIS Success: A Review of the Empirical Literature," *Management Science,* 25, no. 10 (1978), 966–79.

9

AN INVESTIGATION OF DATABASE REQUIREMENTS FOR INSTITUTIONAL AND Ad Hoc *DSS*

Carleen Garnto,
Hugh J. Watson

INTRODUCTION

A growing number of organizations have developed decision support systems (DSS). The applications include financial planning [19], portfolio management [6], marketing-mix decision making [13, 14], plant capacity planning [17], and joint venture analysis [12]. As one studies various DSS applications, it becomes clear that decision support systems can differ considerably. They can be used for operational control, management control, or strategic planning. They can vary in the structuredness of the decision-making task which they support. They can be used for one time or recurring decision making. Because of the variations which exist, one might expect to find differences in their component parts, including the database component.

The authors recently investigated four decision support systems developed for budgeting and resource allocation, train dispatching, pricing, and acquisition applica-

Carleen Garnto and Hugh J. Watson, "An Investigation of Data Base Requirements for Institutional and Ad Hoc DSS," *DATABASE,* Summer 1985.

tions. Two of the DSS studied are used on a recurring basis while the other two were used for a one-time decision. Donovan and Madnick [4] refer to these as institutional and ad hoc DSS, respectively. The primary area of investigation was whether there are differences in the database component of the DSS based on the institutional and ad hoc distinction. This study suggests that there are differences with practical implications for DSS designers.

THE CONCEPTUAL FRAMEWORK

Gorry and Scott Morton [7] combined Anthony's [2] categories of managerial activity (that is, operational control, management control, and strategic planning) with Simon's [15] concepts of structured and unstructured decision making to provide a framework for viewing information systems. This framework has proven useful in understanding information requirements and the type of information system needed to support decision making. For example, information requirements vary with managerial activity. Keen and Scott Morton [11] identify accuracy, age of information, level of detail, time horizon, frequency of use, source, scope of information, and type of information as aspects of information requirements which vary with managerial activity. In another example, the type of information system needed that is, electronic data processing (EDP), management information system (MIS) or (DSS) is related to the structuredness of the decision-making task. While EDP and to a great extent MIS are recognized as useful for supporting structured decisions, DSS are appropriate for supporting semi-structured and unstructured decision making. And as a final example, the type of information system needed is related to managerial activity. Most frequently, EDP best serves operational control, MIS is oriented to management control, and DSS supports strategic planning.

While Gorry and Scott Morton's framework suggests useful generalizations, there are many exceptions. Of particular interest to this study is that DSS can be used for operational control, management control, or strategic planning. This being the case, it follows that different types of DSS may be appropriate for various managerial activities. The work of Donovan and Madnick supports this contention. They suggest that DSS can be divided meaningfully into two categories: institutional DSS which deal with decisions of a recurring nature, and ad hoc DSS which deal with specific decisions which are not usually anticipated or recurring. The characteristics of each type of DSS are summarized in Table 9.1. Donovan and Madnick suggest that these characteristics of institutional and ad hoc DSS lead to the conclusion that institutional DSS are most appropriate for operational control applications, ad hoc DSS are most useful for strategic planning applications, and there is an area of overlap in regard to management control applications.

Keen and Scott Morton indicate that just as information requirements vary with managerial activity, so do data requirements. Because institutional and ad hoc DSS tend to be associated with different managerial activities, it might be expected that the database component would differ. While DSS database requirements have been considered in a variety of contexts, no research has been conducted on the specific database

TABLE 9.1 Comparison of Institutional and Ad Hoc Decision Support Systems

	INSTITUTIONAL DSS	*Ad Hoc DSS*
Number of decision occurrences for a decision type	many	few
Number of decision types	few	many
Number of people making decisions of same type	many	few
Range of decisions supported	narrow	wide
Range of users supported	narrow	wide
Range of issues addressed	narrow	wide
Specific data needed known in advance	usually	rarely
Problems are recurring	usually	rarely
Importance of operational efficiency	high	low
Duration of specific type of problem being addressed	long	short
Need for rapid development	low	high

SOURCE: J. Donovan and S. Madnick, "Institutional and Ad Hoc DSS and Their Effective Use," *DATABASE*, 8, no. 3 (Winter 1977), 82.

requirements for institutional and ad hoc DSS. Given that the institutional and ad hoc DSS dichotomy seems to be a useful way of looking at DSS, such research might potentially provide helpful guidelines for DSS database design. Sprague and Carlson [16] have developed a list of general requirements common to DSS databases which is presented in Table 9.2. It is used in this study as a basis for exploring the database requirements for institutional and ad hoc DSS.

THE STUDY METHOD

Purpose

The purpose of this study was to gather and analyze data about the database component of institutional and ad hoc DSS based on the general requirements proposed by Sprague and Carlson. This information is used to suggest generalizations about database

TABLE 9.2 General Requirements for DSS Databases

■ Support for Memories	■ Varying Degrees of Accuracy
■ Data Reduction	■ Set Operations
■ Varying Levels of Detail	■ Random Access
■ Varying Amounts of Data	■ Support for Relationships and Views
■ Multiple Sources	■ Performance
■ Catalog of Sources	■ Interface to Other DSS Components
■ Wide Time Frame	■ End-User Interface
■ Public and Private Data Bases	

SOURCE: Ralph H. Sprague, Jr., and Eric D. Carlson, *Building Effective Decision Support Systems* (Englewood Cliffs, N.J.: Prentice Hall, 1982).

requirements for institutional and ad hoc DSS. The findings should prove helpful to interested researchers and to those considering the development of decision support systems.

Research Methodology

The research method selected for this study was the field study. A structured interview was conducted with a knowledgeable individual in the company about a specific application of an institutional or ad hoc DSS in order to gain information related to each of the database requirements identified by Sprague and Carlson.

Sample Selection

Four companies in Atlanta, Georgia, who are developing and using DSS participated in the study. The criteria for including a specific DSS in the study was the same as that used by Hogue and Watson [9] in their study of management's role in the approval and administration of DSS. Each of the four companies had developed a DSS which met the following essential criteria:

- Supports but does not replace decision making.
- Directed toward semistructured and/or unstructured decision-making tasks.
- Data and models organized around the decision.
- Easy to use software interface.

In addition, each of the four DSS satisfied most of the following additional criteria:

- Interactive processing.
- DSS use and control determined by the user.
- Flexible and adaptable to changes in the environment and decision maker's style.
- Quick ad hoc DSS building capabilities.

The DSS was judged to be either institutional or ad hoc based on the characteristics provided by Donovan and Madnick. For the purpose of the study, two institutional and two ad hoc systems were identified. Each was considered successful by users and developers.

The Interview

Interviews were conducted at each organization with a member or members of the DSS development team. The interviews were tape recorded so that the information could be carefully analyzed and categorized.

The interviews consisted of two parts. The first part was designed to gather background information on the company and on the development and use of the DSS. It included questions related to the corporate business sector, conditions that led to the creation of the DSS, developmental history, and usage patterns. The second part of the interview focused on the database component of the DSS. Specific questions were designed to obtain information related to each of the general requirements proposed by Sprague and Carlson. This information was used to prepare case studies, descriptions, and summary tables regarding institutional and ad hoc database requirements.

FOUR CASE STUDIES

Brief descriptions follow for the four DSS, two institutional and two ad hoc, selected for this study of database requirements. All DSS met the requirements for DSS as defined by Hogue and Watson, each could be classified as institutional or ad hoc based on the characteristics set forth by Donovan and Madnick, and each was considered successful.

Collectively, the systems support all of Anthony's levels of managerial activity. The train dispatching system aids in the area of operational control, while a majority of AIMS capabilities focus on managerial control. Both ad hoc systems, the pricing model and the acquisition model, support strategic planning.

Train Dispatching System

The train dispatching system used by the Norfolk Southern Corporation is an example of an institutional DSS. It is an on-line, real-time, operational DSS that is used daily by train dispatchers of the Norfolk and Southern Railroad. It was developed to assist dispatchers on the northern portion of the Alabama Division and is now being expanded to include the nine other divisions of the Norfolk and Southern Railway.

Each dispatcher is typically responsible for the movement of twenty to thirty trains over three to six hundred miles of track. Most of this is single track and requires that the routes of opposing trains be safely coordinated so that the trains meet at strategically placed passing sidings. In addition, the dispatcher must safely coordinate the movement of work and inspection crews along these same tracks. The dispatcher is also in constant contact with freight terminals for information regarding trains that will move over the division and for information on trains that have arrived at their destination. The system developed by the operations research staff was designed to assist the dispatchers with these activities.

The train dispatching system now in use provides for more accurate and timely entry of federal reporting information directly into the system by the dispatchers and allows the dispatchers ready access to the information needed for train and work crew dispatching.

Specialized algorithms and models were developed by the operations research staff specifically for train dispatching and related decisions. The models take into account thousands of possible meet/pass combinations that could occur for the trains and suggest the optimal solution. As information is entered regarding changes in track or train conditions, a new optimal solution is displayed along with projections of future conditions over a six-to-eight hour period. All train information is current and changes as conditions change. While the system offers an optimal solution for each dispatching decision, the dispatcher has the ability to override each plan to reflect his experience and judgment. His decision can be entered into the system which results in new projections.

The minicomputer based system involved approximately three years of prototype work. The system at a division office includes four color CRTs. Two display track layout and the movement of trains along the tracks. A third CRT displays screen formats which serve as work sheets for updating the train data by the dispatchers. The fourth CRT displays how trains should be routed based on calculations of the models.

Automated Information Management System (AIMS)

In January 1984, BellSouth began operation as the parent company for Southern Bell and South Central Bell. This brought the two divisions which supply local telephone service to the southern United States under a single managing body separate from American Telephone and Telegraph. This proved to be a great opportunity and challenge for BellSouth. Top management saw the need for an extensive management support system to aid largely in management control decision making. As a result, a systems analysis group was formed at BellSouth to develop such a system. The first prototype of the Automated Information Management System (AIMS) was installed approximately six weeks later. AIMS is a corporate planning model used for budgeting, resource allocation, and strategic planning. It utilizes forecasting, graphics, and spreadsheet packages along with a sophisticated database management package to provide needed information and analysis capabilities at different managerial levels. It has approximately 4000 users at the district, state, and headquarters level and combines features of office automation and information resource management as well as decision support.

At the district level, managers use the system to evaluate daily operations. They can analyze present performance in terms of past performance and can view projected performance generated from preprogrammed models. This information is used to keep service to customers in line with company standards and to see that budget restrictions are maintained. The district data is used by managers at the state level to prepare preliminary budgets and to forecast resource needs using additional models.

At the corporate level managers consolidate the state budgets and develop a corporate budget and corporate resource forecasts. They serve as intermediaries for the CEO by preparing reports, identifying problem areas, and exploring "what if" performance and budgeting scenarios. These budgets and reports are stored in a private database accessible only by the CEO and used at his discretion for strategic planning decisions.

Pricing Model

Coca-Cola USA is the producer and marketer of all Coca-Cola domestic beverages. Rather than marketing a finished product, however, Coca-Cola USA supplies the beverage syrup and sweetening agent to individual bottling franchises and fountain operations where it is then mixed for bottling and final sale.

In early 1983 Coca-Cola USA geared for the introduction of Diet Coke, a new diet product, into the market. All market research and testing had been completed for the product, but the Vice President of Strategic Planning faced a problem. What price would bottlers be charged for the Diet Coke syrup and Aspartame sweetener? Would the syrup be priced at the Tab rate, the rate for Coca-Cola USA's other diet product, or would it be priced, as the bottlers hoped, at the rate for original Coke? There were also questions about the pricing of the sweetener Aspartame. The Vice President for Strategic Planning also had to consider how the pricing of the Diet Coke syrup and sweetener would affect Tab's market share.

To assist him in making the pricing decision, the Vice President requested the creation of a model that would allow him to manipulate the model's parameters in order to evaluate possible pricing combinations. As a result of working with the model, a pricing proposal would then be prepared and presented to the bottlers. A three-person, in-house team was selected to develop the model. The group was composed of a financial analyst, a builder/intermediary, and the Vice President for Strategic Planning. The Vice President was important in determining the parameters necessary for the decision and was the ultimate user of the information provided by the model. The financial analyst determined the financial relationships necessary for the model, and the builder/intermediary actually created and coded the model using available tools. The builder intermediary also operated the model to obtain results for the Vice President.

The model was created using EXPRESS, a DSS generator equipped with a high level, non-procedural programming language, financial and statistical analysis capabilities, graphics, and database management capabilities. The initial creation of the model took approximately one week. The model was refined as new parameters were identified and as additional considerations were raised by the bottlers.

Acquisition Model

Since its founding in 1933, Gold Kist, Inc., has become the leader in the Southeast's agribusiness industry. At the present time, Gold Kist is considering adding to its holdings through the acquisition of a company in a related area of business. The Executive Committee instructed the Director of Corporate Planning and Economic Research to recommend the best company for such an acquisition. The Executive Committee provided the Director with basic parameters the selected company should meet, including the price range Gold Kist would pay to acquire the company, the volume of business the company should maintain, and the company's contribution to the Gold Kist profit picture. Even with these guidelines the Director faced a big job. Many companies met the requirements specified by the Executive Committee. Selecting the one best company from as many as twenty-five possibilities would require careful analysis of each company's performance based on information from knowledgeable individuals at all levels within the company, as well as financial information.

The Director wanted financial information that reflected the company's future performance should an acquisition by Gold Kist take place. This information could be easily identified and analyzed once basic fundamental reports such as balance sheets and income statements had been prepared. Therefore, the Director wanted a model that would formulate these reports for each company under study. Using PROFIT II, a DSS generator that combines a high level programming language with financial and statistical analysis capabilities, graphics, and data management capabilities, the Director set out to develop such a model. After one week, the Director had a working model that produced an income statement, cash flow statement, working capital statement, and source and use of funds statement, as well as financial ratios and forecasting ratios for each company being considered.

FINDINGS AND DISCUSSION

As was expected, differences were found in the database component of the four DSS studied. In general, the differences can be explained by the institutional and ad hoc DSS distinction. Of course, the differences are also related to the managerial activity supported by the DSS. Consider now the database differences using the general DSS database requirements suggested by Sprague and Carlson.

Multiple Sources

Data for the train dispatching system is largely transaction data gathered as a result of daily dispatching operations. The remainder of the data is also internal. The data for AIMS comes from a variety of sources. It includes transaction data obtained from operations, internal data from corporate personnel databases and from corporate planning, and external population data purchased outside of the organization. All the data for Coca-Cola USA's pricing model was internally generated and gathered by different departments within the company. This data reflected external factors such as consumer preferences, market demand, and economic conditions. The data was prepared to reflect total corporate performance before its inclusion in the database. Likewise, all data included in Gold Kist's acquisition model was based on information gained from external sources. This external information was modified during planning and evaluation. The internally generated results were then included in the database.

The use of transaction, other internal, and external data by the institutional and ad hoc DSS is presented in Table 9.3. The general impression is that institutional DSS

TABLE 9.3   Sources of Data for Each System

	TRANSACTION	INTERNAL	EXTERNAL
Institutional			
Train Dispatching System	X	X	
AIMS	X	X	X
Ad hoc			
Pricing Model		X	X
Acquisition Model		X	X

rely primarily on transaction and other internal data while ad hoc DSS employ non-transaction internal data and external data. The data requirements for the four DSS also correspond with what one would expect based on Anthony's levels of managerial activity.

Wide Time Frame

While all data in Gold Kist's acquisition model was based on historical data, the actual data included in the database were projections of performance. A similar situation existed for Coca-Cola USA's pricing model, however, one time period of historical data was included for projection purposes. The train dispatching system relies exclusively on current data, while AIMS uses data from all three time frames: historical, current, and projected.

The time frame for the data used in the four DSS does not appear to be strongly related to the type of DSS. However, as can be seen in Table 9.4, both ad hoc DSS employ projected data. There seems to be a stronger relationship between the data's time frame and the level of managerial activity.

Data Reduction

Based on Sprague and Carlson's definition, very little data reduction took place in the ad hoc systems studied. In the pricing model and the acquisition model all data reduction manipulations were performed on the data before their inclusion in data files. The data management capabilities of the DSS generators serve to limit the extent to which these features can be included in the ad hoc systems.

On the other hand, the institutional systems studied rely heavily on data reduction. AIMS aggregates data at each level of use, while the train dispatching system relies on subsetting and combination to represent the movement of all trains over a division. These capabilities necessitate the use of packaged or in-house created database management systems.

Various Levels of Detail

It follows from the data reduction requirements that institutional and ad hoc systems would vary in the level of detail of data necessary to support the systems. For the ad

TABLE 9.4   Time Frame for Data for Each System

	HISTORICAL	CURRENT	PROJECTED
Institutional			
Train Dispatching System		X	
AIMS	X	X	X
Ad hoc			
Pricing Model	X		X
Acquisition			X

hoc systems no attempt was made to maintain detailed data in the database. A request for this type of information was beyond the scope of each of the ad hoc systems.

The institutional DSS studied do maintain data at different levels of detail. With AIMS, if a question arises regarding a figure in the corporate budget, the data used to arrive at that figure can be traced to the district level through data maintained in the database. Likewise, a question about a division's performance can be investigated by viewing data on each train dispatched in the division during a specific shift. In both cases, the decisions supported by the systems call for this type of capability. The institutional systems have a commitment of resources and technology that make these levels of data easier to maintain.

Varying Amounts of Data

Varying amounts of data are also maintained and used in institutional and ad hoc DSS. This follows from the previous requirements regarding data reduction and varying levels of detail. The ad hoc systems studied maintained only those data which were actually used for the decision-making process. In contrast, the institutional systems maintained a large amount of data. Both AIMS and the train dispatching system maintain a large volume of potentially relevant data in varying levels of detail. As mentioned earlier, this facilitates the explanation of aggregate data should a question arise. It also results in much data being maintained which is seldom used.

Varying Degrees of Accuracy

Absolute accuracy was not required of the data included in the ad hoc systems. It is difficult to verify the accuracy of the data for these systems since both relied on aggregate, projected data.

Related to accuracy is the idea of currency of the data. For both ad hoc systems, all data included were based on historical data. With Gold Kist's acquisition model, data were based on the latest financial reports available for a company. In many cases these were as much as a year old. This data was, therefore, subject to a certain amount of inaccuracy due to the lack of currency of the historical data. The increasing age of the information on which the projections were based would tend to decrease the accuracy.

By the same argument, the institutional systems tended to have a much higher degree of accuracy. The long-range projections included in AIMS and short-range, shift projections included in the train dispatching system are based on current information. The operational natures of the dispatching decision for Norfolk and Southern and district service for BellSouth require a high degree of accuracy.

Support for Memories

Sprague and Carlson suggest four kinds of memory aids that the DSS database should support. Table 9.5 illustrates the types of memory aids that are found in the database component of each of the systems studied.

TABLE 9.5   Memory Aids Provided by Each System

	WORKSPACES	LIBRARIES	LINKS	TRIGGERS
Institutional				
Train Dispatching System	X	X	X	X
AIMS	X	X	X	X
Ad hoc				
Pricing Model	X	X		
Acquisition Model	X	X		

Both the institutional and ad hoc systems were organized around the "scratch pad" concept. All four systems provided workspaces where calculations could be performed and displayed. Each system also provided libraries for saving intermediate results for later use.

The institutional database components provide additional memory support in the form of links and triggers. With the train dispatching system, a particular train can be identified from a list of those dispatched during a shift. All information relevant to that train can be stored in link memory for use with another workspace. A blinking asterisk also appears in the corner of the display screen if changing track conditions result in a new meet/pass plan. This triggers a new decision situation for the dispatcher. Similarly, with AIMS, blinking, reverse screen figures indicate when a budgetary or service figure is out of range.

Support for Relationships and Views

While both types of systems provided support in this area, the ad hoc systems tended to provide the best support for relationships and views. The "what if" capabilities of the DSS generators used by each of the ad hoc systems allowed the managers to test alternate scenarios quickly and with relative ease. This flexibility was essential due to the ill-defined nature of the ad hoc decisions.

The institutional systems studied, on the other hand, do not exhibit this degree of flexibility. Due to the better defined nature of the decision, alternate relationships and ways of viewing the data were designed at the time of system development. While "what if" scenarios may be carried out on AIMS by certain skilled managers at the headquarters level, "what if" options beyond those originally developed for the train dispatching system must be handled by the OR development team.

Random Access

Database components of both the ad hoc and institutional DSS were found to support random access. This access proved to be more sophisticated for the institutional DSS. Their database management capabilities allowed access to data that the decision maker did not expect to need and to data that was not related to the data currently being used.

Security and Private Databases

No specific measures were taken to protect the data included in the database component of either of the ad hoc systems studied. Both systems were designed for personal support for a single user. Therefore, data security was not a primary concern.

The institutional systems studied, on the other hand, are accessible by many people. As a result, measures were taken to secure certain data. While any dispatcher can access and view any train information during his shift, only certain dispatchers can alter specific train data. Likewise, AIMS provides a private database, accessible only by the CEO, where sensitive budgets and reports are stored.

End-User Interface

Differences were observed in the end-user interface for the institutional and ad hoc DSS. The interfaces for the institutional systems were designed to be "transparent" to the user. Users need know nothing of the internal structure of the DSS. Both DSS employ menus and function keys which facilitate the use of each system by many users.

In contrast, no special end-user interfaces were designed for the ad hoc systems studied other than the standard prompt interfaces provided by each DSS generator.

CONCLUSION

Based on the characteristics of the database components of the systems studied, generalizations can be proposed for the specific database requirements for institutional and ad hoc systems. Table 9.6 summarizes these requirements as they apply to the general database requirements for DSS.

From these requirements we see that the nature of the decision, whether or not it is recurring, does indeed affect the type of DSS support chosen and the database

TABLE 9.6 Database Requirements for Institutional and Ad Hoc DSS

	INSTITUTIONAL	AD HOC
Multiple sources	internal	external
Wide time frame	no relationship found	
Data reduction	extensive	minor
Varying levels of detail	many	few
Varying amounts of data	large	small
Varying degree of accuracy	high	low
Security & private databases	common	rare
Support for memories	broad	narrow
Support for relationships and views	limited	extensive
Random access	complex	simple
End-user interface	fixed	variable

requirements for the DSS. Recurring, well-defined decisions call for institutional systems. These are developed by highly technical and experienced development teams using a sophisticated collection of DSS tools. Institutional DSS provides organizational support to a large number of users. Consequently, considerable time and money are spent making the system as complete and easy to use as possible. This is illustrated by the data requirements for memory aids, varying amounts of data, public and private databases, and easy to use end-user interface. As a result, flexibility to change and to create new views of the data is limited.

The one-shot decisions are difficult to anticipate and define and call for ad hoc support. This support must be provided quickly and cost effectively. As a result, the ad hoc system is normally developed by a small development team using a DSS generator. The system's data management capabilities are limited to the data management capabilities of the DSS generator. Therefore, much preparatory work is usually done on the data before it is included in the database.

Ad hoc systems tend to provide personal support to single users. Consequently, only data handling features essential for the decision are included in the system. The user's familiarity with the system or an intermediary to operate the system for the decision maker reduces the data management features necessary, as well as the development time. The DSS generator does provide a great deal of flexibility for making changes and viewing data in many ways. The ill-defined nature of ad hoc problems makes this essential.

The database components for these two types of DSS are different. These differences reflect the nature of the decision involved as well as characteristics of the system itself. These requirements facilitate the storage and transformation of data for decisions unique to each type of system.

QUESTIONS

1. What are the differences between institutional and ad hoc DSS?
2. Describe the general requirements for a DSS database.
3. Describe the database component of the train dispatching DSS at Southern Railway, the automated information management system (AIMS) at BellSouth, the pricing model at Coca-Cola USA, and the acquisition model at Gold Kist.
4. Discuss the differences in database requirements for institutional and ad hoc DSS.

REFERENCES

1. ALTER, STEVEN L. *Decision Support Systems: Current Practices and Continuing Challenges.* Reading, Mass.: Addison-Wesley, 1980.
2. ANTHONY, R. N. *Planning and Control Systems: A Framework for Analysis,* Harvard University Graduate School of Business Administration, Boston, 1965.
3. BENNETT, JOHN L., ED. *Building Decision Support Systems.* Reading, Mass.: Addison-Wesley, 1983.

4. DONOVAN, J., AND S. MADNICK "Institutional and Ad Hoc DSS and Their Effective Use," *Data Base,* 8, no. 3 (Winter 1977), 79–88.

5. FICK, GLORIA, AND RALPH H. SPRAGUE, JR., EDS. *Decision Support Systems: Issues and Challenges.* London, England: Pergamon Press, 1980.

6. GERRITY, THOMAS P. "Design of Man-Machine Decision Systems: An Application to Portfolio Management," *Sloan Management Review,* 12, no. 2 (Winter 1971), 59–75.

7. GORRY, G. A., AND M. S. SCOTT MORTON "A Framework for Management Information Systems," *Sloan Management Review,* 12, no. 1 (Fall 1971), 55–70.

8. HACKATHORN, RICHARD D., AND PETER G. W. KEEN "Organizational Strategies for Personal Computing in Decision Support Systems," *MIS Quarterly,* 5, no. 3 (September 1981), 21–26.

9. HOGUE, JACK T., AND HUGH J. WATSON "Management's Role in the Approval and Administration of Decision Support Systems," *MIS Quarterly,* 7, no. 2 (June 1983), 15–25.

10. KEEN, PETER G. W. "Interactive Computer Systems for Managers: A Modest Proposal," *Sloan Management Review,* 18, no. 1 (Fall 1976), 1–17.

11. KEEN, PETER G. W., AND MICHAEL S. SCOTT MORTON *Decision Support Systems: An Organizational Perspective.* Reading, Mass.: Addison-Wesley, 1978.

12. KEEN, PETER G. W., AND GERALD R. WAGNER "DSS: An Executive Mind-Support System," *Datamation,* 25, no. 12 (November 1979), 117–22.

13. LITTLE, JOHN D. C. "BRANDAID: A Marketing-Mix Model, Part I: Structure," *Operations Research,* 23, no. 4 (July–August 1975), 628–55.

14. LITTLE, JOHN D. C. "BRANDAID: A Marketing-Mix Model, Part 2: Implementation, Calibration, and Case Study," *Operations Research,* 23, no. 4 (July–August 1975), 656–73.

15. SIMON, HERBERT A. *The New Science of Management Decision.* New York: Harper & Row, 1960.

16. SPRAGUE, RALPH H., JR., AND ERIC D. CARLSON *Building Effective Decision Support Systems.* Englewood Cliffs, N.J.: Prentice Hall, 1982.

17. SPRAGUE, RALPH H., JR., AND HUGH J. WATSON "Bit by Bit: Toward Decision Support Systems," *California Management Review,* 22, no. 1 (Fall 1979), 60–68.

18. SPRAGUE, RALPH H., JR., AND HUGH J. WATSON "MIS Concepts: Part II," *Journal of Systems Management,* 26, no. 2 (February 1975), 35–40.

19. SPRAGUE, RALPH H., JR., AND RON L. OLSEN "The Financial Planning System at the Louisiana National Bank," *MIS Quarterly,* 3, no. 3 (September 1979), 1–11.

10

EVOLVING TECHNOLOGY FOR DOCUMENT-BASED *DSS*

Jane Fedorowicz

INTRODUCTION

The data component of the DSS architecture is often viewed as the most important of the three primary components. In fact, it is easy to argue that data are the real raw material for DSS; the modeling component manipulates and analyzes data, while the dialog component provides easy access to the data and allows the user to activate the models. Important concepts for the data component include the following:

- The DSS database should include external data because the kinds of decisions supported by DSS often require an assessment of the situation outside the organization.
- DSS databases should generally be extracted versions, with selections drawn from the production databases for transaction processing, as well as from external sources.
- The database management functions are important for DSS databases but they might be different from traditional production databases, and the organization of the data might be different. The relational data model, for example, tends to be

more relevant for DSS applications, and the query language must be less cryptic if managers and executives are to use it easily.

One underlying assumption seldom questioned is that all the data—whether the source is internal or external, whether the data model is heriarchical or relational—can be described in simple record format. There is always an entity (employee, part number, general ledger account number, for example) that has a set of attributes described by data items or fields (address, social security number, wages earned to date, for example) that contain all the relevant information about that entity. This has not been a particularly limiting assumption for DSS thus far. Indeed, much value has derived from DSS simply through integrating external and internal sources and organizing the data in different ways to permit flexibility and variety in their access.

There is a very large, rich source of data that does not satisfy this assumption, however, and it is becoming increasingly valuable for decision makers. This source includes, for example, written reports, letters from customers, internal memos, news items, electronic mail messages, and conversations among executives. Some of these data are so informal that they may never be captured, stored, and made available through a DSS. Most of them, however, have been excluded from DSS only because it is technologically difficult or impossible to include them. Now there are technological advances that are making it increasingly possible to manage what we will call document-based data.

We define "document" rather broadly here. It is a "chunk" of information usually dealing with a relatively limited topic or subject area. It may contain numbers, but it is predominantly nonnumeric, including text, graphics, image, and perhaps voice or video. DSS that expand the data component to gather, store, manipulate, manage, and provide access to these kinds of data are called document-based DSS (DDSS).

There is, of course, a long history of managing this type of data. Libraries have done it for years, as have computerized bibliographic services. The limitations in these cases have been technical limitations that increase the cost of entering and storing the data and limitations in the ways of representing the content of the data. In fact, a typical approach has been to use an adaptation of the record format described earlier by assigning keywords that become the attributes of a document (the entity).

The limitation of traditional DSS efforts to handle record-based data may be blamed on limitations of its underlying technology. These limitations may finally be dissipating. Office automation, communications, storage, and other technologies provide the tools with which to make the information accessible. Recent developments in artificial intelligence may aid in improving the utility of technology to understand, interpret, and classify the information itself. The technological demands of a document-based DSS will benefit from advances in many related research areas. A document base will require different internal representation and access schemes. This may be possible with new techniques in AI, database management systems, group decision support systems, information retrieval, electronic mail, telecommunications, cognitive psychology, and other areas.

In these and other subjects, technological advances are now emerging to enable the management of document-based data in DSS, making it accessible to managers, executives, and other decision makers. In this article, we examine advances in hardware, software, and application approaches that are leading in this direction.

HARDWARE

Decreasing cost and increasing processing speed are obvious benefits for DDSS, which require much processing of large amounts of stored data. But these alone will not suffice for the volumes of documents that a document base can be expected to contain. What is needed are accompanying improvements in storage technology.

New storage options based on optical disks are burgeoning in the marketplace. The technologies include CD-ROM (compact disk read-only memory) and WORM (write once read many), which enable large amounts of textual information to be stored relatively cheaply, and CD-I, which is a multimedia format that can combine video, audio, and graphics. A related technology, by GE, is DVI (Digital Video Interactive), which mixes motion video, still frames, audio, graphics, databases, retrieval schemes, and interactive processes onto a CD. It can store full-motion video as well. Optical read-write CDs are available that store over 600 megabytes on a standard compact disk.

All of these technologies provide high volume data access but at a slower rate than magnetic disk technology. Only some of them can be rewritten or changed after data are initially placed on them; the read only media are used for historical and reference data.

A DDSS would need to integrate various storage and processing technologies to provide complete document retrieval. Magnetic or optical disks, whether at the PC or centralized, could be used for time-sensitive corporate data. Online database services could be tied in to gather timely external information. CD-ROMs can be used for historical records, including minutes of meetings, digitized voice, videotapes of teleconferences, copies of memos, online databases and search algorithms, and other documents that a decision maker might normally retain.

Another new technology, initially marketed in the desktop publishing arena, will enable the DDSS user to incorporate pictorial or textual documents. Image scanners can copy any image into the PC. The appealing aspect of these scanners is that they will input a textual document in a format manipulatable by word processing software and pictorial images in a form that can be accessed by "painting" programs. Thus, any printed document can be included in the DDSS as if it had been input by hand.

These storage and input technologies, in conjunction with powerful PC processing and telecommunications, provide vital components for building a DDSS. They provide the ease of use, flexibility, and speed of access that decision makers demand. The next sections present an overview of the software advances that will make the system feasible.

ONLINE DATABASES

In an early study of document-based information systems for management, Swanson and Culnan (1978) identified twenty-two document-based systems designed to support managerial planning and control. These systems, as seen in Table 10.1, provide extraorganizational support for strategic level planning and intraorganizational support for control and communications functions. The extraorganizational systems are, as one might expect, online databases. Notably missing are the types of systems that would provide planning support documents within a DSS environment.

TABLE 10.1   Document-based Systems for Managerial Planning and Control

STRATEGIC PLANNING: EXTRAORGANIZATIONAL INFORMATION

1. SDC Search Service (ORBIT)
2. DIALOG
3. New York Times Information Bank
4. INTERFILE
5. DISCLOSURE
6. National Automated Accounting Research Systems (NAARS)
7. WESTLAW
8. LEXIS
9. FLITE

STRATEGIC PLANNING: INTRAORGANIZATIONAL INFORMATION

No illustrations

MANAGEMENT CONTROL: INTRAORGANIZATIONAL INFORMATION

10. Construction Project Management System
11. Intelligence Information System
12. ACDMS (Automated Control of a Document Management System)
13. CDMAN (Computer-based System for Control and Dissemination)

OPERATIONAL CONTROL: INTRAORGANIZATIONAL INFORMATION

14. CUBE Registration System
15. CADM (Configuration and Data Management)
16. Engineering Drawing System

OFFICE COMMUNICATIONS

17. DAISY (Decision Aiding Information System)
18. Augmented Knowledge Workshop (AKW)
19. Paperless Office Project
20. WILTEK
21. Electronic Information Exchange System (EIES)
22. Management Work Stations (MWS)

Source: Swanson and Culnan (1978).

TABLE 10.2   Providers of Online Databases

ADP Network Services
Compuserve, Inc.
Data Resources, Inc. (DRI)
Dialog Information Services, Inc.
Dow Jones News/Retrieval
General Electric Information Services Company
General Videotex Corporation
Mead Data Central
SDC Information Services
I. P. Sharp Associates, Inc.
Source Telecomputing Corporation
Telebase Systems, Inc.
Telescan, Inc.

It is interesting to note that U.S. businesses increased their online database expenditures by 117 percent in three years, according to a recent study by Information Market Indicators, Inc. (Jenkins, 1986a, 1986b). Companies are retrieving more information from databases such as Dow Jones News/Retrieval and The Source. The increased reliance on external market indicators and improved sources of information have dramatically boosted the demand for online database services. Table 10.2 lists many of the current providers of online data services.

Frequent users of these systems are predominantly trained librarians who provide a service within their company and PC users who tie in to general-purpose databases. Most of the time, the results of the search are hard copy reports of bibliographic, financial, or other stored information. Even now, relatively few of these services are tied into other computer tools, such as decision support or word processing applications.

The mechanisms for searching these databases have improved over time. Techniques for information retrieval are the subjects of the next sections.

INFORMATION RETRIEVAL

Document bases have their roots in the field of information retrieval. Bibliographic searching to produce lists of citations and abstracts based on keyword selection has been successfully applied to large indexed files for approximately twenty-five years. These services have been the domain of librarians, as they have been predominantly used as a research support mechanism for academics, corporate researchers, and practitioners who want to be apprised of new developments in their field.

Bibliographic retrieval research comprises a number of related issues, including effective and efficient index term assignment, keyword search schemes, free text search algorithms, file design (Fedorowicz, 1987), specification of adjacency conditions for free text terms, and the use of truncation and synonyms to improve the efficiency of retrieval (Salton, 1986). Recently, improvements in retrieval effectiveness have been made through the application of probabilistic indexing (Kwok, 1985), clustering of documents (van Rijsbergen, 1979), and cognitive modeling of users.

Cognitive modeling has been incorporated into a number of expert systems that adapt knowledge about a user into a personalized retrieval tool (Daniels, 1986). Models can be explicit, demanding answers to a list of questions by the user before the retrieval process can begin. Alternatively, implicit user modeling is based on the answers to a few preliminary questions, after which the system reverts to knowledge about stereotypical users. GRUNDY (Rich, 1979) constructs a user model in this way, and incorporates feedback from the user to update the user profile and hypotheses. User models, in any case, will need to encompass static models reflecting permanent information about the user and dynamic models, which depend on the particular interaction with the system.

Another expert system that employs user models was proposed by Lenat et al. (1983) to provide access to the 300,000 paragraphs composing the *Encyclopaedia Britannica*. This would require a comprehensive user profile that would "appear capable of accounting for every user type, preference, goal, belief, etc. that could ever be encountered. This user model would contain information about types of people (i.e. a kind of subset user modeling) and individual people" (Daniels, 1986:285).

Additionally, artificial intelligence techniques have been advanced as a way to increase the effectiveness of the retrieval process. Fuzzy set theory has been applied to documents to represent the extent that a document is "about" an index term (Buell, 1985). Knowledge representation in linguistics, psychology, and AI exhibits similarities to knowledge representation in information retrieval (Vickery, 1986).

Vickery, Brooks, and Robinson (1985) proposed a prototype expert system that assigns each indexed term entered by the user to one of about two dozen categories. "Knowledge of dependency relations between categories guides the system both in attempting to amplify the initial query and in dropping terms during reformulation of the search statement" (Vickery, 1986:157). The categories, as seen in Table 10.3, enable the system to expand on the meaning of the terms in the query by applying knowledge stored in frames and rules. The frames depict the relationships among the categories.

TABLE 10.3   Semantic Categories from a Reference and Referral Expert System

Objects
Parts (of an object)
Processes (behavior of an object)
Interactions (between objects)
Operations (by humans on objects)
Instruments (used in operations)
Environments (of objects)
Attributes (of any of the above)
Uses (of objects)
Time
Locations (geographical)

Source: Vickery (1986:157).

Other expert systems have also been developed to provide intelligent interfaces for document retrieval systems. Vickery and Brooks (1987) review a number of them, including EXPERT, which uses production rules to select which database to search and provides advice on how to select synonyms and how to combine terms in a query. Other intelligent interface systems include CANSEARCH and I3R.

These and other advances in information retrieval may prove invaluable for DDSS retrieval activities. A DDSS will probably consist of large-scale databases that contain bibliographic, encyclopedic, reference, historical, or other types of documents available in online databases. Current financial data and newspaper clippings could be retrieved using artificially intelligent keyword profiles and user models. If these profiles were sufficiently sophisticated, passive retrieval activities could be incorporated to provide environmental scanning facilities for executives. New concerns could be added or modified from existing profiles when new opportunities or problems arise, making this an active support tool as well.

HYPERTEXT RETRIEVAL

A promising new set of software advances hit the market recently and may have enormous implications for DDBMS feasibility. These products, such as Lotus Development Corporation's Agenda, Search Express by Executive Technologies, Inc., and Apple Computer's Hypercard, appear to be PC-based applications of hypertext retrieval systems that can be integrated with other PC products. These products have attracted a great deal of attention, particularly considering their low purchase price. (At the low end, Hypercard sells for $50 and comes free with the purchase of a Macintosh computer.)

Search Express is marketed as an information retrieval enhancement, featuring fast access to up to 1 million documents. Agenda and Hypercard are sold as techniques for managing various types of user-input documents by cross-referencing and labeling documents stored by assorted software packages. All three incorporate artificial intelligence with hypertext retrieval to aid the user in the assignment and selection of document-level associations.

Hypertext is a way of linking together various computer documents based on user-specified associations. Thus, a phone memo and a related stored report could be linked together by associative labeling, so that a user could easily recall one when referring to the other. Graphs and drawings on the same subject could also be tied in, in line with the user's thought processes. The ability to associate different types of documents in a free-form manner provides the flexibility many decision makers need for ad hoc information retrieval.

ELECTRONIC MAIL

Electronic mail provides a medium for sending mail messages privately over a local area network or worldwide using a public access network. Many companies have adopted internal E-mail systems, with many turning to IBM's PROFS. These systems do not permit receivers of mail to sort messages based on the meaning of their contents prior to reading them. A number of research projects are currently under way to augment these systems with the capability of filtering messages based on their content or header information.

Chang and Leung (1987) propose a knowledge-based message management system in which messages may contain graphic documents, image documents, and voice documents as well as text. The messages are stored in a relational database. A linguistic message filter culls out junk messages and user-defined "alerter rules" process relevant messages. The message filter considers network traffic, message rate, message length, and message relevance. Alerter rules can trigger database retrievals, office activities, filing activities, and mailing actions.

The LENS project at MIT is designed to disseminate information "so that it reaches those people to whom it is valuable without interfering with those to whom it is not" (Malone et al., 1987:390). Dissemination is accomplished through a process of filtering. The researchers on this project have proposed three mechanisms that may be used in filtering messages. Social filtering is based on the organizational relationship between sender and receiver. Economic filtering relies on the cost to the sender of transmitting a message, and proposes a cutoff to the receiver based on the trade-off between quality and personalization. The third type of filtering is the one emphasized in the LENS project. Cognitive filtering is based on sophisticated heuristics combining message contents with the information needs of the receiver.

The LENS project uses the AI techniques of frames, production rules, and inheritance to provide a rich set of semistructured message types and automatic message processing. Message templates are stored as frames, with more specific types of messages inheriting features of parent frames. Rules are used to filter messages based on stored characteristics and slot values.

A prototype electronic mail system has been developed. Future extensions to the project include connections to external information sources, natural-language processing and advanced information retrieval techniques, and forms processing.

The electronic mail projects are important because they provide mechanisms to manipulate the contents of documents based on the meaning of the messages rather than solely manipulating the descriptive information defining their fields (or slots). They represent the application of AI techniques as a way of providing a meaningful interpretation of document contents in a DDSS. The filtering techniques can be adapted to other types of documents as well and perhaps expanded to interpretations not normally found in the electronic mail area. They also demonstrate that multiple types of documents can be supported with a single representational structure.

DOCUMENT-BASED SYSTEMS

In addition to the document-based systems built around hypertext retrieval mechanisms, at least one project is in the works that supports the storage and manipulation of multimedia documents. The MINOS project (Christodoulakis et al., 1986, 1987) uses an object-oriented model of a document that is composed of attributes, text, images

DATE DUE

(line graphs, bit maps), and voice. The objectives of MINOS are to provide the following capabilities (Christodoulakis and Velissaropoulos, 1987:13–14):

1. Concurrent storage and retrieval of unformatted data.
2. Data sharing and duplication control.
3. Appropriate structuring of multimedia objects.
4. Powerful languages for achieving content addressability in formatted and unformatted data types.
5. Access methods for unformatted data.
6. Data retrieval optimization.
7. Efficient browsing through and within multimedia objects.
8. Interactive creation of multimedia objects composed of voice, image, text, attributes, and programs.
9. Extraction of information from existing unformatted data.
10. Comparison of extracted information with other objects or desired objects.
11. Transformations of extracted information from one presentation form to another.
12. Synthesis of new information from extracted or interactively created information.
13. Retrieval of information from previous versions of objects.
14. Effective version control.

Two features of MINOS make these objectives particularly difficult to achieve. First, the objects are stored on optical disk–based technology, so that changes cannot be made to the stored data. Second, the data consist of multiple media, including text, voice, and image, which makes manipulation and addressability issues that much more complex.

Similarities exist between MINOS and the hypertext-based systems. Both allow for multiple types of documents to be represented. Linkages can be made among relevant objects or documents, so that associative browsing among documents and document types is supported. New documents can be constructed from bits and pieces of existing documents, again permitting generation of multiformatted output. Both incorporate artificial intelligence to carry out these complex activities. AI governs the storage and retrieval patterns of the document-based systems.

The role of these systems in DDSS is obvious. The ability to integrate and link multiple media documents is vital to the success of a DDSS. These technological advancements demonstrate the intricacies and magnitude of a DDSS project. These systems permit the active access and reconstruction of many types of documents. In combination with advanced information retrieval mechanisms that promote system-generated associations within and between documents, document-based systems can become a valuable decision support tool.

SUMMARY

Where do we go from here? It is apparent that many of the pieces are in place with which to develop a document-based management system and from that a document-based decision support environment. The hardware technology, long a stumbling block for large document bases needing fast retrieval time, has progressed to a point where microcomputer systems are inexpensively available. Information retrieval has advanced as well, with sophisticated search algorithms and expert system components providing efficient and effective retrieval. Electronic mail and multimedia document systems provide the technological foundations for augmenting passive retrieval techniques.

The missing element is not the technology. Rather, it is the knowledge of how to effectively employ the technology in such a way that executive decision makers will benefit from it. Further study is needed to ascertain whether executives do not use technology because it is cumbersome and inappropriate to their needs, or if the inherent "impersonalness" of an information system as a source of information will persist as a deterrent to its use. Only after determining its potential usefulness and, ultimately, its role in the decision-making process can a DDSS be successfully designed.

QUESTIONS

1. Why is it important to include document-based data in the database for DSS?
2. In what way do hardware advances assist in the process of information retrieval?
3. What is the value of hypertext in DDSS?
4. Develop a decision-making or problem-solving scenario in which the decision maker uses one or more of the features of a DDSS. Explain how each feature is used and why it is valuable.

REFERENCES

HARDWARE

BRENNAN, LAURA   "GE Brings Digital Video Interactive Technology Out of Its Labs," *PC Week,* August 4, 1987, 8.

FAUST, MARGARET   "Image Scanners Are Good...But Could Be Better," *PC Week,* July 14, 1987, 63–74.

GLATZER, HAL   "CD-ROM Is Ready; Are You?" *Software News,* July 1987, 62–69.

GRIGSBY, MASON   "Merging Micrographics and MIS," *Infosystems,* May 1986, 94–97.

KRAMER, MATT   "CD ROM Expands Options for Corporate Research," *PC Week,* June 24, 1986, 89–90.

WEE, DON   "LANscape System Allows Fast Efficient Data-Based Searches," *PC Week,* August 25, 1987, c/11–c/12.

ONLINE DATABASES

JENKINS, AVERY   "Firms Work to Control On-line Database Charges," *PC Week,* March 11, 1986a, 41–42.

JENKINS, AVERY   "On-line Databases," *PC Week,* March 11, 1986b, 83–84+.

SWANSON, E. BURTON, AND MARY J. CULNAN   "Document-based Systems for Management Planning and Control: A Classification, Survey, and Assessment," *MIS Quarterly,* December 1978, 31–47.

INFORMATION RETRIEVAL

BUELL, DUNCAN A. "A Problem in Information Retrieval with Fuzzy Sets," *Journal of the American Society for Information Science,* 36, no. 6 (November 1985), 398–401.

DANIELS, P. J. "Cognitive Models in Information Retrieval—An Evaluative Review," *Journal of Documentation,* 24, no. 4 (December 1986), 272–304.

FEDOROWICZ, JANE "Database Performance Evaluation in an Indexed File Environment," *Transactions on Database Systems,* 12, no. 1 (March 1987), 85–110.

KWOK, K. L. "A Probabilistic Theory of Indexing and Similarity Measure Based on Cited and Citing Documents," *Journal of the American Society for Information Science,* 36, no. 5 (September 1985), 342–51.

LENAT, D. B., A. BORNING, D. MCDONALD, C. TAYLOR, AND S. WEYER "KNOESPHERE: Building Expert Systems with Encyclopedic Knowledge," *Proceedings of the International Joint Conference on Artificial Intelligence,* 8 (1983), 229–35.

RICH, E. "User Modelling via Stereotypes," *Cognitive Science,* 3 (1979), 329–54.

SALTON, G. "Another Look at Automatic Text-Retrieval Systems," *Communications of the ACM,* 29, no. 7 (July 1986), 648–56.

VAN RIJSBERGEN, C. J. *Information Retrieval,* 2nd ed. (London: Buttersworth, 1979).

VICKERY, ALINA, AND HELEN BROOKS "Expert Systems and Their Applications in LIS," *Online Review,* 11, no. 3 (1987), 149–63.

VICKERY, B. C. "Knowledge Representation: A Brief Review," *Journal of Documentation,* 42, no. 3 (September 1986), 145–59.

VICKERY, B. C., H. BROOKS, AND B. A. ROBINSON *Expert System for Referral, Final Report for the First Phase of the Project* (London: University of London, Central Information Service, 1985).

HYPERTEXT

EXECUTIVE TECHNOLOGIES, INC. *SearchExpress* Marketing literature, August 1987.

FIELD, ANNE R., ET AL. "PC Software That Helps You Think," *Business Week,* November 2, 1987, 142.

ELECTRONIC MAIL

CHANG, SHI-KUO, AND L. LEUNG "A Knowledge-based Message Management System," *ACM Transactions on Office Information Systems,* 5, no. 3 (July 1987), 213–36.

MALONE, THOMAS W., KENNETH R. GRANT, FRANKLYN A. TURBAK, STEPHEN A. BROBST, AND MICHAEL D. COHEN "Intelligent Information-Sharing Systems," *Communications of the ACM,* 30, no. 5 (May 1987), 390–402.

DOCUMENT-BASED SYSTEMS

CHRISTODOULAKIS, S., M. THEODORIDOU, F. HO, M. PAPA, AND A. PATHRIA "Multimedia Document Presentation, Information Extraction, and Document Formation in MINOS: A Model and System," *ACM Transactions on Office Information Systems,* 4, no. 4 (October 1986), 345–83.

CHRISTODOULAKIS, S., AND THEODORA VELISSAROPOULAKIS "Issues in the Design of a Distributed Testbed for Multimedia Information Systems (MINOS)," *Journal of Management Information Systems,* 4, no. 2 (Fall 1987), 8–33.

11

MODEL MANAGEMENT SYSTEMS

Robert W. Blanning

INTRODUCTION

Decision support systems (DSS) were created to provide support for poorly structured decision-making tasks. Although this purpose has not changed, the methods for realizing this purpose are changing. In the early days of DSS, methods for handling data were advanced relative to methods for managing models. This situation is changing as important conceptual breakthroughs are taking place in how models can be stored, used, and managed. These systems are commonly referred to as *model management systems*.

The purpose of a model management system is analogous to that of a data management system. Just as data management systems insulate their users from the physical aspects of database organization and processing, so also do model management systems insulate their users from the physical aspects of model base organization and processing. This includes specifying the relationships between models (when the output of one model is an input to another), documenting the models, integrating them in response to a user query, integrating them with data files, and specifying input and output formats for the models.

The seminal literature on model management identified these purposes and suggested in a very general way how they might be accomplished [1, 2]. However, the subsequent literature in this area, which presented theories of model management and descriptions of experimental model management systems developed primarily at universities, began to focus on specific system structures. The first of these is the CODASYL DBTG structure used in many data management systems. Two of the early model management systems were extensions of CODASYL systems written in FORTRAN [3] and APL [4]. That is, the CODASYL framework was enlarged from a framework for describing interactions between files in a database to include interactions between files and models and between the models themselves. Another approach, which has resulted in theoretical literature but not in implemented systems, is based on the relational view of data. A model is viewed as a virtual relation—that is, as a virtual subset of the Cartesian product of the input and output attributes of the model—just as a file is viewed in relational database theory as a stored subset of the Cartesian product of the key and content attributes of a file. Questions of model base organization, accessing, and integration have been addressed in this framework.

In this article we address two major topics. The first is the relational framework for model management just mentioned. The purpose of this framework is both to provide a foundation for the development of model management systems and, in conjunction with the relational framework for data management, to allow for a comparison of files and models as sources of information for decision support. The second topic is the application of artificial intelligence (AI) to model management. AI techniques have been used, primarily on an experimental basis, to assist the users of a DSS in model construction, model base integration, and the interpretation of model outputs. Each of these areas will be examined briefly.

THE RELATIONAL VIEW OF MODELS

The relational view of models, like the relational view of data, is based on the mathematical theory of relations. It is not our purpose here to describe this theory or its application to data and model management. Rather, we will examine, in a nonmathematical way, a central issue raised by the theory and its applications: the similarities and differences between data and models. We will also provide references to the literature for those who wish to investigate any details.

In the relational view of models, a model is viewed as a virtual file. That is, we pretend that a model is a file created by running the model for all possible values of its inputs and recording the inputs and the resulting outputs as records in the file, in which the inputs are key attributes and the outputs are content attributes. This allows us to ignore the physical differences between files and models (e.g., a linear programming algorithm is different from a file processing algorithm) and focus instead on logical similarities and differences—that is, on the similarities and differences seen by the user [5, 6].

An important issue in relational database theory is the organization of databases. Workers in this area have identified a sequence of normal forms, or permissible database structures. The criterion for the construction of the normal forms is the elimination of storage anomalies—that is, problems that can arise in adding records to a file, deleting records from a file, or changing the content of records in a file. Similarly, model base organization is an important issue in relational model management, but the criteria for normal forms in model bases are different from those in databases. The reason is that storage anomalies do not occur in model bases, since records in virtual file are not individually updated. Instead, when a change is made in a model, the entire virtual file is changed. However, there are other anomalies, called processing anomalies, that arise in model management, and these have led to normal forms for model bases that are similar, but not identical, to those that have been found for databases [7].

Another issue is the criteria for relational completeness of model base query languages. Such criteria have been identified for database query languages and are based on the operations that one would like to perform on relational databases. Similar studies have been performed on operations for relational model bases, and these have led to the design (but not the implementation) of three model base query languages. The first is MQL (Model Query Language), a linear language that is similar to the relational database language SQL [8]. The second is called TQL (Table Query Language), a tabular language similar to Query by Example [9]. The third is an unnamed logic-based language similar to PROLOG [10].

A major difference between the operations performed on files and those performed on models is that the operation of sensitivity analysis is frequently performed on models but not on files. That is, one might perform a sensitivity analysis on an order quantity model to determine the sensitivity of order quantity (an output) to demand (an input), but one would not use a payroll file to determine the sensitivity of salary (a content element) to employee identification number (a key element). In each case, an output or content element is functionally dependent on an input or key element—that is, the input or key uniquely determines the output or content at any one point in time. But when the file is a virtual file representing a model, then sensitivity analysis is a useful operation, and when the file contains stored data, then sensitivity analysis is not useful.

The reason is that the type of functional dependencies found in models is quite different from that found in data files [11]. The functional dependencies found in data files (i.e., stored relations) are *assigned dependencies,* and the functional dependencies found in models (i.e., virtual relations) are *causal dependencies.* In relational data management each record in a file corresponds to an entity in the real world (a person, a product, etc.), and functional dependencies represent an association between an identifier assigned to the entity (e.g., an employee identification number) and certain characteristics of the entity (e.g., salary), but there is no causal connection between them. That is, changing an employee's identification number will not change the employee and, hence, will not change her or his salary. In model management, on the other hand, there is a single entity in the real world corresponding to the entire model (a factory, an ordering process, etc.), and the records in the virtual relation collectively represent a causal relationship between input and output elements. That is, changing a demand will change the corresponding order quantity, and in this instance sensitivity analysis is meaningful and often appropriate.

A third issue in relational model management is the meaning and implementation of joins in model banks. A join across two or more files in a database is accomplished by linking corresponding records in the files—for example, linking records in a piece parts file to corresponding records in a finished goods file in order to calculate the demand for piece parts from the demand for finished goods. In relational model management, a join occurs whenever the output of one model is the input to another model. This leads to two differences between joins of files and joins of models. First, in relational model management, joins are transparent to the user and can be implemented in software, because model outputs are pairwise disjoint [12]. Second, cycles may arise in model bases (e.g., the output of an economic supply model may be part of the input to a demand model, and vice versa), which will require that a consistent solution must be found for all of the input and output elements in the collection of models [13]. It appears that this problem does not arise in data management.

We conclude this section by noting that the relational framework described here can be extended beyond the data/model comparison. For example, an entity-relationship framework of the type that has been developed for data management has also been developed for model management. In this framework the relationship sets are used to identify the attributes across which joins can be implemented [14]. In addition, a relational framework has been developed for the management of logic statements, in which the relations are very much like truth tables [15]. It has also been suggested that relational frameworks might be developed for other types of information, which may lead to a better understanding of the similarities and differences among the various types of information used in decision support [16].

EXPERT MODELBASE SYSTEMS: THE APPLICATION OF AI TO MODEL MANAGEMENT

An important trend is occurring in several areas of information processing technology: Certain areas that have previously been considered separate and examined largely in isolation of each other are now being examined jointly so that the interactions between them can be better understood. For example, in computer science the areas of database management and AI are being studied jointly under the title *expert database systems*. These systems might use database systems to support knowledge bases, use AI techniques for database query optimization, or use logic programming to draw inferences from stored data. An expert database system has been defined as "a system for developing applications requiring knowledge-based processing of shared information" [17, p. K2]. Although the information being referred to is stored data, it could also be one or more decision models in a model base.

The relationship between AI and model management is currently being investigated [18], and this area of research has been called *expert modelbase systems* [19]. The area of expert modelbase systems consists of three subareas: (1) the application of

AI to model construction, (2) the application of AI to model base integration, and (3) the application of AI to the interpretation of model outputs. Most but not all of the expert modelbase systems in these three subareas are experimental prototypes developed at universities and industrial research laboratories. However, in the future we may expect to see more systems of the type described below in routine productive use.

Expert Modelbase Systems for Model Construction

Since knowledge and experience are needed to build models (e.g., a linear programming model of an oil refinery or a chemical plant), it should not be surprising that attempts have been made to construct expert modelbase systems to assist in this task [20]. There are three types of models for which this has been done: statistical models, linear programming models, and queueing models. Two examples of the first type are (1) REX, a system that helps a user to perform an ordinary least-squares regression by identifying anomalies in the output and suggesting variable transformations that will eliminate them [21] and (2) ZEERA, a system that helps a user select proper procedures for elementary statistical analyses [22].

There are four examples of expert modelbase systems that help users to construct linear programming models. Each system receives a problem statement from the user and interrogates the user in order to identify the variables, objective function, and constraints in the model. The first is a rule-based system, written in PROLOG, that helps a user to construct a network-based linear programming model [23]. The second is a rule-based system, written in EXSYS (an expert system shell), that helps a user to construct a production planning model [24]. The third is a frame-based system, written in PROLOG, that helps a user to construct a production management model [25, 26]. The fourth system, based on semantic nets, is still in the design stage, but its purpose is to help a user to recognize simple linear programming problem types and to construct an appropriate model [27].

With regard to queueing models, two systems have been developed, one for building GPSS simulations of a queueing system [28] and the other for selecting the appropriate assumptions (e.g., assumptions about probability distributions and queue discipline) for an analytical model and building the model [29].

In addition to the model-specific approaches just described, techniques have also been developed for deciding how to select models or components of models that have similar properties in response to a user query [30] and to control redundancy in a model bank [31]. Although these are based on causal, rather than intelligent, models, they may eventually lead to expert modelbase systems for model selection.

Expert Modelbase Systems for Model Base Integration

When the outputs of some models in a model base are inputs to others, it is necessary that the models be integrated. As stated above, this corresponds to a join in relational data management, and it has been suggested that expert modelbase systems may be constructed to implement the join. It has also been suggested that a relational framework may be useful in constructing a model dictionary that describes the inputs and outputs of the models for model base integration and other tasks [32].

Five AI techniques have been proposed for the implementation of joins. The first is logic programming, in which the inputs and outputs of the models are facts, and the rules describe how models can be linked [32, 34, 35]. The query to be answered is stated in the form of a conclusion to be inferred, and the rules are applied to the input/output facts to determine whether the conclusion can be derived from the facts. It has also been suggested that the efficiency of the integration process would be improved if connection graphs were used to guide the search [36]. In addition, heuristics have been developed to improve the efficiency of model bank integration [37, 38, 39].

The second technique is AND/OR graphs [33], in which the AND operation is used to combine two dissimilar models and the OR operation is used to combine two similar models (i.e., models that have the same outputs but that use different inputs or are based on different assumptions). The remaining techniques are frames [40], semantic nets [41], situation-action rules [42], and a combination of connection graphs and frames [43].

We note that the way in which these techniques are implanted will depend on whether there are any cycles in the model bank, which will occur when the input of one model is the output of another, and vice versa. As was stated in the previous section, if a cycle should exist, then it would be necessary to find a consistent (or equilibrium) set of input and output attributes for the models in the cycle. This is done by creating an additional object (rule, frame, logic statement, etc.) whose purpose is to implement an algorithm that will arrive at a consistent solution.

Expert Modelbase Systems for Model Interpretation

Knowledge and experience are required not only to construct models but also to interpret their results. Models sometimes produce anomalous results, and the user must try to understand them. For example, a model may predict that under certain conditions, both prices and sales will decrease but profits will increase. Although this is quite possible for a number of reasons, the reasons may not always be obvious and further explanation may be necessary. This would occur if the assumptions in the model interact in ways that are counterintuitive or if other assumptions—for example, a substantial decrease in production costs caused by a decline in economic conditions—are responsible. Two expert modelbase systems have been developed thus far to address this problem: one for spreadsheet-based models and one for linear programming models.

The notion that one can construct an intelligent system to explain the results of spreadsheet calculations was first advanced in work done at Carnegie-Mellon University [44, 45]. This led to the development of ERGO, a commercially available system that attempts to identify and explain the causes of apparent contradictions in spreadsheet outputs [46, 47]. ERGO constructs its explanations by performing various sensitivity analyses, such as calculating what the output of the spreadsheet generator would have been if there had been no decline in economic conditions.

The system for interpreting the output of linear programming models is based on a discipline called computer-assisted analysis [48, 49]. This has led to the development of ANALYZE [50, 51], which examines the input (initial tableau) and output (final tableau) in an attempt to explain any anomalies. The anomalies may include an unbounded solution (possibly caused by an incorrect sign in the objective function), the lack of a feasible solution (caused by an overly restrictive constraint or set of constraints), or the use of an unusually expensive resource in a cost minimization problem (which might result from constraints on the use of less expensive resources). ANALYZE attempts to find a simple explanation, such as a single constraint or a small set of constraints that will explain the anomaly.

Other Possible Types of Expert Modelbase Systems

The three types of expert modelbase systems described above do not exhaust all possible types of expert modelbase systems. Here we examine four additional possible types. The first is a system that helps managers or staff analysts to decide whether to initiate a model construction effort in the first place. Presumably, such a system would be similar to the model construction systems described above, but it should also take into account the way in which managers make these decisions in practice.

There are two points of view with regard to this type of decision. The first is an economic one: Managers should consider model construction an example of information purchasing and should initiate a model construction effort if and only if the value of the information generated by the model exceeds the cost of constructing and using it [52]. Thus, managers should try to determine the value of various characteristics of the information (content, timeliness, accuracy, etc.) and the tangible and intangible costs of constructing and using the model.

The other point of view is based on a set of case studies of corporate planning models describing the construction and use of these models in nine corporations and government agencies in the mid-1970s [53]. It was found that the managers made the decision to proceed not by performing formal cost/benefit analyses, but rather by looking for instances in which a model similar to the one being proposed had been implemented elsewhere, sometimes within their own organization and sometimes in other organizations, and extrapolating from this experience. The reason that they did this is that they found it difficult to estimate the benefits and development costs of models not yet constructed.

These points of view do not necessarily conflict. It may be that the second point of view is appropriate for new types of models (as were planning models, in the mid-1970s) and the first is appropriate for more established model types. In any case, this suggests that an expert modelbase system for helping managers decide whether to build a model should perform two functions. First, it should help a manager to estimate the costs and benefits of a proposed model and especially, to ensure that any important costs and benefits have not been overlooked. Second, it should contain information about other model building efforts and help the manager to determine the relevance of these efforts to the proposal being evaluated.

The second possible application of expert modelbase systems is the validation and verification of models. Validation means determining whether the model properly represents the real world, and verification means determining whether the modeling software accurately implements the model (i.e., whether the computer program is correct). The first problem is quite difficult to solve, but a little progress has been made on the second one. Theoretical work has been done on proofs of program correctness, and an expert system, called I-KBS, has been developed for this purpose [54]. I-KBS examines a model, attempts to infer the cause-and-effect relationships in the model, and asks the user whether its understanding is correct. It then examines traces of model executions to verify that the behavior of the program is consistent with what it has learned about the model.

A third possible application is the development of natural-language (e.g., English) query processors for model bases. Such processors have been developed for databases, and there has been some discussion of the possibility of developing them for model banks as well [55]. The principal difference between data and model query processors is that the latter must perform additional functions, especially optimization and sensitivity analysis. A simple prototype model query processor, called MERLIN, has been developed, but it performs only the most basic functions [56, 57].

The fourth application is the integration of model bases with other components of a DSS. Two leading texts in DSS have described the components of a DSS as:

1. a knowledge system, a language system, and a problem processing system [33]; and
2. a data management system, a model management system, and a dialog management system [58, 59].

An expert modelbase system that integrates a model base with other components of a DSS would probably be similar to the ones described in the previous section for integrating the models in a model base. However, it would have to have additional capabilities, and identifying these capabilities would require additional research.

Three such areas of research are currently underway. The first is in the context of linear programming and simulation. Systems have been developed to integrate the components of linear programming, matrix generation, and report writing procedures with each other and with data files [60, 61, 62], and similar systems have been developed for simulation models [63, 64, 65]. The second is the development of interactive systems that allow people to communicate with models, data files, and each other [66, 67, 68, 69]. The third, called *structured modeling* [70, 71, 72] or *structural modeling* [73], views a model as an integrated collection of components, some of which are calculation procedures and some of which are data files.

In order to introduce new technologies, such as those described above, into model management, it is important that an organization or suborganization be created with the responsibility for their implementation. The responsibilities of "model base administrators" have been investigated, both in the seminal literature on model management [1, 2] and in more recent literature [74]. Many of these responsibilities are similar to those that have been proposed in the data management literature for database administrators. One such responsibility is the coordination of modeling efforts, especially when models will exchange information or when there is a potential for unnecessary duplication. Another is coordination with other appropriate persons, especially database administrators. In addition, model base administrators may influence the construction of individual models, formulate modeling policies, provide tools for model construction, and the like. We suggest an additional responsibility: to develop or acquire expert modelbase systems that will improve the effectiveness of their model management efforts.

CONCLUSION: FROM INTELLIGENT *DSS* TO INTELLIGENT ORGANIZATIONS

We have seen that model management can be viewed as an extension of data management to encompass a new type of information source [75]. Similarly, expert modelbase systems can be viewed as an extension of expert database systems. We now ask whether any further extensions might be useful. One possibility is to include the management of knowledge bases [76], and it might eventually be possible to incorporate other types of stored information, such as text and images. We consider here the possibility that the information sources might be enlarged to include people or groups of people.

Three emerging areas of the literature address this issue. The first is a straightforward extension of the work described in the previous section. It has been suggested that expert systems may become a useful paradigm for describing information flows and decision processes in an organization, supplementing the existing organizational paradigms drawn from economics and the behavioral sciences [77]. For example, the subunits in an organization might be viewed as a set of rules in a knowledge base, in which information acquired by a subunit is the antecedent to its corresponding role and information produced by the subunit is the consequent of that rule. Decision processes could then be described by rule processing strategies, such as forward and backward chaining. Alternatively, subunits could be viewed as a collection of frames, in which some frames can inherit information from other frames. A similar view, based on object-oriented programming, has also been developed [78].

The second perspective derives from the notion that the United States and certain other nations are becoming postindustrial societies, and the organizations in them will be postindustrial organizations [79]. It has been suggested that information processing technology—that is, the technology of computers and data communication—will allow greater flexibility of interaction between individuals and organizational subunits and that this in turn will require more sophisticated management of decision processes.

The third perspective is an enlargement of the second one to include considerations of economics as well as information processing technology [80]. Several different strategies for the design of intelligent organizations are presented, in which economic and technological considerations are emphasized in varying degrees.

In summary, we can see that the notion of information management, and also of intelligent (in the AI sense) information management, once confined largely to stored data, has been extended to include decision models, and it may be further extended to include other types of computer-based information. It may even be extended to include the management of human information resources and, as a consequence, provide useful insights into organization design and the structuring of decision processes.

ACKNOWLEDGMENT

This work was supported by the Dean's Fund for Faculty Research of the Owen Graduate School of Management of Vanderbilt University.

QUESTIONS

1. There are similarities and differences in the requirements for managing data and models. Briefly describe several of each.
2. How useful is it to have a common framework, such as a CODASYL DBTG framework or a relational framework, for both data and model management? Are there any disadvantages to doing this?
3. Assume that an organization's budgeting process is performed in the following way. Each department submits its proposed budget on an electronic spreadsheet. The budgets are approved or disapproved at various levels based on their own merits. They are also combined with other budgets and reviewed to ensure that organizational resources are being used appropriately. There are typically several cycles to the process, as revisions are made to departmental budgets and reviewed once again. How might a model management system support this process?

REFERENCES

1. WILL, HARTMUT J. "Model Management Systems," in *Information Systems and Organization Structure,* ed. Edwin Grochla and Norbert Szyperski (Berlin: Walter de Gruyter, 1975), pp. 468–82.
2. SPRAGUE, RALPH II., JR., AND HUGH J. WATSON "Model Management in MIS," *Proceedings of the Seventeenth National AIDS,* November 1975, 213–15.
3. KONSYNSKI, BENN R. "On the Structure of a Generalized Model Management System," *Proceedings of the Fourteenth Hawaii International Conference on System Sciences,* Vol. 1 (January 1981), 630–38.
4. STOHR, EDWARD A., AND MOHAN R. TANNIRU "A Database for Operations Research Models," *International Journal of Policy Analysis and Information Systems,* 4, no. 1 (1980), 105–21.
5. BLANNING, ROBERT W. "Issues in the Design of Relational Model Management Systems," *Proceedings of the National Computer Conference,* June 1983, 395–407.
6. BLANNING, ROBERT W. "A Relational Theory of Model Management," in *Decision Support Systems: Theory and Application,* ed. Clyde W. Holsapple and Andrew B. Whinston (Berlin: Springer-Verlag, 1987), pp. 19–53.
7. BLANNING, ROBERT W. "A Relational Framework for Model Bank Organization," *Proceedings of the IEEE Workshop on Languages for Automation,* November 1984, 148–54.
8. BLANNING, ROBERT W. "Language Design for Relational Model Management," in *Management and Office Information Systems,* ed. S. K. Chang (New York: Plenum, 1984), pp. 217–35.
9. BLANNING, ROBERT W. "TQL: A Model Query Language Based on the Domain Relational Calculus," *Proceedings of the IEEE Workshop on Languages for Automation,* November 1983, 141–46.

10. BLANNING, ROBERT W.   "A PROLOG-based Framework for Model Management," *Proceedings of the First International Workshop on Expert Database Systems,* October 1984, 633–42.

11. BLANNING, ROBERT W.   "Data Management and Model Management: A Relational Synthesis," *Proceedings of the Twentieth Annual Southeast Regional ACM Conference,* April 1982, 139–47.

12. BLANNING, ROBERT W.   "A Relational Framework for Join Implementation in Model Management Systems," *Decision Support Systems,* 1, no. 1 (January 1985), 69–82.

13. BLANNING, ROBERT W.   "The Existence and Uniqueness of Joins in Relational Model Banks," *International Journal on Policy and Information,* 9, no. 1 (June 1985), 73–95.

14. BLANNING, ROBERT W.   "An Entity-Relationship Approach to Model Management," *Decision Support Systems,* 2, no. 1 (March 1986), 65–72.

15. BLANNING, ROBERT W.   "A Relational Framework for Assertion Management," *Decision Support Systems,* 1, no. 2 (April 1985), 167–72.

16. BLANNING, ROBERT W.   "A Relational Framework for Information Management," in *Decision Support Systems: A Decade in Perspective,* ed. Ephraim R. McLean and Henk G. Sol (Amsterdam: North-Holland, 1986), pp. 25–40.

17. SMITH, JOHN MILES   "Expert Database Systems: A Database Perspective," *Proceedings of the First International Workshop on Expert Database Systems,* October 1984, K1–K22.

18. ELAM, JOYCE J., AND BENN KONSYNSKI   "Using Artificial Intelligence Techniques to Enhance the Capabilities of Model Management Systems," *Decision Sciences,* 18, no. 3 (Summer 1987), 487–502.

19. BLANNING, ROBERT W.   "A Framework for Expert Modelbase Systems," *Proceedings of the National Computer Conference,* June 1987, 13–17.

20. HWANG, SYMING   "Automatic Model Building Systems: A Survey," *DSS-85 Transactions,* April 1985, 22–32.

21. GALE, WILLIAM A., ED.   *Artificial Intelligence & Statistics* (Reading, Mass.: Addison-Wesley, 1986).

22. MARCOULIDES, GEORGE A.   "An Expert System for Statistical Consulting," *Proceedings of the 1987 Annual Meeting of the Decision Sciences Institute,* November 1987, 1182–83.

23. MURPHY, FREDERIC H., AND EDWARD A. STOHR   "An Intelligent System for Formulating Linear Programs," *Decision Support Systems,* 2, no. 1 (March 1986), 39–47.

24. EVANS, JAMES R., AND SCOTT M. SHAFER   "An Expert Modeling Assistant for Production Planning Optimization Problems," *Proceedings of the 1987 Annual Meeting of the Decision Sciences Institute,* November 1987, 768–70.

25. BINBASIOGLU, MERAL, AND MATTHIAS JARKE   "Domain Specific DSS Tools for Knowledge-Based Model Building," *Decision Support Systems,* 2, no. 3 (September 1986), 213–23.

26. BINBASIOGLU, MERAL, AND MATTHIAS JARKE   "Knowledge-based Formulation of Linear Programming Models," in *Expert Systems and Artificial Intelligence in Decision Support Systems,* ed. Henk G. Sol, Cees A. Th. Takkenberg, and Pieter F. De Vries Robbe (Dordrecht: Reidel, 1987), pp. 113–36.

27. EVANS, JAMES R., AND JEFFREY D. CAMM   "Structuring the Modeling Process for Linear Programming," *Proceedings of the 1987 Annual Meeting of the Decision Sciences Institute,* November 1987, 957–59.

28. HEIDORN, GEORGE E.   "Simulation Programming through Natural Language Dialogue," in *Logistics,* ed. Murray A. Geisler (Amsterdam: North-Holland, 1975), pp. 71–83.

29. HOSSEINI, JINOOS, XITONG ZHENG, AND ZONGBIN ZHAO   "Stochastic Queuing System: An Artificial Intelligence Approach (Summary)," *Proceedings of the 1987 Annual Meeting of the Decision Sciences Institute,* November 1987, 418–19.

30. KLEIN, GARY, BENN KONSYNSKI, AND PHILIP O. BECK "A Linear Representation for Model Management in DSS," *Journal of Management Information Systems,* II, no. 2 (Fall 1985), 40–54.

31. ORMAN, LEVENT "Flexible Management of Computational Models," *Decision Support Systems,* 2, no. 3 (September 1986), 225–34.

32. DOLK, DANIEL R., AND ALAN R. NOEL "A Relational Dictionary Prototype for Implementing Model Management," *Proceedings of the Nineteenth Hawaii International Conference on System Sciences,* January 1986, 405–15.

33. BONCZEK, ROBERT A., CLYDE W. HOLSAPPLE, AND ANDREW B. WHINSTON *Foundations of Decision Support Systems,* (New York: Academic Press, 1981).

34. DUTTA, AMITAVA, AND AMIT BASU "An Artificial Intelligence Approach to Model Management in Decision Support Systems," *IEEE Computer,* 17, no. 9 (September 1984), 89–97.

35. LEE, RONALD M., AND LOUIS W. MILLER "A Logic Programming Framework for Planning and Simulation," *Decision Support Systems,* 2, no. 1 (March 1986), 15–25.

36. CHEN, MICHAEL C., JANE E. FEDOROWICZ, AND LAWRENCE J. HENSCHEN "Deductive Processes in Databases and Decision Support Systems," *Proceedings of the North Central ACM 82 Conference,* 1982, 81–100.

37. LIANG, TING-PENG "Reasoning in Model Management Systems," *Proceedings of the Twenty-first Annual Hawaii International Conference on System Sciences,* III, *Decision Support and Knowledge Based Systems Track,* January 1988, 461–70.

38. LIANG, TING-PENG "A Graph-Based Approach to Model Management," *Proceedings of the Seventh International Conference on Information Systems,* December 1986, 136–51.

39. KLEIN, GARY "Developing Model Strings for Model Managers," *Journal of Management Information Systems,* III, no. 2 (Fall 1986), 94–110.

40. DOLK, DANIEL R., AND BENN R. KONSYNSKI "Knowledge Representation for Model Management Systems," *IEEE Transactions on Software Engineering,* SE-10, no. 6 (November 1984), 619–28.

41. ELAM, JOYCE J., JOHN C. HENDERSON, AND LOUIS W. MILLER "Model Management Systems: An Approach to Decision Support in Complex Organizations," *Proceedings of the First International Conference on Information Systems,* December 1980, 98–110.

42. BLANNING, ROBERT W. "The Application of Metaknowledge to Information Management," *Human Systems Management,* 7, no. 1 (1987), 49–57.

43. FEDOROWICZ, JANE, AND GERALD D. WILLIAMS "Representing Modeling Knowledge in an Intelligent Decision Support System," *Decision Support Systems,* 2, no. 1 (March 1986), 3–14.

44. KOSY, DONALD W., AND BEN P. WISE "Self-Explanatory Financial Planning Models," *Proceedings of the National Conference on Artificial Intelligence,* August 1984, 176–81.

45. WISE, BEN P., AND DONALD W. KOSY "Model-Based Evaluation of Long-Range Resource Allocation Plans," in *Artificial Intelligence in Economics and Management,* ed. L. F. Pau (Amsterdam: North-Holland, 1986), pp. 93–102.

46. KING, DAVID "The ERGO Project: A Natural Language Query Facility for Explaining Financial Results," *DDS-86 Transactions,* April 1986, 131–50.

47. KOSY, DONALD W., AND BEN P. WISE "Overview of ROME: A Reason-Oriented Modeling Environment," in *Artificial Intelligence in Economics and Management,* ed. L. F. Pau (Amsterdam: North-Holland, 1986), pp. 21–30.

48. GREENBERG, HARVEY J., AND JOHN S. MAYBEE *Computer-Assisted Analysis and Model Simplification,* (New York: Academic Press, 1981).

49. GREENBERG, HARVEY J. "A Tutorial on Computer-Assisted Analysis," in *Advanced Techniques in the Practice of Operations Research,* ed. Harvey J. Greenberg, Frederick H. Murphy, and Susan H. Shaw (New York: North-Holland, 1982), pp. 212–49.

50. GREENBERG, HARVEY J. "A Natural Language Discourse Model to Explain Linear Programming Models and Solutions," *Decision Support Systems,* 3, no. 4 (December 1987), 333–42.

51. GREENBERG, HARVEY J. "A Functional Description of ANALYZE: A Computer Assisted Analysis System for Linear Programming Models," *ACM Transactions on Mathematical Software,* 9, no. 1 (March 1983), 18–56.

52. EMERY, JAMES C. *Management Information Systems: The Critical Strategic Resource,* (New York: Oxford University Press, 1987), pp. 208–39.

53. BLANNING, ROBERT W. "How Managers Decide to Use Planning Models," *Long Range Planning,* 13, no. 3 (April 1980), 32–35.

54. REDDY, Y. V. "The Role of Introspective Simulation in Management Decision Making," *DSS-85 Transactions,* April 1985, 18–21.

55. BLANNING, ROBERT W. "Conversing with Management Information Systems in Natural Language," *Communications of the ACM,* 27, no. 3 (March 1984), 201–207.

56. BLANNING, ROBERT W. "A System for Natural Language Communication Between a Decision Model and Its Users," in *Artificial Intelligence in Economics and Management,* ed. L. F. Pau (Amsterdam: North-Holland, 1986), pp. 77–85.

57. BLANNING, ROBERT W. "A Framework for Structured/Natural Language Model Query Processing," *Proceedings of the Nineteenth Hawaii International Conference on System Sciences,* January 1986, 487–93.

58. SPRAGUE, RALPH H., JR., AND ERIC D. CARLSON *Building Effective Decision Support Systems,* Englewood Cliffs, N.J.: Prentice Hall, 1982).

59. SPRAGUE, RALPH H., JR. "A Framework for the Development of Decision Support Systems," *MIS Quarterly,* 4, no. 4 (December 1980), 1–26.

60. SINGH, INDU SHEKHAR, AND SOWMYANARAYANAN SADAGOPAN "A Support System for Optimization Modelling," *Decision Support Systems,* 3, no. 2 (June 1987), 165–78.

61. DOLK, DANIEL R. "A Generalized Model Management System for Mathematical Programming," *ACM Transactions on Mathematical Software,* 12, no. 2 (June 1986), 92–126.

62. PALMER, KENNETH H., N. KENNETH BOUDWIN, HELEN A. PATTON, A. JOHN ROWLAND, JEREMY D. SAMMES, AND DAVID M. SMITH *A Model-Management Framework for Mathematical Programming,* (New York: John Wiley, 1984).

63. MCINTYRE, SCOTT C., BENN R. KONSYNSKI, AND JAY F. NUNAMAKER, JR. "Automating Planning Environments: Knowledge Integration and Model Scripting," *Journal of Management Information Systems,* II, no. 4 (Spring 1986), 49–69.

64. MILLER, LOUIS W., AND NORMAN KATZ "A Model Management System to Support Policy Analysis," *Decision Support Systems,* 2, no. 1 (March 1986), 55–63.

65. LIANG, TING-PENG "Integrating Model Management with Data Management in Decision Support Systems," *Decision Support Systems,* 1, no. 3 (September 1985), 221–32.

66. APPLEGATE, LYNDA M., BENN R. KONSYNSKI, AND JAY F. NUNAMAKER "Model Management Systems: Design for Decision Support," *Decision Support Systems,* 2, no. 1 (March 1986), 81–91.

67. KONSYNSKI, BENN R., JEFFREY E. KOTTEMANN, JAY F. NUNAMAKER, AND JACK W. STOTT "PLEXSYS-84: An Integrated Development Environment for Information Systems," *Journal of Management Information Systems,* I, no. 3 (Winter 1984–85), 64–104.

68. WANG, MICHAEL SZU-YUAN, AND JAMES F. COURTNEY, JR.   "A Conceptual Architecture for Generalized Decision Support System Software," *IEEE Transactions on Systems, Man, and Cybernetics,* SMC-14, no. 5 (September/October 1984), 701–11.

69. MINCH, ROBERT P., AND JAMES R. BURNS   "Conceptual Design of Decision Support Systems Containing Management Science Models," *IEEE Transactions on Systems, Man, and Cybernetics,* SMC-13, no. 4 (July/August 1983), 549–57.

70. GEOFFRION, ARTHUR M.   "An Introduction to Structured Modeling," *Management Science,* 33, no. 5 (May 1987), 547–88.

71. LENARD, MELANIE   "Representing Models as Data," *Journal of Management Information Systems,* II, no. 4 (Spring 1986), 36–48.

72. DOLK, DANIEL R.   "Data as Models: An Approach to Implementing Model Management," *Decision Support Systems,* 2, no. 1 (March 1986), 73–80.

73. PRACHT, WILLIAM E., AND JAMES F. COURTNEY   "A Visual User Interface for Capturing Mental Models in Model Management Systems," *Proceedings of the Nineteenth Annual Hawaii International Conference on System Sciences,* January 1986, 535–41.

74. DOLK, DANIEL R., AND BENN R. KONSYNSKI   "Model Management in Organizations," *Information & Management,* 9, no. 1 (August 1985), 35–47.

75. BONCZEK, ROBERT H., CLYDE W. HOLSAPPLE, AND ANDREW B. WHINSTON   "The Evolution from MIS to DSS: Extension of Data Management to Model Management," in *Decision Support Systems,* ed. Michael J. Ginzberg, Walter Reitman, and Edward A. Stohr (Amsterdam: North-Holland, 1982), pp. 61–78.

76. BRODIE, MICHAEL L., AND JOHN MYLOPOULOS, EDS.   *On Knowledge Base Management Systems,* (New York: Springer-Verlag, 1986).

77. BLANNING, ROBERT W.   "Expert Systems as an Organizational Paradigm," *Proceedings of the Eighth International Conference on Information Systems,* December 1987, 232–40.

78. BLANNING, ROBERT W.   "An Object-Oriented Paradigm for Organizational Behavior," *DSS-87 Transactions,* June 1987, 87–94.

79. HUBER, GEORGE P.   "The Nature and Design of Post-Industrial Organizations," *Management Science,* 30, no. 8 (August 1984), 928–51.

80. MARSDEN, JAMES R., AND DAVID E. PINGRY   "The Intelligent Organization: Some Observations and Alternative Views," *Proceedings of the Twenty-first Annual Hawaii International Conference on System Sciences,* III, *Decision Support and Knowledge Based Systems Track,* January 1988, 19–24.

12

INTERACTIVE VISUAL DECISION MAKING

Efraim Turban,
John G. Carlson

INTRODUCTION

Business graphics is one of the fastest-growing and most diversified areas of computer graphics. Once a specialized product, business graphics is now a standard feature of many DSS generators, such as Lotus 1-2-3. Dramatic cost reductions and ease of use have made business graphics available to executives in any functional area of the organization. Computer-generated graphs, charts, and drawings are commonly used to support financial analysis, marketing studies, and production planning. Graphics help managers to plot trends, analyze investments, compare costs and product characteristics, locate potential customers, and adjust sales territories. Business graphics is also a powerful tool in presenting information to others. For an overview and list of products and vendors, see Austin (1985).

One of the most recent uses of graphics is in the support of decision making, especially in the areas of quantitative analysis and decision support systems (DSS).

Computer technology and quantitative analysis for managerial decision making are well developed in many areas. However, because managers are reluctant to use these tools, there is a major gap between what is available and what is being used. Many believe that computer graphics tend to reduce this gap by making information available to managers in a form that they better understand. That is, computer graphics improve the dialog between the users and the computers.

Although research results show little impact of graphics on decision-making performance (see DeSanctis, 1984; Ives, 1982; Remus, 1984), decision makers clearly prefer graphics, as evidenced by the billions of dollars in annual sales of computer graphics. Furthermore, industry reports (e.g., see Paller, 1986; Lembersky and Chi, 1984) point to millions of dollars saved that can be directly attributed to graphics.

An emerging area in business graphics is interactive visual decision making (IVDM). IVDM allows a manager to visually create or modify a model of complex decision situations. Furthermore, the manager can experiment with various decision alternatives and *see,* on the computer's screen, the effect of different alternatives, in a graphical, even dynamic, form on the system's measures of performance. In addition, results of solutions derived by the computer (e.g., by using mathematical models) can be displayed, and the manager can validate or modify such solutions. Finally, artificial intelligence (AI) techniques were incorporated into IVDM, providing it with extended capabilities. IVDM can be viewed as an emerging dialog option for DSS. Preliminary studies conducted by the authors indicate that managers value IVDM more than any other dialog option.

The purpose of this article is to describe IVDMs, survey their current applications, and discuss their managerial implications.

DEFINITION AND CHARACTERISTICS

Interactive visual decision making is a technique that uses computer-generated graphic displays to show interactively the impact of different decisions. These displays can be either representational summaries of data (bar charts, pie charts, etc.) and/or iconic displays of processes or systems (e.g., parts, tools, machines, persons).

The IVDM is based around a *visual model* that is used as an *integral part* of the decision-making process. Manual visual models have been used to support decision making for a long time. For example, planning city bus routes can be made easier if colored pins are used to denote bus stops on a city map, with stops on the same bus route shown in the same color. Route changes can be tried out by changing pin colors until the overall routings meet acceptable criteria. In this application, the map, pins, and the managerial criteria constitute a visual model. This same route planning has been done with interactive computer terminals (Bell et al., 1984). The computer version enables much faster experimentation and analysis, and thus the solution can be developed faster and better results expected (because more alternatives can be checked in a short time).

An even better analysis can take place when AI technology is added. Stefik et al. (1986), for example, simulated a city with icons showing city blocks, cars, buses, and traffic lights. The simulator represents the dynamics of traffic. When a traffic light turns green, it sends messages to start traffic. Cars move and stop; an emergency vehicle arrives and all other cars pull aside, and so on. The user can interact with and control the view in the traffic windows. For example, the location of the bus stop can be changed, the time for a green light can be modified, and a street can be made one-way. The results (in terms of travel time, waiting time, and even accidents) are displayed within seconds.

In general, IVDM involves decision making with an interactive visual model, which displays the effect of different decisions in graphic form on a computer screen. The more advanced IVDM, which are AI-supported, can be also used as *programming tools to construct* models (both symbolic and numerical) of managerial systems.

The interactive visual model can represent static or dynamic systems. Most other graphical systems represent only static situations. Dynamic models display systems that *evolve over time*. The evolution is represented by a flicker and/or animation. The *flicker* technique uses programmed color changes to depict changing states of the system. For example, if a machine in "on," the color is green; if a machine is "off," the color is red. In an *animation,* the images or icons that represent moving objects are actually moving about the display. For example, in a factory assembly line, one can see parts and materials moving from one production station to the next.

VIDEO GAMES: PINBALL MACHINE CONSTRUCTION AND PLAY

The basic concept of IVDM can be explained by using the analogy of micro software that enables a player not only to play pinball machines but also to construct such machines and set up their parameters. This software works as follows:

- *Building a system.* A pinball machine is composed of coils, bulbs, and other items that are organized in certain layouts. These items are represented on the computer screen by icons that look like the items in a real pinball machine. These icons are stored at one side of the computer screen. The player *selects* icons from the inventory and *positions* them inside the frame of the "pinball machine." This is done with the help of joysticks, a mouse, or selected keys on the keyboard. Then the player determines the number of points at each icon, the speed at which a ball will move once it hits an item, and any other parameters that may influence the results of a game.
- *Playing.* Once the system is ready, the player plays the pinball machine. Balls are visually entered into the system and points are accumulated when the ball hits the coils and the other items. Simulated noise and flashing lights are added. The game can be played by one or several players taking turns.
- *Control.* The player-builder can *change* the configuration of the pinball machine easily. Icons can be added or deleted, the speed of the traveling ball can be changed, the number of points earned can be modified, and so on.

FROM VIDEO GAMES TO *IVDM*[1]

The pinball machine example illustrates the graphical interface functions in IVDM and its capabilities. The following list includes the function and characteristics of advanced IVDMs:

■ *Constructing the system.* In a manner similar to the one used in the pinball construction, one can "build" manufacturing plants, service facilities, engines, or other desired systems. The more capable systems will have many different icons that can be arranged in many configuration. For example, a factory may be constructed to include ten different types of machines, two production lines, three types of conveyors, two storage facilities, and a maintenance shop. Using a mouse, items are selected and positioned. Then parameters that numerically describe the system, such as the speed of the production lines, are inputted or selected from menus.

■ *Viewing a system (monitoring the system).* Reflecting the *state* of a system and/or its components in any given time is another property of IVDM. For example, in a factory simulation, one can see the size of the inventories and the magnitude of delays for any configuration of factory layout or for any desired speed of the production lines. Using colors it is possible to show if machines are "on" or "off." The user can see, for example, aspects of operations that one cannot normally witness in a real organization,—for example, the flow rates in pipes or the level of customers' satisfaction. In addition, one can see *results,* such as total profit, amount of products or the anticipated number of complaints, which are associated with each decision alternative. Viewing can be static or dynamic. For example, one can see how inventories or waiting lines are *being changed with time* (i.e., during the simulation process).

■ *Controlling a system.* The IVDM permits the control of the system, its components, and its mode of operation. Thus, one can change the output rate of the machines, the number of operators, the space available for storage, or the price of a product. Controlling is an extremely important property in managerial systems because it allows the user to conduct sensitivity analysis (e.g., "what-if" analysis) and receive an immediate visual feedback.

■ *Experimentation.* The capabilities just discussed allow the user to conduct experiments with different systems and different configurations of the systems. These capabilities are especially important for planning and for problem solving because they permit the user to evaluate proposed solutions. All of this is done graphically. The graphical experimentation is done with a special editor, such as a flavor, which enables the construction of diagrams and their interfacing with an underlying mathematical model.

■ *Simulation vs. other decision situations.* Most existing IVDMs employ the technique of simulation, some employ other mathematical models such as linear programming, and others combine simulation and other quantitative models.

---

[1] It is interesting to note that, historically, society has used mass media innovations first as toys. Then inventors find work-related ways to employ these innovations. This situation occurred, for example, in both the film and television industries.

Simulation plays a major role in many DSS, especially for decisions that are unstructured and complex. Simulation models are commonly found in DSS. As a matter of fact, employing the "what-if" capability of a DSS means the use of simulation.

INTERACTIVE VISUAL DECISION SIMULATORS

The most applied class of interactive visual decision making is the interactive visual decision simulator. Two types of visual simulators exist, those that are incorporated with mathematical models (usually optimization models) and those that work as regular simulation models.

The origin of visual simulation can be traced to computerized games. One of the most popular computer games that executives play is Flight Simulator (Bell, 1985). This game was developed out of real-life flight simulators, an important training technique in aviation. Currently in its second version, Flight Simulator II includes full flight instrumentations and avionics and provides a full-color, animated, out-the-window view. Instruments are arranged in the format standard to modern aircraft. This game, when supported by an instruction manual, can be used for supporting actual initial pilot training.

Several other visual simulation games are available for home use (see box).

Popular Visual Simulation Games on Microcomputers*

Balance of Power
Flight Simulator II
GATO (WWII-class submarine simulation)
Kennedy Airport Approach
Jet Simulator
NFL Challenge
Wall Street

USE IN SYSTEM DYNAMICS

An interesting area of simulation where dynamic display is important is system dynamics (Forrester, 1971; Roberts, 1978). System dynamics is a simulation modeling technique that deals with very complex systems. Such systems are viewed as chains of causes and effects. A decision or a policy in one area (the cause) produces a result (effect) in another area.

System dynamics has been used to model social, political, corporate, governmental, and even worldwide systems. As with any other simulation, the method permits

---

*Source: Bell (1985)

experimentation with a model of the system under study. System dynamics models allow a manager to formulate several different policies and observe their effect through feedback loops.

System dynamics is composed of flowcharts coupled with equations that describe how the various elements of the system interact. For example, in addition to information feedback loops, other flows, such as inventory, inventory reorders, inventory backlog, and manufacturing processes, can be displayed. A policy that one might test is whether to supply a backlog by manufacturing or by using a stock.

System dynamics models are generally associated with large computer simulations and are constructed with a special language such as DYNAMO. However, visual interactive simulation software called STELLA (Structural Thinking, Experimental Learning, Laboratory with Animation) not only brings the technique into microcomputers (currently on the Macintosh) but also adds the ability to construct and modify the flowcharts and the diagram. STELLA is a system dynamics "expert system" development tool that embodies expertise in the areas of computational and structural logic, conceptualization, equation formulation, and model analysis. It enables those lacking computer experience or a quantitative orientation to conceptualize, construct, and analyze high-quality system dynamic models, while accelerating the development of an intuition for dynamics. For further details see Richmond (1985).

INTERACTIVE VISUAL SIMULATION
AND ARTIFICIAL INTELLIGENCE

The IVDM and especially the simulation approach are appropriate not only for quantitatively oriented algorithms but also for symbolically oriented procedures typically found in artificial intelligence. An example of such systems is the U.S. Navy's STEAMER project.

The STEAMER project is a research effort concerned with exploring the use of AI technology in the implementation of intelligent computer-based training systems for the U.S. Navy. A major component in this system is an intelligent graphical interface that simulates physical systems. This interface makes possible new approaches of instructional interactions by allowing one to control, manipulate, and monitor simulations of dynamic systems. The key idea of STEAMER is the conception of an *interactive inspectable* simulation. This inspectable system provides graphical views of ship engines (steam propulsion plant) and also allows the user to *inspect* various aspects of the procedures for operating the system. More than 100 views are available, ranging from an abstract representation of the entire steam plant to a picture of gauge panels. In addition, there exist *conceptual* diagrams constructed to reveal aspects of the system not normally available in a real plant but that might be beneficial for understanding some aspect of the plant's operation. The system reduces required training time by about 40 percent. For further details see Hollan et al. (1984).

IVDS development software, called SIMKIT, is available from IntelliCorp (Mountain View, Calif.). SIMKIT, a knowledge-based visual simulation tool, enables the rapid construction of expert systems that are combined with visual simulation. The builder creates libraries of graphically displayed simulation objects (icons). Non-programmers can then easily configure or alter simulations by manipulating the graphical displays with a few mouse-and-menu operations. While the user graphically configures the elements of the simulation, an appropriate knowledge base is created using a development tool called KEE (Knowledge Engineering Environment). Because KEE knowledge bases can interact with one another, SIMKIT simulations can be used as graphics drivers to KEE-based expert systems to create intelligent simulations— simulations that offer solutions, not just descriptive information. SIMKIT allows a quick "what-if" mechanism to test scenarios; thus, it provides an ideal way of explaining and validating expert system performance.

APPLICATIONS AT WEYERHAEUSER COMPANY

Weyerhaeuser Company (Tacoma, Wash.) is a large timber processor. The company developed several IVDS applications (two of which will be described here). The company estimates the annual increase in profit contribution to top $7 million due to the introduction of IVDS.

Case A: Log-Cutting Decisions (Lembersky and Chi, 1984)

Timber processing involves harvesting trees that are then delimbed and topped. The resulting "stems" are crosscut into logs of various lengths. These logs are allocated among different mills, each of which makes a different end product (e.g., plywood, lumber, paper). For each tree there may be *hundreds* of reasonable cutting and allocation combinations. The cutting and allocation decisions are the *major* determinant of revenues of the company and its profitability. The decisions are made on a stem-by-stem basis since each tree is physically different from every other one. Many variables determine the manner in which a stem is cut. Because costs are not affected much by these decisions, the larger the revenue generated, the larger is the profit.

Management scientists had developed a theoretical optimization model for the cutting and allocation decisions, using the technique of dynamic programming. However, the employees in the field were reluctant to use solutions that resulted from an unfamiliar, somewhat intimidating, "black box" algorithm. Furthermore, like any other mathematical model, the model was based on several assumptions that do not always fit reality, and, on occasion, its recommended solutions proved to be incorrect. Thus, the operators had had a legitimate reason for not following the computer's recommendations that seem to be inferior to the intuitive solutions that are based on experience.

The visual simulator enables the operators now to deal with the proposed solutions on their own terms. This is done by allowing them to simulate, on a video display, a realistic representation of each stem. The operator can roll, rotate, cut, and allocate each stem any way and see the result on the computer screen. The operator can *visualize* the end product and the resultant profit contribution of the suggested solution. The operator can then compare it with the profit resulting from the recommendation of the dynamic programming model. If not satisfied, the operator can recut the same stem repeatedly (on the computer screen, of course) to explore alternate decisions. The final decision, how to cut, is always made by the operator; therefore, the system is non-threatening. Furthermore, the repeated cutting experiments on the screen improve the operator's decision-making skills. The system is used also by management to evaluate alternative stem-processing strategies.

Case B: Facility Design (Garbini et al., 1984)

The design of log-processing facilities is a key factor in the determination of the productivity and the profitability of the company. The company is continuously engaged in such designs and they are impacted by many variables. The decision simulator in this case supports a computer-aided design (CAD) of the various facilities.

The design process involves a numerical simulation combined with a graphical animation. The designer can evaluate design alternatives by observing the proposed layout of equipment on the computer screen. In addition, the designer can observe the flow of materials, backlogs, queues of products and work orders, and delays that usually happen during production, as well as the inventories accumulated at various stages of production. Combined with product mix (production plans), the simulation can show graphically the profit associated with each design alternative. The designer can interactively adjust design parameters and watch their effects on various measures of performance. Adjustments can be made graphically using the CAD feature or numerically using the simulator. Many errors in facility design and modeling, difficult or impossible to predict from numerical results alone, are quickly detected in the animation. Similar to the log-cutting situation, the designer can use optimization techniques and compare the results with intuitive solutions.

OTHER APPLICATIONS

Most current applications of visual simulation are in operations management. Representative applications are listed in Table 12.1.

TABLE 12.1   Applications of Interactive Visual Simulation

	TOPIC
Regular	Road traffic at a signal-free intersection
Visual	Transportation system planning
Simulation	Hospital construction planning
	Design forest equipment
Visual	Locating service centers
Simulation	Water supply planning
plus	Urban transportation planning
Operations	Vehicle scheduling
Research	Truck dispatching and routing
Models	Scheduling of employees

Source: Bell et al., 1984.

A REPRESENTATIVE SOFTWARE: THE PC MODEL

In addition to STELLA, which runs on PCs, there are several other packages in development. Of special interest is the PC Model developed by Simulation Sofware Systems, Inc. (San Jose, Calif.). Simulated time displays of iconic objects move across a standard computer screen following user-specified routes, much like video games. The objects can be slowed down to sense the real-time action of queues, processing, gates, and the like. The screen can be output to the printer at any time and all the statistical data relating to the control points can be automatically and continuously saved to diskette for offline analysis. Symbolic variables can be used to allow global changes of the parameters directly from the keyboard. The IF instruction allows real-time decision making, or the simulation can be halted awaiting user keyboard response.

Through this simulation, managers, planners, and researchers can quickly see the processes being represented and the effect of parameter changes made online. The package has several demonstrations, including a study of a robot feeding parts to four machines; see Figure 12.1. The robot in the center acts as a transfer device for moving nine different parts through their sequences of operation performed by up to four different machines. The robot picks up the part at an entry point and moves it to the IN queue; if the first tool allows time for the operation and its entry into the OUT queue, the robot then moves the part to the IN queue of the next machine for its processing and queue time. Finally, the robot moves the part to the EXIT station. Each batch of parts is unique and visits the machines in different order. Utilization data are available at the ENTRY, ROBOT, EXIT; and various points at each machine, or a total of 14

FIGURE 12.1 Machine Shop Model

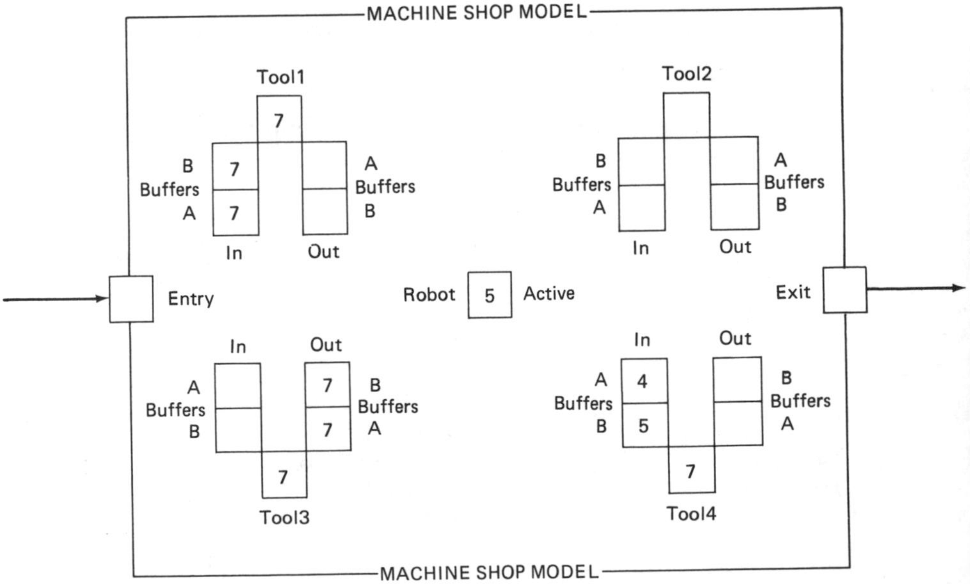

locations. The processing time, wait time, and robot handling time can be manipulated by the user.

CONCLUSIONS AND MANAGERIAL IMPLICATIONS

Interactive visual decision-making systems are in their infancy, yet they could greatly impact managerial decision making (see box).

How Can Interactive Visual Decision Making Help a Manager?*

The first exposure to IVDM sets the manager on unfamiliar ground. A large color screen lights up with a graphic display that may include moving icons and blinking colors. The first response is usually a comparison to a video-game and, indeed, the program creating the display has much in common with game software. The comparison is, however, short-lived. The power of the technique emerges in stages:

Stage 1: The manager recognizes the screen display as a graphic representing a familiar process or situation.

State 2: The manager observes the screen carefully, perhaps also several other screen displays, and accepts the picture(s) as a sufficiently detailed image of the real process, with any motion showing realistic process evolution.

Stage 3: The manager interacts with the model, and observes that the screen image responds in accordance with his understanding of the real system.

Stage 4: Through experimentation and observation, the manager gains confidence in the visual model, and becomes convinced that the model producing the displays is a valid representation of the real system.

Stage 5: Once convinced of the validity of the visual model, the manager can begin to ask "what if," and the visual model becomes a powerful decision-making aid.

The power of IVDM as a decision-making tool comes from the *confidence* in the model that grows as the manager sees the model confirms his understanding of the real system. Managerial validation of the model occurs because:

- A picture is recognizable as a model of the real world more readily than a table of numbers; a street map of a city is easier to recognize as the city than a list of the coordinates of street intersections.

- A visual model is not a "black box." The interior workings of the model are in full view and nothing has to be taken on trust.

- Dynamic visual models show the same transient behavior of the process that the manager sees every day, rather than average behavior over a long period of time.

- IVDM enables the manager to interact directly with the model rather than working with a mathematical model through an analyst.

Once confidence in the visual model is achieved, IVDM provides the manager with a decision-making environment very like that of a scientist working in a laboratory. The manager chooses experiments to be conducted, and evaluates them using results provided by the model. Explicit measures of the quality of alternative solutions can be incorporated into the model; for example, in a bus-routing problem it may be desirable to keep the routes as short as possible and so, after changing stops around, the total length of the routes can be computed and displayed. Optimizing procedures can also be built into the model: when a stop is moved from one route to another, the routes can be redrawn so that the distance travelled is a minimum.

IVDM is particularly powerful when the decision maker has multiple decision criteria, or where decision criteria are implicit or difficult to formalize. IVDM allows the decision maker to choose a best solution, using whatever criteria he thinks appropriate. IVDM is also a powerful *training* device, allowing an exposure to operations which can be very like the real thing—a flight simulator, for example, is an advanced form of IVDM application.

*Source: Bell et al. (1984).

The following are some of the characteristics that make interactive visual decision-making so valuable and viable:

- An IVDM provides a believable representation of the actual decision-making environment. It does not require detailed replication, but just enough realism to be credible to the ultimate user. It is also helpful in presenting only that portion of reality that is appropriate to the problem at hand. Balancing the objectives of realism for the user and an accurate portrayal of the underlying quantitative model or algorithm is an important challenge in designing an IVDM. The visual representation should include real-time dynamics and, where appropriate, animation. This aids in creating a believable decision-making environment.
- An IVDM is highly interactive and provides immediate feedback on the effect of decisions. These characteristics are very important for both user acceptance and improved decision making. An IVDM also emphasizes "seeing" the impact of decisions in motion, rather than just displaying data about the decisions (as in tabulations or bar charts).
- An IVDM is easy to use, and it requires minimal training. The goal is to create systems that the typical user can successfully operate with a minimum of instruction and with little user support. Almost every good video game demonstrates that this goal is achievable. IVDM users should not need to learn new specialized skills or a special vocabulary (such as command languages and their associated syntax), nor deal with devices that are not already part of their operational experience.

These three characteristics can be translated into five major areas of application:

- *Understanding systems operation.* IVDM allows the presentation of aspects that cannot be viewed in the actual systems (e.g., logical relationships and flow of information). This can be used to make much of the causal topology of a system directly apparent. Such a capability is important for assisting an individual attempting to build a conceptual model of systems operations. That is, it enables the building of better DSS.

- *Designing systems.* Design of factories, facilities, products, and services can be enhanced with IVDM. Various design configurations can be tested. The design can be interconnected with CAD systems or even with both CAD and CAM (computer-aided manufacturing). One area in which system design of this type can be particularly helpful is capital-intensive projects, such as flexible manufacturing systems (FMS).

- *Training.* IVDM and especially animated simulation could play an important role in computer-aided instruction (CAI) and computer-aided training. Adding AI capability enables the improvement of the *explanation* capability of the computerized system. The concept of flight simulators can be expanded to many other systems involving motions and dynamics. Significant savings of training costs can be realized by using this type of system.

- *Dynamic simulations.* Decision situations in real-time systems are difficult to model, experiment, and implement. IVDM could be helpful in such cases. The results at the Weyerhaeuser Company point to possibilities of significant savings. This capability pushes the bounderies of DSS into the real-time environment.

- *System dynamics animation.* The use of such tools as STELLA offers interesting modeling capabilities using system dynamics animation. This approach could be used for both training purposes and for improved decision-making capabilities.

IVDM promises much, but it should be treated with caution. Very few general-purpose development software packages are currently available on the market (e.g., SEE-WHY and SIMKIT for the mainframe and PC Model for micros and a micro-SIMKIT). The mainframe packages cost over $50,000, while the micro packages cost only a few hundred dollars. As an alternative to a development tool, the user can build a system from scratch. However, such an approach can be both expensive and time consuming. The benefits of IVDM are not always tangible, and therefore, it may be difficult to justify financially such a system. An exception, of course, is a micro-based system. The micro packages are not as powerful as the mainframe product, but for a cost of only a few hundred dollars, the user is able to animate and simulate many aspects of real-life systems for greater effectiveness and improved decision-making capabilities.

QUESTIONS

1. If a teenager became a senior executive overnight, would he or she be impressed with the graphics used in a typical organization? Why?

2. Drawing on your experiences with video games, how might a cash flow analysis be depicted if a video game approach were used?

3. Should there be concern that IVDS creates a false sense of security in regard to the validity of a model?

REFERENCES AND BIBLIOGRAPHY

AUSTIN, S. "The Graphic Edge," *Business Computer Systems,* October 1985.

BELL, J. "Games—The New Breed," *Personal Computing,* December 1985.

BELL, P. C., ET AL. "Visual Interactive Problem Solving—A New Look at Management Problems," *Business Quarterly,* Spring 1984.

BELL, P. C., ET AL. "A Visual Decision Support Systems for Workforce (Nurse) Scheduling," *INFOR,* May 1986.

BHATNAGAR, S. C. "Locating Social Service Centres Using Interactive Graphics," *OMEGA,* 11, no. 2 (1983).

DEMETRESCH, S. "Moving Pictures," *Byte,* November 1985.

DESANCTIS, GERARDINE "Computer Graphics as Decision Aids: Direction for Research," *Decision Sciences,* 15, no. 4 (Fall 1984).

FOLEY, JAMES D., AND ANDRIES VAN DAM *Fundamentals of Interactive Computer Graphics* (Reading, Mass.: Addison-Wesley, 1982).

FORRESTER, J. W. *Industrial Dynamics* (Cambridge, Mass.: MIT Press, 1971).

GARBINI, J. L., ET AL. "Merchandiser Design Using Simulation with Graphical Animation," *Forest Product Journal,* April 1984.

HOLLAN, J. D., ET AL. "STEAMER: An Interactive Inspectable Simulation-Based Training System," *AL Magazine,* Summer 1984.

IVES, B. "Graphical User Interfaces for Business Information Systems," *MIS Quarterly,* special issue, December 1982.

KHATOR S. "Computer Assisted Plant Layout Using Graphic Editor," *Computers and Industrial Engineering,* 8, no. 3 (1984).

LAW, A. M. "An Introduction to Simulation; A Powerful Tool for Analyzing Complex Manufacturing Systems," *Industrial Engineering,* May 1986.

LEMBERSKY, M. R., AND U. H. CHI " 'Decisions simulators' speed implementation and improved operations," *Interfaces,* July–August 1984.

MELAMED, B., AND R. J. T. MORRIS "Visual Simulation: The Performance Analysis Workstation," *Computer,* August 1985.

NAGY, D. "Dynamic Simulation Using Pascal," *Journal of Pascal,* May/June 1984.

NOF, S., ET AL. "Computerized Physical Simulators are Developed to Solve Industrial Engineering Problems," *Industrial Engineering,* October 1980.

PALLER A. "Million-Dollar Graphics (Visual Information Systems)" *COMPUTERWORLD,* April 1986; see also *Information Center,* February 1986.

PERRY, TEKLA S. "Video Games: The Next Wave," *IEEE Spectrum,* 20, no. 12 (December 1983).

REMUS, W. "An Empirical Investigation of the Impact of Graphical and Tabular Data Presentations on Decision Making," *Management Science,* May 1984.

RICHMOND, B. "STELLA: Software for Bringing System Dynamics to the Other 98%," working paper, Dartmouth College, 1985.

ROBERTS, E. D., ED. *Managerial Applications of System Dynamics,* (Cambridge, Mass.: MIT Press, 1978).

STEFIK, M. J., ET AL. "Integrated Access-Oriented Programming into a Multiparadigm Environment," *IEEE Software,* January 1986.

STIEFEL, M. L. "Surveying Interactive Graphic Systems," *Mini-Micro Systems,* December 1980.

PART 4

Creating the DSS Environment

DSS activity can begin in a variety of ways in an organization. At one extreme an individual may build decision support systems on an entrepreneurial basis, while at the other extreme the organization may commit itself to supporting and encouraging DSS as part of its corporate strategy. Whatever approach is taken, there normally comes a time when management realizes that a systematic approach must be used in order to create an appropriate DSS environment. This endeavor is a major undertaking that involves human as well as physical resources.

This section of the book contains five readings on creating the DSS environment. It ranges from broad selections such as how to develop a DSS corporate strategy to narrower ones such as how to select DSS software. It includes both conceptual ideas and actual illustrations of how organizations are creating an environment for DSS. The end result should be an enhanced understanding of how to develop a setting in which DSS activities can flourish.

Lawrence Young, in "A Corporate Strategy for Decision Support Systems" (Reading 13), describes why it is necessary to develop a DSS corporate strategy and how it is related to the corporate strategy for MIS. The seven major components that a DSS corporate strategy must deal with are identified. He also considers the steps in developing a DSS corporate strategy, who should be involved in the process, and their roles and responsibilities.

An important part of the DSS environment is the organizational environment within which the DSS will be developed and revised. Hugh Watson and Houston Carr in Reading 14 discuss the principal elements of this organizational environment and explain how the DSS support team can be organized for maximum effectiveness. Another important environment is the political, cultural, and problem-solving environment, which is especially important for the support of high-level strategy formulation and policy setting. In their award-winning article "Issue-Based Decision Support Systems for the Egyptian Cabinet," Omar El Sawy and Hishim El Sherif in Reading 15 show how a DSS can be structured to provide valuable support in an environment characterized by turbulence and ambiguity.

Special-purpose DSS software can do much to facilitate the building of decision support systems. Lawrence Meador and Richard Mezger, in "Selecting an End User Programming Language for DSS Development" (Reading 16), discuss how to evaluate and select DSS software for an organization. They recommend that a multidisciplinary task force follow a seven-step process.

Some firms have changed their information systems organization structure in order to better accommodate end-user computing, office automation, decision support systems, and other areas that have changed or evolved because of advances in computer hardware and software technology. The Mead Corporation is one of these firms. Ralph Sprague and Barbara McNurlin, in "The Mead Corporation" (Reading 17), describe how Mead has organized its information systems activities and what services are provided. They also discuss the benefits and problems of Mead's current organization structure.

13

A CORPORATE STRATEGY FOR DECISION SUPPORT SYSTEMS

Lawrence F. Young

WHAT IS A DECISION SUPPORT SYSTEM?

Decision Support Systems (DSS) have been described as computer-based aids for management decision-makers dealing with semi-structured problems (Keen and Scott Morton, 1978). The mode of DSS usage differs from other MIS applications in that DSS seeks to establish a symbiosis of human mind and computer by allowing for a high degree of human-computer interaction and by enabling the manager-user to maintain direct control over the computer's tasks and their outcome.

Early in the computer era Simon (1960) recognized that many aspects of the decision-making process, and many decision problems in their entirety, were not "programmable." These unstructured or "open" problem tasks were characterized as requiring much human judgment and often some creativity. Keen and Scott Morton (1978) point out that Simon had expected an increasing number of management decisions previously found to be unprogrammable would rapidly become structured and programmed for computer solution, but that this did not happen. The computer, they claim, "has had minimal impact on tasks involving judgment, ambiguity, creativity, and volatility of environment." The newer DSS approach needed to increase the computer's impact on such tasks has subsequently been evolved by a number of practitioners (Little, 1970) attempting to overcome past limitations.

The DSS approach is supposed to succeed where previous efforts failed because it does not require either the complete automation of decision-making or the computerization of an isolated task, unconnected with the human processing that must follow it. It instead breaks the decision process into a menu of selectable modules, each of which is understood by the user, adjusted and controlled by the user, and interwoven into the decision-maker's own step by step human processing sequence.

The broad charter of DSS is to support the more intuitive and less structured aspects of decision-making but we do not have a precise borderline delineation between "structured" vs. "unstructured." We can, however, recognize the degree of structure, which depends on how much is known of the three basic components of any decision problem:

    a. Objectives: in less structured problems not all objectives may be known at the outset; multiple objectives exist rather than one, and the trade-offs or relative utilities of the objectives are largely unknown.

    b. Outcome affecting variables: in less structured problems the identity of all of the important variables (both controllable and uncontrollable) that affect the outcomes may not be known at the outset of the decision process and therefore complete models cannot be specified in advance.

    c. Relations between affecting variables and between variables and outcomes: in less structured problems these relations are not all well-known in advance or may vary according to different plausible assumptions.

All of these conditions require a different approach to computer support and development than the more traditional MIS projects characterized by high-volume, fixed processing logic and repetitive, fixed frequency, fixed content reporting.

DSS development cannot be approached by completing hard application design specifications through the usual "life cycle" approach of systems analysis and design. Instead, DSS development requires the selection or development of very flexible model generators and/or information generators whose use and processing logic evolves and varies with usage and the user learning process. DSS software modules need to be generic rather than application specific and the system/user interface needs to be sufficiently "user friendly" so that it will present no barriers to interactive usage. "User friendliness" is especially critical because the applications of DSS are generally optional for users: they do not *have* to use the system in order to do their work, unlike many more traditional computer applications.

Most potential DSS applications have never surfaced in the past as part of the visible MIS application backlog because neither users nor traditional MIS specialists have been able to identify these functions as being appropriate for computer support. Only recently have some MIS planners taken them into account because of the push of technological advances. These advances are manifested in two primary tools of DSS.

1. User friendly DSS "generators," such as ad hoc query languages and planning modeling languages;
2. Micro-computers with user-friendly interfaces, low price tags, and inexpensive software (such as Lotus 1-2-3, SuperCalc, etc.) with some of the features of the more powerful mainframe software packages (such as IFPS, Express, System W).

All of the above described characteristics of DSS and its spontaneous growth have posed new questions for MIS planners and have led to the recognition of a need for formulating a corporate strategy for the introduction and effective use of DSS.

A *DSS* CORPORATE STRATEGY

A planned corporate strategy for DSS must deal with similar components to those relevant to MIS plans and policy, but, because of the different nature of DSS, must deal with these components in different ways.

The seven major components a DSS strategy must deal with are:

1. Staff Support
2. Software
3. Hardware
4. Data Bases
5. Information Integrity and Security
6. Communication Facilities
7. Definition of Authority and Responsibility (of Users vs. Information Systems and other Corporate Units)

The details of a particular strategy must, of course, be tailored to the organization. Some general features that are often found to be useful in fostering effective use of DSS include:

■ Creating a central group of DSS consultants to advise users (but not to centrally control) on the selection of micro-computers and software packages;

■ Distributing DSS consultants among user groups in various functional departments so that at least one resident support person provides a focus for educating and advising inexperienced computer users as well as serving as a liaison to central MIS and DSS support groups;

■ Providing DSS hardware, software and some data bases as part of the central information center facility;

■ Sending out advisory reports from the MIS department on DSS software evaluations, data base availabilities, microcomputer evaluations, etc.;

■ Setting up in-house educational seminars and workshops on DSS for users to attend;

■ Establishing a policy on microcomputer acquisition (that may limit choices and specify CP/M2.2 for example) in order to ensure compatibility of software and communications;

- Establishing a standard set of DSS generators to be used as planning languages such that a common language is used at each particular level of power and sophistication that may be required;
- Establishing a users liaison group for the exchange of information and as a network to be used as required.

It can be seen from the above that the common denominator of DSS strategy features is a large degree of user flexibility and autonomy within a larger framework of corporate boundaries and supporting facilities.

The need for a DSS strategy is again similar, but not identical to, the need for an MIS strategic policy. The reasons a DSS strategy is needed are:

Systems Integration and Compatibility

As in MIS, early applications are often developed as stand alone, independent systems. As usage matures, however, DSS users begin to demand direct access to corporate data bases rather than relying on their own private data bases and/or the local re-entry of previously processed computer output. The need to down-load data from a centrally maintained data base to individuals' micro-computer files makes compatibility of hardware, software, communications, and data base structures a critical issue.

Information Resource Economics

The proliferation of micro-computers, micro software packages, local use of outside time sharing services, uncoordinated local creation and maintenance of data bases, local acquisition of staff specialists or outside consultants, raises questions as to the cost-effectiveness of allowing an unplanned, largely invisible, ad hoc approach to the infiltration of DSS applications. Moreover, the lack of a centrally focused responsibility inhibits the exchange of information between users and does not facilitate organizational learning and development. The multitude and variety of approaches of independently operating users also diminishes the value of informal user communications. One user's sophistication gained in the use of a particular software package or micro or data base is of little or no value to a peer using a different set of facilities.

In addition, the local uncoordinated use of data bases and planning models may increase accessibility of information for unauthorized persons. The extent to which information integrity and security is affected by DSS proliferation needs to be analyzed and treated in a consistent manner throughout the organization so that realistic economic trade-offs are made between the utility of access and potential losses.

On the other hand, tight central control over all aspects of DSS by an MIS department or any other corporate unit is inappropriate to fostering the initial growth and development of DSS and the broad range of tools needed to support the full scope of tasks and users. The need to foster and loosely control the early growth stage of MIS has been observed by Gibson and Nolan (1974) and DSS needs no less encouragement and nurturing. Even more than early MIS growth stages, DSS needs a higher degree of local control in its early stages and even in its more mature stages, because the DSS approach is inherently concerned with serving individual decision processes in less structured tasks that cannot and should not be standardized.

A middle ground of coordination policies and facilities can be worked out to suit the individual corporate structure and culture. Such coordination should seek a more economic use of scarce staff expertise, computing power, and software, without imposing uniformity and forcing centralization of acquisition or use of supporting staff or facilities.

Organizational and Group Decision-making Support

Many if not most initial DSS applications are oriented to the use of individual users working on their own planning or evaluation problems. The organization, however, ultimately requires the integration of individual decision processes into larger organizational processes. The linkages between the various separate sub-processes, in most current modes of DSS, are left outside the boundaries of computer support to other organizational procedures. Again, as usage matures, it seems inevitable that a higher degree of integration of organizational decision processes will be demanded of computer support systems.

For example, a brand or product manager works out a marketing plan with his DSS but must communicate not only the results but also the assumptions made in the planning process to other brand managers and to the marketing manager so that all brand/product plans can be integrated into a total corporate plan. Often this requires a group process in order to formulate compromises among individual proposals. Similarly, unit financial plans need to be integrated into consolidated plans. To facilitate the integration process it may be far more useful to enable both downward and upward as well as multi-lateral communications between individuals and modeling systems at all levels to take place so that a team approach to decision-making can be used. Technical integration merely ensures that the output of the lower-level plan is compatible with the input format requirements of the higher level planning support system. Organizational process integration requires a common modeling language so that a multi-level, multi-lateral group process of planning can be supported when that is desired.

The nature and degree of need for this kind of integration depends, of course, on the practices of each organization. If group processes such as those characterizing the Japanese management practice that has been called "Theory Z" predominate, then group decision support systems will become essential. In any case, unless such needs are identified and planned for as part of the DSS strategy, they are unlikely to be effectively supported to any degree.

The above three need factors represent the criteria that a DSS strategy can be measured against by answering the following questions:

- Does the strategy provide technical systems integration and compatibility without imposing unnecessary uniformity?
- Does the strategy make the most economical use of resources and safeguard against losses without imposing stifling, bureaucratic control?

■ Does the strategy consider the ultimate need to support organizational and group decision processes as well as provide for individual support?

In summary, a DSS strategy must meet the above criteria by means of specifying the desired "mix" of the seven major components of 1) Staff support, 2) Software, 3) Hardware, 4) Data bases, 5) Information integration and security practices, 6) Communications facilities, and 7) Definitions of authority and responsibility;

■ the scheduling or phasing of the development and implementation of the identified mix so that the transition from the current status to the ultimate target situation is accomplished in digestible degrees with minimal organizational strains and so that some payoffs and confidence are gained early in the process;
■ estimated costs and the budgeting of financial resources required;
■ the assignment of responsibility for the continuing development, maintenance, implementation and control of DSS strategic planning.

GETTING STARTED: WHO DOES WHAT?

The impetus for a DSS corporate strategy must originate with some person or department that recognizes the need for coordination and planning, recognizes the legitimate demands on the part of those users who already know that some of their previously unmet needs can now be served by DSS software, and recognizes the benefits of further education of potential users and of the identification and fostering of DSS applications throughout the organization.

Recognition of the need and the benefits, however, is not enough. The impetus must come from the *right place* in the organization. Ideally, this will be from those most directly responsible for the planning of information services for the entire organization, if such a function exists. DSS planning can thereby be seen as a component of MIS planning and not a rival or independent undertaking. MIS planners and managers with foresight will not see DSS and the end-user computing and user control it entails as a threat to their traditional preserves, but as an opportunity to serve the organization in a new and different manner.

If DSS applications require less central programming support and central processing than traditional MIS processing, where is the threat? The new DSS applications were previously unsupported at all so nothing real has been lost to MIS departments. If it is the precedent of users by-passing MIS that is feared, this fear is ultimately also groundless. If MIS is by-passed for some traditional services, DSS usage ultimately fosters new kinds of demands on MIS departments such as:

1. Software package and applications consulting instead of taking over full responsibility for the development process;
2. DSS education of users, including the selection and use of packages, data bases, and micros, as well as modeling and analysis skills;

3. "Toolsmith" kinds of support such as tying micros into communications networks via modems, the need for and use of data base and software interfaces to assure compatability between system components, the maintenance and maintenance management of hardware and software, etc.

Thus no real conflict should exist and the managerially oriented MIS professional who sees DSS as a new opportunity requiring a new kind of response is the best sponsor and focal point for the responsibility of DSS strategy planning.

The first steps to getting started generally include the following:

- Obtain sponsorship for the strategy planning effort at the highest level.
- Identify key persons who should be involved in developing a strategy for DSS, including user management representing a broad spectrum of organizational functional areas.
- Provide an orientation and introductory educational program on DSS for the key people.
- Set up a DSS Steering Committee comprised of the key people, and preferably as an interlocking unit or sub-group of the MIS Steering Committee.
- Set short range target dates for completing the first general statement of goals, objectives, and main policy elements for DSS in the organization.
- In parallel to the above, get a broad coverage survey of the organization underway to identify a) the low risk, high leverage initial DSS application opportunities and b) other second phase, DSS application opportunities.
- Prepare to move rapidly into implementing the identified low risk, high leverage applications by contacting software vendors, running demonstrations, training or providing materials to key users, etc.
- Identify current staff members who have the necessary technical skills, consulting orientation, and knowledge of the organization and its managers, and would thereby have the qualifications to comprise the nucleus of a new DSS support unit. At the same time, identify gaps in these human resources that will need to be filled from outside the organization by hiring new personnel, using consultants, and developing others from anywhere in the organization with the potential needed.

In combination, the steps outlined above can accomplish two things:

1. Get the longer term strategy planning effort underway on a sound basis of support and organizational scope.
2. Enable the organization to move as rapidly as possible toward getting results through some immediate implementation as well as to be ready to carry out the new DSS strategy that will emerge.

The right blend of this kind of two-pronged effort provides a pragmatic middle ground between caution and planning on the one hand, and action producing faster payoffs on the other.

QUESTIONS

1. Why is a DSS corporate strategy important?
2. Describe the seven major components that a DSS corporate strategy should cover.
3. Discuss the first steps that are required in order to develop a DSS corporate strategy.
4. Should DSS be viewed as a threat by MIS professionals? Discuss.

REFERENCES

GIBSON, C. F., AND R. L. NOLAN   "Managing the Four Stages of EDP Growth," *Harvard Business Review,* 52, no. 1 (January–February 1974), 76–88.

KEEN, P. G. W., AND M. S. SCOTT MORTON   *Decision Support Systems: An Organizational Perspective*. Reading, Mass.: Addison-Wesley, 1978.

LITTLE, J. D. C.   "Models and Managers: The Concept of a Decision Calculus," *Management Science,* 16, no. 8 (April 1970), 466–85.

SIMON, H. A.   *The New Science of Management*. New York: Harper and Bros., 1960.

14

ORGANIZING FOR DECISION SUPPORT SYSTEM SUPPORT: THE END-USER SERVICES ALTERNATIVE

Hugh J. Watson,
Houston H. Carr

INTRODUCTION

Decision support systems (DSS) are being used in an increasing number of organizations, and with this development comes the need to support DSS efforts. This includes helping users evaluate hardware and software products, providing access to data, and participating in application development. First, however, it must be decided which organizational unit(s) is (are) responsible for DSS support. This decision has a potentially significant impact on the success and direction of DSS efforts in an organization. It is not an easy decision because there are many alternatives, there is no conventional wisdom, an organization's past history influences the choices, and organization structure decisions are frequently difficult to make.

Our purpose is to explore the issue of where to locate DSS support. We will discuss the evolution of DSS, especially in regard to how organizations have handled

Reprinted from the *Journal of Management Information Systems,* Vol. 4, No. 1, 1987. By permission of M. E. Sharpe, Inc., Armonk, NY.

it. We will also examine the evolution of end-user computing (EUC) because it has many parallels with DSS and offers an emerging placement alternative. In order to evaluate the placement alternatives, their advantages and disadvantages are considered. Given this background, we will explore the end-user services alternative and describe how one company, the Oglethorpe Power Corporation of Atlanta, Georgia, is organized. The discussion and case study should help senior-level information systems managers and executives understand the issues and alternatives which exist and stimulate researchers to investigate this relatively unexplored area.

DSS AND *EUC*: PARALLEL LINES OF EVOLUTION

DSS activity can be traced to the late 1960s when the first decision support systems began to appear [9]. Their emergence can be associated with hardware and software advances (e.g., timesharing terminals) and the realization that traditional management information systems (MIS) or operations research/management science (OR/MS) approaches to supporting poorly structured decision making were unlikely to succeed. During the early to mid 1970s there were further hardware and, especially, software advances (e.g., DSS generators) and the conceptual foundation (e.g., iterative design) for DSS was laid. From the late 1970s to the present, hardware and software advances (e.g., PCs, integrated software packages) facilitated DSS application development and an increasing number of books, articles, and conferences spread the DSS doctrine.

Today, DSS activity may be found in most large organizations. This activity can have a variety of origins, it can change over time, and different organizational units may be involved with it. However, as DSS activity spreads in an organization, there is normally a growing awareness that DSS efforts need formal organizational support. This typically results in one or more organizational units assuming DSS responsibilities. Independent of which choice(s) is (are) made, responsibility for the activities listed in Table 14.1 needs to be assumed. The importance of supporting these activities by one or more groups tends to change over time as DSS activity in an organization moves through the stages of growth [3, 5].

During the same timeframe, end-user computing was developing. The first end users were in engineering where direct access to the computer made it possible to avoid

TABLE 14.1   Responsibilities of a Decision Support System (DSS) Group

- Plan, organize, staff, direct, and control DSS activities
- Provide hardware, software, and data
- Promote the use of DSS
- Build DSS for end users
- Conduct training programs
- Provide DSS consulting services
- Evaluate DSS hardware and software products
- Provide technical support

the delays and backlogs of formal development. The engineering departments had a well-defined organizational structure and charter, an established power base, access to financial resources, and trained personnel and could often acquire their own computing equipment. The engineers also had the aptitude and inclination to support themselves.

Business-oriented EUC did not appear until the early 1970s. At this point, the backlog of requests was intolerable, hardware and software advances were such that business end users were better able to address their own needs, and colleges were producing more computer literate graduates. Even so, business-oriented EUC did not advance rapidly due to the nature of the end users. They often did not have the attitude, aptitude, and training to support themselves as did the engineers.

Near the end of the 1970s, software and hardware developments, as well as vendor attitudes, combined to make resources, support, and training available. This occurred at a time when the data services department and company management began to recognize the value of EUC and as data services became less and less able to respond to the demand for application development. Not all users gained access and support through the usual path to the firm's computer. Many sought faster routes through the purchase of packaged software, the use of outside timesharing services, and the departmental purchase of personal computers. In each case, the user's objective was to gain access to the computer and computer-resident data to make queries, analyze data, and generate reports.

The establishment of formal EUC support groups did not occur until the early 1980s. Unlike that of DSS, EUC support customarily comes from designated members of the application development department, who work with technical services and data administration for the users. Part of the impetus to formally support end users was to reduce the expenditures for outside timesharing services and to control the purchase of personal computers. As formal EUC support developed, both of these practices have either declined or been more generally controlled [4]. Table 14.2 lists the responsibilities of an EUC support group.

Many organizations are making EUC support groups full-fledged brothers to technical support, application development, and operations. There are many advantages to this organizational arrangement. It provides a central, visible place where end users can go for a variety of support. When end users seek support, they find personnel with the right mix of education, experience, and personal attributes. The existence of an EUC support group naturally separates those development tasks which

TABLE 14.2   Responsibilities of an End-User Computing Group

- Plan, support, market, and control end-user computing
- Provide consulting and troubleshooting services
- Conduct end-user training
- Support end users in interfacing with other data processing departments
- Help provide access to corporate data
- Perform hardware and software evaluations
- Assist in acquiring and installing hardware
- Promote aspects of security

are large, complex, lengthy, and costly and which are best handled by IS development from those which are small, simple, quick, or hard to cost-justify and which can be best handled by end users given appropriate support. It also reduces interruptions to other IS personnel by end users.

As one considers the responsibilities of DSS and EUC groups, many similarities are seen in the support services that each provides. These similarities suggest the possibility that both types of support might be provided by a common organizational unit. Though this general concept has its merits, the differences between DSS and EUC groups must be considered before any support is organized. These issues are discussed next as the various placement alternatives for DSS support are explored.

DSS ORGANIZATIONAL PLACEMENT

Organizations use a variety of organizational placements for DSS. Some placements remain where they began originally. At the other extreme, some placements reflect careful thought and consideration. For example, one company's financial planning group used a financial planning language for application development and became the major source of DSS support in the organization. At another company, a decision support systems unit was created to lead the organization's DSS efforts.

There is no organizational placement for DSS which is best for all organizations. Each alternative has pros and cons which need to be considered in light of an organization's past and current situation. As with many organizational structure decisions, a number of alternatives can be used if appropriate care is taken.

An organization can choose to centralize or distribute DSS responsibilities. In the first case, a single organizational unit is charged with the responsibility for formally supporting DSS. In the latter case, DSS responsibilities are spread over several organizational units. Once again, each alternative is potentially viable. However, a danger with distributing DSS responsibilities is that important DSS activities may be neglected.

Sprague and Carlson [10] suggest a number of origins for DSS groups in organizations:

1. a special purpose team of applications systems analysts,
2. a reoriented tools group,
3. a management science or operations research group,
4. a planning department, and
5. a staff analysis group from one of the functional areas.

Each of these origins can become an organization's primary DSS support group. There are also other possibilities:

6. a formally chartered DSS group,
7. the information center, and
8. a DSS group within end-user services.

There is some evidence that shows which alternatives are most common in organizations. In view of empirical data and the authors' own observations, a planning department or specialized staff analysis group seems to be the most popular choices [6]. There is no reason to believe, however, that the most popular current placements will remain the same over time given the speed with which computer-related activities change.

There are advantages and disadvantages to the various placement alternatives. Several of the alternatives are grouped together because of their similarities. Only the most distinguishing advantages and disadvantages are discussed in order to highlight the differences among the alternatives.

Alternatives 1–2: Applications Systems Analysts and Reoriented Tools Groups

Alternatives 1–2 involve placing DSS support in the hands of data-processing professionals. There are several advantages to this choice. Personnel in these groups are skilled in the use of computer hardware and software technology, are experienced in developing computer applications, and are capable of providing strong technical support.

There are also disadvantages with this selection. Data-processing professionals tend to be oriented toward traditional information systems methods and applications, and their training and experience may have limited transferability to DSS work. Also the group does not contain the mix of personnel with the skills needed for supporting DSS activities. They may only have a limited understanding of the nature of the decisions faced by managers and functional area personnel. They may speak in jargon alien to many potential users. For these reasons, they do not enjoy the confidence of management and functional area users. For most organizations, the disadvantages of alternatives 1–2 outweigh the advantages.

Alternative 3: Operations Research/Management Science Groups

Operations research/management science (OR/MS) groups are highly skilled in modeling and providing computer-based decision support. Unfortunately, many OR/MS groups are not held in high regard by management. The OR/MS people and their methods seem remote from the problems and decisions in the functional areas. In fact, the trend in many organizations is to distribute rather than centralize OR/MS talent [12]. Traditional OR/MS approaches are best suited for structured decision making rather than the semistructured and unstructured decision making which characterizes DSS. Their organizational ties to data services may be loose, and OR/MS personnel also are frequently criticized for their specialized jargon.

Once again the disadvantages outweigh the advantages. However, we should point out that the OR/MS field is reconsidering its usefulness and organizational role. These deliberations may produce a new orientation more closely associated with the DSS approach. If this happens, the disadvantages associated with the OR/MS alternative would decrease.

Alternatives 4–5: Planning Departments and Staff Analysis Groups

Alternatives 4–5 (planning departments and staff analysis groups) are similar in that both are specialized staff groups. Both are also popular choices for housing DSS activities. They have the advantage of being where many of the potential DSS applications are located. They have frequent contact with management and functional area personnel. Their mindset is that of an end user, and they speak in the language of potential DSS users.

There are also disadvantages associated with this choice. The interest of planning departments and staff analysis groups in DSS may be greater in their own applications than in the applications of other potential users. They may have trouble perceiving themselves as a DSS support group and, hence, ready to accept the full range of DSS support responsibilities. They are likely to be relatively weak in their ability to provide technical support and may have only weak ties to the data services department.

Though these are popular choices for housing DSS work, there are significant problems with these alternatives. The most serious are a possible lack of support for DSS efforts outside of the group and the group's low visibility as a focal point for DSS activities.

Alternative 6: Formally Chartered DSS Groups

Some organizations have created new, formally chartered organizational units responsible for DSS activities. This approach has a number of appeals. A staff can be assembled with the correct combination of skills necessary for DSS work, including the ability to communicate effectively with users. A range of DSS support responsibilities is easily assigned to the group, and they can take an organization-wide approach to DSS.

The disadvantages are less obvious than with the other alternatives, but they do exist. As a new, small, specialized staff group, they may not have a strong base of political support. Depending on their placement in the organization's structure, they may not be highly visible to potential users. In an ideal arrangement for fostering DSS, the DSS group should be placed high in the organization's structure and support upper management. However, this arrangement is not always easy to sell to top management because management may be uncertain about what DSS has to offer and may feel that DSS is just another set of computer applications. Also, the appealing nature of their work and their potential contacts with top management and other important organizational personnel may foster resentment from the data services group.

The separate DSS group has considerable appeal. Safeguards need to be installed, however, to minimize disadvantages.

Alternative 7: Information Centers

Many organizations have created information centers (IC) to formally support end-user computing. Their responsibilities are similar to those listed for an EUC group. Both groups have administrative responsibilities, provide consulting services, supply technical support, evaluate hardware and software products, and provide training. Consequently, it makes sense to consider placing DSS activities in the information center. There are other points in favor of this placement alternative. It is more efficient to have a single group. Information centers are well received, highly visible, and familiar with organization-wide information needs. They tend to be service-oriented and capable of serving a variety of computing and information needs.

The use of the information center has disadvantages that, like those of the formally chartered DSS group, may not be obvious immediately. Information centers tend to be understaffed relative to the amount of work and customer base they support. The backgrounds, educational levels, and training of IC and DSS groups differ. IC staff support to top management may be limited, and they may be more familiar with tools than with potential applications.

Information centers ultimately may be an attractive home for DSS activities. To date, there is little evidence about how well this alternative is working. There is another alternative, however, that has the advantages of the IC but fewer of the disadvantages.

Alternative 8: A DSS Group within End-User Services

The last alternative, and one that we believe has great potential, is the end-user services (EUS) group. With this organizational arrangement, the DSS group becomes a department within EUS along with the IC and other user support staffs. This alternative has many advantages, overcomes most of the disadvantages associated with the other alternatives, and is compatible with current trends in providing computer services. EUS advantages include high visibility, accessibility, a formal organization charter, support for fast application development, a management and a functional area orientation, a firm base of support, and close ties to data services.

Separating DSS from the IC eliminates many of the disadvantages of an IC placement. The DSS group would not be affected by the existing workload of IC staffs. The DSS staff would have the right mix of education, skills, and experience. This staff could possess an exceptionally strong management and functional area orientation. They would have the time, opportunity, and charter to stay current with DSS developments.

There are some disadvantages to this placement alternative. Because placement of an end-user services group in the overall organization structure is relatively low, upper management may not fully perceive and utilize this support. This problem might be reduced, however, by aggressive promotion of DSS services. Another potential problem is how the data services group treats the DSS group. There may be jealousy within the application development department because of the attractiveness of DSS work and the contacts that such work provides throughout the organization. Data services management might fail to recognize the contribution of DSS to the organization because of the difficulty of measuring many of the benefits of DSS. One key to managing this potential problem is to make data services management understand the role and value of DSS to an organization. Another is to protect the DSS group.

The following case study illustrates the value of an end-user services group for the support of DSS as well as more generic end-user computing activities.

THE OGLETHORPE POWER CORPORATION

Oglethorpe Power Corporation (OPC) is a not-for-profit power supply cooperative formed in 1974 to provide electricity to 39 of Georgia's 42 consumer-owned Electric Membership Corporations (EMCs). These EMCs serve businesses, farms, homes, and institutions in many of Georgia's rural and suburban areas. Oglethorpe Power's member-EMCs provide electricity to more than 1.6 million Georgians living in about 71% of the state's geographic area.

The corporation employs more than 400 people, 40 of whom are in the MIS department. The end-user services group is a relatively recent addition to the MIS organization. It is a result of splitting the systems development group to provide better management and control of both operational and end-user-developed applications and to formally acknowledge the difference in these applications. End-user services contains three separate functions: corporate model, decision support systems, and the information center. The corporate model and decision support systems groups support OPC's efforts at modeling the demand and supply of electrical energy and translating this analysis into financial terms. The information center provides the classic (i.e., the IBM concept) set of IC services. Figure 14.1 shows the present organization structure for supporting EUC.

Corporate Models

Work on a corporate planning model was begun in 1977. A team of financial planners, engineers, and consultants used SIMPLAN in creating it. The model was first used by the planning department in 1979.

The corporate model unit consists of three people who assist in support and development. The model is updated on a project basis using a team consisting of EUS

FIGURE 14.1 Organization Structure for Supporting End-User Computing

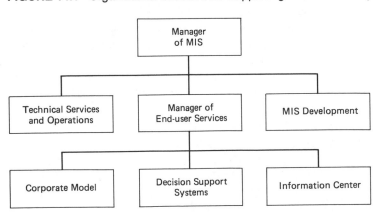

personnel and staff from the user department. The model is especially important to the functioning of the planning department.

Decision Support Systems

The three members of the DSS staff support the development of DSS by end users. Personnel from planning, contracts, and finance are the primary users of DSS. Most of the DSS applications are for planning purposes. As the manager of MIS has said, "Planning is our major emphasis."

A variety of services are provided by the DSS staff. Most DSS applications at OPC are detailed, complex, and mainframe-oriented. This requires that the DSS staff works closely with end users who are the primary DSS developers. Training must be provided for the use of products such as XSIM, Easytrieve, SIMPLAN, Tel-a-graph, SAS, and Megacalc. Many of the DSS applications utilize large amounts of historical data, and users frequently need assistance in accessing this data. The DSS staff provides technical support in utilizing the mainframe. It also assists in model development.

Information Center

The information center is staffed by two individuals who provide classic IC services. Most of the IC work is PC-oriented and requires no support for modeling efforts. Much of the staff's time is spent answering end users' questions. Lotus 1-2-3, Symphony, dBase III, and a variety of specialized software are used, and training is provided on the use of these products. Users frequently require assistance in obtaining needed data. The IC is expanding in size and scope, and the IC staff is responsible for managing this growth. New products must be evaluated, purchased, installed, and implemented.

How It Is Working

The organizational arrangements at OPC for supporting DSS are working out well. Both the manager of MIS and end users feel that strong DSS support is being provided. The DSS group has an organizational charter to help users develop their own DSS applications. An appropriate range of DSS services is being provided. The group is visible within the organization. Its separation from the IC staff allows the group to focus its attention on DSS activities. The EUS staff is received well by the user community. In a recent survey, EUS in general and DSS in particular received good grades from the people they support.

CONCLUSION

Many organizations are reorganizing for the delivery of information systems products and services. This change is the result of growing awareness that the role of the data services organization is moving from that of a provider of products to a supplier of products *and* services. With the likelihood that end-user computing will become the dominant form of computing in the 1990s [7], this added attention to the service dimension is entirely appropriate. In order to better accommodate EUC, many organizations are adding end-user computing support groups to the systems development, operations, and technical support departments within the data services department.

Information systems applications can be categorized as operational, end-user-developed, and third-environment [7]. Operational applications are company wide, use corporate data, and serve many users. These are the types of applications developed by IS professionals. End-user-developed applications are found in organizational sub-units, use private as well as corporate data, and serve one or only a few users. Third-environment applications are departmental, employ data from one or only a few departments, and serve users at the same level. The development of these applications is jointly shared by end users and IS professionals.

End-user services groups within data services support EUC and third-environment application development. In order to provide this support, several departments may be placed within EUS. The most common, of course, is the information center. Other logical candidates include office automation and decision support systems because of the nature of the applications they support.

Eight organization placement alternatives for DSS have been discussed. The major advantages and disadvantages associated with each alternative are summarized in Table 14.3. We have argued for placing DSS in a separate department within data services, called end-user services. This alternative currently is being used quite well by the Oglethorpe Power Corporation, as the case study showed.

The placement of DSS support in a separate group within end-user services is a new development. Not only does it suggest an interesting option for MIS managers, but it also provides a new area for MIS researchers. In a few years we should better understand how this placement alternative is working out.*

TABLE 14.3   The Advantages and Disadvantages of Decision Support Systems (DSS) Organization Placement Alternatives

DSS ALTERNATIVES 1–2: APPLICATIONS SYSTEMS ANALYSTS AND REORIENTED TOOLS GROUPS

Advantages	Disadvantages
Skilled in the use of computer hardware and software technology	Oriented toward traditional IS applications and methods
Experienced in application development	Staff does not have an appropriate mix of backgrounds and experiences
Capable of providing strong technical support	Not familiar with many potential applications

*The authors would like to thank Margaret Schultz, manager of MIS at Oglethorpe Power Corporation, for providing the information on which this case is based.

TABLE 14.3   (Continued)

DSS *ALTERNATIVE 3: OPERATIONS RESEARCH/MANAGEMENT SCIENCE GROUPS*

Advantages	*Disadvantages*
Skilled in the use of models	May be more oriented toward providing solutions rather than supporting decision making
Experienced in providing computer-based support	May not have the confidence of management and functional area users
	May not communicate in terms understandable to managers and functional area users
	Has only loose ties to IS

DSS *ALTERNATIVES 4–5: PLANNING DEPARTMENTS AND STAFF ANALYSIS GROUPS*

Advantages	*Disadvantages*
Many DSS applications are located here	May not be as interested in other DSS applications as in their own
High level of contact with management and functional area users	May not perceive themselves as having responsibility for the full range of DSS support responsibilities
Communicates in the language of managers and functional area users	May offer only weak technical support

---

DSS *ALTERNATIVE 6: FORMALLY CHARTERED DSS GROUPS*

Advantages	*Disadvantages*
The staff has the appropriate mix of skills for performing DSS work	May not have a firm base of support
Understands the role and nature of DSS	May not be highly visible in the organization
Fully responsible for supporting DSS activities	May be resented by IS
Can take an organization-wide approach to supporting DSS	

DSS *ALTERNATIVE 7: INFORMATION CENTERS (ICs)*

Advantages	*Disadvantages*
High visibility with management and functional area users	May be understaffed for supporting DSS
Many of the responsibilities of ICs correspond with DSS responsibilities	The staff typically does not have the appropriate mix of background and experiences

TABLE 14.3 (Continued)

DSS ALTERNATIVE 7: INFORMATION CENTERS (ICs) (Continued)

Advantages	*Disadvantages*
Very accessible to managers and functional area users	May have limited contact with top management
Good technical support for DSS	Staff may be unfamiliar with potential applications
Familiar with organization-wide information needs	
Has a service orientation	

DSS ALTERNATIVE 8: A DSS GROUP WITHIN END-USER SERVICES

Advantages	*Disadvantages*
High visibility with management and functional area users	May be too much under the influence of data services
Many of the responsibilities of EUC correspond with DSS responsibilities	Low organization placement may limit its use by top management
Very accessible to managers and functional area users	
A firm base of support	
Good technical support for DSS	

QUESTIONS

1. It appears that the responsibilities of the DSS and end-user support groups are very similar. What are the important characteristics that differentiate them?
2. Eight alternatives are given for the support of DSS in an organization. One view is that the groups can be placed on a continuum ranging from a technical to a managerial orientation. Draw this continuum and place the eight groups in their proper places. (If appropriate, you may wish to place some of them at a vertical distance from the horizontal continuum line to show an additional dimension.)
3. Discuss the advantages and the disadvantages of the organization structure shown in Figure 14.1.
4. Potentially, DSS could be developed at any level of the organization—that is, operational, management control, or strategic. Would different qualities or resources be required to support the building of DSS at these different levels? If so, what would they be?

REFERENCES

1. ALLOWAY, R. M., AND QUILLARD, J.A.   User managers' systems needs. *MIS Quarterly,* 7, 2 (June 1983), 27–41.

2. EDELMAN, F.   The management of information resources—A challenge for American business. *MIS Quarterly,* 5, 1 (March 1981), 17–27.

3. GIBSON, C. F., AND NOLAN, R. L.   Managing the four stages of EDP growth. *Harvard Business Review,* 52, 1 (January–February 1974), 76–88.

4. HARRAR, G.   Information center, the user's report. *Computerworld* (December 26, 1983–January 2, 1984), 70–74.

5. HENDERSON, J. C., AND TREACY, M. E.   Managing end user computing. CISR working paper No. 114. Massachusetts Institute of Technology Center for Information Systems Research, Cambridge, MA, May 1984.

6. HOGUE, J. T., AND WATSON, H. J.   Management's role in the approval and administration of decision support systems. *MIS Quarterly,* 7, 2, (June 1983), 15–26.

7. ROCKART, J. F., AND FLANNERY, L. S.   The management of end user computing—A research perspective. CISR working paper No. 100, Massachusetts Institute of Technology, Cambridge, MA, February 1983.

8. ROSENBERGER, R. B.   The productivity impacts of an information center on application development. *Proceedings GUIDE 53.* Dallas, TX, 1981, 918–932.

9. SCOTT MORTON, M. S.   Management decision systems: Computer based support for decision making. Division of Research, Harvard University, Cambridge, MA, 1971.

10. SPRAGUE, R. H., JR., AND CARLSON, E. D. *Building Effective Decision Support Systems.* Englewood Cliffs, NJ: Prentice Hall, 1982.

11. TARGLER, R.   Information center. *Information Processing,* 2, 1 (March 1983), 12–14.

12. THOMAS, G., AND DA COSTA, J. A.   sample survey of corporate operations research. *Interfaces* (August 1979), 103–111.

15

ISSUE-BASED DECISION SUPPORT SYSTEMS FOR THE EGYPTIAN CABINET

Omar A. El Sawy,
Hisham El Sherif

THE CHALLENGE OF PROVIDING INFORMATION AND DECISION SUPPORT FOR STRATEGIC DECISION-MAKING PROCESSES

The effectiveness of strategic decisions can have enormous impacts on organizations and their successful functioning. Consequently, it is a critical priority for information systems professionals to effectively provide organizations with information and decision support systems that support and enhance the strategic decision-making process. The process of managing the design and delivery of such systems is what we report and examine in this article.

Information systems professionals generally agree that—despite the advances in the design and implementation of decision support systems (DSS) in the last decade, despite the rapid strides in information technology capabilities, despite the

Reprinted by special permission of the *MIS Quarterly,* Volume 12, Number 4, December 1988. Copyright 1988 by the Society for Information Management and the Management Information Systems Research Center.

relatively widespread acceptance of DSS by professionals and middle managers, and even despite the recent emergence of executive information systems (EIS)—the provision of effective DSS for strategic decision making remains a challenge that we have yet to overcome. While there are examples of successful DSS used for strategic decision making by top managers in such decision contexts as mergers and acquisitions, plant location, and capital expenditures, they tend to focus on limited well-structured phases of specific decisions. However, when it comes to supporting the whole strategic decision-making process over time with competing and changing strategic issues, multiple decisions, and changing participants, we have made much less progress. Our motivation here is to contribute one more step toward overcoming that challenge.

A large part of the challenge comes from the messy and complex nature of the strategic decision-making process itself and the accompanying encumbrances that it brings to the DSS design and delivery situation:

- Strategic decision making is a murky, ill-structured process that can be drawn out over weeks and months, yet often requires very rapid response capabilities in crisis situations.

- Strategic decision making is usually a group effort rather than an individual one, and it involves activities such as cooperative ideation, cooperative problem solving, conflict resolution, negotiation, crisis management, and consensus building (Gray, 1988).

- Strategic decision making in turbulent and dynamic environments is accompanied by a large environmental scanning component which has its own information requirements for early warning about potential discontinuities, surprises, threats, and opportunities (El Sawy, 1985).

- A strategic decision involves multiple stakeholders with different implicit assumptions that need to be surfaced and made explicit (Mason and Mitroff, 1981).

- Strategy formation in dynamic environments takes place in a somewhat less deliberate and a much more emergent fashion than conventional descriptions of strategic management suggest, bringing with it a large serendipitous discovery component whose support requirements are difficult to forecast (Mintzberg and Waters, 1985).

- Since a large proportion of information needed for strategic decision making comes from a virtually unlimited external environment, the key problem that the decision maker faces is information overload with multiple and conflicting interpretations, rather than solely the absence of relevant information (Zmud, 1986).

- Much of the information that is used for strategic decisions is qualitative, verbal, and poorly recorded.

- Because the stakes in strategic decision making are very high, there is much more situational vulnerability to both political maneuvering and stressed emotional behavior, which may call for additional considerations in DSS implementation.

Another part of the challenge comes from the nature of the decision maker who typically engages in the strategic decision-making process as one of the central participants. He or she is usually:

- A top manager, executive, or policymaker whose time is very valuable.
- Older and more resistant to technological change.
- Comfortable relying on intuition and gut feeling.
- Unwilling to spend time learning to personally use computer-based DSS.
- Powerful enough to require and enforce quick response to his or her demands.

The call for designing and delivering DSS for such a demanding class of decision-making situation and decision maker has not gone unheeded in the information systems community. Various efforts have been made to advance the state of the art, each of which has moved us closer toward overcoming that challenge. These include:

- Focusing on the decision maker and providing generalized support tailored to senior executives in the form of EIS (see Houdeshel and Watson, 1987, for a description of the MIDS system at Lockheed-Georgia; Rockart and DeLong, 1988).
- Focusing on the provision of EIS generators with user-seductive technology platforms suited to executives with fancy graphics, pop-up menus, touchscreens, and optical mice (Paller, 1988; typical examples include products from software vendors such as Comshare, Execucom, and Pilot).
- Focusing on better understanding of the decision context (see Stabell, 1983, who advocates "bringing the D back into DSS").
- Focusing on information requirements determination methodologies that foster the fit between the executive decision maker and the strategic decision context (Henderson, Rockart, and Sifonis, 1987).
- Focusing on the structuring of fit between the decision context and the decision makers by building decision rooms and group decision support systems (Gray, 1987).
- Focusing on the simultaneous advancement of the "squeakiest wheels" in DSS design and implementation (see Keen, 1987, and his call to action for "a redressing of the balance between D, S, and S").

The approach that we take in this work builds on the experiences gained from the above. However, our approach tries to make progress toward overcoming this challenge through focusing on the process of *managing* the design and delivery of DSS while preserving the fit among the decision makers, the form of support provided, and the technologies used in the context of an ongoing strategic decision-making context. Our application context is the cabinet of Egypt.

DECISION MAKING IN THE EGYPTIAN CABINET

The Egyptian Cabinet comprises the prime minister, thirty-two ministers, and four sectoral ministerial committees assisted by staff. Decision making at the cabinet level addresses a variety of national socioeconomic and infrastructural concerns, such as reducing the deficit in the balance of payments and national budget, debt management, performance improvement of public sector organizations, ways of promoting the development of small- and medium-scale private industries, and the allocation of resources to solve urban housing problems and overpopulation.

Depending on the scope, urgency, and criticality of an issue, it is addressed either through the ministerial committees or by the full cabinet. The decision-making process involves much debate and group discussion, requires much preparation of position papers and studies, and is subject to public accountability and media attention. A simplified view of the cabinet decision-making process showing key participants, deliberation forums, and information flows is shown in Figure 15.1.

FIGURE 15.1 The Cabinet Decision-making Process before IDSC

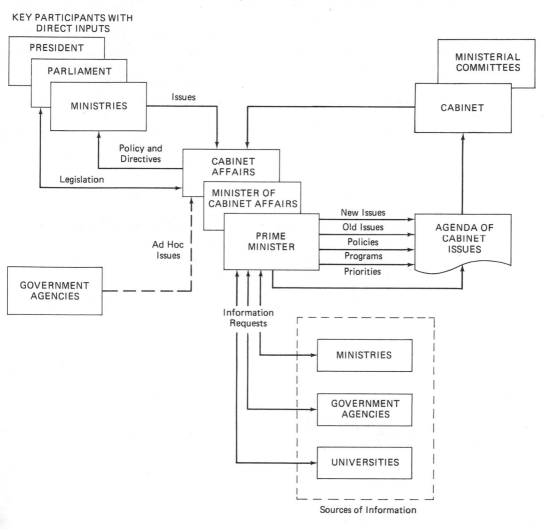

As is the case with any decision-making setting, the cabinet has its own jargon and mental constructions. Labels indicative of deliberate structured logic (such as objectives, outcomes, directives, and decrees) and rational decision making (such as decisions, alternatives, choices, problems, and solutions) are used in both written and oral communication. However, a closer examination of those reveals that the decision-making process is best and most comfortably viewed by the participants as a process of attention to sets of *issues* with varying and shifting priorities; the cabinet world is chunked primarily into issues, rather than decisions. As indicated in Figure 15.1 by the closed loops, sets of issues circulate continuously and are managed over time. They enter and exit circulation through the key participants. When some of them are resolved (or dissolved) by decisions, actions, political maneuvering, or environmental shifts, they fade from circulation. Similarly, they can reappear and also become more salient. Of course, decisions are made, but the focal point of deliberation is the issue rather than the one of many decisions made around it.

The decisions around issues considered by the cabinet are usually complex, ill-structured, interdependent, and multisectoral, with strategic impacts at the national, regional, and international levels. The nature of the information environment can be characterized as one that is data rich but information poor, in which there is an overload of information of questionable reliability, which often yields multiple and murky interpretations, and which is often qualitative and disjointed. The cabinet is the epitome of strategic decision making at the group level under complex and turbulent conditions which cries out for information and decision support systems (IS/DSS).

After Egypt's peace agreement with Israel, the cabinet of Egypt embarked on a program of economic revival and was faced with formidable infrastructural and socioeconomic development challenges in the early 1980s. In addition, the turbulence of the regional and international economy and politics was causing major shifts in Egypt's traditional sources of GNP such as Suez Canal revenues, remittances from Egyptians working in oil-rich countries, and tourism. This created a heightened awareness of the increasing complexity of the environment and the vulnerability of static plans and slow decision making at the strategic level. It also brought into focus the critical importance of making available in an integrated form the information needed for supporting the decision-making process of the cabinet through the use of the most appropriate information technologies and services. In 1985, as part of a broader intensive national plan for administrative development, an information systems project for the cabinet was initiated, and it has evolved into what is now the Information and Decision Support Center (IDSC) for the cabinet.

THE CABINET INFORMATION AND DECISION SUPPORT CENTER (*IDSC*)

Since its inception, the IDSC was guided by three strategic objectives. First and foremost was the development of information and decision support systems (IS/DSS) for the cabinet and top policymakers in Egypt. Second was to support the establishment of end-user–managed information and decision support centers in the individual ministries. Third and more indirect was to encourage, support, and initiate informatics projects that would accelerate the development of Egyptian government ministries and agencies.

To achieve these strategic objectives, a trilevel architecture for information infrastructure and decision support was conceived:

- IDSC level   Building of IDSC base at the cabinet to provide a focal point for cabinet issues support, information and decision support, multisectoral analysis, and integration.

- National nodes level   Linking to and/or supporting the building of local sources of information and decision support at ministries and national agencies.

- International level   Extending telecommunications access to international sources of information and major databases worldwide.

As of November 1985, the IDSC started providing information and decision support services for the cabinet and developing this trilevel architecture. Figure 15.2 shows the positioning of the IDSC as a facilitative conduit, integrator, and expediter of information from various sources to the cabinet. New information sources such as sectoral information centers and international databases have been added, and since then, the computer-based component has been growing.

The IDSC has evolved rapidly from a three-person start-up with a handful of personal computers to an organization of over 150 people in mid-1988, which provides an array of information and decision support services specifically targeted to the strategic decision-making level. It has since implemented twenty-eight IS/DSS projects. Learning how to effectively provide information and decision support for strategic decisions in the cabinet context while managing rapid growth and response to an impatient and increasing service demand—and simultaneously developing the poor information and technological infrastructure of Egyptian government organizations—provided many managerial, technological, and contextual challenges for the IDSC.

With respect to the design and delivery of IS/DSS for cabinet decision making, the IDSC was convinced that not only was there a need for a process different from that used for traditional DSS, but that it was also important to create an organization design that could facilitate the effective management of such services. Initially, the IDSC thought that the answers were "out there somewhere" and sought comparative information from other countries with similar projects. While these inputs were very helpful, it became painfully obvious to the IDSC that it would have to devise both the design and delivery process and the organizational design through its own contextual learning in the Egyptian cabinet strategic decision-making environment.

To deal with this challenge, the IDSC's strategy had several components. First, to maximize the chances of implementation success, it saw the need to improve the fit among the users in their decision-making context, the form of support provided, and

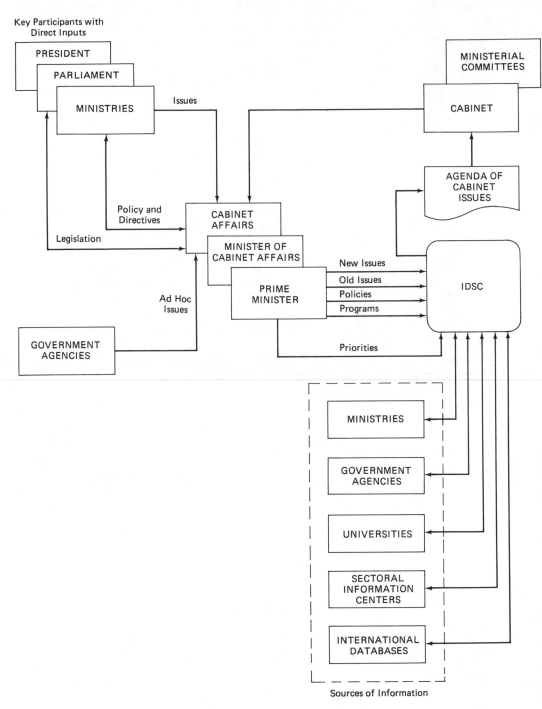

FIGURE 15.2 The Cabinet Decision-making Process after IDSC

TABLE 15.1   Examples of Contextual Fit Improvement Strategies Used by IDSC

DESCRIPTION	EFFECTS
Reverse Distributed Processing Approach for developing technology infrastructure which started with islands of personal computers, then linked them together and built a network infra-structure and finally added a mainframe.	Bridged user-technology gap and allowed accelerated implementation of applications. There are now 110 PCs and a data network of national nodes at various ministries.
Two-Tiered Teams IDSC design team always includes two two types of members: *One who is technically competent (typically a young college graduate) *Another who is fully experienced with the bureaucracy (an older person with government experience)	Bridged translation gap between DSS builders and typical bureaucrats whose inputs are sought and needed. Improved communication and minimized risk of technical failures.
Arabization of Software Linguistic and cultural adaptation of user interfaces to the Egyptian decision-making environment. The IDSC has also championed incentives for a "Pyramids Technology Valley" project for software start-ups.	Bridged user-application gap. Custom applications and many standard tools (such as dBase III, Lotus 1-2-3, FOCUS) are fully Arabized. Bilingual (English/Arabic) electronic mail in beta test.
Chauffeured IS/DSS Use Use of staff intermediaries for supporting senior policymakers, rather than having him or her directly online.	Kept focus on providing support for strategic decision making, rather than draining IDSC resources in supporting nonstrategic office applications.

the technologies used (examples of ways that the IDSC used for contextual fit improvement are shown in Table 15.1). Second, it would use an iterative prototyping strategy for IS/DSS design and delivery. Third, the organizational design would emerge and develop as the process for managing the design and delivery of IS/DSS became more apparent.

The IS/DSS design and delivery process was initially conceived as shown in Figure 15.3. While deliberation inside the cabinet decision-making forum revolves around issues, formal communications outside it are expressed in terms of policies, programs, and objectives. Thus, IS/DSS project definitions are handed down to the IDSC in either a broad mission-driven form (such as "we need to build a DSS to help formulate, develop, and monitor the industrial sector strategic and tactical plans") or

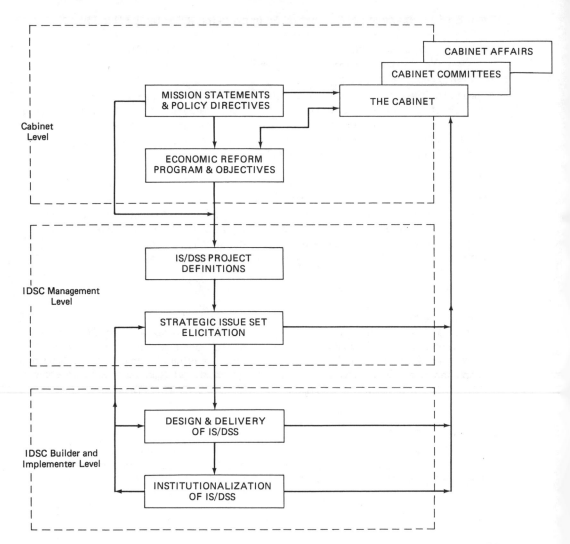

FIGURE 15.3 Supporting and Shaping Cabinet Strategic Decision Making through IS/DSS

in a directive data-driven form (such as "we want you to establish an information base about all companies in the industrial sector in Egypt"). At the IDSC management level, this is translated through interactions with policymakers to a set of better articulated strategic issues around which IS/DSS are defined. Design, delivery, and in-stitutionalization are carried out at the IDSC builder and implementer level as the process goes through iterative prototyping cycles. The tactical details of this procedure, its requisite management processes, and supporting organizational design evolved as more was learned from each successive IS/DSS project.

LEARNING ABOUT THE MANAGEMENT OF *DSS* FOR STRATEGIC DECISION MAKING THROUGH ILLUSTRATIVE *IDSC* PROJECTS

Episodes from five example IS/DSS projects from the IDSC experience are presented to illustrate the generic lessons that were learned for managing the design and delivery of DSS for strategic decision making.

Illustrative Case 1: Customs Tariff Policy Formulation DSS

For many years there was much effort by the cabinet to overhaul a complex customs tariff structure that encompassed too many inconsistent regulations. That concerted effort had evolved into initial agreement on a formulation of three broad reform objectives: a homogeneous consistent tariff structure, increasing revenues to the treasury, and minimum impact on low income groups. In early 1986, the "new customs program" was announced as in prefinal form. But six months later, despite initial agreement and good intentions, interministerial debates and conflicts about policy form and perceived sectoral impacts grew. In June 1986, the services of the IDSC were requested by the cabinet.

A joint IDSC/Ministry of Finance crisis team developed an initial PC-based DSS model using the written tariff reform proposal. The team consisted of thirty-two people: two IDSC managers, two undersecretaries, six builders/implementers, and twenty-two data entry/validation personnel. Data were collected from fragmented sources with difficulty. As development progressed, the team shuttled daily to the six most affected ministries and met with senior policymakers to gather input and feedback and build consensus. Initially, conflicts were sharp, discussions heated, and one-sided theories prevailed. For example, the Ministry of Industry, wanting to encourage local manufacturing, sought to raise import tariffs on auto spare parts. The Ministry of Economy agreed because it would reduce foreign currency expenditures, but the Ministry of Finance disagreed because this would reduce a sizable source of customs revenue.

However, as the model became more explicit through the prototyping effort, the strategic issues were better articulated, assumptions were uncovered, and the impacts of various "what-if" scenarios for structural alternatives were demonstrated with numbers rather than abstract opinions. The focus gradually moved from objection to constructive input and considerate accommodation. After one month of intense effort, a consensus was reached and a new customs tariff policy was in place.

Lessons 1 and 2 for the Management of DSS for Strategic Decision Making

Lesson 1:   Structuring and articulating strategic issues is an integral, critical, and very time-consuming portion of the design/delivery of DSS for strategic decisions. It should be labeled as an explicit "rewardable/billable" activity in the design/delivery cycle. It includes conflict resolution and consensus building and may involve shuttle diplomacy.

> **Lesson 2:** Providing DSS for strategic decision making is most often coupled with both urgency and criticality, making crisis management a frequent mode of operation. This requires an organization design and human resource policy for the support organization that explicitly includes a crisis management component. It is a type of crisis management that has large unexpected variance in tempo and task (i.e., more like a fire department than an overnight package delivery business). The IDSC has added crisis management teams to its organization design (see Figure 15.4). These can be quickly put together in response to crisis requests.

Impacts The customs tariff DSS facilitated a group decision-making process by reducing conflict and promoting consensus by clarifying the trade-offs and potential impacts of tariff structures on individual sectors and on the overall economy. It has proved to be an excellent negotiation tool, and the decision-making process was conducted with more information and less misplaced emotion. It has also made it possible to provide an equitable uniform tariff structure. Furthermore, the originally estimated £E 500 million increase in customs revenues ($1 = about £E 2) were shown by the DSS "what-if" process to be unlikely and that any realistic scenarios would generate about £E 50 million. A year later the actual increase turned out to be £E 56 million.

Illustrative Case 2: Production IS/DSS

Initiated in late 1985 and developed jointly with the General Organization for Industrialization (GOFI), the project was identified by the cabinet as having two main objectives: establishing an information base about all industrial companies in Egypt

FIGURE 15.4 Organization Chart for IDSC

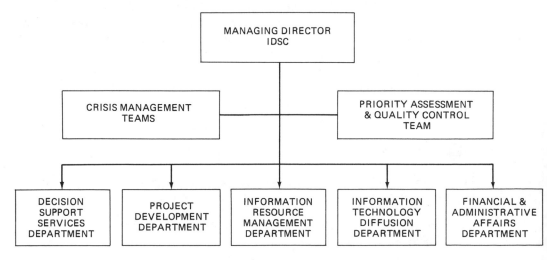

and building a DSS to help formulate, develop, and monitor the industrial sector's strategic and tactical plans. The IDSC's data collection efforts from four main data centers (one at GOFI) were met with subject databases with incomparable structures, nonstandardized data definitions, and contradictory definitional assumptions. Furthermore, examination of redundant data indicated uneven updating and unreliable integrity. Rebuilding of an integrated database was a massive effort that detracted from decision support.

This prompted the IDSC to have separate decision support services (DSSV) and project development (PD) departments (see Figure 15.4). DSSV provides frontline decision support services to the cabinet, and is staffed by about twenty-five multidisciplinary user consultants. If an IS/DSS project is initiated that requires massive systems development, database building, or infrastructure development at the ministry/agency level, then PD takes over. PD is staffed by project managers, DSS builders/implementers, and application programmers. A third department, information resources management (IRM), provides technical support and manages databases. It comprises technical staff, database administrators, and systems programmers. For better interdepartmental coordination and crisis management peak demands, there is some staff rotation among DSSV, PD, and IRM.

Lesson 3 for the Management of DSS for Strategic Decision Making

Providing information and decision support for strategic decision making often requires much effort in building and integrating databases from diverse extraorganizational sources. The frontline decision support consultants should not get sucked into this activity at the expense of reduced decision support. The organizational design should reflect that.

As the issue-based structuring process moved forward, several other specific strategic issues were articulated. These focused the database building effort on a much smaller extracted database which was built much faster. For example, at one point, the issue of import substitution with local production surfaced as critical and focused database building on imported industrial commodities.

Lesson 4 for the Management of DSS for Strategic Decision Making

The structuring of one strategic issue begets other strategic issues and these can be used to focus the database building effort.

Impacts   A prototype PC-based DSS showed that 248 commodities represented 90 percent ($7 billion) of Egypt's 1985 total commodity imports of which 112 were industrial commodities. That further revealed that ninety-two of these had not been promoted locally by the Ministry of Industry since 1974. Further DSS prototypes showed that eighty-seven commodities out of these ninety-two could be manufactured locally with favorable economics. Based on this diagnosis, the national industrial five-year plan was changed by the cabinet. This diagnostic also resulted in identifying another strategic issue—idle capacity. Using simple bar chart comparisons for each of the eighty-seven commodities that compared local production, idle capacity, and imports, another DSS component allowed the identification of idle and/or underutilized capacities for about 55 percent of public sector industrial companies and the "what-if-fing" of many scenarios.

Because of the initial data reliability problems, this project accentuated the importance of having explicit quality indicators for critical information in IS/DSS. It also brought to the IDSC's attention the importance of decision methods that could enhance the effectiveness of information "beyond the information given." Methods such as the examination and surfacing of critical assumptions underlying the information, transforming data from table to chart form, comparing rates of change, and sensitivity analysis of variables needed to be made more salient to users. To accentuate to users the fact that decision-making effectiveness depends on much more than information, the IDSC made a distinction between information services support and decision methods support within its DSSV organization design (see Figure 15.5). Furthermore, to emphasize the importance of surfacing assumptions, the IDSC has integrated them within its IS/DSS designs and includes an "assumption key" (similar to a help key).

Lesson 5 for the Management of DSS for Strategic Decision Making

It is key to articulate explicitly to users that effective decision making depends on more than information. For decisions around strategic issues, information is usually partial and its quality questionable. Rather than just trying to improve information quality, it may often be more useful to use more decision methods/heuristics on it.

Illustrative Case 3: Debt Management DSS

In its massive effort to rebuild the economy, Egypt has accumulated a staggering foreign debt of $33 billion. Servicing this debt involves pegging sources of funds, renegotiating terms and interest rates, managing payment schedules, and monitoring transactions for over 5,000 loans with a large number of creditor countries, banks, and international agencies. Previously, a decision or renegotiation on a loan payment was done on a case-by-case basis (often through telex responses), data related to each loan were fragmented, global planning for matching sources of funds was not possible, and the aggregate debt portfolio details were not accurately known.

A debt management IS/DSS project was established to centralize and computerize all foreign debt data in the Central Bank of Egypt and to develop a management tool

FIGURE 15.5 Organization Chart for Decision Support Services Department

to support and facilitate the registration, control, and analysis of debt. Over eighteen months a comprehensive debt validated database for government loans and a transaction processing system for debt management was built with DSS capabilities for examining the impacts of different scenarios. The DSS includes a multiperiod forward-looking component that provides overall debt status in the future, and includes "what-if" functions for queries related to such things as refinancing. A rescheduling mo le that allows users to dynamically track and mark status changes on any loan in the tal portfolio has also been added.

Lesson 6 for the Management of DSS for Strategic Decision Making

If recurring decisions are to be made around a strategic issue, there is critical need for setting up a management system for tracking and monitoring changes in the critical parameters of the issue.

The rescheduling activities carried out during the last eight months of 1987 showed that it is still difficult to maintain and manage the loans database, especially with dispersed negotiation for 5,000 loans. This project also experienced technical difficulties that eventually were resolved but that caused delay and aggravation. These included a classic transaction processing situation: Off-the-shelf mainframe software is adapted but does not deliver, modification efforts delayed, sphagetti code and inadequate documentation, switch to PC-based system, prototype appears quickly and works but much too slowly.

Lesson 7 for the Management of DSS for Strategic Decision Making

The dynamic tracking component of an issue-based DSS has the usual technical demands of transaction processing systems and requires more demanding technological capabilities.

Impacts   However, technical performance problems, while frustrating, did not hinder the debt management DSS from having strategic impacts. Rescheduling negotiations with fourteen countries have been smoothly managed because of the detailed convincing information support made available to negotiators (such as preemptive assessment of alternatives). A key impact on the strategic decision-making process is that loans are now viewed as part of a dynamic and integrated portfolio rather than being managed on an isolated case-by-case basis.

Illustrative Case 4: Electricity DSS

"I would like to have a computer system on my desk" was the triggering statement by the minister of electricity and energy at a meeting in August 1987 to which the IDSC director was summoned. The seemingly symbolic statement was quickly followed by: "The cost of providing electricity is increasingly contributing to the deficit in the national budget and balance of payments. Most investment in electric power generation requires foreign currency. Besides, the current tariff structure still requires government subsidies."

It was clear that there was a set of strategic issues around which an IS/DSS was needed, and there was a top policymaker who was championing it. Again, the need had been expressed initially around strategic issues rather than specific decisions. Further probing with the minister identified several critical sets of information and decision support needs such as daily information about the production and consumption of electricity in Egypt, ability to assess the impact of tariff changes on different income groups, ability to manage debt effectively, monitoring large electricity sector projects, and access to studies and legislation relevant to this sector.

Lesson 8 for the Management of DSS for Strategic Decision Making

The issue-based approach to DSS provides a solid base for easy transition to EIS in the future.

A joint IS/DSS team was quickly formed by the IDSC and the ministry. Because of the multiplicity and diversity of data sources needed for this project, the desire to build an internal information and decision support center inside the Ministry of Electricity and the minister's expressed long-term interest in having EIS-like capabilities, the IDSC saw a much greater need in this project to focus on the process of managing the delivery of the system with its requisite support infrastructure rather than just the design of the IS/DSS itself. However, the process by which this effort would be managed was prototyped and adjusted on the fly: The ministry team would be responsible for gathering data around the issues identified by the minister, and the IDSC team would be responsible for issue structuring, DSS development, hardware selection, training, and managing the process. However, these roles changed as the project progressed and was adapted to the contextual requirements of DSS implementation.

Lesson 9 for the Management of DSS for Strategic Decision Making

It was not only DSS design that could be prototyped; the management of delivery could be prototyped as well.

A working prototype was developed, methods for providing information support services were devised, and decision heuristics to assess the impact of various tariff structures and production and consumption patterns were implemented. As the design and delivery activity proceeded, a related strategic issue of crisis proportions surfaced: Drought in the source regions of the Nile River and its overuse in irrigation was causing peak hydroelectric power generated by the Aswan Dam to drop precipitously; $500 million were needed to quickly build three generating stations. There was now a crisis dimension that had appeared suddenly. Furthermore, the strategic issue had now drawn in the Ministry of Water Resources as a critical stakeholder in DSS design. The process by which the effort was managed also changed at this point: A team of six people were selected from the ministry as a core group for its own information and decision support center, and seven user committees were formed by the ministry's undersecretary to manage data collection and analysis.

Impacts The DSS is still evolving and so is the process by which it is being managed. The management process had to be changed when two of the six undersecretaries were unwilling to accept the DSS. However, the impacts of the DSS have already been felt, and the water level crisis is in full focus and much better understood. The DSS has also helped to assess the different tariff alternatives and the impact of each on citizens and total revenue, and a new electricity tariff is in place since January 1988.

Case 5: Document-based DSS

Various IDSC projects accentuated the role of textual documents as key sources used in the strategic decision-making process. For example, the legislation and decrees project was initiated to respond to the access problems related to the retrieval and classification of all Egyptian government legislation and decrees since legislation was first passed in Egypt in 1824. The project to date has classified all legislation and decrees from 1957 to 1987. This document database has been used in conjunction with other DSS such as the electricity DSS. The IDSC has established a fully staffed documentation center as part of its information support services unit (see Figure 15.5).

Lesson 10 for the Management of DSS for Strategic Decision Making

Providing decision support for strategic decision making will require much textual and document-based information sources. Organizational design should reflect that capability.

ASSESSING IMPACTS AND VALUE

In general, DSS benefits are often very uncertain and are elusive to assess. In the cabinet case with a prototyping approach where development is evolutionary, and when benefits can appear very early (while structuring an issue) or much later (crisis response in a future negotiation), this is especially the case. The ongoing group strategic decision-making context with multiple interrelated DSS in shifting environments makes it even more so. Orthodox cost/benefit analysis will not work. However, at the strategic level, the leverage of a few big obvious "hits" can also justify the whole effort many times over. Some of the examples presented have illustrated the magnitude of a few "hits." The IDSC has implemented a total of twenty-eight IS/DSS projects for the cabinet, and while some projects may not have been as successful as others, and in some cases the benefits were not as obvious, the cumulative leverage that IS/DSS has provided through the obvious "hits" has been estimated by the cabinet to be at least in the tens and possibly in the hundreds of millions of dollars. For the cabinet, the leverage is now overwhelmingly clear.

However, even without the track record of a few big hits, the *potential* leverage is sufficient to justify the investment in IS/DSS to support strategic decision making. It is difficult to ignore the potential leverage of effective IS/DSS for debt management when negotiating a 1 percent interest rate difference on a $33 billion debt is a whopping $330 million. In contrast, the IDSC's total operating costs (excluding overhead borne by the Ministry of Cabinet Affairs) have been around $2 million. In order to enable IS/DSS for strategic decision making to be delivered successfully in any organization, that balance must be very clear to top management; otherwise, it will be difficult to generate strong and sustained top management commitment. The IDSC project could not have gone forward without that understanding and strong commitment and support from the minister of cabinet affairs. The IDSC director reports directly to him.

The "bottom line" impacts of IS/DSS at the cabinet level have been mediated through process changes and qualitative valuation criteria. In the examples given, the valuation criteria in each case were different, usually qualitative, context-dependent, and in many instances they blurred the difference between process and outcome: quicker and more effective consensus on a group decision, uncovering hidden assumptions, better crisis response, better understanding of the interaction among industry forces, preemptive generation of alternatives for better negotiation, and identification of new strategic issues. Cumulatively, these impacts have also changed the way that the cabinet views the role and value of IS/DSS: There is a deeper realization of its potential leverage for helping the decision-making process, as evidenced by the increasing requests and resulting growth of IDSC services.

Finally, this experience has convinced us that, contrary to stereotypical depictions, computer-based DSS do not necessarily have to move the decision-making process away from emotional deliberation. Rather, the IDSC management process for the design and delivery of issue-based DSS accommodated and took advantage of (rather than denied) the social, visceral, political, and intuitive aspects of the strategic decision-making process. The metaphor used at the IDSC is that the group decision-making forum has changed from "a darkened room to a more illuminated one" where assumptions are more visible, potential impacts are better seen, quality of information is made more explicit, and competing scenarios can be made clearer. This extra illumination still allows emotional views to be aired and the intensity of values and commitments to be expressed and considered; but now it takes place with less misplaced emotion and in an information context in which more effective strategic decision making can be realized.

A PROCEDURE FOR MANAGING THE DESIGN AND DELIVERY OF ISSUE-BASED *DSS* FOR STRATEGIC DECISION MAKING

This work has resulted in a generalized procedure for managing the design and delivery of issue-based DSS for strategic decision making. It evolved through lessons learned from the IDSC's cumulative experience with twenty-eight cabinet IS/DSS projects. In addition, the procedure was more formally articulated and the process expertise more thoroughly captured through a six-day participative workshop in late 1987 attended by over twenty professional IDSC staff (El Sawy and El Sherif, 1987).

The unconventional nature of the Egyptian cabinet setting has helped to stimulate our approach. Strategic decision making is the major cabinet activity, thus affording an opportunity to observe the process with an intensity that is unequaled in more conventional settings. Coupled with the Egyptian cultural penchant for debate around focal points (rather than talking directly at them), it accentuated the notion that strategic decision making primarily revolved around issues rather than riveted on decisions. The inadequate reliability of the information infrastructure, coupled with the need for crisis response, led to the idea of prototyping the delivery process as well as the design. However, while the setting's cultural and environmental uniqueness helped to shape our approach, we believe that both the tactical essence of the procedure and its underlying concepts are transferable to other types of organizational settings.

Parallels are easily mapped from the cabinet to corporate settings, whether for executive roles, IS management, issue "downloading/uploading" between levels, or potential interaction between strategic decision making and IS/DSS (compare Figure 15.6 to Figure 15.3). The use of issues management is not alien to corporations (King, 1987), and has also been applied to planning for the MIS organization (Dansker et al., 1987). While strategic decision making in the corporate world may be more closely linked to competitive advantage, that does not seem to change any of its process features.

Figure 15.7 shows the basic building blocks of the procedure for managing the design and delivery of issue-based DSS for strategic decision making; Table 15.2 illustrates its tactical essence. The procedure has the following distinctive features:

FIGURE 15.6 Supporting and Shaping Corporate Strategic Decision Making through IS/DSS

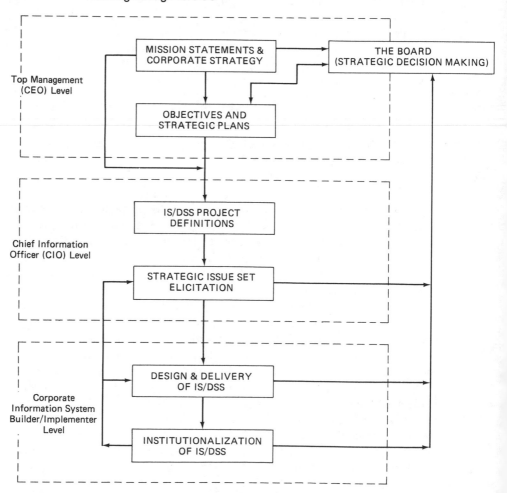

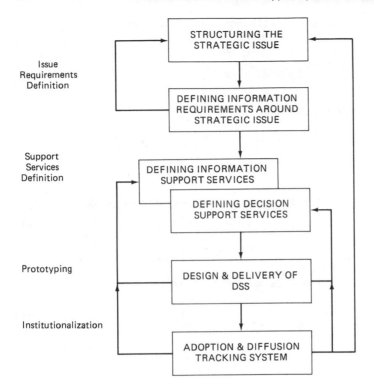

Issue
Requirements
Definition

Support
Services
Definition

Prototyping

Institutionalization

FIGURE 15.7 Procedure for Managing the Design and Delivery of Issue-based DSS for Strategic Decision Making

- It is *based on issues* rather than primarily on decisions.
- It is a *management process* rather than solely a systems development life cycle.
- It has a strategic *issue structuring front-end* that is sizable, explicitly identifiable, and consequently rewardable and billable.
- It explicitly *distinguishes between information support* services *and decision support* services.
- As well as prototyping the DSS design, it also *prototypes the DSS delivery process.* Its "delivery" stance implies a service view of implementation with continuous user support. This maximizes contextual fit and accommodates crisis response.
- As part of the institutionalization process for the DSS, it includes setting up a *dynamic tracking back-end* for monitoring shifts in critical issue parameters. This is key for recurring decisions and also makes transition to EIS much easier.

The procedure, as shown in Figure 15.7 and elaborated in Table 15.2, is highly iterative and consists of both nested and intersecting process loops:

- *Issue requirements definition loop:* Cycles between structuring the strategic issue and defining the requirements around strategic issues.
- *Support services definition loop:* Cycles between defining information support services and decision support services. In combination, this component roughly parallels Sprague and Carlson's (1982) ROMC approach.

TABLE 15.2   Tactical Essence of Procedure for Managing the Design and Delivery of Issue-based DSS for Strategic Decision Making

OUTCOMES	TYPICAL ACTIVITIES	REPRESENTATIVE METHODS AND TOOLS	TYPICAL KEY PARTICIPANTS
1. Structuring the Strategic Issue			
Reformulated issue	Assumption surfacing	Shuttle diplomacy	Issue stakeholders
Emergent objectives	Negotiation	Interviews Group meetings	Key decision makers
Issue articulation	Conflict resolution	Brainstorming and idea processing tools	CIO
Stakeholder consensus	Stakeholder identification	Empathy	
2. Defining Information Requirements around Strategic Issues			
Critical information	Defining initial information needs	Modified variants of extended CSF methods	Key decisions makers
Critical assumptions	Determining information quality requirements	Delphi methods	DSS user consultants
Decision scenarios	Defining information format requirements	Interviews	Staff intermediaries
Crisis scenarios			
3. Defining Information Support Services around Strategic Issue			
Scope and type of information support services that need to be provided	Providing access routes to information	Data dictionaries	Staff intermediaries
	Integrating information from multiple sources	Bibliographic searches	DSS user consultants
	Providing information views	External information utilities	DSS builders
4. Defining Decision Support Services around Strategic Issue			
Scope and type of decision support services that need to be provided	Providing "what-if" analysis capabilities	Modelling software	Staff intermediaries
	Scenario generation	Assumption surfacing tools	DSS user consultants
			DSS builders

TABLE 15.2 (Continued)

OUTCOMES	TYPICAL ACTIVITIES	REPRESENTATIVE METHODS AND TOOLS	TYPICAL KEY PARTICIPANTS
5. Prototyping the Design and Delivery of DSS Related to Strategic Issue			
DSS delivery methods Working DSS prototypes	Infrastructure development Database development DSS design and delivery	Prototyping tools	Key decision makers Staff intermediaries DSS user consultants DSS builders Toolsmiths
6. Managing Institutionalization of DSS			
DSS adoption DSS diffusion Dynamic tracking system	Cultural adaptation User support	Training workshops Newsletters Exception reporting	DSS consultants Trainers Staff intermediaries

- *Prototyping design and delivery loop:* The design prototyping iterations are nested in a delivery process envelope that is also prototyped. Iterates with support services definition loop.
- *Institutionalization loop:* Encompasses both organizational adoption and diffusion, including the setting up of an issue tracking system. Iterates with all other loops.
- *Evaluation and prioritization envelope* (not shown in Figure 15.7): The procedure is enveloped by continuous evaluation and prioritization, which enables shifting and/or intensifying effort and resources between issues and/or DSSs as appropriate.

COMPARING THE CONVENTIONAL AND ISSUE-BASED *DSS* APPROACHES

We have shown how the issued-based DSS approach has been successfully implemented in response to the need for supporting strategic decision making at the cabinet level in Egypt. We have also presented a procedure for managing the design and delivery process for such DSS. In Table 15.3 we provide a brief comparison of the conventional and issue-based approaches to DSS. The table may be useful to both information systems practitioners and researchers in clarifying the advantages and limitations of the issue-based approach to various situations and organizational settings. It is also meant to suggest how the issue-based view of DSS may be the missing

TABLE 15.3   Comparing the Conventional and the Issue-based DSS Approaches

	CONVENTIONAL	ISSUE-BASED
Focus:	On decision maker On single decision Decision making Alternative generation	On issue On groups of interacting issues Attention focusing Agenda setting
Favored domains:	Tactical and operational decisions One-shot decisions Functional applications Departmental applications	Strategic decisions Recurring strategic decisions Cross-functional applications Transorganizational applications

Design and delivery:	Promotes customization
	  to individual decision maker
	Interaction between decisions
	  not incorporated
	Prototypes design
	Design approach becomes
	  the system
		Promotes consensus around
		  group issue
		Integration and consensus
		  drives process
		Prototypes design and delivery
		Delivery approach becomes
		  the system

EIS readiness:	No tracking component
	Emphasizes convergent
	  structuring
	Major transformation
		Incorporates tracking component
		Balances divergent exploration
		  and convergent structuring
		Easy transition to EIS

Emerging leveraging technologies:	Expert systems	Idea processing and associative
		  aids (hypertext)
		Multimedia connectivity platforms
		  (video conferencing)
		Object-oriented languages

stepping-stone to advancing the state of the art in the definition, design, and delivery of EIS.

CONCLUSIONS

The use of information and decision support systems has significantly leveraged the strategic decision-making process in the Egyptian cabinet. Ministers and senior policymakers have increasingly realized that information systems and information technologies are not convenient luxuries for times of prosperity, but rather can be vital necessities in times of turbulence and adversity.

Strategic decision making is a very messy process, but it can still be made more effective by information and decision support systems. However, the IDSC cabinet experience suggests that it may be necessary for us to change our conventional views about DSS *and* our ways of managing them, if we are to make more progress in the strategic decision-making arena. The issue-based view that we have presented and its accompanying design and delivery procedure is one way of doing that.

Finally, we hope that this narrative provides the international information systems profession with a compelling example to show that there are things that can be learned to advance the field and its practice through information systems implementations in international contexts with less advanced technological infrastructures. We also hope that this will encourage SIM to continue to become more international.

QUESTIONS

1. Explain the difference between prototyping the design of a DSS and prototyping the delivery system.
2. What is the most significant impact or value of the ISDC effort? What does this say about efforts to justify or evaluate DSS?
3. Explain how each of the "lessons" evolved from one or more of the projects.

REFERENCES

DANSKER, B., J. S. HANSEN, R. LOFTIN, AND M. VELDWEISCH "Issues Management in the Information Planning Process," *MIS Quarterly,* 11, no. 2 (June 1987), 223–232.

DUTTON, W., AND K. KRAEMER *Modeling as Negotiating: The Political Dynamics of Computer Models in the Policy Process.* Norwood, N.J.: Ablex, 1985.

EL SAWY, O. A. "Personal Information Systems for Strategic Scanning in Turbulent Environments: Can the CEO Go On-line?" *MIS Quarterly,* 9, no. 1 (March 1985), 53–60.

EL SAWY, O. A., AND H. EL SHERIF, "Partnership Workshop on Providing Information and Decision Support Services for Top Level Decision Makers," Information and Decision Support Center, Cabinet of Egypt, Cairo, 1987.

EL SHERIF, H. "The Cabinet Information and Decision Support Systems Project," Ministry of Cabinet Affairs, Cairo, Egypt, 1985.

EL SHERIF, H. "Managing Large Information and Decision Support Systems Projects," IFORS Conference Proceedings, Argentina, August 1987.

GRAY, P. "Group Decision Support Systems," *Decision Support Systems,* 3 (September 1987), 233–242.

GRAY, P. "Using Technology for Strategic Group Decision Making," Working Paper, Claremont Graduate School, Claremont, Calif., January 1988.

HENDERSON, J., J. ROCKART, AND J. SIFONIS "Integrating Management Support Systems into Strategic Information Systems Planning," *Journal of MIS,* 4 (Summer 1987), 5–24.

HOUDESHEL, G., AND H. WATSON "The Management Information and Decision Support (MIDS) System at Lockheed-Georgia," *MIS Quarterly,* 11, no. 1 (March 1987), 127–140.

KEEN, P. G. W. "Value Analysis: Justifying Decision Support Systems," *MIS Quarterly,* 5, no. 1 (March 1981), 1–15.

KEEN, P. G. W. "Decision Support Systems: The Next Decade," *Decision Support Systems,* 3 (September 1987), 253–265.

KEEN, P. G. W. AND H. EL SHERIF   "An Accelerated Development Strategy for Applying DSS in Developing Countries," paper presented at DSS-82 Conference, San Francisco, 1982.

KING, W. R.   "Strategic Issue Management," in *Strategic Planning and Management Handbook,* ed. W. R. King and D. I. Cleland. New York: Van Nostrand Reinhold, 1987, pp. 252–264.

LASDEN, M.   "Decision Support Systems: Mission Accomplished?" *Computer Decisions,* April 6, 1987, 41–42.

MASON, R. O., AND I. I. MITROFF   *Challenging Strategic Planning Assumptions.* New York: John Wiley, 1981.

MINTZBERG, H., AND J. WATERS   "Of Strategies, Deliberate and Emergent," *Strategic Management Journal,* 6, no. 3 (1985), 257–272.

MOORE, J. H., AND M. G. CHANG   "Meta-Design Considerations in Building DSS," in *Building Decision Support Systems,* ed. J. L. Bennett. Reading, Mass.: Addison-Wesley, 1983, pp. 173–204.

PALLER, A.   "Executive Information Systems Should Do More than Just Identify Problems," *Information Center,* 4, no. 2 (February 1988), 16–17.

PIEPTEA, D., AND E. ANDERSON   "Price and Value of Decision Support Systems," *MIS Quarterly,* 11, no. 4 (December 1987), 515–528.

ROCKART, J. F., AND D. W. DELONG   *Executive Support Systems.* Homewood, Ill.: Dow Jones-Irwin, 1988.

SPRAGUE, R., AND E. CARLSON   *Building Effective Decision Support Systems.* Englewood Cliffs, N.J.: Prentice Hall, 1982.

SPRAGUE, R. H., AND H. J. WATSON   eds., *Decision Support Systems: Putting Theory into Practice,* Englewood Cliffs, N.J.: Prentice Hall, 1986.

STABELL, C. B.   "A Decision-Oriented Approach to Building Decision Support Systems," in *Building Decision Support Systems,* ed. J. L. Bennett. Reading, Mass.: Addison-Wesley, 1983, 221–260.

TURBAN, E., AND D. SCHAEFFER   "A Comparative Study of Executive Information Systems," in *DSS-87 Transactions,* ed. O. A. El Sawy. Providence, R.Is.: Institute of Management Sciences, 1987, pp. 139–148.

ZMUD, R.   "Supporting Senior Executives through Decision Support Technologies: A Review and Directions for Future Research," in *Decision Support Systems: A Decade in Perspective,* ed. E. R. Mclean and H. G. Sol. Amsterdam: Elsevier Science, 1986, 87–101.

16

SELECTING AN END USER PROGRAMMING LANGUAGE FOR *DSS* DEVELOPMENT

C. Lawrence Meador,
Richard A. Mezger

Decision support systems (DSS) represent a relatively new way of thinking about managerial use of computers. A decision support system is a computer-based information system that is designed to help managers in private corporations and policymakers in public sector organizations solve problems in relatively unstructured decision-making environments. Long-range and strategic planning, merger and acquisition analysis, policy formulation, policy evaluation, new product development, marketing mix planning, research and development, and portfolio management are a few areas where the DSS concept has been successfully applied [see 6, 9, 14, and 19].

   Unstructured decision-making environments are those where the global problem is not well enough understood for a complete analytical description. A DSS is a system which provides computational and analytical support in situations where it is necessary to integrate judgment, experience, and insight of managerial or policy decision makers along with computer-supported modeling and presentation facilities. DSS focuses on achieving productivity improvements from managers and policymakers, rather than from the reduction of clerical and administrative costs.

As used in this article, a DSS language is one very important example of the generic set of computer application development tools generally known as end user programming languages (or in some cases, fourth generation languages). Other examples include relational database facilities with powerful report generation and ad hoc inquiry facilities; general purpose statistical data analysis languages; and broad based graphics generation languages. While each of these four types of languages usually address different user needs, they often share some subset of similar capabilities and characteristics such as:

- Integrated database management (sometimes relational)
- User friendliness to nontechnicians
- Both procedural and nonprocedural command structures
- Interactive on-line utilization
- Support of prototyping and adaptive development
- Modest training requirements for end users
- Easy debugging and intelligent default assumptions
- Quantity of code required only a fraction of Cobol, Fortran, etc.
- Internal documentation generation support
- Understandable code for non-developers [5].

The methodology presented here has been developed and used in software selection projects in a wide range of fourth generation software—including software for the emerging microcomputer marketplace. The DSS languages have been chosen as an example to illustrate the language selection methodology. This article deals with the process by which an organization acquires a DSS language (i.e., a tool to be used by end users and/or by analysts to develop DSS applications).

INTRODUCTION

Today's managers and policymakers are confronted with an overwhelming range of choices of computer software to develop decision support systems for many of the important corporate applications referred to previously. Making the right choice of software for a particular organizational context can have a profound impact on the success of a DSS. A new, more powerful, cost-effective, productive, and flexible generation of software has now been developed and made commercially available for DSS applications. These so-called fourth generation languages are so much better than prior languages (such as Fortran, Cobol, Basic, PL/1, etc.) that we believe DSS developers should only consider utilizing the prior generation of software tools in very unusual circumstances.

The purpose of this article is to address significant managerial issues in the evaluation and selection of a DSS language. Attention is focused on the critical areas of DSS end user characterization, problem diagnosis, and needs assessment along with their implications for the software evaluation and selection process. The role of top-level managers as well as data processing staff in the evaluation and selection process is also considered. (Some of these topics are also discussed in Meador and Mezger, "Decision Support Systems for Minis and Micros," [13] and in Meador, Rosenfeld and Guyote, "Decision Support Planning and Analysis: The Problem of Getting Large-Scale DSS Started" [15].)

The selection and acquisition of a decision support language is too complex and important to exclude end users from the evaluation process. Top-level managers and their analytical support staff, who will be in the DSS user community, must participate in the evaluation and selection process in order to ensure that their needs are adequately addressed by the language selected. This discussion presents a range of methodologies and criteria which should be carefully considered by every organization embarking on a serious DSS development process.

A MULTI-STEP PROCESS

The selection of an appropriate DSS language is an important and challenging undertaking. The necessity of matching the range of language capabilities to the range of organizational needs is crucial in light of the cost of computer and professional resources required to develop and effectively utilize the language. In addition, a formal process for DSS language evaluation and selection is an educational process. In the end the organization has a much better appreciation of what it needs, what it is buying, and the costs and benefits of accomplishing the planned improvement in managerial decision support. This education process not only improves the odds that the organization is making a good choice, it also provides a broad base of knowledge and appreciation of the facility being acquired and the process of deploying it. Thus, the educational component enhances the probability of successfully using DSS.

A multi-step process of DSS language evaluation and selection is needed. The individual steps within the process are shown in Table 16.1 and discussed in the remainder of this article. It may not be necessary to perform each step in order to complete an effective evaluation process. However, it is important to note that each step addresses different aspects of the planned use of the DSS language. Thus, each step provides additional knowledge that improves the chances of success (also see Keen [5]).

TABLE 16.1 Steps in DSS Language Evaluation

- End user needs assessment and problem diagnosis (decision support analysis)
- Critical success factor identification
- Feature analysis and capability review
- Demonstration prototype development
- External user surveys
- Benchmark and simulation tests
- Programmer productivity and end user orientation analysis

Organizing for DSS Language Evaluation and Selection

It is often useful to establish a multi-disciplinary task force to accomplish the DSS language evaluation and selection process. Our experience has shown that such a task force can accomplish its work in six to twelve weeks if the application domain is not extremely broad and if the number of people on the task force is kept small. We have observed such evaluation projects taking considerably more time in some organizations. We recommend that the group of individuals involved in the process include at least one senior manager and at least one representative of each of the major functional user areas which are designated to be DSS application areas (e.g., finance, marketing, research, sales, and so forth). There also needs to be representation from the data processing community so that all issues and consequences of hosting a responsive DSS environment can be adequately considered. In many cases, substantial computer systems resources are required for model utilization, data storage, and output display in a timely and responsive manner. Finally, the task force needs to include the individual(s) who will form the nucleus of the DSS support group (see Figure 16.1). This multi-disciplinary task force may be comprised of six to ten individuals who will play important roles in the evaluation and selection process (see also [2]). In most situations a core group of three, at most four, members of the task force should be charged with the primary responsibility for data gathering and analysis.

End User Needs Assessment and Problem Diagnosis

It is important to involve the DSS user community in the language evaluation and selection process. While the "user requirements" phase of a traditional data processing project is

FIGURE 16.1   Organizing to Evaluate DSS Languages

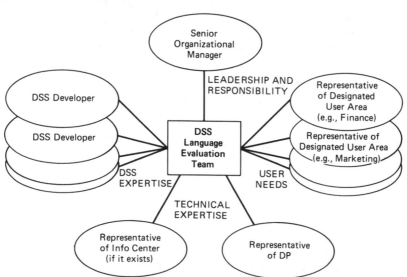

always critical to success, the involvement of the intended DSS end users in this process is ever more important. This is because many DSS languages are directly used by the decision makers or their immediate staff, individuals who are not computer systems analysts. Thus, in the context of trends toward more emphasis on end user computing, involving the end users in the early stages of analysis of requirements is crucial.

End user needs assessment and problem diagnosis is a systematic, organized, and structured procedure for identifying and evaluating features necessary for the DSS language. It involves direct contact with the intended users to understand the general nature of the business decisions which they are making and to identify the modeling, analytic, data manipulation, and display functions needed to support the business decision processes. Information is gathered by interviews and questionnaires: mechanisms that permit an experienced DSS analyst to understand the users' needs and to place these needs in the context of the facilities and features of DSS languages. (Research on DSS end user needs assessment is described in Meador, Guyote and Keen [11] and a structure for the process is recommended in [5].)

The end user needs assessment and problem diagnosis activity of the language evaluation process is similar to, but less detailed or intensive than the planning and analysis phase of the development life cycle. Both processes involve a DSS analyst exploring the nature of planned applications with its user community. For language selection, the objective is to determine the general nature and extent of the language functions and features which will be required to build the applications. Language functions and features which are not required are also identified. For actual DSS application development, the more detailed end user needs assessment and problem diagnosis is concerned with specific data structures, computational algorithms, and presentation contents and formats (reports and graphics).

End user education is an important component of the needs assessment and problem diagnosis process. In some situations, it may turn out that manual calculations of informal models are already in use to support the decision-making process—perhaps even with the use of alternative scenarios and "what-if" calculations. In such situations the educational process formalizes concepts and terminology to facilitate the dialogue. In other situations there may be little or no quantitative support of the decision-making process—manual or otherwise. It is necessary to introduce decision support system concepts and to explain to the manager how they might effectively be applied. It is important to keep in mind that the quality and quantity of the DSS support is expected to increase over time based upon the capabilities of the language being used and to the successful application of DSS concepts within the organizational unit and across the organization as a whole.

Thus, we see end user needs assessment and problem diagnosis as a means of improving the reliability of the statement of functional needs and requirements specification. This statement becomes the basis for the Feature Analysis and Capability Review stage. In addition, the interviews, questionnaires, and educational activities enhance the legitimacy of the feature specification and feature analysis part of the evaluation process. Finally, the process initiates communication between the decision-making managers and the technical specialists, a continuing two-way communication that is essential to success.

Critical Success Factor Identification

After performing the assessment of user and organizational needs, it is important to prioritize the decision criteria to be addressed in the language selection process. This is done by identifying the factors which are critical for accomplishing the objectives of the DSS applications (and thus, by implication, the objectives of the key managers). These factors are referred to as Critical Success Factors (CSF), a concept introduced by John Rockart [17]. Critical Success Factors help to determine the key language features for which satisfactory performance will ensure overall project success.

Critical Success Factors for the DSS language selection process should reflect information gained in the interviews with users, executives, and technical personnel within the organization. By incorporating the input of personnel at all levels of DSS involvement, the CSF's address user needs in addition to economic factors such as budgets and projected growth, and technological factors such as system capacities and trends in hardware and software.

For each of the Critical Success Factors, a minimum level of performance is established and adequacy of each alternative language environment should be evaluated with respect to these criteria.

Feature Analysis and Capability Review

General Features   The purpose of the DSS language feature analysis is to match the capabilities of the candidate DSS languages with the requirements determined in the user needs assessment and problem diagnosis activity. To do this, it is first necessary to select a number of candidate DSS languages for the evaluation. This process is a difficult one because of the large number of choices available. One of two situations is likely to exist. The first is that the host computer systems hardware has been selected—and in fact is installed and operational. In this situation it is necessary to determine the spectrum of DSS languages that are available to run on the selected computer systems hardware and within the operating system of that computer environment. In some cases, this process substantially narrows the choices of available DSS languages. The other situation is where the hardware selection is to be made upon the completion of the software selection. The latter situation presents substantially more language choices and also provides more latitude and flexibility for the language to quite closely meet the requirements of the organization.

In both cases there are a number of general considerations relative to language features which are important to the evaluation and selection process. These are listed in Table 16.2. These general considerations cover a broad range of areas of interest and are introduced briefly here. *Compatibility* deals with the manner in which the DSS language fits into the ongoing corporate computer systems environment, and whether it meets hardware, operating system, and data structure specifications. *Availability* issues are concerned with whether the language can be accessed on more than one hardware configuration and whether it can be used via remote computing services, and service bureau facilities as well as in-house. Frequently, the ability to begin DSS development out-of-house and then bring it in-house when usage increases and

TABLE 16.2   Language Features—General Considerations

- Compatability
- Availability
- Maintainability
- Reliability
- End user orientation
- Programmer productivity

economics dictate can be very valuable. *Maintainability* considerations are concerned with how much effort is required to support ongoing use of the language. *Reliability* issues have to do with failure rates and recovery characteristics, and of the software's ability to perform all variations of its functions and to do so through the series of upgrades of the language which occur over time.

Two related topics are *end user orientation* and *programmer productivity.* They both involve the ease-of-use of the language and the amount of systems orientation, design, and programming skill required to use the language. Important issues here include whether the language has a procedural or non-procedural orientation. Some "languages" are essentially two-dimensional spreadsheet calculators with relatively restricted notations to refer to the rows and columns of the "model"; other DSS languages have comprehensive relational data management capabilities and substantially more powerful conventions and mechanisms for addressing data. Non-procedural languages with easy symbolic references to data and goal-oriented control conventions represent more of an end user orientation. Similarly, these features, representing more powerful and logically concise functions, are expected to improve programmer productivity during the initial development of a model and during the ensuing maintenance and modification cycle.

Specific Language Features   There are a number of technical considerations relative to evaluating DSS language features which are briefly summarized in Table 16.3 (a more detailed list is given in Appendix 1). One of these deals with the design of the interface between the machine and the user, and the abilities of the language to provide a friendly and supportive environment for both novice and experienced users. In this regard, one needs to consciously distinguish between various "levels" of users as to

TABLE 16.3   Language Features—Technical Considerations

- Interface design
- Data management—external, internal
- Data analysis
- Modeling
- Data display—reports, graphics
- Hardware/operating software environment
- Multi-user interaction/sharing
- Security and integrity protection

how efficient they wish the system to be. (For a discussion of the user/system interface, see Sterling [18].)

Multidimensional data management is often considered an important requirement of the DSS language. While there exists a substantial class of decision support problems involving only a two-dimensional analysis, it is more and more common to see three-dimensional and more than three-dimensional problems being modeled to support important organizational decisions. When the activities of a company are viewed by product line and geographic area, as well as by time and specific business variables (sales, depreciation, etc.), a four-dimensional problem exists. DSS languages approach the multidimensional manipulation of data in different ways, which is sometimes reflected in the level of complexity of the language code when developing a model to access the data. In other words, if multidimensional data models are to be constructed, the multidimensional data manipulation features of the DSS language should be powerful and easy to use.

Access to *external data* may also be an important requirement for a DSS language. External data for a model may come from other transaction processing or management information databases within the organization, on the same computer system, or on another one. Alternatively, it may be economic and demographic databases which are external to the organization and available on a subscription basis. The ability and ease with which a DSS facility can access these databases can be an important element in its successful use. The system-to-system interface to support this access needs to be "black boxed" because the day-to-day user of the application is often not a systems specialist.

Data analysis is the collective term applied to statistical and forecasting applications and requirements. There are numerous standard statistical and forecasting functions, many of which may need to be available for frequent use. Checklists for these statistical and forecasting functions generally exist in DSS literature or can be provided by the vendor of a DSS language. One should be modestly cautious here. User needs assessment activity may mistakenly identify requirements for more complex and sophisticated statistical and forecasting algorithms than are really needed. The issue here is to avoid selecting (or rejecting) a DSS language on the basis of the presence (or absence) of an advanced feature which, in reality, is likely never to be used. Alternatively, when such a sophisticated feature is required, but on an extremely infrequent basis, it may be appropriate to access that feature from a statistics language within a remote computing services (RCS) environment.

The *modeling function* is generally acknowledged to be the heart of a DSS application. Modeling is a process of representing, through mathematical equations and logical expressions, aspects of the organization's business activities. By representing important parts of the organization and/or the competitive and external environments in which it operates, the model is able to support a careful study and analysis of alternative courses of action and outcomes. Such models often require complex sets of simultaneous equations where automatic equation reordering and simultaneous solution functions of a modeling facility are needed. "What-if" analysis evaluates the effect of changes in critical parameters. "Goalseeking" provides a backwards calculation capability which, in essence, determines the parameters of the problem given the parameters of the solution. Hierarchical processing and consolidation across products, regions, and geographical entities frequently must be modeled. On occasion, multi-dimensional equations permit solution of highly complex models representing diverse and numerous parts of an organization. In some cases mathematical optimization routines (linear, nonlinear, integer, mixed integer, and goal programming, for instance) may be useful components of the language.

Data display of the results of analysis and modeling activity is, of course, essential. Results are usually printed in hardcopy or as video display outputs. Printed output is frequently needed in a rough format which permits the examination of intermediate values. When the analysis is complete, presentation-quality reports may be needed with appropriate formatting, labeling, and text. In graphics, features generally offered are line charts, scatter plots, bar charts (or histograms) and pie charts with options for multiple charts per page and various color, display, sizing, and labeling options (see [16] and [20]).

In a production environment, providing for access by more than one user at a time may be important. Options should exist to allow *multiple users* to execute the same model (program) to access different personal databases as well as for multiple users to access parts of a common historical database by the same or different programs at the same time. An important capability relating to simultaneous access is the ability to prevent simultaneous attempts to modify a database's contents. In general, a user community should have broad flexibility in terms of sharing models (programs) and databases [12].

Database security and integrity protection features are important to the successful use of a DSS language. It is common for many users to share the same computing system environment. Password control at the model and database levels is needed to protect the privacy of users, models, and data.

Vendor Support Considerations   In evaluating a DSS language, it is also necessary to consider the capabilities of the vendor who supports the language. Table 16.4 represents a number of vendor capability and support issues which need to be considered. All of the vendor capabilities shown are quite important; substantial deficiencies in any one of them could produce a painful and nonproductive experience. *Training* and *documentation* are related capabilities which directly address the process of learning how to effectively use the DSS language. Training and documentation need to be available for

TABLE 16.4   Vendor Capabilities

- Training
    - vendor facilities
    - in-house
- Application systems development
- Consultation
- Crisis reaction
- Error/bug correction
- Documentation

---

a variety of levels and types of users so that first-time and infrequent users obtain adequate training in the basics of using the language while more sophisticated users are able to receive advanced training and have access to detailed reference documentation. In order to minimize the computer resources consumed, the efficient use of a DSS language becomes very important for large and/or multi-user models.

Two other related capabilities are *crisis reaction* and *error/bug correction*. There will be occasions, without doubt, when the application written in the DSS language does not work. The error diagnostics produced under such circumstances may be mysterious, or they may point to the DSS language itself as the source of the problem. In either case, there may indeed be a fault in the DSS language, or the model may have exceeded the capabilities of the language in some ill-defined manner. Crisis reaction or hot-line support means that the vendor has qualified systems personnel available on a standby basis to respond rapidly to such problems and to research and correct the difficulty. It may call for a suggestion as to how to program around the error or it may be a high priority activity to correct the problem and to provide updated software so that development and operation of the model can continue.

Finally, there are situations where it may be appropriate to look to the vendor for assistance in the design and programming of a DSS application. After all, the vendor is likely to be (and in fact should be) highly qualified and thoroughly experienced in designing and building applications using the language. *Consultation* involves relatively small amounts of support, more likely in the areas of design review or of designing and/or programming particularly difficult model segments. Application systems development support, unlike consultation, usually involves the full spectrum of development activities from design through deployment and is typically performed on a contractual basis. As to costs, application systems development support is almost always performed under contract and for a fee. Consultation may be for a fee or without fee—some vendors have limits below which the consultation is free and above which a fee is assessed. However, one should reasonably expect that brief periods of consultation via the hot-line support mechanism will be provided without fee. In this regard, there is typically an annual maintenance fee for ongoing support of a DSS language. In addition to providing updates to the DSS language and its documentation, the fee should include access to new language features and to training opportunities.

Acquisition Cost Considerations   One of the important features of a DSS language is its direct acquisition and utilization cost. Usually the cost factor which is given the most consideration is the initial acquisition cost. Important considerations when comparing the costs of DSS languages include the features of the language that are included, or not included, in the basic license cost. Some languages come in a totally bundled format while others are available in major functional segments (unbundled). Also, vendor support capabilities may or may not be bundled into the license fee; thus, there may or may not be a training allowance, a complement of technical documentation, and access to the hot-line. Even where there is an initial allowance, the cost evaluation should consider the costs of additional training, documentation, and start-up consultation support.

Other cost factors need to be considered. The cost of additional licenses for second and subsequent CPU systems are typically considerably less than for the first.

The availability of the DSS language in a time-sharing or remote computing services environment, where it can be used and paid for on a fee-for-use basis, is often attractive. This is especially the case if models and databases can be moved from the remote environment to an in-house environment without costly conversion activities.

Another extremely important cost factor is that of the ongoing maintenance fee which frequently runs in the range of 1% of the license fee per month (e.g., a $75,000 license fee for a DSS language might well have a monthly maintenance cost of $750). The maintenance fee often guarantees receipt of the latest versions of the software and documentation. Further, it may very well provide for receipt of new and expanded features of the DSS language as they become available through the vendor's continued program of support and enhancement.

Two related cost considerations are worthy of discussion. The first is the cost of the computer system's hardware required to operate the organization's models when developed in the selected language. On the surface, the host computer environment may seem to be an almost limitless resource relative to the anticipated usage by the DSS community, although such a view is often deceiving. Experience shows that the use of a facility expands to meet the resources available. Models and databases grow in size, complexity, and frequency of use. In general, a DSS language which will permit twenty busy users to obtain good throughput and response time in the host environment is substantially more desirable than one which only supports ten users with the same quality and range of performance capabilities.

The other cost consideration concerns the personnel costs needed to develop and maintain models written in the selected language. As will be seen, different levels of programmer productivity are possible when the same quality of individual uses different DSS languages. Consider that it might be substantially less expensive overall to invest funds in a more powerful host computer environment than to permit the use of an inefficient DSS language (in terms of computer resources consumed) if the language is very efficient in programmer productivity.

Demonstration Prototype Development

Experience has shown that there can be significant value from using a language on a trial basis to develop a meaningful application before a decision is made to select the language for a major application or for corporate-wide deployment [1, 7, 8]. This approach involves the development and operation of a demonstration prototype. This prototype model should be based on a real need and should accomplish the major objectives of some planned DSS application.

There are several reasons why the development of a prototype application has significant value in the DSS language evaluation and selection process. It serves to:

- Verify the size and complexity of a meaningful DSS application as programmed in the target language.
- Quantify and measure the computer system resources needed to develop and operate the application.
- Determine the characteristics and qualifications of the personnel needed to develop the application.

- Understand the training requirements for the use of the language.
- Test the vendor's technical documentation and hot-line support necessary for effective model development and utilization.
- Determine estimates of programmer productivity with a given language.
- Demonstrate the feasibility of the DSS application and obtain operational experience in the application area.
- Experience the entire DSS application development process from an educational perspective in what is clearly a realistic setting for future uses of the DSS language.
- Obtain at least some real decision support value in a limited timeframe, i.e., actually build, deploy, and use a DSS application which has immediate value to corporate management.

It is often true that in-house professional staff will be used to design, develop, and deploy the prototype DSS application with support from the vendor. It is possible that support from outside consultants specializing in DSS software evaluation, selection, and application implementation would provide assistance on a cost effective basis in the prototype development as well.

External User Survey

An external user survey is an evaluation of the experience of other organizations using the DSS languages being considered. The user survey is of particular value in an important business undertaking such as DSS development since it provides insights into key considerations and potential problems. Specifically, the objectives of conducting an external user survey are to:

- Obtain independent and unbiased information on the performance of the DSS language and of the vendor.
- Identify potential problems as well as sources of strength and weakness of candidate DSS languages and of their operation in particular host hardware environments.
- Verify computer systems hardware and support software requirements across a range of DSS applications.
- Develop realistic implementation planning information including an understanding of training requirements and implementation productivity considerations.
- Access the end user managerial and technical staff satisfaction with the candidate DSS language.

This process of performing an intensive reference check can be done in stages as the DSS languages move closer to final selection and as some candidates are eliminated. Initially, an informal, but organized, one-half to one hour telephone conversation with the DSS coordinator of an organization using the candidate DSS language will suffice to obtain a useful impression. As the finalists emerge from the selection process, more in-depth interaction with heavy users of the language, including an on-site visit, can be quite valuable and is definitely encouraged. The vendor can be helpful in providing

TABLE 16.5 External User Survey

HIGH PRIORITY INFORMATION REQUIREMENTS OF:	
DP	*Users*
Programmer Satisfaction	Management Satisfaction
Installation Impacts of Language	User Orientation of Language
Hardware/Software Implications	Functional Analysis Implications
■ Memory	■ Graphics
■ Disks	■ Modeling
■ CPU	■ Report generation
■ Operating systems	■ Data analysis
■ Lines of execution code	■ Data access/manipulation
Programmer Characteristics	Direct User Characteristics
■ Background in DP	■ Range of potential users
■ Training required in language	■ Ease of learning
■ Organizational location (DP?)	■ Ease of use
Cost	Cost/Effectiveness

names of candidate organizations to choose from, as can be a user's group. Picking a reference organization with similar applications and/or in the same industry is especially worthwhile.

A major objective of the external user survey is to determine overall satisfaction with the DSS language. Dimensions of "satisfaction" include ease of learning and use, quality of documentation, programmer productivity, and efficiency of performance. Table 16.5 presents an overview of the information which is sought in the external user survey process.

Vendor performance is to be examined in two areas: 1) the timing and smoothness of the initial installation and any modifications and upgrades subsequently provided; and 2) the overall quality and quantity of ongoing vendor assistance. Aspects of vendor assistance to be examined include: initial installation, user support, product maintenance and upgrades, technical competence in providing support, reliability of product, cooperativeness and availability of support, and availability and timing of training. The analysis of vendor assistance should be summarized by determining and understanding both the strongest and the weakest points, as the organization will seek to maximize the vendors strength and to minimize or bypass vendor weaknesses.

Experience has shown that many corporate users of DSS languages are quite receptive to participating in such an extensive reference check. They have an opportunity to demonstrate their success as well as to discuss potential DSS applications and how the applications provide decision support assistance to their management. A well-organized approach with specific information-gathering objectives is likely to be most successful in developing a receptive and cooperative relationship and in obtaining the desired information.

Benchmark and Simulation Tests

At first glance it might appear that benchmarks and simulation tests are similar to, or even redundant with, a demonstration prototype project. While there is a general similarity in the objectives, the two activities are quite different in an important and meaningful way. A benchmark is a series of simulated tests of a comprehensive set of the features of the DSS language. It seeks to determine the level of computer systems resources utilized by the various capabilities of the DSS language (see Table 16.6). With these objectives, the programs or models which comprise the benchmark do not, in general, solve real DSS applications problems; rather, they are specially constructed to exercise various features or capabilities of the DSS language in a known manner. For example, a benchmark program may seek to shed light on the amount of computer main memory consumed by a typical model and the way in which the memory is managed by the support software. This benchmark program is constructed to consume a predetermined amount of memory, although the way in which it uses the memory only approximates the manner in which a real model uses memory. All of this contrasts with the demonstration prototype approach where the emphasis on solving a real DSS application problem may very well require only a small subset of the total DSS language features and capabilities to be exercised.

The objectives of a benchmark evaluation are to:

1. Measure computer systems resources consumed by the DSS language in typical user operation (see Table 16.6 for resources to be measured).
2. Determine cost of computer resources consumed (where costs are understood to be determined to be a usage algorithm intended to simulate the utilization of specific computer resources).
3. Learn about programming with the DSS language.
4. Check and verify the operation of a number of important language features and capabilities.
5. Evaluate the user friendly or English-like features of the DSS language.
6. Improve confidence in the DSS language's features and capabilities to meet the needs of the organization's DSS applications.
7. Improve confidence in feasibility of DSS application development.
8. Develop a series of sample programs for analysis of programmer productivity and user orientation.

TABLE 16.6 Benchmark Evaluation

Measure Computer Systems Resources Consumed by DSS Software in Typical User Operations

- CPU Cycles
- Main Memory—including virtual memory paging load
- Large-Volume Disk Input/Output
- Input/Output Activity
- Response Time

In essence, the benchmark activity enhances the user needs assessment activity by forcing the analyst and the user to think through in more detail the specifics of the needs. It permits exploration of important systems features and often exposes multiple ways of meeting a user requirement. It also requires the use of the DSS language's technical documentation and provides an opportunity to test the vendor's technical support. Finally, when the benchmark is run on an in-house computer, it allows for an observation of the installation process, and quite likely provides experience in moving DSS models and their data from one computer system environment to another. In summary, Table 16.7 presents one possible set of benchmark components for consideration.

Programmer Productivity and End User Orientation Analysis

Two additional issues of importance in the selection of computer software for DSS development, maintenance, and enhancement include the extent of programming development effort that must be expended to achieve a given set of objectives (a function of programming language productivity), and the range of types of individuals who directly use the language who may reasonably access the software (a function of simplicity and end user orientation of the language). These are the issues which, among others, tend to differentiate fourth generation languages and distinguish them from third generation languages.

Unfortunately, no set of agreed-upon criteria exists which allows an absolute comparison of the relative productivity and degree of end user orientation of various

TABLE 16.7   Benchmark Components

Databases:

- Statistical and Financial

Benchmarks:

- Data entry
- Financial model calculations
- Goal seeking (backwards iteration)
- Aggregation
- Data communications
- Large-model startup
- Linear regression
- Basic descriptive statistics
- T Test
- Matrix correlation
- Exponential smoothing and moving averages
- Growth rates
- Volume data transfer
- Report output
- User interface

computer languages. However, several useful measures have been constructed and tested which lead to insights on these issues for specific instances of utilization of different languages.

In general, it can be stated that "more productive languages" support the achievement of end user application goals with less total program development effort (and thus cost) than would be expected of less productive languages. More end user oriented languages are accessible by a wider range of users (because the languages are more like the "natural" language of the users and thus are more "user friendly" [4]).

More productive languages tend to require less specification of the detailed procedures by which desired goals are achieved. These highly productive languages are often referred to as goal-oriented or non-procedural languages for this reason. They tend to require the specification of fewer lines of executable code and fewer lexical items (shorter and simpler lines of code) to accomplish a given purpose. User-oriented languages tend to emphasize logical names of entities such as variables, commands, labels, locations, logic, and dimensions, rather than numeric codes or highly constrained acronyms.

Some fundamental criteria related to productivity and end user orientation which can be applied to DSS applications are:

- Executable lines of source code in an application program—excluding program comments.
- Lexical entities in the programs—excluding program comments, where a lexical entity is any continuous character string of one or more characters with meaningful definition such as a variable name, command, label, data item, logical or arithmetic operator, etc.
- Average number of lexical entities per line of code in each program.
- Numeric string ratio in each program—defined as the total number of numeric strings divided by the total number of lexical entities.

The number of executable lines of source code and the number of lexical entities are taken to be measures of the quantity of code that has to be produced to achieve the application objective (with programmer productivity implications). The average number of lexical entities per line of code is a conservative measure of statement complexity (with both productivity and end user orientation implications). The numeric string ratio is an approximation of the relative use of numeric codes rather than logical names of variables, labels, locations, etc., (with end user orientation implications for non-programmers).

Programmer productivity analysis is an important part of the language evaluation process that can reveal potentially large hidden costs in language acquisition. Dunsmore and Gannon [3], for example, show that significantly different levels of programming effort can exist between almost-identical languages. However, it should also be noted that much disagreement exists among both academics and practitioners on the proper metrics for measuring programmer productivity and end user orientation characteristics of different languages.

MULTICRITERIA ASSESSMENT

It would seem that much of the language evaluation process could be facilitated by some sort of multicriteria scoring or weighting scheme. We have observed, and sometimes used, schemes which assigned weights and point scores to different functions of the language and to outcomes of other aspects of the evaluation process. The merit of such an approach is that it collapses results and evaluations among several dimensionally incompatible criteria into a single metric, and produces a simple scalar comparison to rank candidate languages. But in presenting recommendations to user management, we think that relevant summarized raw data in its native dimensions should still be presented. User managers may have differing weights which will change over the evaluation timeframes as they learn more and more about the issues that count.

SUMMARY

The selection of an appropriate DSS language is a challenging and important task for organizations that are starting to focus on information technologies to improve the effectiveness and productivity of managers and policymakers.

Both the process and the structure of the language evaluation activity are likely to impact its effectiveness and its success. The software technology for decision support is changing rapidly and substantial variance exists in the quality and relevance of the hundreds of products designed for potential decision support applications. Investment in a careful, well thought out and credible user-driven evaluation process is likely to be worthwhile but care should be taken to avoid studying the alternatives so long that the decision support opportunity evaporates.

QUESTIONS

1. What are the recommended steps in a DSS language evaluation?
2. Who should participate in a DSS language evaluation? Why?
3. Once a DSS language evaluation has been completed, how can and should the findings be presented to user management?

REFERENCES

1. ALAVI, M. "An Assessment of the Prototyping Approach to Informative Systems Development," *Communications of the ACM,* 27, no. 6 (June 1984), 556–63.
2. ALTER, S. L. *Decision Support Systems: Current Practice and Continuing Challenge,* 38, 149–53, 173–74. Reading, Mass.: Addison-Wesley, 1980.
3. DUNSMORE, H. G., AND J. D. GANNON "Analysis of the Effects of the Programming Factors on Programming Effort," *Journal of Systems and Software,* 1, no. 2 (February 1980), 141–54.

4. HARRIS, L. R.   "Natural Language Front Ends," in *The Al Business,* ed. P. H. Winston and K. A. Prendergast, 149–62. Cambridge, Mass.: M.I.T. Press, 1984.

5. KEEN, P. G. W.   "Computer-Based Decision Aids: The Evaluation Problem," *Sloan Management Review,* 16, no. 3 (Spring 1975), 17–29.

6. KEEN, P. G. W., AND M. S. SCOTT MORTON   *Decision Support Systems: An Organizational Perspective.* Reading, Mass.: Addison-Wesley, 1978.

7. KEEN, P. G. W.   "Adaptive Design for Decision Support Systems," *Database,* 12, no. 132 (1980) 15–25.

8. KEEN, P. G. W.   "Value Analysis: Justifying Decision Support Systems," *MIS Quarterly,* 5, no. 2 (1981), 1–15.

9. LITTLE, J. D. C.   "Brandaid, an On-Line Marketing Mix Model, Part 2: Implementation, Calibration, and Case Study," *Operations Research,* 23, no. 4 (1975), 656–73.

10. MARTIN, J.   *An Information Systems Manifesto,* 19–38. Englewood Cliffs, N.J.: Prentice Hall, 1984.

11. MEADOR, C. L., M. J. GUYOTE, AND P. G. W. KEEN   "Setting Priorities for DSS Development," *MIS Quarterly,* 8, no. 2 (June 1984), 117–29.

12. MEADOR, C. L., P. G. W. KEEN, AND M. J. GUYOTE   "Personal Computers and Distributed Decision Support," *Computerworld in Depth,* XVIII, no. 19 (May 7, 1984), ID/7-ID/16.

13. MEADOR, C. L., AND R. A. MEZGER   "Decision Support Systems for Minis and Micros," *Small Systems World,* 11, no. 3 (March 1983), 27–31.

14. MEADOR, C. L., AND D. N. NESS   "Decision Support Systems: An Application to Corporate Planning," *Sloan Management Review,* 15, no. 2 (Winter 1974), 51–68.

15. MEADOR, C. L., W. L. ROSENFELD, AND M. J. GUYOTE   "Decision Support Planning and Analysis: The Problem of Getting Large-Scale DSS Started," M.I.T. Working Paper MERG-6, Cambridge, Mass., October 1983, 1–35.

16. REMUS, W.   "An Empirical Investigation of the Impact of Graphical and Tabular Data Presentations on Decision Making," *Management Science,* 30, no. 5 (May 1984), 533–42.

17. ROCKART, J. F.   "Chief Executives Define Their Own Data Needs," *Harvard Business Review,* 57, no. 2 (March–April 1979), 82–88.

18. STERLING, T. D.   "Humanized Computer Systems," *Science,* 190, no. 4220 (December 19, 1975), 1168–72.

19. URBAN, G. L., AND R. KARASH   "Evolutionary Model Building," *Journal of Marketing Research,* 8 (1971), 62–66.

20. VANDAM, A.   "Computer Graphics Comes of Age," *Communications of the ACM,* 27, no. 7 (July 1984), 638–48.

17

THE MEAD CORPORATION

Ralph H. Sprague, Jr.,
Barbara McNurlin

Mead Corporation, with headquarters in Dayton, Ohio, is a paper and forest products company. It has over one hundred mills, offices, and distribution centers throughout the United States and Canada. Since the mid-1970s, Mead has also been in the electronic publishing business, with NEXIS, its news information retrieval service, LEXIS, its on-line legal research service, and several other on-line and database services. The company is highly decentralized, with four operating groups—forest products, consumer and distribution, specialty, and Mead Data Central. Each group has one or more divisions.

INFORMATION SYSTEMS ORGANIZATION—PRE-1980

In the 1960s, Mead's corporate information systems department provided all Mead divisions with data processing services. By 1967, the department's budget had become so large that management decided to spin off some of the functions to the divisions.

Reprinted by permission of Canning Publications, Inc., from Sprague and McNurlin (eds.), *Information Systems Management in Practice* (Prentice Hall, 1986), and the *EDP Analyzer,* June 1985.

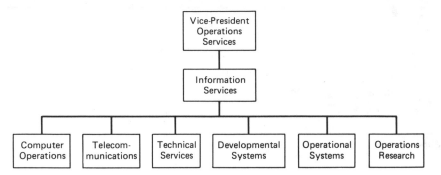

FIGURE 17.1 Mead Corporation's Pre–1980 Information Services Department (from Mead Corporation)

Divisions could establish their own data processing and process engineering groups if they so desired. Or they could continue to purchase data processing services from the corporate information services department. Many of the divisions did establish their own information systems departments, but all continued to use the corporate data center for their corporate applications.

In the late 1970s, the corporate information services department had six groups, as illustrated in Figure 17.1. The director reported to the vice-president of operations services, and under the director were the following:

- Computer operations—responsible for managing the corporate data center
- Telecommunications—responsible for designing the telecommunications network and establishing standards
- Technical services—responsible for providing and maintaining systems software
- Developmental systems—responsible for traditional systems development
- Operational systems—responsible for maintaining systems after they become operational
- Operations research—responsible for performing management science analysis

CURRENT ORGANIZATION

In 1980, management realized that the existing organizational structure would not serve the needs of the rapidly growing end-user computing community. In addition, in order to become an "electronic-based" organization, management needed to build a corporate-wide network. Thus, they reorganized into three departments, as shown in Figure 17.2. In this new structure, the corporate information resources group not only creates the hardware, software, and communication standards for the entire corporation but runs the corporate data center and operates the network. All the divisions use the network and corporate data center. They follow the corporate standards, and some operate their own small distributed systems as well, which link into the corporate network.

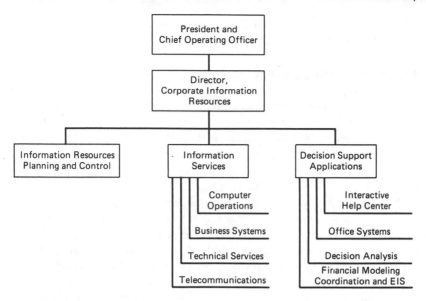

FIGURE 17.2 Mead Corporation's 1980–1984 Corporate Information Resources Group
(from Mead Corporation)

The director of the corporate information resources group now reports directly
to the company president—not through the vice-president of operations, as in the
former structure. This change signaled an increase in the importance of information
resources to the company. There are three departments within the new group:

- Information Resources Planning and Control—responsible for planning future
  information systems and technology
- Information Services—responsible for most of the traditional information systems
  functions from the previous information services department
- Decision Support Applications—responsible for "marketing" and supporting end-
  user computing

The Information Resources Planning and Control Department

The information resources planning and control department grew out of the company's
strong planning culture. The decentralization of the 1970s pointed out the need for a
coordinating body for information systems planning. Although it is a small department,
it plays two important roles. First, it takes the corporate perspective for information
systems planning to ensure that Mead's information resources plans mesh with the
business plans. Second, it acts as planning coordinator for the various groups and
divisions, helping them to coordinate their plans with corporate and information
resources plans. The information resources planning department is currently concentrating on planning in six areas: networking, office automation, end-user comput-

ing, database management, manufacturing systems, and automating the system development process.

The Information Services Department

The information services department handles the traditional computing functions for Mead. It manages computer operations and traditional system development of corporate-wide systems. It also provides technical services—database administration, system software support, and technical support for end-user computing, such as creating micromainframe communication links. The department also provides all the telecommunications services to the company.

The question of database management required special consideration. At the time of the 1980 restructuring, Mead believed it needed a separate function to provide centralized database administration. The value of centralized data became apparent in 1978 when a takeover attempt required Mead to combine and analyze divisional data rapidly. However, further investigation revealed that there was little need for data sharing between the divisions on a day-to-day basis; consequently, there was little need for permanent corporate databases. The database administration function, therefore, was left within technical services. Their role is to guide the use of standard data definitions throughout Mead. Thus, data from the many divisions can be pulled together on an ad hoc basis when needed.

Most divisions develop their own applications, following the guidelines created by the information services department. The *EDP* steering committee—composed of the president and group vice-presidents—has established the policy that applications should be transportable among the various computing centers and accessible from any Mead terminal. The company's telecommunications network sets the guidelines for making this interconnection possible.

The Decision Support Applications Department

The decision support applications (DSA) department provides all end-user computing support for the company. The corporate information resources director sees it as the "marketing arm" of his group. The DSA department "sells" and trains Mead employees on end-user computing, whereas the information services department provides the technical support for the end-user systems.

At the time of the 1980 reorganization, DSA had no users, no products, no common-use applications among its multiple locations, and only five staff members in operations research and two in its office systems support group. In 1985, this department was serving fifteen hundred users in some thirty Mead locations, with ten people in its own department. DSA offers fourteen products and eight corporatewide common-use applications. Its purchased products include SAS, IFPS, PROFS, APL, and Focus. An example of a proprietary common-use system is its corporate planning resources mode, which is used to cost-justify projects and purchases.

DSA consists of four groups that provide end-user computing support:

- Interactive Help Center
- Office Systems
- Decision Analysis
- Financial Modeling Coordinator/*EIS*

Mead's *interactive help center* provides the "customer relations" type of on-going support for end-user computing. It focuses on introducing end-user computing to Mead employees at various types of company meetings. One main function is to hold an annual user group conference. It also evaluates new end-user computing products, provides training for the various end-user products, and offers consulting and hot-line assistance to end users.

The *office systems group* provides services to end users who are interested in using IBM's Professional Office System (PROFS) or Four Phase's dedicated word processing systems. It also provides consulting to groups contemplating putting in an office system. Divisions are free to select any office system, but most of them have followed the recommendations of this group to ensure corporatewide interconnection.

Mead sees PROFS as the "gateway" through which users can access all other end-user computing products. PROFS runs on an IBM 4341 under the IBM VM/CMS operating system and is menu-driven. It allows users to create on-line calendars and tickler files, view others' calendars to schedule meetings and conference rooms, perform limited word processing and electronic filing and retrieval, and send electronic mail—both formal documents and informal messages. Mead has enhanced PROFS by creating an on-line telephone directory, writing various enhancements to the calendar and scheduling systems, and adding an executive information system, which we describe shortly.

The *decision analysis group* uses operations research tools to develop linear programming models and simulations for users needing such sophisticated analysis tools. It has also built a number of companywide decision support systems, such as a corporate budgeting model and a graphics software system.

The *financial modeling coordination group* is in charge of Mead's integrated financial system. It also supports executive computing. This support takes two forms. First, this group supports the IBM PCs that are used by corporate executives. Second, it has developed an executive information system (EIS), which is accessed through PROFS. EIS was developed exclusively for use by top management. The first version was developed in 1982 as an easy-to-use system to introduce top management to potential managerial uses of computers. Using menus of commands and questions, executives can retrieve monthly summary operating reports, financial statements, forecasting data, and so forth.

Mead had few requests for personal computers before 1985, because employees found the company's systems met their needs. Since 1985, Mead has gradually introduced PCs, where they are cost-justified. The group generally recommends PCs be able to communicate with their network.

Mead's new structure presented both benefits and problems. It separated the more people-oriented activities under DSA from the more technical activities under the information services department. Professional staff in each department spent more time doing what they did best—technical people developed and managed the technology, and DSA people worked with end users. The technology was better managed, and relations with users improved. However, this split in responsibilities caused two problems. One, traditional programmers and system analysts felt that the DSA group was receiving all the new and exciting development work. The second problem was coordinating the two departments.

A matrix arrangement has evolved at Mead to handle both problems. Most projects now have both information services and DSA people on project teams; staff from both groups now work on all kinds of projects. For example, a version of the executive information system required the services of a traditional programmer. The programmer was involved with both the system development and the unveiling presentations made to top management.

The new structure has been in place since 1984, and despite the coordination problems that it presented, the company is pleased with the corporate-wide view it is giving to information resources.

CURRENT ORGANIZATION—1985 TO PRESENT

The departmental organization that was put in place from 1980 to 1984 has remained essentially intact through 1988, with two main changes. In early 1988, the vice-president of information resources began reporting directly to the chairman and chief executive officer of Mead. And, two, the DSA group has been reorganized, as shown in Figure 17.3

In 1985, as users became more computer literate, the focus of the DSA group began to shift from marketing products to supporting end users. As the needs of the users became more sophisticated and less generic, the department found itself creating small groups with expertise in specific areas. So their support groups have become more specialized and focused. They now serve over 5,000 users corporate-wide in three ways—service center help, application development consulting, and local area experts.

The *service center* people continue to introduce new users to technology and provide telephone hot-line assistance to experienced users.

The *application development* consultants help users develop more sophisticated applications. They also get involved in guiding maintenance of user-written applications, which has become a noticeable problem. They are also updating traditional applications to permit access to data for end user systems.

The *local area experts* work out in the departments and support users in their area. They report directly to their area manager and indirectly to the information resources department. Due to the growing number of user-written applications, they, too, have become more involved in helping users keep their applications up-to-date.

Their most dramatic new development in end-user computing has been the introduction of a natural language for database query. It has been very popular and has become the platform for developing their executive information systems.

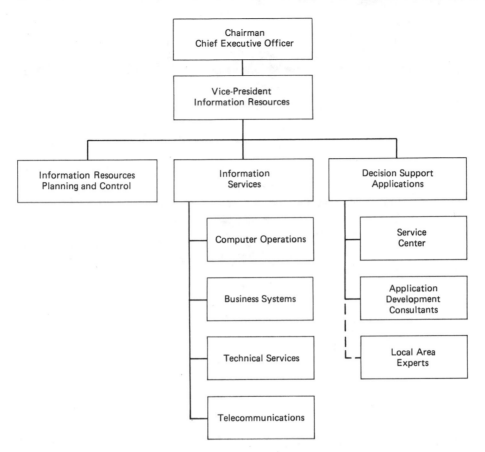

FIGURE 17.3 Mead Corporation's Current Corporate Information Resources Group

So, from 1985 to the present time, Mead has found its end-user computing focus shifting from introducing new technology to making more effective use of the technology already in place. Mead is concentrating on harvesting its investment in information technology by using it as a lever to change the way it does business.

QUESTIONS

1. Describe Mead's pre-1980 information systems organization.
2. Describe Mead's 1980–1984 information systems organization.
3. Discuss the factors that have caused Mead to change the information systems organization structure over the years.

PART 5

The Evolving DSS Domain

Decision support systems were a revolutionary concept in computer support for decision making when they first appeared in the 1970s. Now they are used in a large number of organizations. DSS is not a stagnant field, and it continues to evolve. New applications expand the way that decision support is provided.

Group decision support systems (GDSS) are used to improve the efficiency and effectiveness of groups of people working together. Because of the amount of time people spend in group activities, GDSS has tremendous potential value. GDSS software is now beginning to emerge from university and corporate research centers.

Gerardine DeSanctis and Brent Gallupe, in "Group Decision Support Systems: A New Frontier" (Reading 18), provide an overview of GDSS. They discuss what a GDSS is, the technology used to create it, four scenarios that show how a GDSS capability can be delivered, and design and implementation issues.

Paul Gray and Jay Nunamaker, in "Group Decision Support Systems" (Reading 19), provide a second look at GDSS. After giving background information on GDSS, they consider a specific type of GDSS environment, the decision room, a special facility for GDSS sessions. They describe several decision rooms in current use and what we are learning about this new approach to supporting group activities.

Historically, the attempts to help meet the information needs of senior executives through computer technology have fallen short of expectations. The latest efforts are executive information systems (EIS). These systems provide easy access to internal and external information that is critical to executives in carrying out job responsibilities.

In "A Comparison of Executive Information Systems, DSS, and Management Information Systems" (Reading 20), Efraim Turban and Donna Schaeffer provide a foundation for understanding this new type of information system. They define and give the characteristics of an EIS, discuss the information needs of executives, explore the hardware and software used with EIS, discuss how an EIS is developed, and describe the relationships between EIS and other types of computer-based systems.

One of the oldest and most successful EIS is used by seventy senior executives at Lockheed-Georgia. George Houdeshel and Hugh Watson describe this EIS in "The Management Information and Decision Support (MIDS) System at Lockheed-Georgia" (Reading 21). They describe how it is used; how it has evolved over time; its component parts, features, and capabilities; its benefits; and the keys to its success.

Expert systems are computer applications that contain the knowledge, experience, and judgment of skilled professionals. They suggest decisions and often the reasoning behind their recommendations. While the concept of an expert system is not new, recent developments in expert systems hardware and software have fueled a large interest in them.

Fred Luconi, Thomas Malone, and Michael Scott Morton, in "Expert Systems: The Next Challenge for Managers" (Reading 22), provide an introductory look at expert systems. They discuss what they are, their component parts and how they function, and a framework for understanding how expert systems fit into the information systems constellation of applications. They also describe their benefits, problems, risks, and other important issues.

The development of expert systems is explored by John Sviokla in "Business Implications of Knowledge-Based Systems" (Reading 23). He discusses the key development issues, available expert systems tools, and important implementation issues.

18

GROUP DECISION SUPPORT SYSTEMS: A NEW FRONTIER

Gerardine DeSanctis,
Brent Gallupe

INTRODUCTION

During the past decade, much attention has been given to the area of decision support systems by both industry and academia. The concept of a DSS as originally articulated by Gerrity (1971) involves "an effective blend of human intelligence, information technology and software which interact closely to solve complex problems." In theory this means that either an individual or a group of decision makers might benefit from a DSS. In practice, however, most systems have been designed for use by single decision makers. Although a DSS operating in a mainframe or micro computer environment might be available to many users simultaneously, the software itself accommodates the individual user faced with a particular decision for which he or she is responsible. Support of the individual decision maker undoubtedly is important for effective managerial functioning, but many organizational decisions are made by groups of people, particularly at the strategic or executive level. Moreover, as organiza-

Gerardine DeSanctis and Brent Gallupe, "Group Decision Support Systems: A New Frontier," *DATABASE*, Winter 1985.

tions become increasingly complex, fewer decisions are made by single individuals (Gannon, 1979). Responsibility for organizational actions becomes diffused, resulting in more decision making that involves input from two or more individuals. These group decisions may also benefit from support by a computer-based information system.

A few researchers have acknowledged the need for a group-level focus in DSS (e.g., Hackathorn & Keen, 1981; Keen, 1984; Turoff & Hiltz, 1982). Huber (1984) recently presented some ideas regarding the design of information systems to support electronic meetings. But additional thought must be given to this perspective, particularly with regard to the definition of group decision support and issues related to the design and implementation of computer-based systems for use by groups. The purpose of this paper is to present a conceptual foundation for research and development of decision support systems for group-level decision making. We begin by defining the concept of group decision support systems (GDSS) and outlining the characteristics of these systems. Fundamental features of GDSS technology, including both hardware and software aspects, are described. Four "scenarios," or types of group DSS environments, are proposed. Finally, some specific questions in need of investigation by researchers are identified.

WHAT IS A *GDSS*?

The concept of a "decision support system" has been widely discussed in the MIS literature. Although various definitions have been proposed, there appears to be general agreement that a DSS is an interactive computer-based system which facilitates solution of unstructured problems (Bonczek, Holsapple & Whinston, 1979; Neumann & Hadass, 1980; Sprague, 1980; Vazsonyi, 1978). The concept of "group decision support" builds on the now well-known idea of a DSS. A group decision support system (GDSS) is an interactive computer-based system which facilitates solution of unstructured problems by a set of decision makers working together as a group. Components of a GDSS include hardware, software, people and procedures. These components are arranged to support a group of people, usually in the context of a decision-related meeting (Huber, 1984). Important characteristics of a GDSS can be summarized as follows:

1. The GDSS is a specially designed system, not merely a configuration of already-existing system components.
2. A GDSS is designed with the goal of supporting groups of decision-makers in their work. As such, the GDSS should improve the decision making process and/or decision outcomes of groups over that which would occur if the GDSS were not present.
3. A GDSS is easy to learn and easy to use. It accommodates users with varying levels of knowledge regarding computing and decision support.
4. The GDSS may be "specific" (designed for one type, or class, of problems) or "general" (designed for a variety of group-level organizational decisions).
5. The GDSS contains built-in mechanisms which discourage development of negative group behaviors, such as destructive conflict, miscommunication, or "groupthink."

The definition of GDSS is quite broad and, therefore, can apply to a variety of group decision situations, including committees, review panels, task forces, executive/board meetings, remote workers, and so forth. Appropriate settings for a GDSS range from an executive group meeting which occurs in a single location for the purpose of considering a specific problem (such as a merger/acquisition decision), to a sales managers' meeting held via telecommunications channels for the purpose of considering a variety of problems (such as hiring of sales representatives, product offerings, and sales call schedules). Because the contexts of group decision making vary so greatly, it is useful to think of a GDSS in terms of the common "group" activities which it supports. The basic activities which occur in any group and which, therefore, are in need of computer-based support are: information retrieval, information sharing, and information use (Huber, 1984). *Information retrieval* includes selection of data values from an existing database, as well as simple retrieval of information (including attitudes, opinions, and informal observations) from other group members. *Information sharing* refers to the display of data to the total group on a viewing screen, or sending of data to selected group members' terminal sites for viewing. *Information use* involves the application of software technology (such as modeling packages or specific application programs), procedures, and group problem-solving techniques to data for the purpose of reaching a group decision.

THE TECHNOLOGY OF *GDSS*

A pictorial representative of a typical GDSS is shown in Figure 18.1. In this generalized model, a group of decision makers has access to a data base, a model base, and GDSS applications software during the course of a decision-related meeting. There is at least one computer processor, one input/output device, and one viewing screen. A "group facilitator" coordinates the group's use of the technology, and there is a flexible, friendly user-interface language available for use by the facilitator or each group member. As we shall see later, many different configurations of a GDSS are possible. However, the basic components of any GDSS include hardware, software, people and procedures. Each of these components is now considered in some detail.

Hardware

Regardless of the specific decision situation, the group as a whole, or each member, must be able to access a computer processor and display information. The minimal hardware requirements of the system include: an input/output device, a processor, a communication line between the I/O device and the processor, and either a common viewing screen or individual monitors for use in displaying information to the group. More sophisticated systems may contain I/O terminals or desktop computers for each group member, several central processors, long-distance communications equipment, and several large viewing screens. A design which allows each participant to work independently of the others, to publicly demonstrate personal work, and to see the work of other individuals and the group as a whole is preferred. Since "keyboarding" is a

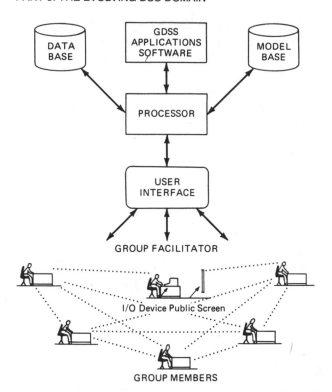

FIGURE 18.1 A Model of a GDSS

skill not totally accepted by managerial personnel in organizations, touch-sensitive screens or a facility to input hand-written communication (such as a graphics tablet) or voice communication may be desirable. Preferably, the viewing screen or monitors should be capable of displaying graphics and text, and should have color as well. Graphics can be used to summarize data or to display voting information in the group; color can be used to add attention value to the visuals or text which are displayed (Tullis, 1981). If a public viewing screen is used, it should be large enough to be seen by all members of the group. The screen would facilitate group discussion and take the place of flipchart or blackboard. It also could be used for video conferencing between subgroups in dispersed locations.

The amount of processing power necessary to support group decision making depends on the software being used, the number of members in the group, and the extent to which networking or teleconferencing are used. If the group members have microcomputers or workstations, then central processing can be used to manage communication among them and to store common databases, model bases, or applications software. With regard to communications, the requirements vary according to the setting in which the GDSS is used. In the confines of the traditional meeting room, hardwire links between an I/O device, a central processor, and display monitors or the public screen may be all that is necessary; more elaborate configurations might link microcomputers with one another and perhaps a central processor. For dispersed groups, a local area network, telephone lines, satellite, or microwave relay may be required to allow group members to communicate with one another. Electronic mail, computer conferencing, audio and video conferencing might also be integrated into the GDSS environment.

Software

The software components of the GDSS include a database, a model base, specialized application program(s) to be used by the group, and an easy-to-use, flexible user interface. Some highly specific GDSS systems may not require a database; for example, those that merely collect, organize, and communicate members' opinions about a problem. However, most sophisticated systems will include databases, along with model bases, very high-level languages for program writing, and interfaces with standard managerial-level software (graphics, statistical/OR packages, spreadsheets, etc.). The GDSS software may or may not interface with individual DSS software.

The most distinguishing technological component of the GDSS is specially-developed applications software that supports the group in the decision process. The precise features of this software will vary extensively but may include the following:

Basic Features

- Text and data file creation, modification, and storage for group members
- Word processing for text editing and formatting
- Learning facilities for naive GDSS users
- On-line "help" facilities
- Worksheets, spreadsheets, decision trees, and other means of graphically displaying numbers and text
- State-of-the-art database management which can handle queries from all participants, create subschemas as necessary for each participant, control access to public, or corporate, databases, etc.

Group Features

- Numerical and graphical summarization of group members' ideas and votes
- Menus which prompt for input of text, data, or votes by group members
- Program(s) for specialized group procedures, such as calculation of weights for decision alternatives; anonymous recording of ideas; formal selection of a group leader; progressive rounds of voting toward concensus-building; or elimination of redundant input during brainstorming.
- Method of analyzing prior group interactions and judgments
- Text and data transmission among the group members, between the group members and the facilitator, and between the group members and a central computer processor

The GDSS software may be designed to support a specific decision or a class of decisions. In some cases the software will be built around a particular decision-making technique, while in other cases it will be more generalized. At the present time few GDSS software products are available. A great deal of development effort is needed before organizations will have a choice of systems for use in group decision making.

People

The "people" component of the GDSS includes the group members and a "group facilitator" who is responsible for the smooth operation of the GDSS technology when it is in use. The facilitator's role is a flexible one. He or she may be present at all group meetings and serve as the group's "chauffeur," operating the GDSS hardware and software and displaying requested information to the group as needed. On the other hand, the facilitator may be physically located in the MIS department or information center and act only on an on-call basis when the group experiences difficulties in using the technology. When the GDSS is first installed this person can be expected to be relied upon quite heavily to coordinate the group's activities and serve as the interface between the group and the technology. As group members become familiar with the technology and its use in their work, the facilitator's responsibilities may diminish, or even be eliminated.

Procedures

The final component of the GDSS consists of procedures which enable ease of operation and effective use of the technology by group members. These procedures may apply only to the operation of the hardware and software, or they may extend to include rules regarding verbal discussion among members and the flow of events during a group meeting. In the latter case, the GDSS may be designed to accommodate a specific group decision-making technique, such as the nominal group technique (Delbecq & Van de Ven, 1974), brainstorming (Osborn, 1957), the Delphi method (Dalkey, 1972), or social judgment analysis (Cook & Hammond, 1982).

CATEGORIES OF *GDSS*: 4 SCENARIOS

An overview of the types of support systems which are needed for group decision making in organizations is presented in Figure 18.2. This framework emphasizes that the purpose and configuration of a GDSS will vary according to the duration of the decision-making session and the degree of physical proximity of group members. The cells that are shown should *not* be considered as independent of one another but as ends of two continua.

Scenario 1—Decision Room   The first scenario is similar to Gray's "Decision Room" (1981) and may be thought of as the electronic equivalent to the traditional meeting. The organization sets up a room (much like a boardroom) with special facilities to support group decision making. Each participant is seated around a horseshoe-shaped

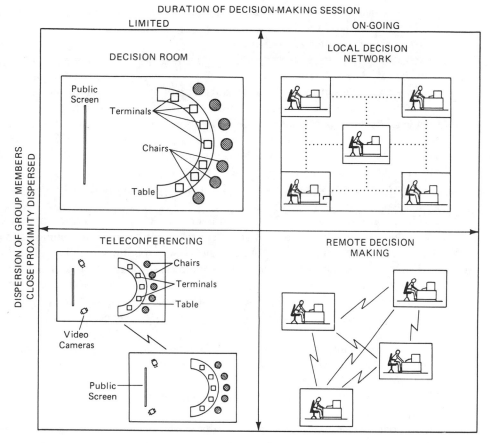

FIGURE 18.2 Framework: Group Decision Support

desk facing a large screen. In a very simple configuration of a GDSS, only the group facilitator would directly interact with the computer. A more typical design would have a display monitor and terminal in front of each participant. Communications may be transmitted verbally or via computer messaging. The public display screen is used to enumerate ideas and to summarize and analyze data. Face-to-face verbal interaction combines with technology-imposed formalization to make the decision meeting more effective and efficient.

To illustrate this type of GDSS, consider a group of high-level managers who must decide on a marketing mix for the coming year. A variety of decision making approaches could be used, such as ordinary group process or nominal group technique, but essentially the process would involve using the GDSS to show the decision makers the current situation in terms of markets and finances, etc., and to facilitate the generation and evaluation of ideas. There is continual interaction among group members, both verbally and through the communication network. Modeling software is used which is capable of being changed to adapt to the group's view of the problem. A number of alternative marketing mix strategies are tested via models and discussed before a specific strategy is selected.

Scenario 2—Local Decision Network   The GDSS may take on a somewhat different configuration in a setting in which a fixed group of decision makers, who work in close proximity to one another, must deal with certain problems on a regular basis. Rather than establishing a permanent "decision room" for group meetings, a "Local Decision Network" (LDN) could be developed to support group members as they work in their individual offices. Each decision maker would have a workstation, or what Dickson (1983) refers to as a "managerial support facility," located on their desk or worktable. A central processor would store common GDSS software and databases, and a local area network would provide member-to-member and member-to-central-processor communication. In the LDN environment, group participants communicate via electronic messaging on the local area network. They can access common and private databases or DSS software as required, and view a "public screen" on their own CRT as needed. Decision makers engage in their day-to-day work and set up "group meetings" or conferences as needed. The approach offers greater flexibility in that the one-place/one-time constraint of scenario 1 is removed. There is the disadvantage of removing face-to-face communication, but face-to-face meetings could be held when necessary.

As an example, consider a scenario found at the head offices of a large insurance company where decisions regarding corporate investments must be made on an ongoing basis. Financial managers, investment managers, and analysts are linked together in a local network that enables them to jointly make decisions in an interactive mode. GDSS software enables the group to analyze investments through the use of in-house investment models. The interactive nature of this "local decision network" provides group members with information on what the others are doing.

Scenario 3—Teleconferencing   A third type of GDSS is needed for groups whose members are geographically distant from one another but who nevertheless must come together for the purpose of making a decision. In this case two or more decision rooms are connected together by visual and/or communication facilities. For example, suppose that Company X, a large computer vendor with offices throughout the world, has decision rooms located in several major cities. Using teleconferencing technology, meetings could be arranged so that decision making could occur without all of the participants having to be in a single location. The approach is essentially the same as in scenario 1 except that teleconferencing is used to supplement the communication component of the GDSS. Reduced travel costs (time, money, productivity loss), and flexibility in terms of time and duration of holding a meeting are advantages.

Scenario 4—Remote Decision Making   The fourth scenario is not yet commonplace but offers possibilities for the near future. Here there is uninterrupted communication between remote "decision stations" in a geographically dispersed organization which has a fixed group of people who must regularly make joint decisions. Part of the problem with scenario 3 is that meetings must be scheduled and coordinated in order to take place. This scenario, along with scenario 2, removes the constraint of meeting location and addresses the needs of decision makers who must work together on a regular basis.

An example of this scenario is a project development team of, say, 5 members which is dispersed in many parts of the country due to facilities at each location (or for whatever reasons that make it inappropriate to bring them all together in one place). Suppose that any changes made by one member will affect other members, and that a group decision is necessary before changes are made. In a remote decision making network, one group member could send a message to the CRT or workstation screens of the other members noting that a decision session is scheduled in, say, 10 minutes. All members are then informed of the problem and decisions to be made. A structured decision technique can be used by the group or a special GDSS application program may aid in the group decision. A long distance communication system, using telephone, microwave, or satellite transmission, would provide communication among the group participants. Eventually, a decision is made by some voting scheme and each member notes the changes that must be made to his or her part of the project.

Summary

This section has presented a framework for categorizing group decision support systems. The precise configuration of a GDSS will vary considerably depending on the type of problem to be solved and the organizational context in which the problem is addressed. Nevertheless, there are design and implementation issues which are common to all categories of GDSS. Several of these are considered in the next section.

DESIGN AND IMPLEMENTATION ISSUES

Existing research on the dynamics of group decision making (Thibaut & Kelley, 1959; Cartwright & Zander, 1968; Bennis & Shepard, 1963; Hackman & Morris, 1975; Shaw, 1971; Guzzo, 1982) has several implications for the design and use of GDSS. Three design implications drawn from the group dynamics literature are first discussed, followed by a summary of implementation options available for GDSS.

First, *an objective of GDSS should be to encourage the active participation of all group members*. An overwhelming amount of research on groups indicates that the major barrier to effective group decision making is any condition which prevents the free expression of ideas in a group (Janis, 1972; Kolasa, 1975; Van de Ven & Delbecq, 1974). A number of events may lead to this problem. For example, group members may feel a strong pressure to conform, thus stifling the input of non-conforming ideas to the decision process, or certain members may regard other members as more competent or higher in status than they are (Hoffman, 1965). The extent to which group members are active in the group is also affected by the group's initial evaluation of the contributions of various members. People whose ideas are initially accepted by the group are likely to increase their participation, while those whose suggestions are rejected may withdraw from the discussion (Oakes et al., 1960; Pepinsky et al., 1958). The implication here is that a computer-based information system should be configured to facilitate group members' communication while reducing bias and prejudice, to enhance participation of all group members. An important feature of a GDSS may be the facility of allowing anonymous input and evaluation of ideas. In addition, GDSS software might have features that actively encourage group members to voice dissent opinions or play a "devil's advocate" role before a critical decision is made.

Second, *special accommodations are needed for groups who have no prior experience working together.* In groups that have never worked together before, members may feel uncertain about the exact goals of the group or their individual responsibilities and expectations. Newly-formed groups usually lack cohesion and a structure for operating (Klein & Ritti, 1980). The GDSS should support the group during the initial phases of group formation. For example, the group meeting room can be set up so that members are in a circle or semi-circle, facing one another. Terminals or other hardware should not obstruct their view or ability to easily interact verbally with one another. Special software might be used to query members on their expectations of how the group should function, and to feedback points of agreement and disagreement among members.

Third, *a useful feature of a GDSS would be to aid high-level management in selecting people to serve as group members for a given decision or problem.* All other things being equal, the quality of a decision made by a group is a function of the skills, abilities, and organizational status of the individual group members (Hoffman, 1965). Data from a human resource information system, or other similar source, could be used along with an appropriate model or selection criteria, to help structure the task of choosing people to serve on committees, boards, panels or task forces.

Extensive developmental work is needed before decision support systems for groups become widely available and useful to organizations. At the present time only a handful of systems have been developed for in-house use by organizations or are available for purchase (Kraemer & King, 1984). Because of their relative novelty, the importance of careful pilot testing of these systems cannot be overemphasized. Systems which fail to provide useful, easy-to-use facilities will quickly result in negative attitudes toward GDSS on the part of users. The role of attitudes in determining system success has been well documented (DeSanctis, 1984; Lucas, 1975; Robey, 1979; Swanson, 1974). We can anticipate that unrealistic expectations or frustrating experiences with GDSS on the part of even a few individuals could result in negative attitudes and poor use of these systems by decision-making groups.

With regard to installation, three options are possible (Huber, 1984): (1) install the system permanently at the user site; (2) rent the system on an on-call basis from the vendor; and (3) access the system remotely from the vendor site. Option 3 may be the best alternative today since option 1 is very costly and option 2 can be impractical. In years to come, however, option 1 may be the installation method of choice as GDSS systems become more sophisticated, more reliable, and less costly to organizations.

SUMMARY

Computers are increasingly being used in organizations for group communication, and all indications are that this trend will continue (Turoff & Hiltz, 1982). With increasing pressure to use the group as a decision-making body in organizations, there is a need for development and study of computer-based systems to support group decision making. The introduction of decision support technology for groups probably will not occur on a wide scale for quite some time. In this sense, GDSS may be an idea whose time has not yet come. But many of the components of such systems are available currently, and a few GDSS products have been produced. Systems developers and researchers should begin now to consider exactly how much systems can be designed, how they might be used in organizations, and what their impacts will be.

QUESTIONS

1. What is a group decision support system? What are its characteristics?
2. Discuss the components of a group decision support system.
3. Describe the four types of support systems that are needed for group decision making.
4. Summarize the three design implications for group decision support systems that can be drawn from the study of group dynamics.

REFERENCES

BENNIS, W. G., AND H. A. SHEPARD   "A Theory of Group Development," *Human Relations,* Summer 1963, 415–57.

BONCZEK, R. H., C. W. HOLSAPPLE, AND A. B. WHINSTON   "Computer-Based Support of Organizational Decision Making," *Decision Sciences,* 10 (1979), 268–91.

CARTWRIGHT, D., AND A. ZANDER   *Group Dynamics* (3rd ed.). Evanston, Ill.: Row, Peterson, 1968.

COOK, R. L., AND K. R. HAMMOND   "Interpersonal Learning and Interpersonal Conflict Reduction in Decision-Making Groups," in *Improving Group Decision Making,* ed. R. A. Guzzo, 13–72. New York: Academic Press, 1982.

DALKEY, N. C.   *Studies in the Quality of Life: Dephi and Decision Making.* Lexington, Mass.: Lexington Books, 1972.

DESANCTIS, G.   "A Micro Perspective of Implementation," in *Implementing Management Science,* ed. R. Schultz and M. Ginzberg, Greenwich, Conn.: JAI Press, 1984.

DICKSON, G. W.   "Requisite Functions for a Management Support Facility," in *Processes and Tools for Decision Support,* ed. J. G. Sol. Amsterdam: North Holland Publishing, 1983.

GANNON, M. J.   *Organizational Behavior: A Managerial and Organizational Perspective.* Boston: Little, Brown, 1979.

GERRITY, T. P.   "Design of Man-Machine Decision Systems: An Application to Portfolio Management," *Sloan Management Review,* Winter 1971, 59.

GRAY, P., et al. "The SMU Decision Room Project," *Transactions on the First International Conference on Decision Support Systems,* Atlanta, June 1981, 122–29.

GUZZO, R., ed. *Improving Group Decision Making,* 13–72. New York: Academic Press, 1982.

HACKATHORN, R. D., AND P. G. W. KEEN "Organizational Strategies for Personal Computing in Decision Support Systems," *MIS Quarterly,* 5, no. 3 (1981), 21–27.

HACKMAN, J. R., AND C. G. MORRIS "Group Tasks, Group Interaction Process, and Group Performance Effectiveness: A Review and Proposed Integration," in *Advances in Experimental Social Psychology,* ed. L. Berkowitz, vol. 8. New York: Academic Press, 1975.

HOFFMAN, L. R. "Group Problem Solving," in *Advances in Experimental Social Psychology,* ed. L. Berkowitz, vol. 2, 99–132. New York: Academic Press, 1965.

HUBER, G. P. "Issues in the Design of Group Decision Support Systems," *MIS Quarterly,* 1984.

JANIS, I. L. *Victims of Groupthink: A Psychological Study of Foreign Policy Decisions and Fiascoes.* Boston: Houghton Mifflin, 1972.

KEEN, P. G. W. "DSS & DP: Powerful Partners," *Office Automation: Computerworld,* 19, no. 7A (1984), 13–15.

KEEN, P. G. W., AND M. S. SOTT MORTON *Decision Support Systems: An Organizational Perspective.* Reading, Mass.: Addison-Wesley, 1978.

KLEIN, S. M., AND R. R. RITTI *Understanding Organizational Behavior.* Boston: Kent Publishing, 1980.

KOLASA, B. J. "Social Influence of Groups," in *Motivation and Work Behavior,* ed. R. M. Steers and L. W. Porter. New York: McGraw-Hill, 1975.

KRAEMER, K. L., AND J. L. KING "Computer-Based Systems for Group Decision Support," unpublished paper, University of California, Irvine, August 1984.

LUCAS, H. C., JR. "Performance and the Use of an Information System," *Management Science,* 20 (1975), 908–19.

NEUMANN, S., AND M. HADASS "DSS and Strategic Decisions," *California Management Review,* 22, no. 2 (1980), 77–84.

OAKES, W. F., A. E. DROGE, AND B. AUGUST "Reinforcement Effects on Participation in Group Discussions," *Psychological Reports,* 7 (1960), 503–14.

OSBORN, A. F. *Applied Imagination.* New York: Scribner's, 1957.

PEPINSKY, P., J. K. HEMPHILL, AND R. N. SHEVITZ "Attempts to Lead, Group Productivity, and Morale under Conditions of Acceptance and Rejection," *Journal of Abnormal Social Psychology,* 57 (1958), 47–54.

ROBEY, D. "User Attitudes and MIS Use," *Academy of Management Journal,* 22 (1979), 527–38.

SHAW, M. *Group Dynamics.* New York: McGraw-Hill, 1971.

SPRAGUE, R. H. "A Framework for the Development of Decision Support Systems," *MIS Quarterly,* 4, no. 4 (1980), 1–26.

SWANSON, E. B. "Management Information Systems: Appreciation and Involvement," *Management Science,* 21 (1974), 178–88.

THIBAUT, J., AND H. KELLEY *The Social Psychology of Groups.* New York: John Wiley, 1959.

TULLIS, T. S. "An Evaluation of Alphanumeric, Graphic, and Color Information Displays," *Human Factors,* 23, no. 5 (1981), 541–50.

TUROFF, M., AND S. R. HILTZ   "Computer Support for Group versus Individual Decisions," *IEEE Transactions on Communications,* 30, no. 1 (1982), 82–90.

VAN de VEN, A. H., AND A. L. DELBECQ   "The Effectiveness of Nominal, Delphi, and Interacting Group Decision Making Processes," *Academy of Management Journal,* 17 (1974), 605–21.

VAZSONYI, A.   "Information Systems in Management Science," *Interfaces,* 9, no. 1 (1978), 72–77.

19

GROUP DECISION SUPPORT SYSTEMS

Paul Gray,
Jay F. Nunamaker

INTRODUCTION

At the First International Conference on Decision Support Systems, Peter G. W. Keen [12] pointed out that the fundamental model of DSS—the lonely decision maker striding down the hall at high noon to make a decision—is true only in rare cases. In real organizations, be they public or private, Japanese, European, or American, most decisions are taken only after extensive consultation. Although it is possible on occasion for decision makers to go counter to the consensus of their organization, this is not a viable long-term position for them. Decision makers out of tune with the people in their organization either depart the organization or the organization undergoes massive personnel turnover.

This reading is based on portions of two papers: "Group Decision Support Systems" by Paul Gray, which appeared in the *DSS Journal*, 3 (1987) and "Computer-Aided Deliberation: Model Management and Group Decision Support" by J. F. Nunamaker, L. M. Applegate, and B. R. Konsynski, which appeared in *Operations Research*, 36 (1988). The present version was prepared in August 1988 specifically for this book.

In this article we consider group decision support systems, usually referred to as GDSS. This is an emerging subfield within DSS in which there has been a marked increase in activity since the mid-1980s. The evolution of GDSS has been rapid. To a first approximation, the evolution can be characterized in terms of a chronology having some very short time intervals (Ahituv [1]):

1981–83   Initial papers describing group decision support systems (e.g., Gray et al. [7], Huber [10], Konsynski and Nunamaker [13]).

1982–85   Survey papers and research agendas (e.g., Kraemer et al. [14], Huber [11], DeSanctis and Gallupe [4]).

1982–86   Initial experimentation and experimental results (Kull [15], Gray [8], Lewis [16], Gallupe [6]).

1987–   Building of advanced facilities (DeSanctis and Gallupe [5], Gray and Borovits [9], Manteii [17], Nunamaker et al. [20], Stefik et al. [22] and formal experimentation (e.g., Applegate et al. [2], Nunamaker et al. [19], Watson [24], Zigurs [25]).

As indicated by this chronology, GDSS is still in the laboratory stage. In the past, when these systems were installed in industry and government, they often behaved like shooting stars. They were put in by one senior executive and used during his or her tenure. However, as soon as that individual was replaced, the system was dismantled or fell into disuse. The classic "not-invented-here" syndrome held sway. The major problem is that at this point we do not know

- How to use these systems effectively, nor
- How to train people (particularly middle-aged executives) how to use them.

It is appropriate, therefore, that GDSS activity be centered in university research laboratories. Although we are now certain that GDSS is a solution that works, we have not yet established for which problems it is the most appropriate solution. There is growing evidence, however, that group decision support systems will be able to improve both the efficiency and the effectiveness of organizational group processes.

THE NATURE OF GROUP DECISION MEETINGS

Although most business organizations are hierarchical, decision making in an environment involving choices among alternatives and assessment of risks is usually a shared process. Face-to-face meetings among groups of senior executives (or boards of directors) are an essential element of reaching a consensus. The group may be involved in a decision or in a decision-related task such as creating a short list of acceptable alternatives or creating a recommendation for approval at higher level. These group meetings are characterized by the following activities and processes:

- The meetings are a joint activity, engaged in by a group of people of equal or near equal status, typically five to twenty or more individuals.
- The activity, as well as its outputs, is intellectual in nature.
- The product depends in an essential way on the knowledge, opinions, and judgments of its participants.
- Differences in opinion are settled either by fiat by the ranking person present or, more often, by negotiation or arbitration. The results lead to action within the organization.

Another way of looking at group decision meetings is in terms of what groups do. Specifically, groups

- Retrieve (or generate) information,
- Share information among members, and
- Use information to reach consensus or decision.

DEFINITION

Definitions of GDSS have been offered by both Huber [11] and DeSanctis and Gallupe [4]. These definitions are more than adequate for our purpose here:

- "A GDSS consists of a set of software, hardware, and language components and proccdurcs that support a group of people engaged in a decision related meeting." (Huber [10])
- "An interactive, computer-based system which facilitates solution of unstructured problems by a set of decision makers working together as a group." (DeSanctis and Gallupe [3])

An important point to note is that the group using the GDSS may not make the ultimate decision. It may be creating and/or reviewing alternatives to be submitted as a short list to the next level in the organizational hierarchy.

GDSS TECHNOLOGY

Although most group decision meetings are face-to-face, technology is starting to be applied to make it possible for participants to be separated in space and/or time. These technologically enhanced meetings include computer conferences (either online or extended in time) and audio and video teleconferences. DeSanctis and Gallupe [4] discuss the four combinations of proximity and separation in space and in time. In this article we will concentrate on one form of technological enhancement, the "decision room," in which the participants are in the same room at the same time.

The motivation for creating a decision room comes from the observation that in almost all organizations office automation has resulted in terminals being ubiquitous in work areas. However, as soon as one steps into a conference room, technology is a telephone and high technology is a speakerphone. The personal and online computer capabilities used routinely elsewhere are not available.

In a typical decision room, terminals (or personal computers) are provided at some or all of the seating positions at a conference table. Input to these terminals is by keyboard, mouse, touchscreen, bit pad, or some combination of these. Participants can do "private work" at their individual displays. One member of the group (either the group leader or a staff member acting as a "chauffeur") operates the software needed to create the "public" display (e.g., a projection TV) that can be seen by everyone. In some rooms, multiple public screens are provided where one screen is used for the current discussion and the others for reference or slowly changing information.

Because decision rooms are designed for senior managers, they tend to have an "executive feel" to them. Even the experimental laboratories are being created with plush carpeting and quality furnishings.

The equipment in the decision room is typically connected to a central computer (usually a minicomputer) and to peripheral equipment, including printers to provide hard copy, file servers to act as dedicated storage, and local area networks to interconnect the terminals.

Appendixes 1 and 2 describe two installations, those at the University of Arizona and at the Claremont Graduate School.

GDSS SOFTWARE

GDSS provide software to support the individual and to support the group. To allow each individual to do private work, the usual collection of text and file creation, graphics, spreadsheet, database, and help routines is provided at the individual workstations. For the group as a whole, in addition to providing information retrieval and display, a GDSS provides software for summarizing group opinion. Thus, for example, the public screen can be used to present a cumulative list of all suggestions (such as from a nominal group technique session) or to show the aggregated results of voting and ranking or ratings of alternatives. Votes and preferences can be either identified by individual or aggregated so that individuals need not expose themselves if they hold views contrary to the consensus or to those of the senior person present. This last feature allows managers to obtain a truer set of advice, since people need not fear retribution if they do not follow the prevailing group opinion.

As discussed later, introducing GDSS hardware and software into a conference changes the content of the discussions. By being able to do private work, a participant can examine an alternative (e.g., a "what-if") on his or her private screen and, if it is good, send it to the public screen for discussion. However, if the alternative is poor, it can be quietly buried without embarrassment. The recording of information on the public screen reduces the redundancy of the conversation. People do not keep bringing the same ideas up over and over if they are displayed. As a result, communications focuses on what participants know and on the rationale that led them to hold their views.

GDSS COMMUNICATIONS

A GDSS must have a communications base as well as the model base, database, and interface required in conventional DSS (Bui and Jarke [3]). This is particularly true for a GDSS distributed in time and space. However, even for a decision room where everyone is present at the same time, communications links are required. For example, a participant may want to send a message "for your eyes only." These links provide electronic mail among participants, access to remote computers, and the ability to send information from a workstation to the public screen via the chauffeur.

A TYPOLOGY OF *GDSS* FACILITIES

Table 19.1 lists some representative GDSS facilities. Such facilities can be characterized by the delivery mode and the range of tasks supported. Delivery modes include:

TABLE 19.1   Selected Group Decision Support System Facilities

---

University-based Facilities

University of Arizona	New York University
Claremont Graduate School	University of Minnesota
University of Georgia	Southern Methodist University (*)
University of Indiana	State University of New York at Albany
University of Louisville	Western Washington University

Corporate-based Facilities

Electronic Data Systems	Gould, Inc.
Execucom Systems Corporation (*)	Xerox Palo Alto Research Center
IBM Corporation	

Commercial Facility Vendors

ICL	Metapraxis

For-Hire Commercial Systems—
Permanent Installations

Decisions and Designs, Inc.

For-Hire Commercial Systems—
Portable

Applied Future, Inc.	Perceptronics, Inc.
K. R. Hammond	Wilson Learning Systems

(*) denotes facilities no longer in use.

1. *Permanent installations at the user's site.* Here a conference room is equipped with terminals and dedicated to GDSS use. For such a system to be successful, it must be used frequently; otherwise, it is not cost-effective and falls victim to one of the periodic cost-cutting efforts in organizations. (The asterisks in the table denote facilities no longer in use.) Most of the permanent facilities are located at universities. Two systems at corporate installations—Xerox Palo Alto Research Center (Stefik et al. [22]), which is referred to as COLAB, and at Electronic Data Systems (Mantei [17])—are developmental systems being used for research.

2. *Portable installations brought to the user's site on an on-call basis.* In these situations, the equipment and the services of support staff to run the meeting are rented from a vendor. K. R. Hammond Associates and Wilson Learning Corporation provide such services. The skills of the vendor's staff in facilitating meetings are often as important as the equipment in such arrangements.

3. *Permanent installation at the vendor's site.* Here the group travels to the vendor to hold its meeting. The vendor supplies the software, hardware, and support staff for a fee. The support staff usually acts as the chauffeur. Such a system is offered by Decisions and Designs, Inc. Some universities are also offering this service.

4. *Facilities designed and sold by commercial firms.* Two organizations in England, ICL (a computer manufacturer) and Metapraxis (a consulting firm and software house), sell permanent GDSS facilities that they have designed and developed. These firms will build a decision room at a company's location.

Tasks supported range for one or a few to a "full service" GDSS. An example of the former are the rooms at Decisions and Designs and SUNY-Albany which support only interactive decision analysis sessions that allow users to create decision trees and utility functions and in which the system does Bayesian statistics. A full service GDSS contains a broad range of software and the ability to support a diversity of tasks from financial decision making to crisis management to personnel selection to project review to long-range planning and forecasting. Appendixes 1 and 2 describe the full service GDSS research facilities at the University of Arizona and at the Claremont Graduate School.

COMMERCIAL EXPERIENCE WITH *GDSS*

The number of group decision support systems built and/or offered for sale is quite small. Facilities that are single purpose and have been offered for rent by vendors seem, thus far, to have survived longer than permanent single site installations at user locations. The reason appears to be that single site installations typically have not offered a broad enough range of services to make them economically viable. A system that has low frequency of use does not survive.

RELATION OF *GDSS* TO *DSS*

GDSS can be viewed as subsuming conventional DSS within it. That is, the concepts of model base, database, and human interface (see Sprague and Carlson [21]) all apply. Thus, as group size shrinks to one, a GDSS reduces to a DSS. Conversely, in moving from a DSS to a GDSS, some new requirements are introduced:

1. The addition of communications capabilities.
2. Enhancement of the model base to provide voting, ranking, rating, and so on, for developing consensus.
3. Greater system reliability.
4. Enhanced physical facilities.
5. Increased setup before use of the system.

The first two requirements have already been discussed. System reliability has to be much greater for a GDSS than for a DSS. If a GDSS goes down, many people are affected, not just one. Since these people are high-level executives and well paid, there is a much greater loss both in terms of financial costs and trust in the system. A GDSS requires much more setup before the system can be used because both the people and the facility must be scheduled, an agenda must be prepared, participants must be able to prepare for the meeting by seeing its data files and models and the like, and, if necessary, create any additional knowledge bases that are needed.

A GDSS requires capital investment in physical facilities. If the GDSS is located in a decision room, the room has to be elegantly furnished and have the feel of the executive conference room that it is. A GDSS also requires much more display and communications hardware.

GAMING AND OTHER NONSTANDARD APPLICATIONS

Gray and Borovits [9] discuss the use of gaming in GDSS environments, with special emphasis on its use for risk assessment and crisis management. They point out that

- Gaming is a form of training that improves both the intuition and skills of a manager in facing real-life situations, particularly high-stress, high-stakes situations such as crises and difficult negotiations.
- The experience and data gained from extensive gaming of a particular situation under laboratory conditions provides a basis for understanding how to cope with "surprise" and with outcomes of low probability.
- Gaming involves highly complex situations in which decision makers respond in novel and unanticipated ways. The iterative nature of the design process for GDSS thus makes it possible to use the results of gaming to increase their ability to handle complex conditions and cope with low probability events.
- Gaming can assist senior managers both in understanding what consensus exists within their organization and in creating consensus. As such, it provides a basis for decision making that takes into account the internal viewpoint of the organization.

Other applications of GDSS include:

- Supporting negotiations, as, for example, in international situations where two or more groups that speak different languages and have different cultural backgrounds are negotiating a contract.

- Supporting cooperative teams involved in design work (the Xerox Palo Alto Research Center facility is used primarily in this way) or quality control reviews.
- Supporting visual decisions such as selecting packaging for a new product.

WHAT HAS BEEN LEARNED

The experimentation with the use of decision rooms is still in its early stages. A number of papers have appeared (e.g., Applegate et al. [2], Gallupe [6], Gray [8], Kull [15], Lewis [16], Watson [24], Zigurs [25]) that report observations, field research, action research, and laboratory experiments. These papers indicate the high potential for the contribution of computer and communication-based mediation, facilitation, and support in creating effective group decision support. The following summary of what has been learned thus far is based on these and other papers and our own observations.

The research results have underscored the need to review and examine the theories and hypotheses on group decision making that have been developed in the past. There is reason to believe that many previously held assumptions about the conduct of group deliberation are subject to review in the new electronically based forum. Factors such as speed, anonymity, recording of group processes, voting, and other facilitated activities change the group environment significantly.

Anonymity

The anonymity facilitated through use of nominal group techniques (Van de Ven and Delbecq [23]) and other tools for electronic brainstorming is a positive factor in encouraging broad-based participation. Anonymity is important when sensitive issues being discussed can easily be confounded with personalities in the group. Anonymity also provides a sense of equality and encourages participation by all members in the group, independent of perceived status. Problems of "group think," pressures for conformity, and dominance of the group by strong personalities or particularly forceful speakers are minimized even though the participants are face-to-face. Group members can contribute without the personal attention and anxiety associated with gaining the floor and being the focus of a particular comment or issue.

Anonymity does tend to heighten conflict within the group because members tend to become more blunt and assertive in their comments and often are not as polite when speaking face-to-face. Further, in any written medium, the richness of voice inflections and facial expressions is lost, which can lead to misunderstanding. Occasional face-to-face discussions, as well as breaks and social time, are important as issues become more politically charged and sensitive.

Facility Design

The lighting and physical organization of the decision room affect outcomes. Better results are obtained when the facility has aesthetic appeal and provides a comfortable, familiar setting for executives. Carpeting, wall coverings, executive style furniture, and quality acoustics provide an atmosphere that is well suited to long sessions over a number of days.

Inadequate lighting control and arrangement of lights result in poor legibility of screens both on the public screen and at the individual workstations. For example, front screen projector images are washed out by fluorescent lighting and can reduce the effectiveness of a meeting.

The decision room should be full service in order to meet the needs of various groups. Thus the decision room should be designed to accommodate a range of group sizes and be able to support tasks that range from passive to active. Breakout rooms adjacent to the decision room that provide computer-based support make it possible to divide a large group into smaller working groups and are useful for changing the environment during a meeting.

Multiple Public Screens

More than one public screen increases group productivity. Not all information can be displayed adequately in the standard 25 line by 80 character format of current computer screens. Windowing on a single screen allows the presentation of multiple sets of data but further reduces the amount of information that is shown about individual items. In a multiple screen setup, the group can view both the current information being discussed and reference information (e.g., sales trends, finances) at the same time. They can see the existing version and the proposed alternative side by side. In rank ordering, they can see the unordered and ordered items simultaneously.

Knowledge Bases and Databases

The documentation of meeting activities, the creation of working papers, and the recording of decisions and commitments are particularly useful by-products of GDSS. These outputs are provided without detracting from meeting activities. File servers handle the knowledge bases and databases, facilitate coordination and management of input from individual decision makers, and serve as "organizational memory" from session to session. The file server functions as a knowledge base repository and provides access to organizational data that are relevant to a particular meeting. A key to effective use of GDSS in supporting planning is the continuity from planning session to planning session provided by an ongoing, expanding knowledge base that is integrated through the output from software tools. This continuity and integration provide the opportunity for analysis from multiple perspectives.

Communication Network Speed

Users become impatient if they must wait more than one or two seconds for a screen. Experience has shown that users expect to receive subsecond response for all activities. A wide bandwidth local network is needed to maintain these high levels of network response.

Fixed vs. Customized Tools

In planning, groups usually start with idea generation, followed by the development of alternatives, and conclude by converging on a course of action through forming a consensus. A group can go through this process in either of two modes:

1. It can create a customized methodology from the set of available tools, or
2. It can follow a standard sequence for using the tools.

Some groups prefer to adopt a standard methodology, whereas others feel that their needs are very different from anyone else's and therefore prefer to generate the sequence. Both approaches have given excellent results.

Software Design: Ease of Use and User Friendly

The best GDSS software helps rather than frustrates individual users. It supports a continuum of modes of working ranging from electronically based, self-directed participation to facilitator-directed discussion. However, a minimum amount of instruction and direction is still required. In the system designed by the University of Arizona, for example, it takes less than five minutes to explain how to use each software tool. Efforts to increase software ease of use are particularly worthwhile. Techniques that use color, overlays, windowing, consistent interfaces, and on-demand help screens all help the user (particularly the novice and computerphobic) to master the software. One or two group members who have difficulty with the software can affect the productivity of the entire group.

Consistency in the dialog interface protocols permits effective dialog management, ease of introduction of participants to new support tools, and ease of tool building. Common keystroke assignments, window layouts, use of color, messaging, and icon semantics facilitate this dialog management.

Screen sharing across and among participants opens new opportunities for particular decision tasks. Activities such as local editing of shared screens, help and monitoring activities, and personal messaging create alternative forms of communication. Using the keyboard as an input device has proven to be much less an inhibitor of active participation than initially had been hypothesized.

Group Size and Composition

Groups numbering from three to twenty or more of differing composition have used GDSS facilities to accomplish a variety of tasks. One finding is clear: Individual satisfaction increases with the size of the group. Computer support assists groups in building toward a consensus. Larger groups appreciate the inherent structuring that keeps the group from becoming bogged down or subject to domination by personalities. Small groups find that the fixed overhead associated with using the computer-based systems eats up the gains from using the system. Small groups are less likely than large groups to conclude that the computer-aided support is more effective or efficient than an unstructured face-to-face meeting. The various electronic brainstorming approaches do not work effectively with groups of less than four. Such techniques are more effective for groups of eight or more persons. Many other techniques, such as stakeholder identification and assumption surfacing, also increase in satisfaction with group size.

The increase in satisfaction with group size is due in part to "human parallel processing." That is, in many situations, participants are entering information into the computer simultaneously. They are functioning in parallel rather than in sequence. In a typical meeting that follows, say, Roberts' Rules of Order, verbal input is sequential. As a result, if a group of ten meets for an hour, each participant has the floor for only six minutes on the average. In parallel processing, the group can finish in twenty minutes and each individual (even slow typists!) have made a larger individual contribution.

Satisfaction

Individual satisfaction is reflected in user reports on the positive aspects of the group decision-making process in a computer-based support environment. Group participants conclude that they are not blocked out of the group and, as a result, they support the group solution with increased confidence.

THE FUTURE OF *GDSS*

The foregoing discussions have been based on the assumption that GDSS is an emerging technology that will succeed. As indicated at the beginning of this article, this assumption needs to be proven. One can argue just as strongly that people meeting in a group need to have a free flow of ideas and that the technology—with its typing, pointing of mice, and other mechanical interruptions—acts as a barrier and a delayer rather than a facilitator of thought. Certainly the present technology is not as user-friendly or as transparent as it ought to be. One of the dangers in the development of GDSS is that, like many other computer-based solutions offered previously, it overpromises and underperforms in its early stages and winds up being discarded. The research programs now under way should help to determine the long-term viability of GDSS.

Suppose GDSS is successful. What can we expect? Group decision support systems today use relatively standard computer, communications, and display technology. Physically, the decision rooms that have been built look very much like conventional conference rooms with terminals and projection screens added. This is to be expected. When a new technology is introduced into an existing situation, it tends to look like and be used in the same way as the technology it replaces. The early automobile looked like and was used in the same way and over the same roads as the carriage, with only the horse replaced by a motor. GDSS provides an enhanced environment for performing existing tasks and will, in the short term, be used the way conference rooms are used now. As understanding of GDSS develops, the nature of group decision making itself can be expected to change. The idea of human parallel processing is such a change.

One potential direction of change comes from the changes going on in the workplace. As large companies decentralize more and more, and as computer and communications costs continue to decrease relative to transportation costs, we can expect that many people will telecommute (e.g., Nilles et al. [18]) to meetings just as they telecommute to work. That is, they will stay where they are and will be brought into the decision conference electronically, through video and computer conference. It is also possible to use these technologies to call experts on a particular subject into the meeting, obtain their advice, and let them go without their ever leaving their place of work.

Another potential direction of change comes from the expert/knowledge-based system realm. As expert systems become more pervasive, one or more of them will be brought into meetings to assist in deliberations. In effect, they become the $(n + 1)$st person in a meeting of n people. Their role can range from retrieving information to synthesis of new alternatives to helping resolve conflicts of opinions.

The present approach of using the technology to mechanize group processes such as voting, Delphi, and nominal group techniques is crude and rudimentary at best. We can anticipate that new ways of gaining group interaction and group consensus will be developed that take advantage of the capabilities offered by GDSS. We are at a very early and a very exciting point in GDSS. The level of activity is building as more researchers start to explore the problem. The next ten years should bring innovation and lead to maturity.

APPENDIX 1: THE UNIVERSITY OF ARIZONA PLANNING LABORATORY

The Planning Laboratory established in 1985 at the University of Arizona's Management Information Systems Department was specifically constructed to aid groups in planning and decision making. The laboratory currently has two decision rooms. The smaller of the two (Figure 19A.1) uses NCR PC4 microcomputers, NCR PC2PC networking, NCR interactive videodisc, and Barco large screen projection technology. As shown in Figure 19A.1, a large U-shaped table is equipped with networked microcomputers recessed into the table to facilitate interaction among participants. The public screen is run off the network through a microcomputer. Microcomputer-equipped breakout rooms provide space for working sessions. The second facility (Figure 19A.2), opened in 1987, uses inner and outer rows of PS/2 model fifty workstations and gallery seating. The facility can accommodate up to sixty people at twenty-five workstations. It provides two large public screens.

Among the software in the Planning Laboratory are facilities for (1) electronic brainstorming, which enhances a form of the nominal group technique; (2) stakeholder identification and analysis, which examines planning issues and looks for discrepancies between stakeholder and organizational interests; and (3) an enterprise analyzer used to determine the relationships among organizational components and to determine the potential impacts that stakeholders have on the organization.

APPENDIX 2: THE CLAREMONT GRADUATE SCHOOL DECISION LABORATORY

The Decision Laboratory at the Claremont Graduate School is a research facility for studying group decision support. The laboratory consists of a decision room, an observation area, and a practicum/preparation room. The decision room (Figure 19A.3)

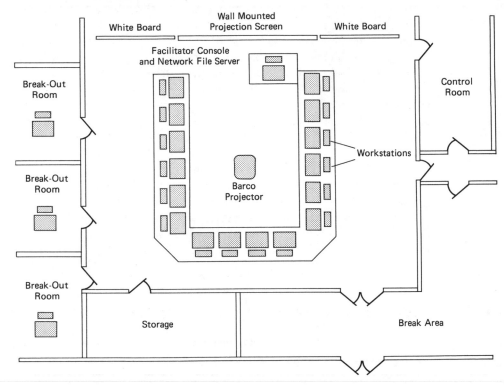

FIGURE 19A.1   University of Arizona Small GDSS Facility

is divided into two parts, each containing a GDSS. Each GDSS has a conference table with individual workstations embedded in it that permit participants to do private work during the conference. The individual workstations are provided with a mouse, touchscreen, and/or bit pad to provide as typewriterless an environment as possible. They are interconnected through a local area network that allows communication and connection with a mainframe. Information can also be displayed to all participants through large public screens at the front of the room. Software is provided to aid reaching consensus through voting, ranking, and rating. The room itself is elegantly furnished to provide the appearance and comfort levels appropriate for executive conferencing. One-way glass and television cameras allow researchers in the observation area to monitor and record what happens during a conference. The practicum room, adjacent to the decision room, contains space for program development and experimental support.

One GDSS uses HP-150 touchscreens supported by an HP-3000 and an Ethernet; the other uses IBM PC/ATs supported by a VAX 11/785 and IBM System/38 mainframes operating on a Sytek local area net. High resolution projection screens serve as public screens.

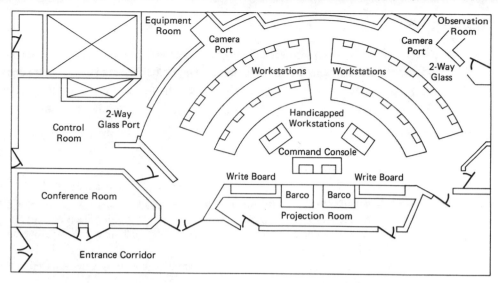

FIGURE 19A.2   University of Arizona Large GDSS Facility

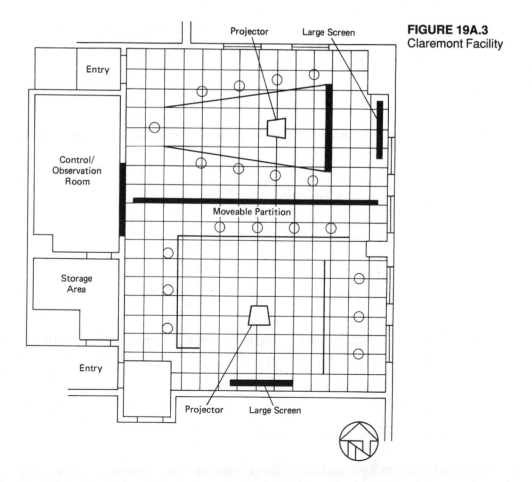

FIGURE 19A.3
Claremont Facility

QUESTIONS

1. Do you believe that GDSS has high or low potential for use in organizations? Why?
2. What are the various types of GDSS facilities? What are the keys to their success?
3. What has been learned from the GDSS experiments that have been conducted?

REFERENCES

1. AHITUV, N. personal communication, 1985.
2. APPLEGATE, L. M., ET AL. "Knowledge Management in Organizational Planning," *Journal of Management Information Systems,* 3 (1987), 20–38.
3. BUI, T., AND M. JARKE "Communications Requirements for Group Decision Support Systems," *Proceedings of the 19th Hawaii International Conference on Systems Science,* Honolulu, January 1986, 524–533.
4. DESANCTIS, G., AND R. B. GALLUPE "Group Decision Support Systems: A New Frontier," *Data Base* (Winter 1985), 3–10.
5. DESANCTIS, G., AND R. B. GALLUPE "A Foundation for the Study of Group Decision Support Systems," *Management Science* (May 1987), 589–609.
6. GALLUPE, R. B. "Experimental Research into Group Decision Support Systems: Practical Issues and Problems," *Proceedings of the 19th Hawaii International Conference on Systems Science,* Honolulu, January 1986, 513–523.
7. GRAY, P., ET AL. "The SMU Decision Room Project," *Transactions of the First International Conference on Decision Support Systems,* Atlanta, June 1981, 122–129.
8. GRAY, P. "Initial Observations from the Decision Room Project," *Transactions of the Third International Conference on Decision Support Systems,* Boston, June 1983, 135–138.
9. GRAY, P., AND I. BOROVITS "Gaming and Group DSS," *Transactions of the Sixth International Conference on Decision Support Systems,* Washington, D.C., April 1986.
10. HUBER, G. P. "Group Decision Support Systems as Aids in the Use of Structured Group Management Techniques," *Transactions of the Second International Conference on Decision Support Systems,* San Francisco, June 1982, 96–108.
11. HUBER, G. P. "Issues in the Design of Group Decision Support Systems," *MIS Quarterly,* 8 (1984), 195–204.
12. KEEN, P. G. W. "Remarks," Closing Plenary Session, *First International Conference on Decision Support Systems,* Atlanta, June 1981.
13. KONSYNSKI, B. R., AND J. F. NUNAMAKER "Plexsys: A System Development System," in J. Daniel Courger et al. *Advanced System Development/Feasibility Techniques.* New York: John Wiley, 1982.
14. KRAEMER, K., ET AL. "Computer-based Systems for Group Decision Support," Working Paper, University of California at Irvine, Public Policy Research Organization, December 1983.
15. KULL, D. "Group Decisions: Can a Computer Help?" *Computer Decisions,* 14 (1982), 14ff.
16. LEWIS, L. F. II, "FACILITATOR: A Microcomputer Decision Support Systems for Small Groups." Ann Arbor, Mich.: University Microfilms, 1983.
17. MANTEI, M. M. "Capturing the Capture Lab Concepts: A Case Study in the Design of Computer Supported Meeting Environments," Research Paper 030988, Center for Machine Intelligence, Electronic Data Systems Corporation, 1988.

18. NILLES, J. M., ET AL. *Telecommunications-Transportation Tradeoff: Options for Tomorrow.* New York: John Wiley, 1976.

19. NUNAMAKER, J. F., L. M. APPLEGATE, AND B. R. KONSYNSKI "Facilitating Group Creativity: Experience with a Group Decision Support System," *Journal of Management Information Systems,* 3 (1987), 5–19.

20. NUNAMAKER, J. F., D. R. VOGEL, AND B. R. KONSYNSKI "Interaction of Group Characteristics, Task and Technology," *DSS Journal,* 4 (1988).

21. SPRAGUE, R. H., JR., AND E. D. CARLSON *Building Effective Decision Support Systems.* Englewood Cliffs, N.J.: Prentice-Hall, 1982.

22. STEFIK, M., ET AL. "Beyond the Chalkboard: Computer Support for Collaboration and Problem Solving in Meetings," *Communications of the ACM,* 30 (1987), 32–47.

23. VAN DE VEN, A. H., AND A. L. DELBECQ "Nominal versus Interacting Group Processes for Committee Decision Making Effectiveness," *Academy of Management Journal,* 14 (1971), 203–212.

24. WATSON, R. A. "Study of Group Decision Support Use in Three- and Four-Person Groups for a Preference Allocation Decision," doctoral dissertation, University of Minnesota, 1987.

25. ZIGURS, I. "Interaction Analysis in GDSS Research: Description of Experience and Some Recommendations," *DSS Journal,* 4 (1988).

20

A COMPARISON OF EXECUTIVE INFORMATION SYSTEMS, *DSS,* AND MANAGEMENT INFORMATION SYSTEMS

Efraim Turban,
Donna M. Schaeffer

INTRODUCTION

The term executive information systems (EIS), also labeled executive support systems, was coined at MIT in the late 1970s. Hailed as a new technology (see Rockart and Treacy [28]), the concept has spread slowly into dozens of large corporations. A recent study conducted at MIT's Center for Information Systems Research showed that about one-third of the large U.S. corporations now have some kind of EIS installed or underway. Another study [29] also indicated that about 50 percent of all EIS were directly used by top executives (CEOs, CFOs, CHOs, and COOs). That is, about one of every six top executives is online with EIS. This figure is confirmed in a survey conducted by *Personal Computing* [9]. Several recent studies provide excellent descriptions of EIS, in general (e.g., Brody [3], McNurlin [21]), and in specific organizations (e.g., Houdeshel and Watson [12], Fedorowicz [8], *Information Center* [33]).

Lately, the concept of EIS has been related to DSS. The Institute for Management Sciences, for example, incorporated in its DSS 1986 and 1987 conferences a special EIS track, which attracted about one-third of the participants (El Sawy [5], Fedorowicz [8]). An EIS track is now a regular feature of the DSS conference.

In spite of all this, many practitioners and academicians believe that EIS is a fad. They claim that there is no new technology, and that, like many other buzzwords, the term will eventually disappear. The purpose of this article is to discern EIS's role as a unique information system and review its relationship with conventional management information systems and with DSS. Specifically, the article is divided into the following parts:

- Definition and characteristics of EIS,
- Information needs of executives,
- Software and hardware needed and available for EIS,
- Comparison of EIS with MIS and DSS,
- The integration of EIS with other computer-based information systems (CBIS) and EIS system development,
- Proposed research issues, and
- Conclusions.

This study drew information from three sources: a review of the literature, communication with users, and communication with EIS vendors.

DEFINITION AND CHARACTERISTICS OF *EIS*

The term executive information systems refers to computer-based systems specifically designed to meet the needs of top executives and eliminate the need for intermediaries between executives and computers. EIS possess the following characteristics:

- Designed to meet the information needs of top executives.
- Principally used for tracking and control.
- Tailored to the individual executive's decision-making style.
- Contains superb graphics capabilities so that information can be presented graphically in several ways and implications of the data presented are highlighted.
- Designed to provide rapidly information for decisions that are made under pressure; that is, timely information is a critical attribute of EIS.
- Designed to be very user-friendly, so that the executive can use it with very little training. When an intermediary operates the system, he or she need not be a computer specialist but may be an executive assistant.
- Designed to fit the corporate culture and decision-making orientation.
- Provides status access, that is, rapid access to current information.
- Provides quick access to detailed information behind text, numbers, or graphs; that is, the information is organized in a top-down fashion.

- Filters, compresses, and tracks critical data.
- Extensively uses data on the organization's environment (competitors, customers, industry, markets, government, international) from online databases, wire services, stock market and financial institutions reports, and other suppliers of information.

These characteristics should be viewed as design criteria for a successful EIS.

INFORMATION NEEDS OF EXECUTIVES

Information systems are designed around information requirements or needs. Can the information needs of executives be provided by an existing corporate information system? Several studies were conducted to identify the information needs of executives, as, for example, that of Rockart [26]. Several other studies were conducted by McLeod and Jones. In one of their studies [19], the researchers asked five executives to keep careful track of the sources of their information. Furthermore, the executives were asked to assign an importance value to the activity or transaction for which the information was secured. The activities logged by the executive were divided into four categories. Table 20.1 shows the nature of these activities and the percentage of information transactions that were used to support those activities.

These and similar studies (e.g., Jones and McLeod [13]) clearly show that executives have unique information needs. However, most existing information sys-

TABLE 20.1   Executive Activities and Information Support

NATURE OF ACTIVITY (DECISION ROLE)	PERCENTAGE OF SUPPORT
Handling disturbances. A disturbance is something that happens unexpectedly and demands immediate attention, but it might take weeks or months to resolve.	42
Entrepreneurial activity. Such an activity is intended to make improvements that will increase performance levels. They are strategic and long term in nature.	32
Resource allocation. Managers allocate resources within the framework of the annual and monthly budgets. Resource allocation is tied with budget and activity planning tasks.	17
Negotiations. The manager attempts to resolve conflicts and disputes, either internal or external to the organization. Such attempts usually involve some negotiations.	3
Other	6
	100

tems do not have the capabilities required to support these information needs. For example, traditional MIS usually have a slow response time because they do not have a separate EIS database. (Companies have been known to dismiss EIS packages because they could not deliver the desired screen output in less than thirty seconds!) Another reason why many existing MIS cannot meet executives' needs is that these systems are designed primarily to meet the needs of functional areas, such as accounting, marketing, manufacturing, or finance. Furthermore, managerial decision making, especially that of a strategic nature, is complex and multidimensional. Conventional MIS is usually designed to deal with fairly structured and much simpler situations.

Executive information systems are designed to gather, process, and display the following five types of information that help senior executives assess their organization's success (Kogan [15]):

1. *Key Problem Narratives*. These reports highlight overall performance and key problems and their causes within an organization. Explanatory text often appears with tables, graphs, or tabular information.
2. *Highlight Charts*. These are summary displays that are designed from the user's perspective. These displays quickly highlight areas of concern and visually signal the state of organizational performance against critical success factors (CSFs).
3. *Top-Level Financials*. These displays provide information on the overall financial health of the organization in the form of absolute numbers and comparative performance ratios.
4. *Key Factors*. These factors, which are denoted as key performance indicators (KPIs), provide specific measures of CSFs at the corporate level. These are flagged as problems on the highlights chart when they fail to meet some predefined standards, usually according to exception reporting.
5. *Detailed KPI Responsibility Reports*. These displays indicate the detailed performance of individuals or business units in areas critical to the corporation's success.

SOFTWARE AND HARDWARE

To exhibit the above types of information and to provide the capabilities discussed earlier, it is necessary to use the latest available software and hardware.

Software

Software for EIS is an extension of typical office automation programs (such as word processing and electronic mail) plus strong database and communication systems. A serious EIS requires a distributed system that involves at least a minicomputer and PCs with specialized software. A representative list of EIS software products, costing $50,000 to $200,000 per system, is given in Table 20.2.

The internal structure of one of these products, the Command Center, is shown in Figure 20.1. Note that the system is built around a central database on a mainframe. This ensures the integrity of the information. The Command Center distributes processing between a mainframe computer and several PCs. The PCs sometimes operate in a

TABLE 20.2   Representative List of EIS Products

PRODUCT	VENDOR
CADET EIS	Southern Electricity International, Atlanta
Commander EIS	Comshare, Inc., Ann Arbor, Mich.
Command Center	Pilot Executive Software, Inc., Boston
Executive Edge	EXECUCOM Systems Corporation, Austin, TX
METAPHOR	Metaphore Computers, Inc., Mountain View, Calif.
OPN	Lincoln National Information, Fort Wayne, Ind.
PC/Forum	Forum Systems, Santa Barbara, Calif.

nonkeyboard environment using only a mouse or touchscreen. Thus, the user has the best of both worlds: the superior displays, quick response, and highly interactive capability associated with PCs and the database and the system logic controller capabilities of a mainframe.

The Command Center includes sophisticated communications software on both the mainframe and PCs. Consequently, performance is exceptionally fast even over lower speed communications links (such as 1,200-baud dial-up lines). Additionally, the Command Center supports off-site users connected to the mainframe via voice-grade-quality links.

Note that, in contrast with a DSS, the Command Center does not have a model base. This is typical of all EIS commercial software. However, a good EIS package will have an interface that allows it to receive and transmit data to and from DSS, freestanding model(s), or CBIS. Since data analysis is not a thrust of an EIS, there is no need for a separate model base.

Hardware

To achieve the capabilities outlined earlier, a serious EIS requires *at least* a minicomputer and PCs. A typical system includes:

- Mainframe: IBM, DEC, PRIME, or Data General.
- PC: Any micro compatible with the mainframe with modem, mouse, graphics, and communication ports; a printer and a plotter are essential.

Some or all of these pieces of hardware are already available in most large organizations. Thus, there is usually no need to purchase special EIS hardware. However, some EIS have their own minicomputers and, of course, executives have their own PCs.

COMPARISON OF *EIS* WITH *MIS* AND *DSS*

As stated earlier, EIS is viewed by some people as not possessing sufficient unique features to be classified as a distinct information system. This situation is analogous to the evolution of DSS. In the early days of DSS there was a considerable debate as to

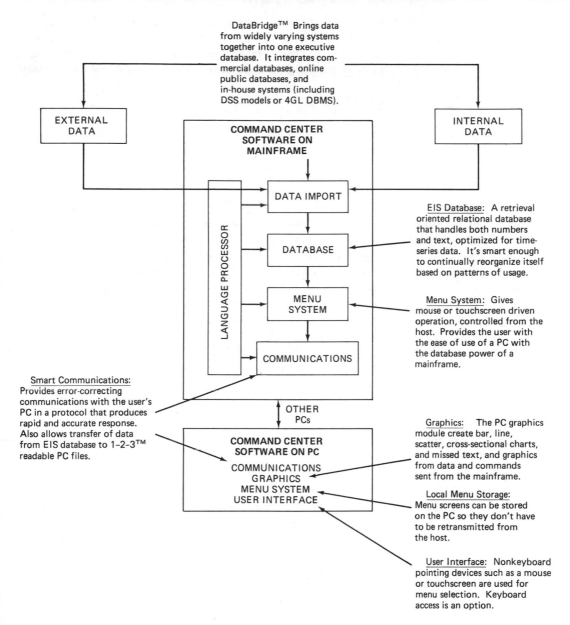

FIGURE 20.1 Command Center
Source: Courtesy of Pilot Executive Software, Boston.

whether DSS had sufficient characteristics to be an entity unto itself. One reason for this debate, as well as for the disagreement regarding what an EIS is, stems from the fact that concepts such as MIS, DSS, and EIS are content-free; that is, they mean different things to different people. Therefore, there exist several definitions of MIS, DSS, and EIS.

In this article we adopt the point of view that MIS and DSS are two different types of information systems (see Kroeber and Watson [16]). This point of view differs from the broad definition of MIS (such as that provided by Ahituv and Neumann [1]) that defines DSS as a *subset* of MIS.

EIS vs. MIS

A major difference between EIS and MIS is the number of users. EIS is designed for senior executives and, therefore, it has a very small number of users. For example, the Gillette Company, which employs over 30,000 employees in twenty-seven countries and fifty-seven manufacturing plants, has only fifty senior managers on its EIS system. In contrast, a few thousand employees access the MIS system regularly. The information needs of the company's top executives were not provided by its MIS, so a decision to build a special EIS was made and implemented. Similarly, Houdeshel and Watson [12] report about seventy users in Lockheed-Georgia.

In addition to the number of people served, EIS is different from traditional MIS along several dimensions. Table 20.3 shows these differences as well as a comparison with a DSS.

TABLE 20.3   A Comparison of EIS, MIS, and DSS

DIMENSION	EIS	*CONVENTIONAL* MIS	DSS
Focus	Status access	Information processing	Analysis, decision support
Typical users served	Senior executives	Middle and lower levels, sometimes senior executives	Analysts, professionals, managers (via inter- mediaries)
Impetus	Expediency	Efficiency	Effectiveness
Application	Environmental scan- ning, performance evaluation, identify- ing problems and opportunities	Production control, sales forecasts, financial analysis, human resour- ces management	Diversified areas where managerial decisions are made
Database(s)	Special	Corporate	Special
Decision support capabilities	Indirect support, main- ly high-level and un- structured decisions and policies	Direct or indirect support, mainly structured routine problems, using stand- ard operations, research, and other models	Supports semistructured and unstructured decision making; mainly ad hoc, but some repeti- tive decisions

TABLE 20.3   (Continued)

DIMENSION	EIS	CONVENTIONAL MIS	DSS
Type of information	News items, external information on customers, competitors, and the environment; scheduled and demand reports on internal operations	Scheduled and demand reports; structured flow, exception reporting of mainly internal operations	Information to support specific situations
Principal use	Tracking and control	Control	Planning, organizing, staffing, and control
Adaptability to individual users	Tailored to the decision-making style of each individual executive, offers several options of outputs	Usually none, standardized	Permits individual judgment, what-if capabilities, some choice of dialog style
Graphics	A must	Desirable	Integrated part of many DSS
User-friendliness	A must	Desirable	A must if no intermediaries are used
Treatment of information	Filters and compresses information, tracks critical data and information	Information is provided to a diversified group of users who then manipulate it or summarize it as needed	Information provided by the EIS and/or MIS is used as an input to the DSS
Supporting detailed information	Instant access to the supporting details of any summary	Inflexibility of reports, cannot get the supporting details quickly	Can be programmed into the DSS
Model base	Can be added, usually not included or limited in nature	Standard models are available, but are not managed	The core of the DSS
Construction	By vendors or IS specialists	By vendors or IS specialists	By users, either alone or in combination with specialists from the IC or IS department
Hardware	Distributed system	Mainframe, micros, or distributed	Mainframe, micros, or distributed
Nature of computing packages	Interactive, easy access to multiple databases, online access, sophisticated DBMS capabilities, complex linkages	Application oriented, performance reports, strong reporting capabilities, standard statistical financial, accounting, and management science models	Large computational capabilities, modeling languages and simulation, application and DSS generators

The comparison of EIS to the conventional MIS shows major differences. EIS is tailored to a small number of top executives, whereas an MIS is usually designed to support all managerial levels. MIS concentrates on control (e.g., exception reporting) and on analysis of structured problems. EIS concentrates on identified problems and opportunities.

For these reasons it is difficult to design an information system that will serve the needs of top executives and at the same time provide the services of the traditional MIS. The question, then, becomes: Can we provide the needs of top executives with an existing DSS?

EIS vs. DSS

EIS has been frequently associated with DSS and considered by some to be a DSS for executives. To examine such an association, we looked at several typical definitions of DSS. Table 20.4 lists the portions of those definitions that are relevant to a comparison of DSS and EIS.

After evaluating Table 20.4, it is fairly clear that EIS fails to meet some of the major requirements of DSS—for example, the use of models, iterative design, and the ability to change the program quickly. Table 20.4 supports the conclusion of Table 20.3, namely, that there are substantial differences between the two systems.

In a general sense, EIS is really a part of the decision support field; that is, it supports the management decision process. However, in a functional sense, EIS and DSS are two different (but complementary) products. The differences are simple but profound. Fundamentally, EIS is a structured automated tracking system that operates in a continuous fashion to keep management abreast of events in all important areas (both inside and outside the corporation). Furthermore, the system itself maintains this tracking without management intervention.

DSS complements this process when more complex analysis is required to understand why things are happening the way they are. These appraisals are performed

TABLE 20.4   EIS in the DSS Definitions

AUTHOR	RELEVANT PORTION OF DSS DEFINITION	COMPARISON TO EIS
Bonczek et al. [2]	CBIS consisting of three subsystems: a problem solving subsystem...	No problem-solving subsystem exists in an EIS
Keen [14]	DSS can be developed *only* through an adaptive process	EIS is not usually developed through an adaptive process
Little [17]	Model-based set of procedures	EIS is not model based
Moore and Chang [22]	Extendable system,...supports decision modeling,...used at irregular intervals	EIS is not extendable, does not have modeling capabilities, and is used at regular intervals
Scott Morton [31]	Utilizes data and models...	EIS does not utilize models

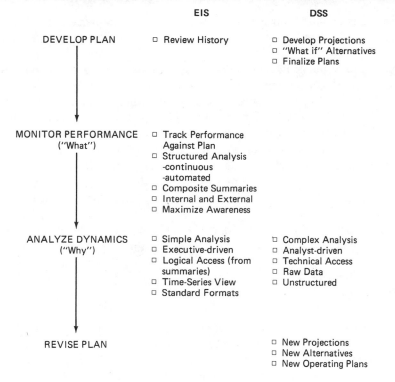

	EIS	DSS
DEVELOP PLAN	□ Review History	□ Develop Projections □ "What if" Alternatives □ Finalize Plans

MONITOR PERFORMANCE
("What")
	□ Track Performance
	  Against Plan
	□ Structured Analysis
	  -continuous
	  -automated
	□ Composite Summaries
	□ Internal and External
	□ Maximize Awareness	

ANALYZE DYNAMICS ("Why")	□ Simple Analysis □ Executive-driven □ Logical Access (from summaries) □ Time-Series View □ Standard Formats	□ Complex Analysis □ Analyst-driven □ Technical Access □ Raw Data □ Unstructured
REVISE PLAN		□ New Projections □ New Alternatives □ New Operating Plans

FIGURE 20.2 EIS/DSS Interrelationship
Source: Courtesy of Pilot Executive Software, Boston.

as needed, usually require evaluation of much raw data, consume considerable time, and almost always require an analyst who is technically proficient with quantitative modeling and analysis. The evaluation may require one analyst for one day or many over several months. In this way, DSS supports EIS in keeping the company on track.

Another way to compare DSS and EIS is reflected in Figure 20.2, which shows the complementary nature of the two systems.

INTEGRATION OF *EIS* WITH OTHER COMPUTER-BASED INFORMATION SYSTEMS

An EIS can be integrated with DSS and/or other CBIS. For example, it is very common for an EIS to be a source of data for PC-based modeling systems. For instance, at a large drug company, brand managers download from an EIS the previous day's orders of their products. The download creates Lotus-readable DSS file on their PC disk. They then exit to the PC and run a Lotus model against the EIS data in order to predict end-of-the-month status, or any other analysis. The results of this DSS model are then uploaded to the EIS, where they can be accessed by top management. Thus, by 11 A.M., senior managers can use their EIS to see where each brand manager thinks she or he will be at the end of the month. This is a good example of the complementary nature of EIS and DSS.

Another example of integration is the system at Hardee's, a national restaurant chain. The point-of-sale terminals at 900 Hardees restaurants accumulate detailed sales information, which the mainframe collects every night for the Command Center database. The database also has information on competitors and financial information from online information services. Financial analysts extract and analyze information on a DSS; top executives access the system through their PCs and use the information on their personal DSS to track or devise marketing and other strategies. This EIS/DSS combination can be very useful. For example, if the figures show that sales in a particular region are falling off during a particular time of the day, local advertising might have to be refocused.

When DSS and EIS are combined, they could have a dramatically positive impact on how well a company operates and how quickly it turns opportunities into rewards.

SYSTEM DEVELOPMENT

Like any other system, EIS can be developed in-house or it can be purchased (for a list of vendors, see Brody [2]). If developed in-house, it can be programmed from scratch or developed with special productivity tools. For example, Forthright Systems (Sunnyvale, Calif.) sells a product called Vantage Point that can be used to build EIS.

In addition, several vendors that develop DSS generators are adapting their products so they can be used to build EIS. Of special interest are Execucom Systems Corporation (Austin, Tex.), which combines its IFPS with the Vantage Point software; and Information Resources (Waltham, Mass.), which has modified its DSS generators (Express and PC Express) so they can be used to construct EIS. Combining DSS generators with EIS development software is especially useful in building integrated DSS/EIS systems.

Another approach is to modify an existing information system to serve EIS goals. Several companies attempted to turn their DSS into a dual purpose (DSS/EIS) system, but this usually does not work. The reason is that a DSS that is productive for an analyst may be counterproductive for the executive. Also, all the design criteria and the capabilities are completely different. Therefore, these systems are designed differently and they perform different functions.

RESEARCH ISSUES

When DSS was evolving, it was supported by extensive theoretical and practical research. The work of such researchers as Alavi, Alter, Bonczek, Briggs, Carlson, Elam, Ginzberg, Gorry, Henderson, Holsapple, Keen, Konsynski, Little, Meador, Morton, Scott Morton, Simon, Sprague, Stohr, Watson, Whinston, and Zmud provided sufficient evidence that DSS is indeed a unique information system for which frameworks were developed, hypotheses were tested, and design was recommended.

A similar approach is needed for EIS. Selected research topics are listed below:

DESIGN ISSUES

1. Further clarification of the nature of managerial work with an attempt to classify it somehow (e.g., public vs. private sectors, manufacturing vs. services, financial services vs. health care).
2. Further clarification of the information required to support top level decisions (including sources of information, types of information, desired timeliners).
3. EIS should be designed to *support* the thought process of the executive. The kind of support that is required in each phase of the decision-making process is a vaguely researched area. It would also be interesting to find out how this support is related to the different decision styles.
4. A framework for EIS design, something similar to Sprague's framework for DSS.
5. Executives make many decisions in a group. Should we design a Group EIS (GEIS)?
6. How EIS interfaces with DSS and with other computer-based information systems (such as an expert system and a natural language processor) both functionally and physically could be an important research issue.
7. What is the most appropriate system analysis and development methodology for EIS?

APPROPRIATIONS OF *EIS*

1. How EISs are actually being used. Can we develop guidelines that will enable executives to get the most out of these systems?
2. A methodology for cost-benefit analysis prior to the installation of EIS and a methodology for the evaluation of operating EIS are desperately needed.
3. Analysis of cases where EIS fail (e.g., see Pallet in [5]).

IMPACTS OF *EIS*

1. Implications for IS planning, personnel, and other resources (e.g., see Gleason in El Sawy [5]).
2. Implementation issues (e.g., see Neal in El Sawy [5]).
3. EIS information as a strategic tool (e.g., see Dacephinais in El Sawy [5]).

***EIS* SUCCESS FACTORS**

1. The software/hardware match.
2. Developing measures of success (e.g., response time).
3. User satisfaction and utilization.

MANAGING THE *EIS*

1. Who is going to build the EIS and be responsible for it?
2. EIS and the IS organization: cooperation, conflict, or separation?
3. Planning requirements for EIS.

These and other research topics will occupy the minds of IS researchers over the next few years and will contribute to the advancement and betterment of the EIS area.

EIS is a development of major importance to management for the following reasons: (1) EIS uses the latest computer technology to improve management productivity; (2) EIS acts as an executive's filter, causing information to be compressed and summarized in a manner dictated by each user; (3) EIS matches the personal information preference of the executive; and (4) the system goes beyond advanced technology to provide added value based on an understanding of management's role. EIS supports managerial problem solving. However, it also supports opportunity analysis, or it may simply put an executive in a better position to understand the operations of his or her organization.

We found EIS to possess sufficient distinguishing characteristics to justify its classification as a unique information systems product. EIS, in our opinion, is neither MIS nor DSS; it is a system of its own and it contributes best when designed and used as such.

EIS can be combined with other CBIS and especially with DSS. In such a case, its output information is automatically transferred to some modeling system and the executive (or an analyst) performs some analysis with these data. Such a combination is extremely important because the collection and analysis of information on markets, new technologies, competitors, legislation, and the like are essential.

The emergence of EIS may be signaling a new era in the organizational use of computers by top executives. EIS enables more top managers and their staffs to use computers to access and utilize data. In addition, it is a productivity improvement tool (it can save about an hour a day of an executive's time; see Brody [3]). Therefore, it should be viewed as an important component of a comprehensive management support system.

QUESTIONS

1. Summarize the nature of executive work. Why do you think that computer-based efforts to support executive work in the past have been less than completely successful?
2. Discuss the similarities and differences between DSS and EIS.
3. Describe the hardware and software used for EIS. What are the similarities to and differences from those for DSS?

REFERENCES AND BIBLIOGRAPHY

1. AHITUV, N., AND S. NEUMANN *Principles of Information Systems for Management,* 2nd ed. Dubuque; Iowa: Wm. C. Brown, 1986.
2. BONCZEK, R. H., C. W. HOLSAPPLE, AND A. B. WHINSTON "The Evolving Roles of Models in Decision Support Systems," *Decision Science,* 11, no. 2., April 1980.
3. BRODY, H. "Computers Invade the Executive Suite," *High Technology,* February 1988.
4. DELONG, D. W., AND J. F. ROCKART "Identifying the Attributes of Successful Executive Support System Implementation," in Fedorowicz [8].

5. EL SAWY, O. A., ED. *DSS 87 Transactions,* Seventh Annual Conference on DSS, June 1987, San Francisco, Institute of Management Science.

6. EL SAWY, O. A. "Personal Information Systems for Strategic Scanning in Turbulent Environments: Can the CEO Go On-Line?" *MIS Quarterly,* March 1985.

7. *Executive Information Systems Reporter,* newsletter, AVI Data Grapohics, McLean, Va.

8. FEDOROWICZ, J., ED. *DSS 86 Transactions,* Sixth Annual Conference on DSS, April 22–24, 1986, Washington, D.C., Institute of Management Science.

9. FERSKO-WEISS, H. "Personal Computing at the Top," *Personal Computing,* March 1985.

10. FRIEND, D. "Executive Information Systems: Successes, Failures, Insights and Misconceptions," in Fedorowicz [8].

11. GHOSHAL, S., AND S. K. KIM "Building Effective Intelligence Systems for Competitive Advantage," *Sloan Management Review,* Fall 1986.

12. HOUDESHEL, G., AND H. J. WATSON "The Management Information and Decision Support (MIDS) System at Lockheed-Georgia," *MIS Quarterly,* March 1987.

13. JONES, J. W., AND R. MCLEOD "The Structure of Executive Information Systems: An Exploratory Analysis," *Decision Sciences,* Spring 1986.

14. KEEN, P. G. W. "Adaptive Design for Decision Support Systems," *Data Base,* 12, nos. 1 and 2 (Fall 1980).

15. KOGAN, J. M. "Information for Motivation: A Key to Executive Information System That Translates Strategy into Results for Management," in Fedorowicz [8].

16. KROEBER, D. W., AND H. J. WATSON *Computer Based Information Systems: A Management Approach,* 2nd ed. New York: Macmillan, 1986.

17. LITTLE, J. D. C. "Models and Managers: The Concept of a Decision Calculus," *Management Science,* 16, no. 8 (April 1970).

18. LUCONI, F. L., ET AL. "Expert Systems and Expert Support Systems: The Next Challenge for Management," *Sloan Management Review,* June 1986.

19. MCLEOD, R., JR., AND J. W. JONES "Making Executive Information Systems More Effective," *Business Horizons,* September–October 1986.

20. MCLEOD, R., JR., AND J. W. JONES "A Framework for Office Automation," *MIS Quarterly,* March 1987.

21. MCNURLIN, B. "Executive Information Systems," *EDP Analyzer,* April 1987.

22. MOORE, J. H., AND M. G. CHANG "Design of Decision Support Systems," *Data Base,* 12, nos. 1 and 2 (Fall 1980).

23. RECK, R. H., AND J. R. HALL "Executive Information Systems: An Overview of Development," *Journal of Information Systems Management,* Fall 1986.

24. RINALDI, R. H., AND J. R. HALL "Executive Information Systems—Put Strategic Data at Your CEO's Fingertips," *Computerworld,* October 27, 1986.

25. RINALDI, D., AND T. JASTRZEMBSKI "Executive Information Systems, Put Strategic Data at Your CEO's Fingertips," *Computerworld,* October 27, 1986.

26. ROCKART, J. F. "Chief Executives Define Their Own Data Needs," *Harvard Business Review,* March–April 1979.

27. ROCKART, J., AND D. DELONG *Executive Information Systems.* Homewood, Ill.: Dow Jones-Irwin, 1988.

28. ROCKART, J. F., AND M. E. TREACY "The CEO Goes On-Line," *Harvard Business Review,* January–February 1982.

29. ROCKART, J. F., AND D. W. DELONG　"Executives Support Systems and the Nature of Executive Work," Report WP B5, Center for Information Systems Research, MIT, April 1986.

30. SCHNEIDER, C.　"Developing a Practical Executive Information System," in Fedorowicz [8].

31. SCOTT MORTON, M. S.　*Management Decision Systems: Computer Based Support for Decision Making.* Cambridge, Mass.: Division of Research, Harvard University, 1971.

32. SIRAGUSA, G.　"The Executive Workstation—Fancy Phone or Productivity Tool?" *Administrative Management,* February 1986.

33. EDITORIAL　"Implementing an EIS: Two Stories," *Information Center,* February 1988.

21

THE MANAGEMENT INFORMATION AND DECISION SUPPORT (*MIDS*) SYSTEM AT LOCKHEED-GEORGIA

George Houdeshel,
Hugh J. Watson

INTRODUCTION

Senior executives at Lockheed-Georgia are hands-on users of the management information and decision support system (MIDS). It clearly illustrates that a carefully designed system can be an important source of information for top management. Consider a few examples of how the system is used.

- The president is concerned about employee morale which for him is a critical success factor. He calls up a display which shows employee contributions to company-sponsored programs such as blood drives, United Way, and savings plans. These are surrogate measures of morale, and because they have declined, he becomes more sensitive to a potential morale problem.
- The vice president of manufacturing is interested in the production status of a C-5B aircraft being manufactured for the U.S. Air Force. He calls up a display which

Reprinted by special permission of the *MIS Quarterly*, Volume 11, Number 1, March 1987. Copyright 1987 by the Society for Information Management and the Management Information Systems Research Center.

pictorially presents the location and assembly status of the plane and information about its progress relative to schedule. He concludes that the aircraft is on schedule for delivery.

- The vice president of finance wants to determine whether actual cash flow corresponds with the amount forecasted. He is initially concerned when a $10 million unfavorable variance is indicated, but an explanatory note indicates that the funds are enroute from Saudi Arabia. To verify the status of the payment, he calls the source of the information using the name and telephone number shown on the display and learns that the money should be in a Lockheed account by the end of the day.

- The vice president of human resources returns from an out-of-town trip and wants to review the major developments which took place while he was gone. While paging through the displays for the human resources area, he notices that labor grievances rose substantially. To learn more about the situation so that appropriate action can be taken, he calls the supervisor of the department where most of the grievances occurred.

These are not isolated incidents; other important uses of MIDS occur many times a day. They demonstrate that computerized systems can have a significant impact on the day-to-day functioning of senior executives.

The purpose of this article is to describe aspects of MIDS which are important to executives, information systems managers, and information systems professionals who are the potential participants in the approval, design, development, operation, and use of systems similar to MIDS. As a starting point, we want to discuss MIDS in the context of various types of information systems (i.e., MIS, DSS, and EIS), because its positioning is important to understanding its hands-on use by senior Lockheed-Georgia executives. We will describe how it was justified and developed, because these are the keys to its success. While online systems are best seen in person to be fully appreciated, we will try to describe what an executive experiences when using MIDS and the kinds of information that are available. Any computer system is made possible by the hardware, software, personnel, and data used and these will be described. Then we will discuss the benefits of MIDS. An organization considering the development of a system like MIDS needs to focus on key factors of success, and we will describe those factors that were most important to MIDS' success. As a closing point of interest, future plans for the evolution of MIDS will be discussed.

MIDS IN CONTEXT

Management information systems (MIS) were the first attempt by information systems professionals to provide managers and other organizational personnel with the information needed to perform their jobs effectively and efficiently. While originators of the MIS concept initially had high hopes and expectations for MIS, in practice MIS largely came to represent an expanded set of structured reports and has had only a minimal impact on upper management levels [11].

Decision support systems (DSS) were the next attempt to help management with its decision-making responsibilities. They have been successful to some extent, especially in regard to helping middle managers and functional area specialists such as financial planners and marketing researchers. However, their usefulness to top management has been primarily indirect. Middle managers and staff specialists may use a DSS to provide information for top management, but despite frequent claims of ease-of-use, top managers are seldom hands-on users of a DSS [4, 5].

With hindsight it is understandable why DSSs have not been used directly by senior executives. Many of the reasons are those typically given when discussing why managers do not use computers: poor keyboard skills, lack of training and experience in using computers, concerns about status, and a belief that hands-on computer use is not part of their job. Another set of reasons revolves around the tradeoff between simplicity and flexibility of use. Simpler systems tend to be less flexible while more flexible systems are usually more complex. Because DSSs are typically used to support poorly structured decision-making tasks, the flexibility required to analyze these decisions comes at the cost of greater complexity. Unless the senior executive is a "techie" at heart, or uses the system enough to master its capabilities, it is unlikely that the executive will feel comfortable using the system directly. Consequently, hands-on use of the DSS is typically delegated to a subordinate who performs the desired analysis.

Executive information systems (EIS), or executive support systems as they are sometimes called, are the latest computerized attempt to help satisfy top management's information needs. These systems tend to have the following characteristics which differentiate them from MIS and DSS:

- They are used directly by top managers without the assistance of intermediaries.
- They provide easy online access to current information about the status of the organization.
- They are designed with management's critical success factors (CSF) in mind.
- They use state-of-the-art graphics, communications, and data storage and retrieval methods.

The limited reportings of EIS suggest that these types of systems can make top managers hands-on users of computer-based systems [2, 10, 12]. While a number of factors contribute to their success, one of the most important is ease-of-use. Because an EIS provides little analysis capabilities, it normally requires only a few, easy to enter keystrokes. Consequently, keyboard skills, previous training and experience in using computers, concerns about loss of status, and perceptions of how one should carry out job responsibilities are less likely to hinder system use.

MIDS is an example of an EIS. It is used directly by top Lockheed-Georgia managers to access online information about the current status of the firm. Great care, time, and effort goes into providing information that meets the special needs of its users. The system is graphics-oriented and draws heavily upon communications technology.

THE EVOLUTION OF *MIDS*

Lockheed-Georgia, a subsidiary of the Lockheed Corporation, is a major producer of cargo aircraft. Over 19,000 employees work at their Marietta, Georgia plant. Their current major activities are production of the C-5B transport aircraft for the U.S. Air Force, Hercules aircraft for worldwide markets, and numerous modification and research programs.

In 1975, Robert B. Ormsby, then President of Lockheed-Georgia, first expressed an interest in the creation of an online status reporting system to provide information which was concise, timely, complete, easy to access, relevant to management's needs, and could be shared by organizational personnel. Though Lockheed's existing systems provided voluminous quantities of data and information, Ormsby thought them to be unsatisfactory for several reasons. It was difficult to quickly locate specific information to apply to a given problem. Reports often were not sufficiently current, leading to organizational units basing decisions on information which should have been the same but actually was not. This is often the case when different reports or the same report with different release dates are used. Little action was taken for several years as Ormsby and information services personnel waited for hardware and software to emerge which would be suitable for the desired type of system. In the fall of 1978, development of the MIDS system began.

The justification for MIDS was informal. No attempt was made to cost-justify its initial development. Ormsby felt that he and other Lockheed-Georgia executives needed the system and mandated its development. Over time, as different versions of MIDS were judged successful, authorization was given to develop enhanced versions. This approach is consistent with current thinking and research on systems to support decision making. It corresponds closely with the recommendation to view the initial system as a research and development project and to evolve later versions if the system proves to be successful [7]. It also is in keeping with findings that accurate, timely and new kinds of information, an organizational champion, and managerial mandate are the factors which motivate systems development [6].

A number of key decisions were made early in the design of the system. First, an evolutionary design approach would be used. Only a limited number of displays would be created initially. Over time they would be modified or possibly deleted if they did not meet an information need. Additional screens would be added as needed and as MIDS was made available to a larger group of Lockheed-Georgia managers. Ease-of-use was considered to be of critical importance because of the nature of the user group. Most of the Lockheed-Georgia executives had all of the normal apprehensions about personally using terminals. In order to encourage hands-on use, it was decided to place a terminal in each user's office, to require a minimum number of keystrokes in order to call up any screen, and to make training largely unnecessary. Response time was to be fast and features were to be included to assist executives in locating needed information.

Bob Pittman was responsible for the system's development and he, in turn, reported to the vice president of finance. Pittman initially had a staff consisting of two people from finance and two from information services. The finance personnel were used because of their experience in preparing company reports and presentations to the corporate headquarters, customers, and government agencies. Their responsibility was to determine the system's content, screen designs, and operational requirements. The information services personnel were responsible for hardware selection and acquisition and software development.

Pittman and his group began by exploring the information requirements of Ormsby and his staff. This included determining what information was needed, in what form, at what level of detail, and when it had to be updated. Several approaches were used in making these determinations. Interviews were held with Ormsby and his staff. Their secretaries were asked about information requested of them by their superiors. The use of existing reports was studied. From these analyses emerged an initial understanding of the information requirements.

The next step was to locate the best data sources for the MIDS system. Two considerations guided this process. The first was to use data sources with greater detail than what would be included in the MIDS displays. Only by using data which had not already been filtered and processed could information be generated which the MIDS team felt would satisfy the information requirements. The second was to use data sources which had a perspective compatible with that of Ormsby and his staff. Multiple organizational units may have data seemingly appropriate for satisfying an information need, but choosing the best source or combination of sources requires care in order that the information provided is not distorted by the perspective of the organizational unit in which it originates.

The initial version of MIDS took six months to develop and allowed Ormsby to call up 31 displays. Over the past eight years, MIDS has evolved to where it now offers over 700 displays for 30 top executives and 40 operating managers. It has continued to be successful through many changes in the senior executive ranks, including the position of president. MIDS subsystems are currently being developed for middle managers in the various functional areas and MIDS-like systems are being implemented in several other Lockheed companies.

MIDS FROM THE USER'S PERSPECTIVE

An executive typically has little interest in the hardware or software used in a system. Rather, the dialog between the executive and the system is what matters. The dialog can be thought of as consisting of the command language by which the user directs the actions of the system, the presentation language through which the system provides the response, and the knowledge that the user must have in order to effectively use the system [1]. From a user's perspective, the dialog *is* the system, and consequently, careful attention was given to the design of the dialog components in MIDS.

An executive gains access to MIDS through the IBM PC/XT on his or her desk. Entering a password is the only sign-on requirement, and every user has a unique password which allows access to an authorized set of displays. After the password is accepted, the executive is informed of any scheduled downtime for system maintenance. The user is then given a number of options. He can enter a maximum of four keystrokes and call up any of the screens that he is authorized to view, obtain a listing of all screens that have been updated, press the "RETURN/ENTER" key to view the major menu, access the online keyword index, or obtain a listing of all persons having access to the system.

The main menu and keyword index are designed to help the executive find needed information quickly. Figure 21.1 shows the main menu. Each subject area listed in the main menu is further broken down into additional menus. Information is available in a variety of subject areas, including by functional area, organizational level, and project. The user can also enter the first three letters of any keywords which are descriptive of the information needed. The system checks these words against the keyword index and lists all of the displays which are related to the user's request.

Information for a particular subject area is organized in a top down fashion. This organization is used within a single display or in a series of displays. A summary graph

FIGURE 21.1 The MIDS Main Menu

```
┌─────────────────────────────────────────────────────────────────┐
│  ┌───────────────────────────────────────────────────────────┐  │
│  │              MIDS MAJOR CATEGORY MENU                       │  │
│  │                                                            │  │
│  │  ■ TO RECALL THIS DISPLAY AT ANY TIME HIT 'RETURN-ENTER' KEY. │  │
│  │  ■ FOR LATEST UPDATES SEE S1.                              │  │
│  └───────────────────────────────────────────────────────────┘  │
│                                                                  │
│   A  MANAGEMENT CONTROL              H  HUMAN RESOURCES           │
│         MSI'S; OBJECTIVES;              CO-OP PROGRAM, EMPLOYEE    │
│         ORGANIZATION CHARTS;            STATISTICS & PARTICIPATION │
│         TRAVEL/AVAILABILITY/EVENTS SCHED.                         │
│   CP CAPTURE PLANS INDEX                                          │
│                                      M  MARKETING                 │
│                                         ASSIGNMENTS; PROSPECTS;   │
│   B  C-5B ALL PROGRAM ACTIVITIES        SIGN-UPS; PRODUCT SUPPORT;│
│                                         TRAVEL                    │
│                                                                  │
│   C  HERCULES ALL PROGRAM ACTIVITIES                             │
│                                      O  OPERATIONS               │
│                                         MANUFACTURING; MATERIAL;  │
│   E  ENGINEERING                        PRODUCT ASSURANCE & SAFETY │
│         COST OF NEW BUSINESS; R & T                              │
│                                                                  │
│                                      P  PROGRAM CONTROL           │
│   F  FINANCIAL CONTROL                  FINANCIAL & SCHEDULE      │
│         BASIC FINANCIAL DATA; COST       PERFORMANCE             │
│         REDUCTION; FIXED ASSETS; OFFSET; MS MASTER SCHEDULING MENU│
│         OVERHEAD; OVERTIME; PERSONNEL                            │
│                                                                  │
│                                      S  SPECIAL ITEMS            │
│                                         DAILY DIARY; SPECIAL PROGRAMS │
│                                                                  │
└─────────────────────────────────────────────────────────────────┘
```

is presented at the top of a screen or first in a series of displays, followed by supporting graphs, and then by tables and text. This approach allows executives to quickly gain an overall perspective while providing backup detail when needed. An interesting finding has been that executives prefer as much information as possible on a single display, even if it appears "busy," rather than having the same information spread over several displays.

Executives tend to use MIDS differently. At one extreme are those who browse through displays. An important feature for them is the ability to stop the generation of a display with a single keystroke when it is not of further interest. At the other extreme are executives who regularly view a particular sequence of displays. To accommodate this type of system use, sequence files can be employed which allow executives to page through a series of displays whose sequence is defined in advance. Sequence files can either be created by the user, requested by the user and prepared by the MIDS staff, or offered by MIDS personnel after observing the user's viewing habits.

All displays contain a screen number, title, when it was last updated, the source(s) of the information presented, and a telephone number for the source(s). It also indicates the MIDS staff member who is responsible for maintaining the display. Every display has a backup person who is responsible for it when the primary person is on leave, sick, or unavailable for any reason. Knowing the information source and the identity of the responsible MIDS staff member is important when an executive has a question about a display.

Standards exist across the displays for the terms used, color codes, and graphic designs. These standards help eliminate possible misinterpretations of the information provided. Standard definitions have also improved communications in the company.

The importance of standard definitions can be illustrated by the use of the word "signup." In general, the term refers to a customer's agreement to buy an aircraft. However, prior to the establishment of a standard definition, it tended to be used differently by various organizational units. To marketing people, a signup was when a letter of intent to buy was received. Legal services considered it to be when a contract was received. Finance interpreted it as when a down payment was made. The standard definition of a signup now used is "a signed contract with a nonrefundable down payment." An online dictionary can be accessed if there is any question about how a term is defined.

Color is used in a standard way across all of the screens. The traffic light pattern is used for status: green is good; yellow is marginal; and red is unfavorable. Under budget or ahead of schedule is in green; on budget or on schedule is in yellow; over budget or behind schedule is in red. Bar graphs have a black background and yellow bars depict actual performance, cyan (light blue) is used for company goals and commitments to the corporate office, and magenta represents internal goals and objectives. Organization charts use different colors for the various levels of management. Special color combinations are used to accommodate executives with color differentiation problems, and all displays are designed to be effective with black and white hard copy output.

Standards exist for all graphic designs. Line charts are used for trends, bar charts for comparisons, and pie or stacked bar charts for parts of a whole. On all charts, vertical wording is avoided and abbreviations and acronyms are limited to those on an authorized list. All bar charts are zero at the origin to avoid distortions, scales are set in prescribed increments and are identical within a subject series, and bars that exceed the scale have numeric values shown. In comparisons of actual with predicted performance, bars for actual performance are always wider.

Comments are added to the displays to explain abnormal conditions, explain graphic depictions, reference related displays, and inform of pending changes. For example, a display may show that signups for May are three less than forecasted. The staff member who is responsible for the display knows, however, that a downpayment from Peru for three aircraft is enroute and adds this information as a comment to the display. Without added comments, situations can arise which are referred to as "paper tigers," because they appear to require managerial attention though they actually do not. The MIDS staff believes that "transmitting data is not the same as conveying information" [8].

The displays have been created with the executives' critical success factors in mind. Some of the CSF measures, such as profits and aircrafts sold, are obvious. Other measures, such as employee participation in company-sponsored programs, are less obvious and reflect the MIDS staff's efforts to fully understand and accommodate the executives' information needs.

To illustrate a typical MIDS display, Figure 21.2 shows Lockheed-Georgia sales as of November 1986. It was accessed by entering F3. The sources of the information and their Lockheed-Georgia telephone numbers are in the upper right-hand corner. The top graphs provide past history, current, and forecasted sales. The wider bars represent actual sales while budgeted sales are depicted by the narrower bars. Detailed, tabular information is provided under the graphs. An explanatory comment is given at the bottom of the display. The R and F in the bottom right-hand corner indicates that related displays can be found by paging in a reverse or forward direction.

Executives are taught to use MIDS in a 15 minute tutorial. For several reasons, no written instructions for the use of the system have ever been prepared. An objective for MIDS has been to make the system easy enough to use so that written instructions are unnecessary. Features such as menus and the keyword index make this possible. Another reason is that senior executives are seldom willing to take the time to read instructions. And most importantly, if an executive has a problem in using the system, the MIDS staff prefers to learn about the problem and to handle it personally.

The IBM PC/XT on the executive's desk is useful for applications other than accessing MIDS displays. It can be used off-line with any appropriate PC software. It is also the mechanism for tying the user through MIDS to other computer systems. For example, some senior executives and even more middle managers want access to outside reference services or internal systems with specific databases. Electronic messaging is the most common use of the IBM PC/XTs for other than MIDS displays. The executive need only request PROFS from within MIDS and the system automatically translates the user's MIDS password to a PROFS password and transfers the user from the DEC 780 VAX host to the IBM mainframe with PROFS. After using PROFS'

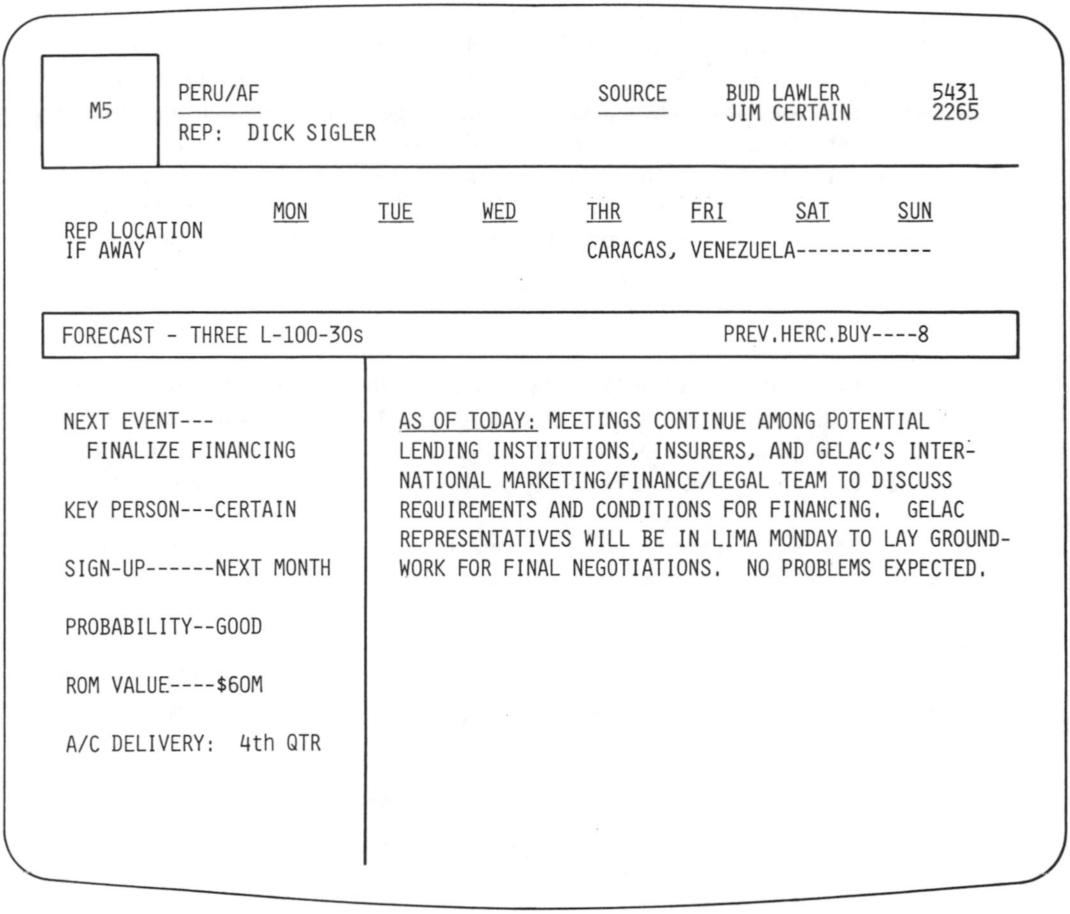

```
┌─────────────────────────────────────────────────────────────────────────┐
│  ┌──────┐  PERU/AF                        SOURCE    BUD LAWLER      5431   │
│  │  M5  │  ─────────                      ──────    JIM CERTAIN     2265   │
│  └──────┘  REP:  DICK SIGLER                                              │
│                                                                           │
│                 MON     TUE     WED     THR     FRI     SAT     SUN        │
│  REP LOCATION   ───     ───     ───     ───     ───     ───     ───        │
│  IF AWAY                                 CARACAS, VENEZUELA-----------     │
│                                                                           │
│  ┌──────────────────────────────────────────────────────────────────┐   │
│  │ FORECAST - THREE L-100-30s                    PREV.HERC.BUY----8   │   │
│  └──────────────────────────────────────────────────────────────────┘   │
│                                                                           │
│   NEXT EVENT---               AS OF TODAY: MEETINGS CONTINUE AMONG POTENTIAL │
│     FINALIZE FINANCING        LENDING INSTITUTIONS, INSURERS, AND GELAC'S INTER- │
│                               NATIONAL MARKETING/FINANCE/LEGAL TEAM TO DISCUSS │
│   KEY PERSON---CERTAIN        REQUIREMENTS AND CONDITIONS FOR FINANCING.  GELAC │
│                               REPRESENTATIVES WILL BE IN LIMA MONDAY TO LAY GROUND- │
│   SIGN-UP------NEXT MONTH     WORK FOR FINAL NEGOTIATIONS.  NO PROBLEMS EXPECTED. │
│                                                                           │
│   PROBABILITY--GOOD                                                        │
│                                                                           │
│   ROM VALUE----$60M                                                        │
│                                                                           │
│   A/C DELIVERY:  4th QTR                                                   │
│                                                                           │
└─────────────────────────────────────────────────────────────────────────┘
```

FIGURE 21.2 Lockheed-Georgia Sales

electronic mail capabilities, the transfer back to MIDS is a simple two keystroke process.

THE COMPONENTS OF MIDS

A number of component parts are essential to the functioning of MIDS: hardware, software, MIDS personnel, and data sources.

Hardware

A microcomputer from Intelligent Systems Corporation was used for the initial version of MIDS. Each day MIDS personnel updated the floppy disks which stored the displays. As more executives were given access to MIDS, it became impractical to update each executive's displays separately, and the decision was made to store them centrally on a DEC 11/34 where they could be accessed by all users. Executives currently interact with MIDS through IBM PC/XTs tied to a DEC 780 VAX. Next year MIDS will be migrated to an IBM 3081 as part of Lockheed's plan to standardize around IBM equipment. Because an objective of MIDS was to reduce the amount of paper, the generation of hard copy output has always been minimized. The only printers are in the MIDS office and include four Printronix 300 (black and white, dot matrix) and Xerox 6500 (color copier, laser unit, with paper and transparencies) printers.

Software

At the time that work on MIDS began, appropriate software was not commercially available. Consequently, the decision was made to develop the software in-house. Even though commercial EIS software such as Command Center and Metaphor are now available, none of it has justified a switch from what has been developed by the MIDS staff.

The software is used for three important tasks: creating and updating the displays; providing information about the system's use and status; and maintaining system security.

Creating and Updating the Displays   Each display has an edit program tailored to fit its needs. Special edit routines have been developed for graph drawing, color changes, scale changes, roll-offs, calculations, or drawing special characters such as airplanes. These edit functions are then combined to create a unique edit program for each display. This approach allows MIDS personnel to quickly update the displays and differs from off-the-shelf software which requires the user to answer questions for all routines, regardless of whether they are needed.

The edit software has other attractive features. There are computer-generated messages to the information analyst advising of other displays which could be affected by changes to the one currently being revised. Color changes are automatically made to a display when conditions become unfavorable. When the most recent period data is entered, the oldest period data is automatically rolled off of all graphs. The edit software has error checks for unlikely or impossible conditions.

Providing Information about the System's Use and Status   Daily reports are generated at night and are available the next morning for the MIDS staff to review. A daily log of system activity shows who requested what, when, and how. The log indicates everything but "why," and sometimes the staff even asks that question in order to better understand management's information needs. The log allows MIDS personnel to analyze system loads, user inquiry patterns, methods used to locate displays, utilization of special features, and any system and/or communication problems. Another report indicates the status of all displays, including the last time each display was updated, when the next update is scheduled, and who is responsible for the update. Yet another report lists all displays which have been added, deleted, or changed.

Weekly reports are generated on Sunday night and are available Monday morning for the MIDS staff. One report lists the previous week's users and the number of displays viewed by each executive. Another report lists the number of displays with the frequency of viewing by the president and his staff and others.

A number of reports are available on demand. They include an authorization matrix of users and terminals; a count of displays by major category and subsystem; a list of users by name, type of terminal, and system line number to the host computer; a list of displays in sequence; a list of display titles with their number organized by subject area; and a keyword exception report of available displays not referenced in the keyword file.

Maintaining System Security   Careful thought goes into deciding who has access to which displays. Information is made available unless there are compelling reasons why it should be denied. For example, middle managers might not be allowed to view strategic plans for the company.

System access is controlled through a double security system. Users can call up only displays which they are authorized to view and then only from certain terminals. This security system helps protect against unauthorized users gaining access to the system and the unintentional sharing of restricted information. As an example of the latter situation, a senior executive might be allowed to view sensitive information in his office, but be denied access to the information in a conference room or the office of lower management.

Personnel

The MIDS staff has grown from five to its current size of nine. Six of the staff members are classified as information analysts, two are computer analysts, and there is the manager of the MIDS group. The information analysts are responsible for determining the system's content, designing the screens, and keeping the system operational. Each information analyst is responsible for about 100 displays. Approximately 170 displays are updated daily by the MIDS staff. The computer analysts are responsible for hardware selection and acquisition and software development. While the two groups have different job responsibilities, they work together and make suggestions to each other for improving the system.

It is imperative that the information analysts understand the information that they enter into the system. Several actions are taken to ensure that this is the case. Most of the information analysts have work experience and/or training in the areas for which they supply information. They are encouraged to take courses which provide a better understanding of the users' areas. And they frequently attend functional area meetings, often serving as an important information resource.

Data

In order to provide the information needed, a variety of internal and external data sources must be used. The internal sources include transaction processing systems, financial applications, and human sources. Some of the data can be transferred directly to MIDS from other computerized systems, while others must be rekeyed or entered for the first time. Access to computerized data is provided by in-house software and commercial software such as DATATRIEVE. External sources are very important and include data from external databases, customers, other Lockheed companies, and Lockheed's Washington, D.C. office.

MIDS relies on both hard and soft data. Hard data comes from sources such as transaction processing systems and provides "the facts." Soft data often comes from human sources and results in information which could not be obtained in any other way; it provides meaning, context, and insight to hard data.

BENEFITS OF MIDS

A variety of benefits are provided by MIDS: better information; improved communications; an evolving understanding of information requirements; a test-bed for system evolution; and cost reductions.

The information provided by MIDS has characteristics which are important to management. It supports decision making by identifying areas which require attention, providing answers to questions, and giving knowledge about related areas. It provides relevant information. Problem areas are highlighted and pertinent comments are included. The information is timely because displays are updated as important events occur. It is accurate because of the efforts of the MIDS staff, since all information is verified before it is made available.

MIDS has also improved communications in several ways. It is sometimes used to share information with vendors, customers, legislators, and others. MIDS users are able to quickly view the same information in the same format with the most current update. In the past, there were often disagreements, especially over the telephone, because executives were operating with different information. PROFS provides electronic mail. The daily diary announces major events as they occur.

Initially identifying a complete set of information requirements is difficult or impossible for systems which support decision making. The evolutionary nature of MIDS' development has allowed users to better understand and evolve their information requirements. Having seen a given set of information in a given format, an executive is often prompted to identify additional information or variations of formats that provide still better decision support.

The current system provides a test-bed for identifying and testing possible system changes. New state-of-the-art hardware and software can be compared with the current system in order to provide information for the evolution of MIDS. For example, a mouse-based system currently is being tested.

MIDS is responsible for cost savings in several areas. Many reports and graphs which were formerly produced manually are now printed from MIDS and distributed to non-MIDS users. Some requirements for special reports and presentation materials are obtained at less cost by modifying standard MIDS displays. Reports that are produced by other systems are summarized in MIDS and are no longer printed and distributed to MIDS users.

THE SUCCESS OF MIDS

Computer-based systems can be evaluated on the basis of cost/benefit, frequency of use, and user satisfaction considerations. Systems which support decision making, such as MIDS, normally do not lend themselves to a quantified assessment of their benefits. They do provide intangible benefits, however, as can be seen in the following example.

Lockheed-Georgia markets its aircrafts worldwide. In response to these efforts, it is common for a prospective buyer to call a company executive to discuss a proposed deal. Upon receipt of a phone call, the executive can call up a display which provides the following information: the aircraft's model and quantity; the dollar value of the offer; the aircraft's availability for delivery; previous purchases by the prospect; the sales representative's name and exact location for the week; and a description of the status of the possible sale. Such a display is shown in Figure 21.3. All of this

FIGURE 21.3 The Status of a Sale

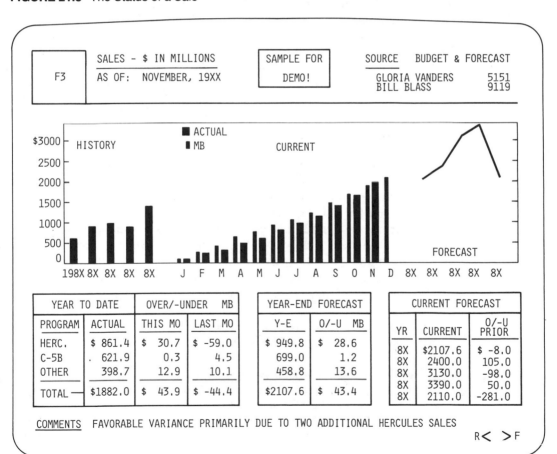

TABLE 21.1   MIDS Users, Displays and Displays Viewed

YEAR	NUMBER OF USERS	NUMBER OF DISPLAYS	MEAN NUMBER OF DISPLAYS VIEWED PER USER/PER DAY
1979	12	69	*
1980	24	231	*
1981	27	327	*
1982	31	397	3
1983	31	441	4
1984	49	620	4.2
1985	70	710	5.5

*Figures not available.

information is available without putting the prospective customer on hold, transferring the call to someone else, or awaiting the retrieval of information from a file.

When a user can choose whether or not to use a system, frequency of use can be employed as a measure of success. Table 21.1 presents data on how the number of users and displays and the mean number of displays viewed per day by each executive has changed over time. The overall picture is one of increased usage; currently an average of 5.5 screens are viewed each day by the 70 executives who have access to MIDS. Unlike some systems which are initially successful but quickly fade away, the success of MIDS has increased over time.

Frequency of use can be a very imperfect measure of success. The MIDS group recognizes that a single display which has a significant impact on decision making is much more valuable than many screens which are paged through with passing interest. Consequently, frequency of use is used as only one indicator of success.

MIDS personnel have felt no need to conduct formal studies of user satisfaction. The data on system usage and daily contact with MIDS users provide ample information on how satisfied users are with MIDS. User satisfaction can be illustrated by the experience of Paul Frech who was vice president of operations in 1979. When MIDS was offered to him, he had little interest in the system because he had well-established channels for the flow of information to support his job responsibilities. Shortly afterwards, Frech was promoted to the corporate headquarters staff in California. When he was again promoted to become the president of Lockheed-Georgia, MIDS had become a standard for executive information and he was reintroduced to the system. He has stated:

> I assumed the presidency of the Lockheed-Georgia Company in June 1984, and the MIDS system had been in operation for some time prior to that. The MIDS system enabled me to more quickly evaluate the current conditions of each of our operational areas and, although I had not been an advocate of executive computer systems, the ease and effectiveness of MIDS made it an essential part of my informational sources.

Because Frech and other senior executives have come to rely on MIDS, middle managers at Lockheed-Georgia and executives at other Lockheed companies want their own versions of MIDS. Within Lockheed-Georgia there is the feeling that "If the boss likes it, I need it." Currently, MIDS personnel are helping middle functional area managers develop subsystems of MIDS and are assisting other Lockheed companies with the development of similar systems.

KEYS TO THE SUCCESS OF *MIDS*

Descriptions of successful systems are useful to people responsible for conceptualizing, approving, and developing similar systems. Perhaps even more important are insights about what makes a system a success. We will identify the keys to MIDS' success here, but it should be remembered that differences exist among executive information systems, organizations, and possibly the factors that lead to success.

1. *A Committed Senior Executive Sponsor*. Ormsby served as the organizational champion for MIDS. He wanted a system like MIDS, committed the necessary resources, participated in its creation, and encouraged its use by others.
2. *Carefully Defined System Requirements*. Several considerations governed the design of the system. It had to be custom-tailored to meet the information needs of its users. Ease-of-use, an absolutely essential item to executives who were wary of computers, was critical. Response time had to be fast. The displays had to be updated quickly and easily as conditions changed.
3. *Carefully Defined Information Requirements*. There has been a continuing effort to understand management's information requirements. Displays have been added, modified, and deleted over time. Providing information relevant to managements' CSFs has been of paramount importance.
4. *A Team Approach to Systems Development*. The staff that developed, operates, and evolves MIDS combines information systems skills and functional area knowledge. The computer analysts are responsible for the technical aspects of the system while the information analysts are responsible for providing the information needed by management. This latter responsibility demands that the information analysts know the business and maintain close contact with information sources and users.
5. *An Evolutionary Development Approach*. The initial version of MIDS successfully addressed the most critical information needs of the company president and strengthened his support for the system. There is little doubt that developing a fully integrated system for a full complement of users would have resulted in substantial delays and less enthusiasm for the system. Over the years, MIDS has expanded and evolved as more users have been provided access to MIDS, management's information requirements have changed, better ways to analyze and present information have been discovered, and improved computer technology has become integrated into the system.
6. *Careful Computer Hardware and Software Selection*. The decision to proceed with the development of MIDS was made when good color terminals at reasonable prices became available. At that time graphics software was very limited and it

was necessary to develop the software for MIDS in-house. The development of MIDS could have been postponed until hardware and software with improved performance at reduced cost appeared, but this decision would have delayed providing management with the information needed. Also affecting the hardware selection was the existing hardware within the organization and the need to integrate MIDS into the overall computing architecture. While it is believed that excellent hardware and software decisions have been made for MIDS, different circumstances at other firms may lead to different hardware and software configurations.

FUTURE PLANS FOR *MIDS*

MIDS continues to evolve along the lines mentioned previously: expansion through subsystems to lower organizational levels; expansion to other Lockheed companies; and hardware changes to make MIDS more IBM compatible. Improvements in display graphics are also planned through the use of a video camera with screen digitizing capabilities. A pilot program for voice input is currently being sponsored by the vice president of engineering.

A number of other enhancements are also projected. A future version of MIDS may automatically present variance reports when actual conditions deviate by more than user defined levels. Audio output may supplement what is presented by the displays. The system may contain artificial intelligence components. There may be large screen projection of MIDS displays with better resolution than is currently available. The overriding objective is to provide Lockheed-Georgia management with the information they need to effectively and efficiently carry out their job responsibilities.

QUESTIONS

1. Why have many senior executives not become hands-on users of a DSS? What raises the hopes for EIS?
2. What screen design features of the MIDS system might be appropriate for any EIS?
3. What methods have been used to document the success of the MIDS system? Are any other methods feasible and desirable? Discuss.

REFERENCES

1. BENNETT, J. "User-Oriented Graphics, Systems for Decision Support in Unstructured Tasks," in *User-Oriented Design of Interactive Graphics Systems,* S. Treu, (ed.), Association for Computing Machinery, New York, New York, 1977, pp. 3–11.
2. DeLONG, D. W. AND ROCKART, J. F. "Identifying the Attributes of Successful Executive Support System Implementation," *Transactions from the Sixth Annual Conference on Decision Support Systems,* J. Fedorowicz (ed.), Washington, D.C., April 21–24, 1986, pp. 41–54.

3. EL SAWY, O. A.   "Personal Information Systems for Strategic Scanning in Turbulent Environments: Can the CEO Go On-Line?" *MIS Quarterly,* volume 9, number 1, March 1985, pp. 53–60.

4. FRIEND, D.   "Executive Information Systems: Success, Failure, Insights and Misconceptions," *Transactions from the Sixth Annual Conference on Decision Support Systems,* J. Fedorowicz (ed.), Washington, D.C., April 21–24, 1986, pp. 35–40.

5. HOGUE, J. T. AND WATSON, H. J.   "An Examination of Decision Makers' Utilization of Decision Support System Output," *Information and Management,* volume 8, number 4, April 1985, pp. 205–212.

6. HOGUE, J. T. AND WATSON, H. J.   "Management's Role in the Approval and Administration of Decision Support Systems," *MIS Quarterly,* volume 7, number 2, June 1983, pp. 15–23.

7. KEEN, P. G. W.   "Value Analysis: Justifying Decision Support Systems," *MIS Quarterly,* volume 5, number 1, March 1981, pp. 1–16.

8. MCDONALD, E.   "Telecommunications," *Government Computer News,* February 28, 1986, p. 44.

9. ROCKART, J. F.   "Chief Executives Define Their Own Data Needs," *Harvard Business Review,* volume 57, number 2, January–February 1979, pp. 81–93.

10. ROCKART, J. F. AND TREACY, M. E.   "The CEO Goes On-Line," *Harvard Business Review,* volume 60, number 1, January–February 1982, pp. 32–88.

11. SPRAGUE, R. H., JR.   "A Framework for the Development of Decision Support Systems," *MIS Quarterly,* volume 4, number 4, December 1980, pp. 10–26.

12. SUNDUE, D. G.   "GenRad's On-line Executives," *Transactions from the Sixth Annual Conference on Decision Support Systems,* J. Fedorowicz (ed.), Washington, D.C., April 21–24, 1986, pp. 14–20.

22

EXPERT SYSTEMS: THE NEXT CHALLENGE FOR MANAGERS

Fred L. Luconi,
Thomas W. Malone,
and Michael S. Scott Morton

Winston defines artificial intelligence (AI) as "the study of ideas which enable computers to do the things that make people seem intelligent."[1] AI systems attempt to accomplish this by dealing with qualitative as well as quantitative information, ambiguous and "fuzzy" reasoning, and rules of thumb that give good but not always optimal solutions. Another way to characterize artificial intelligence is not in terms of what it attempts to do, but in terms of the programming techniques and philosophies that have evolved from it. Specific AI techniques such as "frames" and "rules" allow programmers to represent knowledge in ways that are often much more flexible and much more natural for humans to deal with than the algorithmic procedures used in traditional programming languages.

There are at least three areas in which AI, in its current state of development, appears to have promising near-term applications: robotics, natural language under-

Reprinted from "Expert Systems: The Next Challenge for Managers," by Fred L. Luconi, Thomas W. Malone, and Michael S. Scott Morton, *Sloan Management Review*, Summer 1986, pp. 3–14, by permission of the publisher. © 1986 by the Sloan Management Review Association. All rights reserved.

standing, and expert systems. In this article, we will focus on the realistic potential for the use of expert systems in business. To emphasize our main point about appropriate ways of using these systems, we will exaggerate a distinction between expert systems, as they are often conceived, and a variation of expert systems, which we will call expert support systems.

WHAT DO EXPERT SYSTEMS DO?

Preserve and Disseminate Scarce Expertise

Expert systems techniques can be used to preserve and disseminate scarce expertise by encoding the relevant experience of an expert and making this expertise available as a resource to the less experienced person. Schlumberger Corporation uses its Dipmeter Advisor to access the interpretive abilities of a handful of their most productive geological experts and to make it available to their field geologists all over the world.[2] The program takes oil well log data about the geological characteristics of a well and makes inferences about the probable location of oil in that region.

Solve Problems Thwarting Traditional Programs

Expert systems can also be used to solve problems that thwart traditional programming techniques. For example, an early expert system in practical use today is known as XCON. Developed at Digital Equipment Corporation in a joint effort with Carnegie-Mellon University, XCON uses some 3,300 rules and 5,500 product descriptions to configure the specific detailed components of VAX and other computer systems in response to the customers' overall orders. The system first determines what, if any, substitutions and additions have to be made to the order so that it is complete and consistent. It then produces a number of diagrams showing the electrical connections and room layout for the 50 to 150 components in a typical system.[3]

This application was attempted unsuccessfully several times using traditional programming techniques before the AI effort was initiated. The system has been in daily use now for over four years and the savings have been substantial, not only in terms of saving the technical editor time, but also in ensuring that no component is missing at installation time—an occurrence that delays the customer's acceptance of the system.[4]

WHAT ARE EXPERT SYSTEMS?

With these examples in mind, we define expert systems as *computer programs that use specialized symbolic reasoning to solve difficult problems well*. In other words, expert systems (1) use specialized knowledge about a particular problem area (such as geological analysis or computer configuration) rather than just general purpose knowledge that would apply to all problems, (2) use symbolic (and often qualitative) reasoning rather than just numerical calculations, and (3) perform at a level of competence that is better than that of nonexpert humans.

Expert systems can, of course, include extensive numerical calculations, but a computer program that uses *only* numerical techniques (such as a complex optimization program) would not ordinarily be called an "expert system." The kinds of nonnumerical symbolic knowledge that expert systems use include component/subcomponent relationships and qualitative rules about causal factors.

One of the most important ways in which expert systems differ from traditional computer applications is in their use of heuristic reasoning. Traditional applications employ algorithms, that is, precise rules that, when followed, lead to the correct conclusion. For example, the amount of a payroll check for an employee is calculated according to a precise set of rules. Expert systems, in contrast, often attack problems that are too complex to be solved perfectly; to do this, they use heuristic techniques that provide good but not necessarily optimum answers.

In some ways, of course, all computer programs are algorithms in that they provide a complete set of specifications for what the computer will do. Heuristic programs, however, usually search through alternatives using "rules of thumb" rather than guaranteed solution techniques. A program might consider many different types of geological formations before deciding which type best explains the data observed in a particular case.

WHAT ARE EXPERT SUPPORT SYSTEMS?

While expert support systems and expert systems use the same techniques, expert support systems help *people* (the emphasis is on people) solve a much wider class of problems. In other words, *expert support systems are computer programs that use specialized symbolic reasoning to help people solve difficult problems well.* This is done by pairing the human with the expert system in such a way that the expert system provides some of the knowledge and reasoning steps, while the human provides overall problem-solving direction as well as specific knowledge not incorporated in the system. Some of this knowledge can be thought of beforehand and made explicit when it is encoded in the expert system. However, much of the knowledge may be imprecise and will remain below the level of consciousness, to be recalled to the conscious level of the decision maker only when it is triggered by the evolving problem context.

COMPONENTS OF EXPERT SYSTEMS

To understand how expert systems (and expert support systems) are different from traditional computer applications, it is important to understand the components of a typical expert system (see Figure 22.1). In addition to the *user interface,* which allows the system to communicate with a human user, a typical expert system also has (1) a *knowledge base* of facts and rules related to the problem and (2) a set of reasoning methods—an *"inference engine"*—that interacts with the information in the knowledge

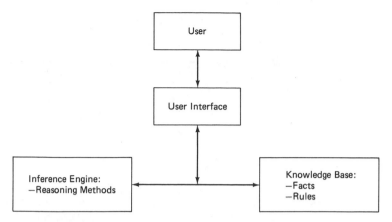

FIGURE 22.1 Expert Systems Architecture

base to solve the problem. As these two components are separate, it makes it much easier to change the system as the problem changes or becomes better understood. New rules can be added to the knowledge base in such a way that all the old facts and reasoning methods can still be used. Figure 22.1 shows in detail the elements of the expert systems architecture.

Knowledge Base

To flexibly use specialized knowledge for many different kinds of problems, AI researchers have developed a number of new "knowledge representation" techniques. Using these techniques to provide structure for a body of knowledge is still very much an art and is practiced by an emerging group of professionals sometimes called "knowledge engineers." Knowledge engineers in this field are akin to the systems analysts of data-processing (DP) applications. They work with the "experts" and draw out the relevant expertise in a form that can be encoded in a computer program. Three of the most important techniques for encoding this knowledge are (1) production rules, (2) semantic networks, and (3) frames.

Production Rules   Production rules are particularly useful in building systems based on heuristic methods.[5] These are simple "if-then" rules that are often used to represent the empirical consequences of a given condition or the action that should be taken in a given situation. For example, a medical diagnosis system might have a rule like:

If: (1) The patient has a fever, and
       (2) The patient has a runny nose,
Then: It is very likely (.9) that the patient has a cold.

A computer configuration system might have a rule like:

If: (1) There is an unassigned single port disk drive, and
       (2) There is a free controller,

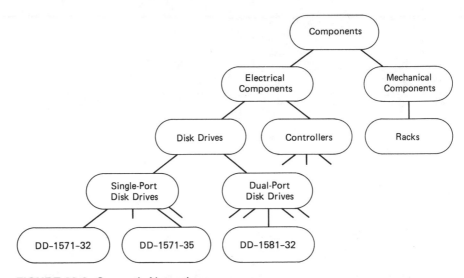

FIGURE 22.2 Semantic Network

Then: Assign the disk drive to the controller port.

Semantic Networks Another formalism that is often more convenient than production rules for representing certain kinds of relational knowledge is called semantic networks or "semantic nets." To apply the rule about assigning disk drives, for example, a system would need to know what part numbers correspond to single port disk drives, controllers, and so forth. Figure 22.2 shows how this knowledge might be represented in a network of "nodes" connected by "links" that signify which classes of components are subsets of other classes.

Frames In many cases, it is convenient to gather into one place a number of different kinds of information about an object. Figure 22.3 shows how several dimensions (such

FIGURE 22.3 Frame

Electrical Component	
Part No.	
Length	
Width	
Height	
Volume	
Voltage	

as length, width, and power requirements) that describe electrical components might be represented as different "slots" in a "frame" about electrical components. Unlike traditional records in a database, frames often contain additional features such as "default values" and "attached procedures." For instance, if the default value for voltage requirement of an electrical component is 110 volts, then the system would infer that a new electrical component required 110 volts unless explicit information to the contrary was provided. An attached procedure might automatically update the "volume" slot, whenever "length," "height," or "width" is changed (see Figure 22.3).

These three knowledge representation techniques—production rules, semantic networks, and frames—have considerable power in that they permit us to capture knowledge in a way that can be exploited by the "inference engine" to produce good, workable answers to the questions at hand.

Inference Engine

The inference engine contains the reasoning methods that might be used by human problem solvers for attacking problems. As these are separate from the knowledge base, either the inference engine or the knowledge base can be changed relatively independently of the other. Two reasoning methods often employed with production rules are *forward chaining* and *backward chaining*.

Forward Chaining   Imagine that we have a set of production rules like those shown in Figure 22.4 for a personal financial planning expert system. Imagine also that we know the current client's tax bracket is 50 percent, his liquidity is greater than $100,000, and he has a high tolerance for risk. By forward chaining through the rules, one at a time, the system could infer that exploratory oil and gas investments should be recommended for this client. With a larger rule base, many other investment recommendations might be deduced as well.

Backward Chaining   Now imagine that we want to know only whether exploratory oil and gas investments are appropriate for a particular client, and we are not interested in any other investments at the moment. The system can use exactly the same rule base to answer this specific question more efficiently by backward chaining through the rules (see Figure 22.4). With backward chaining, the system starts with a goal (e.g., "show that this client needs exploratory oil and gas investments") and asks at each stage what subgoals it would need to reach to achieve this goal. Here, to conclude that the client needs exploratory oil and gas investments, we can use the third rule (indicated in Figure 22.4) if we know that risk tolerance is high (which we already do know) and that a tax shelter is indicated. To conclude that a tax shelter is recommended, we have to find another rule (in this case, the first one) and then check whether its conditions are satisfied. In this case, they are, so our goal is achieved: we know we can recommend exploratory oil and gas investments to the client.

Keeping these basic concepts in mind, we now turn to a framework that puts expert systems and expert support systems into a management context.

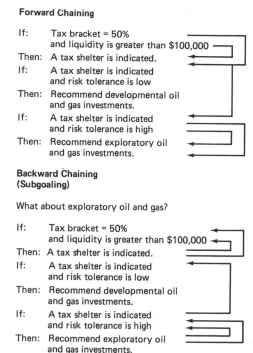

Forward Chaining

If: Tax bracket = 50%
and liquidity is greater than $100,000

Then: A tax shelter is indicated.

If: A tax shelter is indicated
and risk tolerance is low

Then: Recommend developmental oil
and gas investments.

If: A tax shelter is indicated
and risk tolerance is high

Then: Recommend exploratory oil
and gas investments.

**Backward Chaining
(Subgoaling)**

What about exploratory oil and gas?

If: Tax bracket = 50%
and liquidity is greater than $100,000

Then: A tax shelter is indicated.

If: A tax shelter is indicated
and risk tolerance is low

Then: Recommend developmental oil
and gas investments.

If: A tax shelter is indicated
and risk tolerance is high

Then: Recommend exploratory oil
and gas investments.

FIGURE 22.4 Inference Engine

THE FRAMEWORK FOR EXPERT SUPPORT SYSTEMS

The framework developed in this section begins to allow us to identify those classes of business problems that are appropriate for data processing, decision support systems, expert systems, and expert support systems. In addition, we can clarify the relative contributions of humans and computers in the various classes of applications.

This framework extends the earlier work of Gorry and Scott Morton,[6] in which they relate Herbert Simon's seminal work on structured vs. unstructured decision making[7] to Robert Anthony's strategic planning, management control, and operational control.[8] Figure 22.5 presents Gorry and Scott Morton's framework. They argued that to improve the quality of decisions, the manager must seek not only to match the type and quality of information and its presentation to the category of decision, but he or she must also choose a system that reflects the degree of the problem's structure.

In light of the insights garnered from the field of artificial intelligence, Figure 22.6 shows how we can expand and rethink the structured/unstructured dimension of the original framework. Simon separated decision making into three phases: intelligence, design, and choice.[9] A structured decision is one where all three phases are fully understood and "computable" by the human decision maker. As a result, the decision is programmable. In an unstructured decision, one or more of these phases are not fully understood.

	Operational Control	Management Control	Strategic Planning
Structured	Accounts Receivable	Budget Analysis— Engineered Costs	Tanker Fleet Mix
	Order Entry	Short-term Forecasting	Warehouse and Factory Location
	Inventory Control		
Semistructured	Production Scheduling	Variance Analysis— Overall Budget	Mergers & Acquisitions
	Cash Management	Budget Preparation	New Product Planning
Unstructured	PERT/COST Systems	Sales and Production	R&D Planning

FIGURE 22.5 The Original Information Systems Framework
Reprinted from G.A. Gorry and M.S. Scott Morton, "A Framework for Management Information Systems," *Sloan Management Review,* Fall 1971, p. 62.

For business purposes, we can extend this distinction by taking Alan Newell's insightful categorization of problem solving, which consists of goals and constraints, state space, search control knowledge, and operators.[10] We relabel and regroup these problem characteristics into four categories (see Figure 22.6):

1. *Data:* the dimensions and values necessary to represent the state of the world that is relevant to the problem (i.e., the "state space");
2. *Procedures:* the sequence of steps (or "operators") used in solving the problem;
3. *Goals and Constraints:* the desired results of problem solving and the constraints on what can and cannot be done; and
4. *Strategies:* the flexible strategies used to decide which procedures to apply to achieve goals (i.e., the "search control knowledge").

For some structured problems, we can apply a standard procedure (i.e., an algorithm or formula) and proceed directly to a conclusion with no need for flexible problem-solving strategies. For example, we can use standard procedures to compute withholding taxes and prepare employee paychecks, and we can use the classical

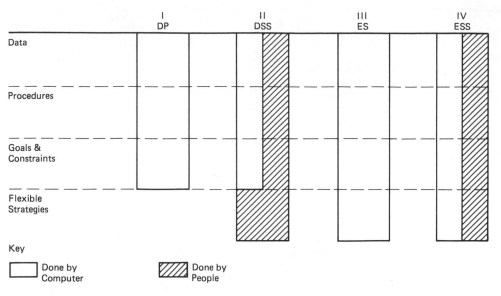

FIGURE 22.6 Problem Types

formula for "economic order quantity" to solve straightforward inventory control problems.

In other less structured problems, no straightforward solution techniques are known. Here, solutions can often be found only by trial and error, that is, by trying a number of possibilities until an acceptable one is found. For instance, for a manager to determine which of three sales strategies to use for a new product, he or she might want to explore the probable consequences of each for advertising expenses, sales force utilization, revenue, and so forth. We will discuss the range of these different types of problems and the appropriate kinds of systems for each.

Type I Problems: Data Processing

A fully structured problem is one in which all four elements of the problem are structured: we have well-stated goals, we can specify the input data needed, there are standard procedures by which a solution may be calculated, and there is no need for complex strategies for generating and evaluating alternatives. Fully structured problems are computable and one can decide if such computation is justifiable given the amount of time and computing resources involved.

Such problems are well suited to the use of conventional programming techniques in that virtually everything about the problem is well defined. In effect, the expert (i.e., the analyst/programmer) has already solved the problem. He or she must only sequence the data through the particular program. Figure 22.6 represents pictorially the class of decision problems that can be solved economically using conventional programming techniques. This class is referred to as Type I Problems—that is, problems historically thought to be suited for data processing.

It is interesting to note that the economics of conventional programming are being fundamentally altered with the provision of new tools such as an "analyst's workbench."[11] These tools include professional workstations used by the systems analyst first to develop flow chart representations of the problem and then to move automatically to testable running code. The more advanced stations use AI techniques, thereby turning these new techniques into tools to make old approaches more effective in classical DP application areas.

Type II Problems: Decision Support Systems

As we move away from problems that are fully structured, we begin to deal with many of the more complicated problems organizations have to grapple with each day. These are cases where standard procedures are helpful but not sufficient by themselves, where the data may be incompletely represented, and where the goals and constraints are only partially understood. Traditional data-processing systems do not solve these problems. Fortunately, in these cases, the computer can perform the well-understood parts of the problem solving, while, at the same time, humans use their goals, intuition, and general knowledge to formulate problems, modify and control the problem solving, and interpret the results. As Figure 22.6 shows, human users may provide or modify data, procedures, or goals, and they may use their knowledge of all these factors to decide on problem-solving strategies.

In many of the best-known decision support systems,[12] the computer applies standard procedures to certain highly structured data but relies on human users to decide which procedures are appropriate in a given situation and whether a given result is satisfactory. Investment managers, for instance, who used the portfolio management system (PMS)[13] did not rely on the computer for either making final decisions about portfolio composition or deciding on which procedures to use for analysis: they used the computer to execute the procedures they felt were appropriate, say for calculating portfolio diversity and expected returns. In the end, the managers themselves proposed alternative portfolios and decided whether a given diversification or return was acceptable. Many people who use spreadsheet programs today for "what-if" analyses follow a similar flexible strategy of proposing an action, letting the computer predict its consequences, and then deciding what action to propose next.

Type III Problems: Expert Systems

We call the problems where essentially all the relevant knowledge for flexible problem solving can be encoded Type III Problems: the systems that solve them are expert systems. Using AI programming techniques like production rules and frames, expert systems are able to encode some of the same kinds of goals, heuristics, and strategies that people use in solving problems but that have previously been very difficult to use in computer programs. These techniques make it possible to design systems that don't just follow standard procedures, but instead use flexible problem-solving strategies to explore a number of possible alternatives before picking a solution. A medical diagnosis program, for example, may consider many different possible diseases and disease combinations before finding one that adequately explains the observed symptoms.

For some cases, like the XCON system, these techniques can capture almost all of the relevant knowledge about the problem. As of 1983, less than 1 out of every 1,000 orders configured by XCON was misconfigured because of missing or incorrect rules. (Only about 10 percent of the orders had to be corrected for any reason at all and almost all of these errors were due to missing descriptions of rarely used parts.)[14]

It is instructive to note, however, that even with XCON, which is probably the most extensively tested system in commercial use today, new knowledge is continually being added and human editors still check every order the system configures. As the developers of XCON remark: "There is no more reason to believe now than there was [in 1979] that [XCON] has all the knowledge relevant to its configuration task. This, coupled with the fact that [XCON] deals with an ever-changing domain, implies its development will never be finished."[15]

If XCON, which operates in the fairly restricted domain of computer order configuration, never contained all the knowledge relevant to its problem, it appears much less likely that we will ever be able to codify all the knowledge needed for less clearly bounded problems like financial analysis, strategic planning, and project management.

In all of these cases, there is a vast amount of knowledge that is *potentially* relevant to the problem solution: the financial desirability of introducing a proposed new product may depend on the likelihood and nature of a competitor's response; the success of a strategic plan may depend as much on the predispositions of the chief executive as it does on the financial merit of the plan; and the best assignment of people to tasks in a project may depend on very subtle evaluations of people's competence and motivation. While it is often possible to formalize and represent any *specific* set of these factors, there is an unbounded number of such factors that may, in some circumstances, become important. Even in what might appear to be a fairly bounded case of job-shop scheduling, often there are many continually changing and possibly implicit constraints on what people, machines, and parts are needed and available for different steps in a manufacturing process.[16] What this suggests is that for many of the problems of practical importance in business, we should focus our attention on designing systems that *support* expert users rather than on replacing them.

Type IV Problems: Expert Support Systems

Even where important kinds of problem-solving knowledge cannot feasibly be encoded, it is still possible to use expert systems techniques. (This dramatically extends the capabilities of computers beyond previous technologies such as DP and DSS.) What is important, in these cases, is to design expert support systems with very good and deeply embedded "user interfaces" that enable their human users to easily inspect and control the problem-solving process (see Figure 22.6). In other words, a good expert support system should be both *accessible* and *malleable*. Many expert support systems make their problem solving accessible to users by providing explanation capabilities. For example, the MYCIN medical diagnosis program can explain to a doctor at any time why it is asking for a given piece of information or what rules it used to arrive at a given conclusion. For a system to be malleable, users should be able to easily change data, procedures, goals, or strategies at any important point in the problem-solving process. Systems with this capability are still rare, but an early version of the Dipmeter Advisor suggests how they may be developed.[17] The Advisor is unable by itself to automatically detect certain kinds of complex geological patterns. Instead it graphically displays the basic data and lets human experts detect the patterns themselves. The human experts then indicate the results of their analysis, and the system proceeds using this information.

An even more vivid example of how a system can be made accessible and malleable is provided by the Steamer Program, which teaches people how to reason in order to operate a steam plant.[18] This system has colorful graphic displays of the schematic flows in the simulated plant, the status of different valves and gauges, and the pressures in different places. Users of the system can manipulate these displays (using a "mouse" pointing device) to control the valves, temperatures, and so forth. The system continually updates its simulation results and expert diagnostics based on these user actions.

SUMMARY OF FRAMEWORK

This framework helps clarify a number of issues. First, it highlights, as did the original Gorry and Scott Morton framework, the importance of matching system type to problem type. The primary practical points made in the original framework were that traditional DP technologies should not be used for semistructured and unstructured problems where new DSS technologies were more appropriate; and secondly that interactive human/computer use opened up an extended class of problems where computers could be exploited. Again, the most important practical point to be made is twofold: first, "pure" expert systems should not be used for partially understood problems where expert support systems are more appropriate; and second, expert systems techniques can be used to dramatically extend the capabilities of traditional decision support systems.

Figure 22.7 shows, in an admittedly simplified way, how we can view expert support systems as the next logical step in each of two somewhat separate progressions.

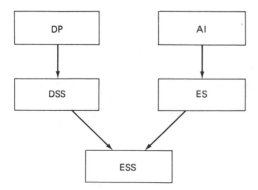

FIGURE 22.7 Progressions in Computer System Development

On the left side of the figure, we see that DSS developed out of a practical recognition of the limits of DP for helping real human beings solve complex problems in actual organizations. The right side of the figure reflects a largely independent evolution that took place in computer science research laboratories. This evolution grew out of a recognition of the limits of traditional computer science techniques for solving the kinds of complex problems that people are able to solve. We are now at the point where these two separate progressions can be united to help solve a broad range of important practical problems.

THE BENEFITS OF *ESS* TO MANAGERS

The real importance of ESS lies in the ability of these systems to harness and make full use of our scarcest resource: the talent and experience of key members of the organization. There are considerable benefits in capturing the expert's experience and making it available to those in an organization who are less knowledgeable about the subject in question. As organizations and their problems become more complex, management can benefit from initiating prototypes ES and ESS. However, the questions now facing managers are when and how to start.

When to Start

The "when" to start is relatively easy to answer. It is "now" for exploratory work. For some organizations, this will be a program of education and active monitoring of the field. For others, the initial investment may take the form of an experimental low-budget prototype. For a few, once the exploration is over, it will make good economic sense to go forward with a full-fledged working prototype. Conceptual and technological developments have made it possible to begin an active prototype development phase.

Where to Start

The second question is "where" to start. A possible beginning may be to explore those areas in which the organization stands to gain a distinct competitive advantage. Schlumberger would seem to feel that their ES used as a drilling advisor is one such example. Digital Equipment Corporation's use of an expert system for "equipment configuration control" is another example. It is interesting that of the more than twenty organizations that we know are investing in ES and ESS, almost none would allow themselves to be quoted. The reasons given basically boil down to the fact that they are experimenting with prototypes that they think will give them a competitive advantage in making or delivering their product or service. Examples of where we can quote without attribution are cases in which an ESS is used to support the cross selling of financial services products (e.g., an insurance salesman selling a tax shelter), or to evaluate the credit worthiness of a loan applicant in a financial services organization.

It is clear that there are a great many problem areas where even our somewhat primitive ability to deal with expert systems can permit the building of useful first generation systems. The development of expert support systems makes the situation even brighter: by helping the beleaguered "expert," the organization will get the desired leverage in the marketplace.

PROBLEMS, RISKS, AND ISSUES

It would be irresponsible of us to conclude without acknowledging that expert systems and expert support systems are in their infancy, and researchers and users alike must be realistic about their capabilities. Already there is an apparent risk that an expert system will be poorly defined and oversold: the resulting backlash may hinder progress.

There is also a danger of proceeding too quickly and too recklessly, without paying careful attention to what we are doing: We may very well embed our knowledge (necessarily incomplete at any moment in time) into a system that is only effective when used by the person who created it. If this system is used by others, there is a risk of misapplication: holes in another user's knowledge could represent a pivotal element in the logic leading to a solution. While these holes are implicitly recognized by the creator of the knowledge base, they may be quite invisible to a new user.

The challenge of proceeding at an appropriate pace can be met if managers treat artificial intelligence, expert systems, expert support systems, and decision support systems as a serious topic, one that requires management attention if it is to be exploited properly. To this end, managers must recognize the differences between Types I and II problems, for which the older techniques are appropriate, and the new methods available for Types III and IV.

CONCLUSION

Although there are some basic risks and constraints that will be with us for some time, the potential of AI techniques is obvious. If we proceed cautiously, acknowledging the problems as we go along, we can begin to achieve worthwhile results.

The illustrations used here are merely a few applications that have been built in a relatively brief period of time with primitive tools. Business has attempted to develop expert systems applications since 1980 and, despite the enormity of some of the problems, has succeeded in developing a number of simple and powerful prototypes.

The state of the art is such that everyone building an expert system must endure this primitive start-up phase to learn what is involved in this fascinating new field. We expect that it will take until about 1990 for ES and ESS to be fully recognized as having achieved worthwhile business results.

However, expert systems and expert support systems are with us now, albeit in a primitive form. The challenge for managers is to harness these tools to increase the effectiveness of the organization and thus add value for its stakeholders. Pioneering firms are leading the way, and once a section of territory has been staked out, the experience gained by these leaders will be hard to equal for those who start later.

QUESTIONS

1. How do expert systems differ from other types of computer applications?
2. What are the component parts of an expert system? Briefly discuss each component.
3. Do expert systems *replace* humans in the decision-making process or *support* humans in decision making? Discuss.
4. What are some of the potential benefits of expert systems to managers?

REFERENCES

1. P. H. WINSTON   *Artificial Intelligence,* 2d ed. (Reading, MA: Addison-Wesley, 1984), p. 1.
2. R. DAVIS ET AL.   "The Dipmeter Advisor: Interpretation of Geological Signals," *Proceedings of the 7th International Joint Conference on Artificial Intelligence* (Vancouver: 1981), pp. 846–849.
3. J. BACHANT AND J. MCDERMOTT   "RI revisited: Four Years in the Trenches," *AI Magazine,* Fall 1984, pp. 21–32.
4. J. MCDERMOTT   "RI: A Rule-based Configurer of Computer Systems," *Artificial Intelligence* 19 (1982).
5. WINSTON (1984).
6. G. A. GORRY AND M. S. SCOTT MORTON   "A Framework for Management Information Systems," *Sloan Management Review,* Fall 1971, pp. 55–70.
7. H. A. SIMON   *The New Science of Management Decision* (New York: Harper & Row, 1960).
8. R. N. ANTHONY   "Planning and Control Systems: A Framework for Analysis" (Boston: Harvard University Graduate School of Business Administration, 1965).
9. SIMON (1960).
10. A. NEWELL   "Reasoning: Problem Solving and Decision Processes: The Problem Space as a Fundamental Category," in *Attention and Performance VIII,* ed. R. Nickerson (Hillsdale, NJ: Erlbaum, 1980).
11. B. SHEIL   "Power Tools for Programmers," *Datamation,* February 1983, pp. 131–144.
12. P. G. W. KEEN AND M. S. SCOTT MORTON   *Decision Support Systems: An Organizational Perspective* (Reading, MA: Addison-Wesley, 1978).
13. Ibid.
14. BACHANT AND MCDERMOTT (Fall 1984).
15. Ibid., p. 27.
16. M. S. FOX   "Constraint-Directed Search: A Case Study of Job-Shop Scheduling" (Pittsburgh: Carnegie-Mellon University Robotics Institute, Technical Report No. CMU-RI-TR-83-22, 1983).
17. DAVIS (1981).
18. J. D. HOLLAN, E. L. HUTCHINS, AND L. WEITZMAN   "Steamer: An Interactive, Inspectable Simulation-based Training System," *AI Magazine,* Summer 1984, pp. 15–28.

23

BUSINESS IMPLICATIONS OF KNOWLEDGE-BASED SYSTEMS

John Sviokla

ISSUES IN *ES* DEVELOPMENT

Looking back on ES development, one finds that notable ES projects were large, long-term research efforts. Dr. Pople, one of the principal designers of the CADUCEUS medical expert system, aptly described early expert systems development.

> One of the generalizations that might be drawn from the first decade of research into expert systems is that a competent performance program will take five to ten years to create, costing from one to two million dollars or more. Certainly if one looks at the developmental history of programs such as DENDRAL (Buchanan and Feigenbaum, 1978), MYCIN (Shortliffe, 1976), PROSPECTOR (Duda, et al., 1978), INTERNIST/CADUCEUS (Miller, et al., 1982; Pople, 1982)—these figures seem about par for the course [29, p. 26].

John Sviokla, "Business Implications of Knowledge-Based Systems," *Data Base,* Fall 1986.

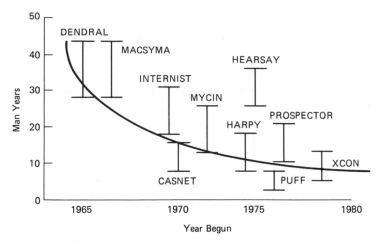

FIGURE 23.1 Development Time of Select ESs
R. Davis, "Amplifying Expertise with Expert Systems." *The AI Business,* P. H. Winston and K. A. Prendergast (eds.), copyright MIT Press. Reprinted by permission of the MIT Press, Cambridge, Massachusetts, 1984, p. 26.

If one looks carefully, the amount of time it takes to create an expert system appears to be decreasing. Davis [11] made a graph for a group of famous ESs [Figure 23.1].

Davis suggests that there is a "learning curve" for ESs. Some of the decrease in development time can be explained by the fact that some of the later ESs deal with more constrained tasks. For example, PUFF concentrates on pulmonary disorders, whereas INTERNIST tries to diagnose internal medicine problems in general. Even accounting for this effect, the graph suggests that the minimum time to create a "usable" system seems to have dropped by 5 years or more—a dramatic improvement. Much of the efficiency is due to increased experience in the field. Later systems used concepts and techniques established by pioneers. Other improvements came from increasingly facile ES tools. But what will future ES development be like and how will it differ from earlier systems?

Insights can be found by comparing ESs to previous IS. Some of the issues which ESs will present are familiar to all IS development. Projects are difficult to manage, good people are hard to find, and project measurement is an art. ESs also bring new challenges. Adding a "domain expert" in the development process increases project pressures and complexities. In addition, an ES has two development efforts embedded within it; the ES shell having one development life cycle, and the knowledge base another.

In order to highlight the special issues which arise in ES creation, I revisit the Problem Types framework [25]. Conceptually, the three Problem Types are points on a continuum of problem structure. Type I problems are at the structured end and Type III at the unstructured. Although these types are artificial distinctions, and practical problems rarely fall into precise categories, the labels are useful for highlighting points of difference or similarity. By distinguishing the old challenges from the new it is hoped that managers will have a better understanding of how to plan for ES project development.

Behaviors

The most obvious difference between an expert system and other systems is the behavior which the ES exhibits (see Table 23.1). These different behaviors have implications for development. In Type I problems the system often performs repetitive, structured tasks with little or no requirement to explain itself. Both the specification of function and the conversion of those functions into software can be accomplished by known techniques. The goal of the system behavior is singular—solve the problem.

In decision support systems, Type II problems, the software is designed to support the user's needs in decision making. The designer arranges models and data, and in the process tailors the behavior of the system to perform complex data retrieval or analysis. But the primary behavior is still to solve the problem.

TABLE 23.1   Issues and Problem Types

ISSUE	TYPE 1 (DP)	TYPE 2 (DSS)	TYPE III (ES)
Behaviors	Perform task, usually transaction processing	Perform task, *support* of decision maker	Perform task, *simulate* expert, explain results, learn, degrade gracefully
Project management	System development life cycle (SDLC)	Prototyping, evolutionary design	Prototyping, knowledge engineering. Two life cycles: knowledge, shell
Development team	Expert and programmer	Expert and programmer	Expert and knowledge engineer
Presentation issues	Known representations	Somewhat known representations	Create new representations
Project life cycle	One life cycle	One life cycle	Two life cycles
Evaluation methods	Established and clear	Some clear, some fuzzy	Fuzzy
Project management tools	Structured programming	Few to none	Very few
Skills: Programming	Cobol, Fortran, Basic	Cobol, Fortran, Basic, 4th generation languages	LISP, PROLOG, ES tools
Other	Conversion of specs, little interpersonal	Conversion of specs, interpersonal	Knowledge engineering, consulting, high interpersonal
Risk	Low to high	Low to high	High

Type III systems exhibit additional behaviors which may introduce complexities in development. In the Karnak case cited earlier, the ES is designed by an expert for use by experts and novices. Only toward the end of development did Karnak's designer realize the complexities of creating an explanation capability. Depending on the target audience, he needed to include entirely different information and presentation methods—a development effort related to, but separate from the problem-solving process.

Project Management

The systems development life cycle, which has proven successful in some IS development efforts, is absent from ES reports. In the literature which discusses ES development, at least three general themes are raised. First, prototyping is essential. Second, most ESs have two parts, (1) a "shell" which is the inference engine and presentation mechanism, and (2) a knowledge base which is developed by knowledge engineering. Third, there is an ES life cycle.

Prototyping In prototyping the designer evolves the system by giving the user a succession of mock-ups which capture most of the appearance and functionality of the proposed software. The method has proven successful for many applications, and especially productive in designing support for semi-structured tasks like DSSs. The concrete example which the prototype provides resolves ambiguity in the specifications.

Unlike ISs, all ESs begin with a prototype due to the ill-structured nature of typical ES tasks. In building ESs the prototype serves two purposes. First, it helps the knowledge engineer and expert design the shell. Second, it becomes the "mental mirror" to help the development team discover the problem-solving methods of the expert. By reviewing and refining the ES prototype, the expert's knowledge and skill becomes expressed and accessible. Challenging development work occurs in the early stages of the prototype as Hayes-Roth, Waterman and Lenat note,

> One of the most difficult aspects of the knowledge engineer's task is helping the expert to structure the domain knowledge, to identify and formalize the domain concepts [19, p. 129].

Knowledge Engineering Knowledge engineering is similar to previous IS efforts in the sense that a technical person interviews an expert (or user) to find out how he or she uses information. However, it differs from other efforts because the knowledge engineer strives to *simulate* the expert's behavior, where a traditional designer tries to *support* the expert.

The minimal development team for an ES includes the knowledge engineer and an expert, both of whom work on the ES (Figure 23.2).

The knowledge engineering process is labor-intensive and expensive; consequently there have been attempts to simplify it. Three solutions are commonly offered. One suggestion is to replace the knowledge engineer with an intelligent editing

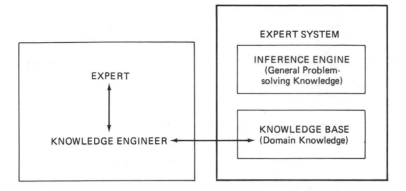

FIGURE 23.2 Expert Systems Development
Hayes-Roth, Waterman and Lenat, *Building Expert Systems,* Copyright 1983, Addison-Wesley Publishing Company, Inc., Reading, Massachusetts. Figure 5.2, on page 131. Reprinted by permission.

program. The best known work on this is TIRESIAS which allows a physician to directly enter knowledge into a knowledge base. The second idea is to have an induction program examine a database from which the ES can extract knowledge. DeDombal has a program which inspects large medical databases and develops rules based on the relationships it finds among diagnoses, treatments and results [4]. The third idea is to replace the knowledge engineer with a text understanding program. In this approach, textbooks are entered into a database from which an ES can extract the information necessary to build a knowledge base. This approach seems unlikely to be successful because books contain theory only, an ES captures practical skills as well. Despite these attempts to remove or augment the knowledge engineer, the prototype method illustrated above is typical.

Managing the Knowledge Engineering Team

Expert systems require more intensive involvement of the expert than most other IS projects. For example, in creating a DSS the user knows the requirements and the programmer knows how to build them. In the creation of an expert system and its knowledge base, the expert helps design both *what* he wants and *how* it should be created.

The ES project manager must manage the expert as well as the knowledge engineer. Even though the programmer tries to explore the problem domain before consulting the expert—via textbooks and other written material—the sessions with the expert can be intensive, prolonged, and frequent.

The knowledge engineering process is "layered" and iterative (Figure 23.3). During this process the ES prototype usually encounters a "paradigm shift"—a notable difference from other IS prototyping. Because an expert cannot reveal his own skill to himself by introspection, his expertise only becomes visible through simulation of his problem-solving behavior. The explication of the problem-solving process generated by ES development often triggers a reformulation of the knowledge and skill—hence

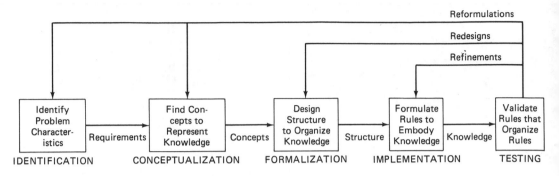

FIGURE 23.3 Stages of Knowledge Acquisition
Hayes-Roth, Waterman and Lenat, *Building Expert Systems,* Copyright 1983, Addison-Wesley Publishing Company, Inc., Reading, Massachusetts. Figure 5.5 on page 139. Reprinted by permission.

the paradigm shift. This effect is so profound that some ES practitioners suggest that the process of knowledge engineering creates the most value; execution of the ES is inconsequential in comparison. Because of this paradigm shift, a knowledge engineer may have to return to the beginning and re-design an entire system. In IS projects the prototype sometimes grows into the actual system; in ES design this rarely happens.

Presentation Issues

Another issue in ES development is design of the man-machine interface. Often, ESs create new representation methods. This occurs in the rule base and in the presentation mechanisms which the system uses. Early in the history of expert systems, Feigenbaum [14] noted the crucial role of the presentation mechanism used by an ES. The ES must present its information in a manner which is understandable to the expert user. For instance, DENDRAL, the ES for mass spectroscopic analysis, had the ability to present data in "ball and stick form," a representation familiar to chemists.

Capturing these presentation mechanisms is challenging. Reide Smith [33] reports that 42% of the code in the DIPMETER ADVISOR system is dedicated to the user interface. It is doubtful that the user interface required 42% of the effort of the entire project because the 30% of the code that makes up the knowledge base and reasoning mechanism is more difficult to create. Yet the interface code was a substantial investment of time.

One could argue that every IS design needs to manage presentation. However, many traditional IS representation mechanisms are known (e.g., balance sheets, organization charts). It is more complex to create new formats to capture the richness of the evolving representations during the process of knowledge engineering. Overall, the subtleties of this presentation problem have yet to be researched well.

In short, knowledge engineering is a labor-intensive process which involves at least two valuable individuals. The outcomes are incremental and the potential of the system can only be found out through experimentation. Thus, one must invest without certain return. As John Clippenger [10] of Brattle Research put it, "Expert systems development is like walking around in a dark room; you don't know where the walls are until you hit them."

Project Life Cycles

Prototyping is the primary development tool used to create ESs. At a higher level of aggregation, one can think of the life cycle of an ES as well. Two ES life cycles are contrasted to the traditional system development life cycle (SDLC); [see Table 23.2].

By putting these side by side one can see some interesting differences. As one would expect, neither of the expert system approaches attempts to perform specification or requirements analysis—prototyping addresses this need. Another difference is that there is little recognition of program maintenance in the ES life cycles. Maintenance is often assumed to be the user's responsibility. For example, in the DEC life cycle the "production model" includes user responsibility to update the knowledge. As was learned in non-ES software, the burden of maintenance can be huge. Fox [15] estimates 60–80% of all current programming effort is expended on maintenance.

Expert systems maintenance needs are probably even greater because there are two parts to maintain—the shell and the knowledge base. Just as other IS systems continually evolve their functionality, so too will ES shells be designed and re-designed by users for different functions. The maintenance job will be doubly demanding because the maintainer must know the code to update the function and be conversant in the domain knowledge to correct the knowledge base.

Two Life Cycles?—One for Prototype, One for Knowledge? It is beneficial to think of development of the shell and development of the knowledge base as two separate development efforts. Each might have its own life cycle and development "shape." The

TABLE 23.2   Life Cycle Comparisons

DEC: ES PROGRAM MANAGEMENT	WATERMAN DEVELOPMENT PHASES FOR EXPERT SYSTEMS	SDLC
Initial program definition	Identification	Feasibility
Build initial prototype	Conceptualization	Requirements
Design program plan	Formalization	Specification
Education and user involvement plan	Implementation	Programming
Design documentation	Testing	Testing
Basic shell		Installation
Adaptive development		Operation
Field test		Maintenance
Release product to production		
Production mode		

life cycle for the shell may be similar to a traditional system; that is, if the function continually changes, the maintenance effort will have to continue.

The following example explores the life cycle for the knowledge base. Digital's XCON is one of the few "old" commercial expert systems. Due to John McDermott's article on XCON one can see the progression of knowledge development over a long period of time [3, 26]. See [Figure 23.4].

Additional shell functions were put into other programs (e.g., the XSITE system generates site diagrams, XSEL helps sell VAX computers, etc.), so it is reasonable to speculate that the function of the XCON shell was relatively stable. Therefore, the changes in the rule base are a good approximation of the maintenance of the knowledge base, distinct from the shell.

Looking at the diagram one sees that during the four years 1980 to 1984, XCON's rule base increased from approximately 850 rules to over 3,200. The dip in the number of rules during late 1980 is interesting because at that time the developers were concentrating on rewriting the rule base. The initial 850 rules had been created by academics at Carnegie-Mellon University, and the practitioners at Digital began to refine the rules with experience. If the number of products had remained stable, the rule base probably would have declined to 500 or less, but the addition of new products kept the base increasing.

Perhaps the knowledge base life cycle for this particular type of problem (computer configuration) is a straight line—a constant effort. For other types of problems it might be a sine wave with each hump being a new development. For others it could be a step function growing more efficient each year. It seems that when the products were held stable, the number of rules declined—achieving a more parsimonious representation of the knowledge and control structure in the program. This might be true of all systems. A system with a stable set of applications might have a life cycle

FIGURE 23.4 Knowledge Development
Banchant, Judith and McDermott, John, "RI Revisited: Four Years in the Trenches," *The AI Magazine,* Volume 5, Number 3, Fall 1985, p. 22.

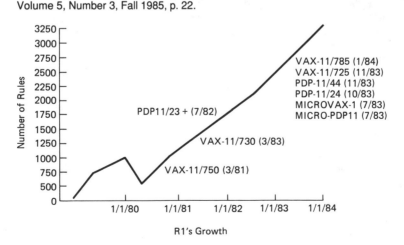

shape of an inverted V. The V occurs because the early rule base is refined with experience and requires less support over time.

There are at least two dimensions which could influence the shape of the life cycle: scope of the system and stability of the knowledge. If the problem is stable and the scope constant, the rule base may shrink as refinements are made. If, on the other hand, the scope increases (as was true in XCON), or the knowledge is unstable (as is true in medical diagnosis), then the rule base might grow indefinitely.

Evaluation Methods

System evaluation for traditional systems is straightforward: "Does it perform to specification?" For DSSs there are many suggested criteria. Keen and Scott-Morton [19], as well as Sprague and Carlson [34], present a smorgasbord of evaluation methods that try to capture both intangible and tangible benefits. These multiple methods are suggested because DSS effects are difficult to demonstrate and virtually impossible to quantify.

Expert systems may inherit some of the evaluation problems which plague DSS. Often there may be no "right answer" for the tasks they solve. In fact, the use of an ES usually implies there are no standard criteria for assessment of the correct answer. Rather, the skill of the analysis and its explanation demonstrates "correctness."

Even with the evaluation of medical ESs which have objective criteria, such as pathology, it is difficult to make the connection between the analysis and the facts. For example, even if an ES correctly diagnoses a disease, it is difficult to validate whether treatment recommendations would have been efficacious.

More commonly, objective measures do not exist and performance evaluation of expert, or ES, is subjective. Also, there are types of behavior which simply do not have metrics. How does one evaluate an explanation capability? When is a mistake acceptable and when unacceptable? The extreme mistakes are easily identified, but methods to measure little mistakes are not available.

The lack of metrics also complicates the management process because it is difficult to assess the state of ES completion. This is true of many software projects, but it is more pronounced in ESs due to goal and task ambiguity.

Evaluation issues will become more important over time as ESs get large and multiple ES modules need to be interconnected. Software developers have noted that integration of modules, and the subsequent debugging of the interconnected system, can amount to two thirds of the development time. Without clear metrics for evaluation of individual modules, this process will be more taxing.

Project Management Tools

Due to the early state of knowledge engineering, there are no standard approaches to program layout, documentation, and execution. In effect, there is no ES analog to structured programming which leads to a number of challenges. There is no standard method to look at a large program and its representation. This causes some programmers to build their own tools in order to be able to examine the logical flow and structure of their knowledge base, and thereby increases development time. Some proponents of rule-based systems suggest that rules are self-documenting because they are readable and understandable. However, flow of execution in a large rule base is at least as opaque as any other computer language. Rules merely have the illusion of being understandable. Also, the lack of intermediate-level representations, like flow charts, makes it difficult to subdivide a task which, in turn, makes projects difficult to track.

Skills Required

The problems associated with getting and keeping good computer professionals are pervasive and ESs present some interesting hurdles in this regard. The process of knowledge engineering is said to require a special mix of skills. The knowledge engineer should be part consultant, part apprentice, and part programmer, for the knowledge engineer attempts to trap the processes and knowledge of the expert without doing too much damage to the expert's intent or finesse.

Needless to say, individuals with the requisite people skills, who also have the programming skills, are difficult to find. Again and again, developers, business people and academics express their concern over the lack of trained people to perform knowledge engineering. The current supply of experienced knowledge engineers is usually estimated to be 100–1,000 [16, 39], far short of the current need and exceedingly small to supply the projected needs.

The appropriate background for knowledge engineering is not standard. Even though ESs are the leading edge of computer software, computer science Ph.D.s may not always make the best knowledge engineers. Taylor, an experienced practitioner, suggests that the best knowledge engineers are an eclectic lot who come from varied backgrounds like English, philosophy, and art [36].

In a similar vein, it is not clear whether knowledge engineers should be business people who learn the technology, or technologists who learn the business. Digital, which has one of the biggest AI training systems in the world, teaches business people the technology—not the other way around. The entire question of what skill set the knowledge engineers should have is an interesting research area.

Risk

Another development issue I want to address is risk. McFarlan and McKenney look at three aspects of risk: size of project, company's relative technology, and structuredness of the problem [27]. Size is an obvious dimension: the larger the project, the more risky it is. The second concept, company's relative technology, is a rating of the company's experience with the technology. One should remember that the important variable is company experience—not industry experience. For example, ESs are not a new technology to DEC, but they are novel to Wells Fargo Bank; therefore ES creation would be more risky at the latter firm. Regarding the last criterion, structuredness, if one knows the steps necessary to solve a problem, it is structured.

If one looks at ESs in light of McFarlan and McKenney's criteria, one finds that most publicized ESs are large, involve a technology which is new to the company, and address ill-structured problems. Therefore, ES projects are often very risky. Companies should take note and try to manage one or more of the dimensions to lower the overall risk. Yet large ES efforts will probably continue to be challenging ventures until more development experience is accumulated and can be assessed.

For this reason, I define successful implementation to be the process of transferring the expert system out of the hands of the designers and builders into the hands of the users.

TOOLS

No discussion of ES creation issues would be complete without considering the evolving tools available. Hardware concerns have always been important to ES development. The early AI programs took a considerable amount of computing power because the instructions of the list-processing languages ran inefficiently and the execution of a list usually gobbled up a considerable amount of main memory.

Despite improvements, this need for processing power continues. Many of the techniques used by ESs to solve problems are computationally intensive. Almost by definition, ESs use weak techniques to examine lots of knowledge to solve problems—making many manipulations. Another facet of this hunger for computer power is created by the graphics which ESs employ. Starting with the Alto machines first developed in the early 1970s by Xerox's Palo Alto Research Center (PARC), most of the ES machines use windows, icons, and other graphic methods to try to make the complexity of the program and its execution more understandable. These schemes are often implemented on bit mapped graphic screens to allow mouse control and high resolution.

The recent drop in the cost of computing power has been a major force in the current interest in ESs. A few years ago the price for a computer capable of running an ES application of any size was as much as $250,000 and up. More recent announcements promise to provide extensive LISP or PROLOG based computing power for individuals at a substantially lower price. In 1985 Digital's VAXstation with VAX LISP start was priced at $48,690 [5]. Symbolic's 3600, a dedicated LISP machine, started at $81,900. Xerox was the bargain basement AI supplier with the 1185 LISP machine priced at $9,995 and up [6]. By 1990 or before, similar or even more powerful machines will be available for $5,000–$10,000—helping to fuel ES development.

Software is also changing rapidly and any assessment of it will soon be out of date. Currently, there are systems which are designed to be run on microcomputers and larger machines. The micro-based packages, like Expert Ease or 1STCLASS, are rather simple tools which create a decision tree. Any application which needs a robust control structure or large knowledge base quickly out-strips the capabilities of micro-based systems. A central issue then in software selection is the trade-off between flexibility and ease of use. In general, those tools which are most flexible, like LISP, also take the most effort because the software engineer must start from scratch. There is a progression of tools which have more and more embedded information.

Barstow has created a helpful categorization scheme [4]. He sees three categories of ES tools: general purpose programming languages, general purpose representation languages, and skeletal systems. General purpose representation languages are specialized languages developed for knowledge engineering. ROSIE, OPS-5, RLL, and HEARSAY-III are examples. These languages are generally more flexible than skeletal systems, but less flexible than general purpose languages. For example, OPS-5 is a rule based, forward-chaining system. The basic control cycle is: recognize, resolve conflict where necessary, and act. The control structure and the inference approach are givens. The programmer can encode more complicated control structures in this system, but it would be inefficient to try to design a completely different approach within this tool. If the intent of the knowledge engineer was to create a frame-based system, OPS-5 would be inappropriate.

Skeletal systems usually begin by taking the inference engine and representation scheme from an existing ES and generalizing them. For example, EMYCIN (van Melle, [37]) is a skeletal system derived from MYCIN (a diagnostic system for rare blood diseases). Skeletal systems provide more structure to the problem approach and are very useful if the problem to be solved has similar characteristics to the original ES. That is, EMYCIN is very effective in modeling diagnostic problems because that is what MYCIN was designed to do. A drawback of these skeletal systems is that they are less flexible. The KAS system was derived from PROSPECTOR to perform knowledge acquisition. KAS represents surface knowledge well, but is poor at creating complex control structures.

A series of other tools are evolving; in particular, "knowledge environments" and knowledge compilers. LOOPS and Knowledge Engineering Environment (KEE) are two examples. These have default representation schemes (frames in this case), and programming aides. Both systems have the ability to trace the implications of a given rule or frame value on the reasoning process which is created. These tools require an experienced user or an extensively trained novice.

One of the best features of the better tools, such as KEE, is the ability to create multiple representation schemes. A given problem might be better expressed in a frame language, or perhaps PROLOG. KEE has the capability to create rules and PROLOG, in addition to its frame representation.

Any serious assessment of ES application should begin with the current hardware and software situation. The market is moving so rapidly at the moment that six months is actually a very long time.

One can see that development of an ES may present some interesting managerial opportunities. In particular, the familiar problems of finding the right people, tracking a project, and measuring success will often be even more challenging with ES technology. Further, real world experience and "war stories" are just beginning to emerge into the public arena. Wisdom should come with practice.

However, successful development is only one facet of creating a useful business tool. Implementation of the system is at least as important. The "implementation issue" has often been noted in previous IS efforts [34, 37, 46, 78]. And upon examination of previous literature one sees some old concerns intertwined with the new ones.

IMPLEMENTATION ISSUES

Implementation—more accurately, the lack thereof—has been a significant problem throughout the history of computer-based systems [2, p. 123].

Managers have increasingly criticized computer professionals for their relative inability to deliver systems that meet user's real needs and that are on time and cost effective. They point to the innumerable instances of models and systems being built but never used. The reasons for this failure in implementation seem rarely to be technical [20, p. 189].

As Keen and Scott-Morton point out above [20], implementation rarely hinges on technical issues; rather, its progress depends on complex organizational dynamics through which new ideas pass from inventors to users.

I conjecture that ES implementations, like those of DSS, are primarily a process of organizational change and learning. Furthermore, ESs may be more difficult to implement than previous information systems because they often change control over knowledge and skill, which in turn alters roles, responsibilities, and power. Therefore, ES implementation may be a formidable task.

Most of the articles in the ES field address technical issues, and avoid questions of implementation and use. As in the development of any field, early energies were devoted to making tools reliable and useful. However, the surge of ES development in commercial organizations makes implementation the critical success factor for the next few years.

In the past, implementation issues were a major challenge for operations research (OR), management science (MS) [13, 32], management information systems (MIS) [24], and decision support systems (DSS) [2, 20, 34]. Often the concern grew from bitter experience.

Schultz and Slevin [34] pointed out that one of the primary problems of early OR/MS efforts was that the builders of the models viewed techniques as an end in themselves, not as a means to an end. Keen and Scott-Morton noted the same difficulty in DSS [20, p. 190]. Today, the computer scientists hold center stage for ESs, and often the technology is viewed as self-fulfilling. It seems that the previous problems of implementation may repeat themselves. However, early articles by practitioners do address some organizational factors. In addition, previous work on DSS sheds light on some issues which are pertinent to, and which may be successfully applied to ES implementation.

Keen and Scott-Morton [20] provide a useful classification scheme for existing MIS research. They see three categories: (1) grand old man research, (2) factor studies, and (3) change process research. Benbasat, in a review of the literature on managerial support system [5], agrees in principle with Keen and Scott-Morton and collapses their view to two categories: factor research and change process research. Yet I will keep the "grand old man" distinction because it is a convenient label for reflections of the practitioners which have yet to be organized and structured extensively.

"Grand Old Man" ES Literature

In reviewing the "grand old man" literature in ESs one sees two types of contributors, academics and business people. These individuals usually created, implemented, or managed an expert system. They often note two important "givens:" (1) pick the right problem and the right people, and (2) evolve the system. These two givens map approximately to the concepts of factors and process. For example, the same lists which help a manager pick the right problem also identify *factors;* and the advice to evolve the system is a general approbation to *manage the process* of creation and implementation. Hence the observations of the grand old man are, in effect, prenascent theories of *factor* and *implementation* research.

Under the banner of picking the *right* problem and the *right* people, many authors have identified three issues to examine: type of task, the nature of the expert who is involved, and organizational attributes (e.g., managerial support within the expert's domain). Some of the important insights are as follows:

- the task should be complex and require symbolic processing, but not be so complex as to be unmanageable;
- the expert should be articulate and interested in the project;
- the expert's management should be supportive of the project;
- the expectations of the management and the user group should not be excessive.

These applications keep the project in the "realm of the possible." In other words, they represent factors which directly influence the implementation process. For example, an articulate expert who is interested in the project can play the role of champion or integrator. By picking a project which can be done in a "few minutes to a few hours" [11] the practitioner is managing the size of the application. When choosing a problem that does not contain "common sense," [8] one is matching technique to task. Each empirical, experienced-based observation tries to capture a kernel of an idea derived from the hands-on knowledge of the practitioner. One should take this advice with some skepticism because there is a penchant for individuals to judge their personal methods as global solutions, though their experience often provides useful direction.

Where these insights are most lacking is in their provision of structure and sense of process. A "bullet" statement from a practitioner is not woven into a model, or an approach to the analysis of a potential ES application.

ESs—Factor Analysis

Dorothy Leonard-Barton [22], in one of the few papers on the implementation of knowledge-based systems, tries to put forth a more complete set of factors which influence implementation. She reviews three case studies to discern the presence or absence of the factors in each case situation, and their relative importance. Leonard-Barton identifies four major factors [22, pp. 3–4]:

1. Perceptions about the technology itself (*Individual*)
   a. Technological readiness
   b. Potential skill impacts
   c. Potential political impacts
   d. Relative advantage
2. Attributes of receiving organization (*Organizational*)
   a. Physical and human resources
   b. Organizational incentive systems
3. Relations between the technology source organization and the user organization (*Inter-Organizational*)
4. The design of the implementation process
   a. Ownership/participation
   b. Roles (*Process*)   (*Italics mine.*)

The three knowledge-based cases she reviewed were LAYOUT, a computer configuration program; ET, a method to electronically transmit design data; and SAD, a structured analysis system for programmers. The latter two systems do not classify as ESs under my definition, but the insights in all three cases are useful to this discussion.

Leonard-Barton found that all but three factors were "critical at the time of the [case] study"—the three missing were 1a., 3., and 4a.—but all of the factors were rated at least "important at the time of the [case] study" [p. 27]. The relative importance varied by setting and stage of development.

It is interesting to note that Leonard-Barton consciously looked for perceptions of the technology. In fact, the first three categories are all perceptions. One could argue that these are subjective, and that objective measures such as system response time and support of top management are more legitimate factors. However, the perception of the computer system may be more important than objective reality. In particular, the user's perceptions of the technology *are* the objective reality from the user's point of view—the important perspective for implementation purposes.

Leonard-Barton's multi-level approach emphasizes the complexity of the issues that need managerial attention. Much of the manager's job is to assess the current state of affairs because only the fourth factor, implementation process, usually falls under control of the manager who implements the knowledge-based system. Looking at each factor one can begin to see some of the things which can be encountered in implementation of an ES.

Perceptions of the Technology Itself Leonard-Barton's first factor is focused on the individual and his or her perceptions of the technology. The many areas of concern—skill, political and technological dimensions—are largely absent in the old man research. This is not surprising because involvement in ES use implies that the writer is a pioneer. Leonard-Barton [21, 22] and Rodgers [30] have both pointed out that early adopters more readily accept problems and obstacles in using technology. More importantly, later users will be less tolerant. This issue is crucial for ES use because the evaluation of an ES is so subjective that fault-finding will often be easy. Consequently, the implementation process could be severely hampered by people who are not technologically ready and therefore continually finding fault.

The next three sub-factors in Leonard-Barton's list—potential skill impacts, potential political impacts, and relative advantage—are three separate dimensions of a similar problem. All have to do with the user's perception of the technology and its influence on the job.

> A technology may be inherently neutral, but its implementation is so only rarely. Technologies tend to empower certain people and enfeeble others, politically. The problem of fighting over "turf" is familiar to all managers who are engaged in attempts to implement new technology [22, p. 12].

With this comment, Leonard-Barton forcefully raises a set of issues which are usually skirted by ES literature. The implicit assumption of the technologist is often that the expert will be willing, the users receptive, and the organization easily molded. It is obvious from experience that this set of assumptions is unfounded.

Before creating an ES, it would be useful to know the expert's perceptions of the ES. If a significant shift in power or responsibility is perceived, the mechanisms for implementing the ES should be considered carefully. The effects can be complex, as Leonard-Barton reports:

> In a study of the introduction of computerized production technologies into a cookie factory, Buchanan and Boddy (1983) found that different computer applications had different effects on jobs. The craft skills of the dough-mixers were devalued when computer-controlled mixing was introduced. However, the bakers were given more control and discretion over their process by the more accurate performance feedback they received from computerized weighing of cookie packages. Their skills were enhanced; the dough-mixers were deskilled [22, p. 9].

New technologies may transfer skill and expertise from one group to another, or it may cause automation of some jobs. It will rarely be a simple process of automating some known task. The subtleties of the shifts which become apparent over time need to be managed.

Attributes of the Receiving Organization   Leonard-Barton highlights two attributes of the receiving organization: physical and human resources, and organizational incentive systems. In ES development there is often a tension between the organizational incentives and the goal of ES implementation.

In the case study on Karnak, Digital's wave soldering expert system [35], the expert was an active participant in the development process even though he was not compensated for his participation. However, secondary experts—not consulted in the project—were not enthusiastic. This could create many potential side effects. First, the ultimate users of the system might have their own careers cut off because the ES might automate their next level of learning. Second, if the ES is designed to augment or replace some part of the user's responsibilities, he or she may be reluctant to participate without a clear road to promotion or new position. Third, it may be difficult to generate new experts with enough field experience to continue to update and extend the system after the first expert moves on.

Popular discussions of ESs have often suggested that the expert might be worried about losing his or her job. In practice it seems that the initial expert participates freely; it is the next line of experts, and apprentices, whose incentives and career paths should be made clear to facilitate successful implementation.

The issue becomes more complex when we examine other important individuals in the ES process like knowledge maintainers. Knowledge maintenance may be a difficult and arduous task. Who should do it? What incentives should be provided? How does the ES affect the skill base of the company? Does it influence the traditional pattern of promotion? For example, if the traditional road into a firm was through field sales because that gave the candidate a "feel" for the business, will the apprenticeship be the same when supported by an ES? Will the skills atrophy or become stronger? These sorts of issues need to be considered.

Infrastructure for support of ESs is another critical element. Due to the newness of the technology and the lack of trained personnel, the establishment of sufficient qualified personnel will be an organizational challenge. Lack of infrastructure might thwart ES implementation. When looking at Digital, one sees the extensive support structures they have built to facilitate the transfer of ES technology. There is a training program open to Digital employees and customers which graduates over 75 knowledge engineers per year. The core group which support XCON is only about 100 individuals, with other knowledge engineers scattered throughout the corporation to seed the transfer of the technology [28]. Digital clearly invests in its technology transfer infrastructure, a critical element in its widespread use of ESs.

Relations between the Technology Source Organization and the User Organization

In practice, the organization which creates the technology is often different from the organization which uses it. The relationship of the user organization to the tool builders influences implementation and if the source organization is the IS department, tension is likely. McFarlan and McKenney note that the needs and drives of IS can be so different from the rest of the organization that it is often wise to run a "business within a business" when managing IS [27].

Focusing on the relationship between the organizations also allows the viewer to discriminate between good and bad user involvement. If established relations are good, then user involvement might facilitate implementation; if relations are tense, user participation may exacerbate problems.

This point is critical for ESs. If the image of the IS department is poor and if there is a history of being ineffective, the ES may have little chance of achieving use in the organization because of lack of faith in its conclusions. This implies that creation of the ES should take into account the previous track record of the IS organization and an assessment of its understanding of the business as a whole.

The Design of the Implementation Process Design of the implementation process is often the only factor under direct control of the manager. In Leonard-Barton's view, the process of implementation equates to ownership and roles. In ES literature the roles encompass technical or functional needs. For example, Waterman envisions four distinct roles: knowledge engineer, expert, user, and toolbuilder [38]. In contrast, Leonard-Barton focuses on managerial and organizational roles, namely: champion, assassin, integrator, sponsor, and project manager [22]. The organizational support and ownership issues are at least as important as the roles of Waterman. As noted above, many of the famous expert systems to date have had a single individual shepherding their advance. In commercial organizations many people may need to get involved to spread the burden of creation and implementation. The complete role set and number of participants which would make for a good ES implementation team is not yet clear.

In short, the observations of Leonard-Barton range through different levels of the organization. Individuals and their relationship to the technology are considered critical. The state of the organization, and its skills and incentives are key. The relationship of the development group to other groups carries history which influences implementation, and ownership of roles and responsibilities looms large. As Leonard-Barton points out, factors are a useful checklist for managing implementation. They should be assessed, regularly sampled, and monitored for changes.

Implementation Research—Change Processes

From a research point of view, factors often lack predictive capability. Keen and Scott-Morton [20] criticize the factor approach to DSS implementation research. They cite Ginzberg's analysis of selected DSS factor research [17]. He found many factors cited, but few that could explain much at all about implementation success, (see Table 23.3).

TABLE 23.3   Factors That Enhance the Likelihood of Implementation Success as Reported in 14 Studies

NO. OF FACTORS	PERCENTAGE	NO. OF REPORTS FACTOR APPEARED IN
102	73	1
23	16	2
12	9	3
2	1	4
1	0.7	5

Ginzberg noted that in fourteen surveys, with over 100 factors, only one factor, top management support, showed up more than four times. Furthermore, the vast majority of the factors appeared only once. From this, Keen and Scott-Morton concluded that the factor approach was contingent on the environment in which the DSS was implemented and that factors are poor explainers of implementation success.

Instead, the duo builds on the familiar ideas of K. Lewin [23; expanded by Schein, 31]. The Lewin-Schein model—unfreeze, move, re-freeze—is the "map" Keen and Scott-Morton use for implementation of DSSs. Given the amount of attention which the Lewin-Schein model has received, both in DSS and elsewhere, it is interesting to note some of the reasons for its appeal.

First, the model posits change as a conscious act with discreet states. This implies that rational factors, by themselves, will not lead to change. Second, change must be planned or caused; unfreezing is prerequisite. Third, after change is done a new order needs to be established. Old habits do not disappear; they are supplanted. In other words, change is an active, sequential process which mediates current reality and future expectations.

From this description, it is easy to see implementation as dynamic—its details evolving. Given this set of insights, the practitioner can see that different approaches to implementation may be necessary at different stages in the implementation process, and that the actual details might evolve.

O'Connor, an ES practitioner, echoes these concerns. In particular he notes the importance of evolutionary design for ESs.

> The management of the technology transfer into the end user group is critical. Preparation is key. One critical lesson is to *start small, build incremental prototypes* that service a real need in your corporate business. Make sure you have identified a real, bounded problem. It is very necessary to demo the prototype Expert System shell early in order to decide if it's the best fit solution. It helps to have lots of patience and persistence, and be willing to fail forward, gracefully, toward success.
>
> User design participation is critical when building any Expert System.
>
> Further, as investment increases, it is important that these systems solve real problems and are capable of being integrated with current, installed traditional MIS systems [28, pp. 8–9]. (*Italics mine*)

Incrementalism, user participation, and integration with current systems—these are O'Connor's three messages. In researching DSS, Alavi and Henderson showed that user participation *increased* the use of the decision support system [1]. Furthermore, Alter [2], in a study of over fifty DSS implementations, showed that successful implementation was preceded by a "felt need" for change. ES demonstrations, as suggested by O'Connor, are one tool to generate interest in the system.

If one accepts the notion that ES implementation is a process, then the management question becomes twofold. How does one foster "good" change? How can we get the organization to adapt progressively and profitably?

Shoshanna Zuboff, in an article which looked at automation in a manufacturing firm, suggested that new technologies can lead to good or bad adaptation. For example, if we assume the ESs provide viable competitive opportunities to organizations then, over time, many decisions will become more structured. The process of "automating" or supporting a decision is similar to automation in general. Zuboff notes that in order to mechanize a task it first must be dissected.

> Any activity, from a clerical transaction to spraying paint on a Chevrolet, if it is to be computerized, must first be analyzed into its smallest components in order that it be translated into the binary language of a computer system. For most organizations, this step prepares the way for automation and simultaneously creates a deeper understanding of the activity at hand [40 p. 5].

She goes on to note that two possible roads lead from this detailed analysis: to automate, or to informate. In "automation" the mechanization of work alienates the workforce. They become passive. In "informatization," workers use new information to augment their understanding and to redesign the work toward more continuity and control. As Zuboff effervescently points out:

> Where information is pursued as a conscious strategy the new information presence infuses every level of organizational activity. It invites organization members to pose questions, generate hypotheses, and construct insights. The organization becomes a learning environment in that work itself becomes a process of inquiry and the contributions that members can make are increasingly a function of their ability to notice, reflect, explore, hypothesize, test, and, to communicate [40, p. 9].

This ringing rendition of the new role of information seems utopian in its zeal. Yet in order to keep a knowledge base active, growing, and current, "informatization," excitement and all, may be needed to stimulate those individuals who keep the knowledge base alive.

This concept cannot be overemphasized. If ESs spread, more decisions will be automated. Structure is seductive. It is easy to avoid investigating assumptions and imbedded reasoning. This lethargy is acceptable if the system is for payroll or other highly structured applications. If the application is an expert system, with a volatile knowledge base, the active review of the system will directly influence its value— hence the need for informatization, not automation. Zuboff notes that progress toward informatization is not guaranteed; its fruition hinges on implementation.

How can we get the organization to adapt well—to informate, not automate? Cash and McLeod note that firms which have the ability to exhibit double-loop learning, in which managers actively manage organizational requirements, norms, and assumptions to continually refine and focus the company's goals, seem better able to incorporate strategically relevant IS applications [9]. Given that ESs are new, and their competitive applications emerging, an organization which can foster good change is more likely to succeed. It is an interesting area of research to discover the relationship of organizational learning to successful ES use.

A MODEL OF *ESs*

As noted throughout the discussion, ESs might influence organizations in many ways. As Leonard-Barton pointed out, implementation is multi-dimensional. In an effort to clarify the discussion I have identified two important dimensions of ES implementation: risk, and incremental improvement.

Here "risk" is the risk of wrong decision. What happens when the ES is wrong? This risk has many dimensions. What happens when a non-optimal decision is made? What happens when a wrong answer is delivered? Clearly the difference between a wrong computer configuration and an incorrect medical diagnosis is significant. The risk of the latter might mean great financial loss, death, and so on.

The "improvement" dimension tries to assess the incremental value of ES support. How much does the ES improve the quality of the task? In a military battlefield situation, tiny improvements might be lifesaving whereas on-board satellite diagnostic ESs might need to approach perfection before they are considered feasible. In general, a user can tolerate more risk of the incremental improvement is significant. Figure 23.5 plots some ESs on the risk/improvement dimensions.

In essence, the graph tries to capture the risk/reward trade-off. When considering the augmentation or automation of a task one should consider the incremental benefit of building an ES. If the application cannot be classified in the low risk, high payoff quadrant, one must carefully evaluate its development potential.

SUMMARY

Expert systems are bold in their goals and subtle in their effects. Simulation of an expert's problem solving behavior is a remarkable objective; the dissection and reassembling of tasks which occurs in knowledge engineering influences the company's

FIGURE 23.5 Risk/Improvement Matrix

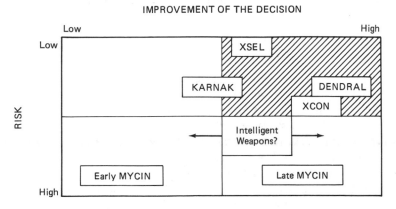

= Interesting Quadrant—Low Risk, High Payoff!

understanding, the task's execution, and the organization's roles. The exact nature of these effects, and the best way to manage them, is still unknown.

Harris and McKinney [18] suggest that the "right road" for some companies is to monitor the technology and wait for future developments. I suggest that a wait and see posture may be risky because ESs may provide defensible competitive advantages. Further, it is difficult to identify opportunities in the abstract—experience with ES technology is a usual precursor to its successful use.

Broadly speaking, information and expertise are assets of the corporation. ESs provide an ability to solve some ill-structured problems—a tool for leveraging those assets. Those firms which implement ESs in their operations may move ahead of their competition.

As mentioned before, ESs are new to industry and many research issues remain open. I suggest three broad categories of investigation for the near future. First, a critical assessment of the current use, based on field observations, should be conducted. Second, the cataloguing of existing systems, tools and their uses should continue. Waterman's *A Guide to Expert Systems* is a recent and comprehensive volume of this type of research [38]. Tracking new developments helps keep possible applications and the current uses in perspective. Third, we need to develop metrics to assess the effects of ESs. What are the economics of knowledge? What are the economies afforded by faster or more effective judgment? How do we begin to think about these issues? These questions may never be completely solved, but their pursuit will yield insight.

QUESTIONS

1. The time required to develop an expert system has decreased. What are some of the reasons for this decrease?
2. Discuss the similarities and differences between developing expert systems and other types of computer applications.
3. What skills should a knowledge engineer process? How can they be developed?
4. Discuss the characteristics of potential expert systems applications.

REFERENCES

1. ALAVI, M. AND HENDERSON, J. C. "Evolutionary Strategy for Implementing a Decision Support System." *Management Science,* volume 27, number 11, November 1981, pp. 1309–1323.

2. ALTER, S. L. *Decision Support Systems: Current Practices and Continuing Challenges.* Addison-Wesley, Reading, Massachusetts, 1980.

3. BACHANT, J. AND MCDERMOTT, J. "R1 Revisited: Four Years in the Trenches." *The AI Magazine,* volume 5, number 3, Fall 1984, pp. 21–32.

4. BARSTOW, D. R., AIELLO, N., DUDA, R., ERMAN, L., FORGY, C., GORLIN, D., GREINER, R., LENAT, D., LONDON, P., MCDERMOTT, J., NII, H., POLITAKIS, P., REBOH, R., ROSENSCHEIN, S., SCOTT, C., VAN MELLE, W., AND WEISS, S. "Expert Systems Tools." In *Building Expert Systems,* F. Hayes-Roth, D. A. Waterman and D. B. Lenat (eds.), Addison-Wesley, Reading, Massachusetts, 1983, pp. 283–345.

5. BENDER, E.   "DEC Unwraps AI Workstation Based on MicroVAX II." *Computerworld,* volume 19, number 33, August 19, 1985, p. 4.

6. BENDER, E.   "Symbolics, Xerox Offer Enhanced AI Workstation." *Computerworld,* volume 19, number 24, August 26, 1985, p. 11.

7. BENBASAT, I.   "An Analysis of Research Methodologies." In *The Information Systems Research Challenge,* F. W. McFarlan (ed.), Harvard Business School Press, Boston, Massachusetts, 1984, pp. 47–88.

8. BUCHANAN, B. G., BARSTOW, D., BECHTEL, R., BENNETT, J., CLANCEY, W., KULIKOWSKI, C., MITCHELL, T., AND WATERMAN, D. A.   "Constructing an Expert System." In *Building Expert Systems,* F. Hayes-Roth, D. A. Waterman and D. B. Lenat (eds.), Addison-Wesley, Reading, Massachusetts, 1983, pp. 127–167.

9. CASH, J. I. AND MCLEOD, P. L.   "Managing the Introduction of Information Systems Technology in Strategically Dependent Companies." *Journal of Management Information Systems,* volume 1, number 4, Spring 1985, pp. 5–23.

10. CLIPPENGER, J.   Personal Communication, Harvard Business School, Spring 1986.

11. DAVIS, R.   "Amplifying Expertise with Expert Systems." In *The AI Business,* P. H. Winston and K. A. Prendergast (eds.), The MIT Press, Cambridge, Massachusetts, 1984.

12. DEDOMBAL, F. T., LEAPER, D. J., STANILAND, J. R., MCCANN, A. P. AND HOLLOCKS, J. C. "Computer-Aided Diagnosis of Acute Abdominal Pain." *The British Medical Journal,* volume 2, 1972, pp. 9–13.

13. DOKTOR, R., SCHULTZ, R. L. AND SLEVIN, D. P.   *The Implementation of Management Science,* North-Holland, Amsterdam, 1979.

14. FEIGENBAUM, E. A., BUCHANAN, B. G., AND LEDERBERG, J.   "On Generality and Problem Solving: A Case Study Using the DENDRAL Program." In *Machine Intelligence 6,* Edinburgh University Press, Edinburgh, Scotland, 1971.

15. FOX, J. M.   *Software and Its Development,* Prentice-Hall, Englewood Cliffs, New Jersey, 1982.

16. FRENKEL, K. A.   "Toward Automating the Software-Development Cycle." *Communications of the ACM,* volume 28, number 6, June 1985, pp. 578–589.

17. GINZBERG, M.   *A Process Approach to Management Science Implementation.* Ph.D. Dissertation, Massachusetts Institute of Technology, Cambridge, Massachusetts, 1974, pp. 51–68.

18. HARRIS, G. AND MCKINNEY, B.   "Managing Artificial Intelligence for Competitive Advantage," unpublished manuscript, 1985.

19. HAYES-ROTH, F., WATERMAN, D. A. AND LENAT, D. B.   *Building Expert Systems,* Addison-Wesley, Reading, Massachusetts, 1983.

20. KEEN, P. AND SCOTT-MORTON, M. S.   *Decision Support Systems: An Organizational Perspective,* Addison-Wesley, Reading, Massachusetts, 1978.

21. LEONARD-BARTON, D.   "The Diffusion of Active Residential Solar Equipment in California." In *Marketing of Solar Energy Innovation,* A. Shama (ed.), Praeger Press, New York, New York, 1981, pp. 145–183.

22. LEONARD-BARTON, D.   "Implementing Innovations: The Automation of Knowledge-Based Production Tasks." *Working Paper* #9-785-003, Harvard Business School, Boston, Massachusetts, July 1984.

23. LEWIN, K.   "Group Decision and Social Change." In *Readings in Social Psychology,* T. M. Newcomb and E. L. Hartley (eds.), Holt, New York, New York, 1947.

24. LUCAS, H. C. JR.   *The Implementation of Computer Based Models,* The National Association of Accountants, New York, New York, 1976.

25. LUCONI, F., MALONE, T. AND SCOTT-MORTON, M. S. "Expert Support Systems." *CISR Working Paper* #122, Massachusetts Institute of Technology, Cambridge, Massachusetts, 1985.

26. MCDERMOTT, J. "RI: The Formative Years." *The AI Magazine,* volume 2, number 2, Summer 1981, pp. 21–29.

27. MCFARLAN, F. W. AND MCKENNEY, J. L. *Corporate Information Systems Management,* Richard D. Iwrin, Homewood, Illinois, 1983.

28. O'CONNOR, D. "Using Expert Systems in a Corporate Environment," unpublished paper, 1985.

29. POPLE, H. E. "Knowledge-Based Expert Systems: The Buy or Build Decision." In *Artificial Intelligence Applications for Business,* Walter Reitman (ed.), Ablex Publishing, Norwood, New Jersey, 1984.

30. ROCKART, J. F. "Chief Executives Define Their Own Data Needs." *Harvard Business Review,* March–April 1979, pp. 81–93.

31. SAMUELS, A. L. "Some Studies in Machine Learning Using the Game of Checkers." In *Computers and Thought,* E. A. Feigenbaum and J. Feldman (eds.), McGraw-Hill, New York, New York, 1963.

32. SCHEIN, E. H. "Management Development as a Process of Influence." *Industrial Management Review,* volume 2, number 2, Spring 1961, pp. 59–77.

33. SMITH, R. "On the Development of Commercial Expert Systems." *The AI Business,* volume 5, number 3, Fall 1984, pp. 61–73.

34. SPRAGUE, R. H. JR. AND CARLSON, E. D. *Building Effective Decision Support Systems,* Prentice-Hall, Englewood Cliffs, New Jersey, 1982.

35. SVIOKLA, J. J. AND MCKENNEY, J. L. "Karnak: The Wave Soldering Expert System." HBS Case #0-186-059, Harvard Business School, Boston, Massachusetts, 1985.

36. TAYLOR, E. C. "Developing a Knowledge Engineering Capability in the TRW Defense Systems Group." *The AI Magazine,* Summer 1985, pp. 58–63.

37. VAN MELLE, W., SHORTLIFFE, E. H. AND BUCHANAN, B. G. "EMYCIN: A Domain-Independent System that Aids in Constructing Knowledge-Based Consultation Programs." In *Machine Intelligence, Infotech State of the Art Report 9,* number 3, 1981, pp. 249–263.

38. WATERMAN, D. A. *A Guide to Expert Systems,* Addison-Wesley, Reading, Massachusetts, 1985.

39. WINSTON, P. H. AND PRENDERGAST, K. A. (eds.) *The AI Business,* The MIT Press, Cambridge, Massachusetts, 1984.

40. ZUBOFF, S. "Automate/Informate: The Two Faces of Intelligent Technology." *Organizational Dynamics,* Autumn 1985, pp. 4–18.

PART 6

DSS Applications

Applications are the reason for the existence of decision support systems. They are the payoff from all the activities required in order to have DSS in an organization. DSS applications vary considerably. Some are mainframe-based while others run on a PC. Some support a single decision maker while others support a group decision-making process. Some support ad hoc decision making while others are used on a planned, repetitive basis. Some are built using a DSS generator while others are created from DSS tools. A variety of DSS applications have been described throughout this book. In this final part, three additional DSS applications are described in depth.

Train dispatchers route trains along the section of tracks for which they are responsible. Richard Sauder and William Westerman in "Computer Aided Train Dispatching: Decision Support through Optimization" (Reading 24), describe a highly successful train dispatching DSS at Southern Railway. They describe the conditions that led to the creation of the DSS, how the system was developed, its architecture, and the benefits that are being realized.

The Louisiana National Bank was experiencing difficulties and, more importantly, was uncertain about how to remedy its problems. In order to obtain information to support management decision making during these troubled times, bank management decided to develop a financial planning DSS. The system that was developed is described by Ron Olson and Ralph Sprague in "Financial Planning in Action" (Reading 25). The financial planning system is credited with turning the bank's decisions and fortunes around.

Robert Breitman and John Lucas, in "PLANETS: A Modeling System for Business Planning" (Reading 26), describe the Production Location Analysis NETwork System developed at General Motors. This comprehensive DSS has been evolving since 1974 and helps individuals make decisions about important issues such as what products to produce; when, where, and how to make these products; which markets to pursue; and which resources to use. In addition to describing the capabilities of PLANETS, the authors share what they have learned about developing applications of this type.

24

COMPUTER AIDED TRAIN DISPATCHING: DECISION SUPPORT THROUGH OPTIMIZATION

Richard L. Sauder,
William M. Westerman

A mini-computer based information system with on-line optimal route planning capability was developed to assist dispatchers on the complex northern portion of Southern Railway's Alabama Division. The routing plan is revised automatically as conditions change. Since implementation in September 1980, train delay has been more than 15 percent lower, reflecting annual savings of $316,000.

The dispatching support system is now being expanded to all other Southern Railway operating divisions with $3,000,000 annual savings expected from reduced train delay.

Southern Railway Company operating throughout the southeastern United States is one of the nation's largest railroads. For years it has been a leader in profitability in the industry. In 1981 Southern's after tax profits totaled $212 million from revenues of $1.87 billion.

In June 1982, Southern Railway and the Norfolk and Western Railway merged to form the Norfolk Southern Corporation. The combined system provides efficient single

Reprinted by permission of Richard L. Sauder and William M. Westerman, "Computer Aided Train Dispatching: Decision Support Through Optimization," *Interfaces,* Vol. 13, No. 6, December 1983. Copyright 1983 The Institute of Management Sciences.

system service throughout the South, East, and Midwest. The Norfolk Southern Corporation is now the nation's fifth largest and most profitable railway system. Had it existed in 1981, it would have produced revenue of $3.59 billion and realized profits of $500 million. Even in the 1982 recession year, after tax profits, on a pro forma basis, amounted to $411 million.

Southern Railway and the Norfolk and Western operate as autonomous organizations whose activities are coordinated at the holding company level. Each railroad is divided into two operating regions, and each region, headed by a general manager, contains five operating divisions.

Daily operations are controlled at the division headquarters level. Although movement of trains between divisions is coordinated through a centralized operations control center, the responsibility for the safe and efficient movement of trains over the division lies principally in the division dispatching office. Directly accountable to the division superintendent, the dispatching office is headed by an assistant superintendent, the "Super Chief"; reporting to him is a chief dispatcher and a staff of train dispatchers.

Dispatching trains is complex and demanding. In a typical eight hour shift, a train dispatcher will control the movement of 20 to 30 trains over territories spanning three to six hundred miles. In most cases, these trains operate over single tracks and opposing trains must meet at strategically placed passing sidings. The dispatcher arranges these "meets" with safety the paramount consideration. He also must safely coordinate movements of roadway maintenance gangs, signal maintenance crews, industrial switch engines, and motor car inspection crews.

The dispatcher is also in constant contact with yard personnel at freight terminals who report essential information regarding trains that will move over the division. Once trains reach their destinations, they report operating and delay statistics for the dispatcher to record. Federal law requires that the dispatcher maintain this "train sheet." Finally, the train dispatcher interacts and coordinates with other dispatchers, as well as the chief dispatcher, giving and taking information about the operation of his territory.

Southern Railway's Alabama Division (Figure 24.1) is a complex operating division. Headquartered at Birmingham, Alabama, its most heavily traveled routes extend from Atlanta through Birmingham to Sheffield, Alabama, near Memphis. It interfaces with other operating divisions at each of these locations. Other major routes extend from Birmingham south to Mobile and from Birmingham southeast to Columbus, Georgia. Altogether, mainline trackage exceeds 800 miles and 80 to 90 trains operate daily. The division employs more than 1,200 persons, mostly in train and engine service.

Two train dispatchers are on duty around the clock at the Birmingham headquarters. One controls the high density Birmingham-Sheffield corridor (the North Alabama District) and the line south to Mobile. The other controls the Birmingham-Atlanta route (the East End District) and the line into southwest Georgia.

Both the North Alabama and the East End Districts operate under Centralized Traffic Control (CTC). This provides a failsafe system of signals and switches in the field controlled centrally by the dispatcher who monitors all field activity on an electronic display board. The other lines on the division have no signal control. In these "dark" territories, train movement is controlled solely by the dispatcher issuing stringent orders to train crews.

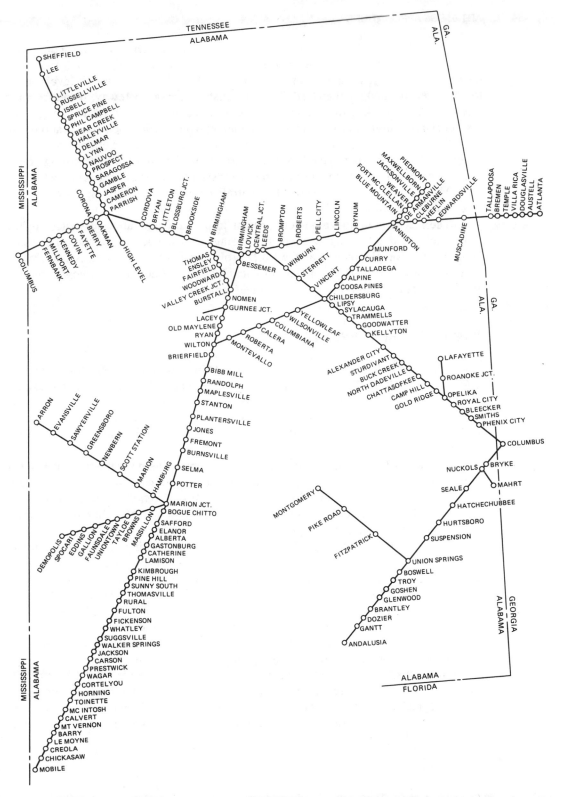

FIGURE 24.1 Southern Railway's Alabama Division

Until the mid-1970s, the operation of the Alabama Division was not overly complex; in fact, there was no centralized traffic control whatsoever. Then in 1974 with the opening of a large freight yard facility at Sheffield, merchandise traffic levels began to grow steadily, making the North Alabama District a major gateway to and from the Midwest. A coal loading facility near Sheffield was opened in 1977, further congesting the line. Unit trains (trains with up to seven locomotives and 96 loaded coal cars) began operating to key power plants in Georgia and Alabama. These trains operate on 40 hour "cycles," that is, moving loaded to their destination, unloading, and returning empty over the reverse route for reloading. Up to four such trains operate concurrently.

Management foresaw the need for centralized traffic control to assist dispatchers and began installation in 1976.

The research and development project to provide computer assistance for the dispatcher was in progress independently during this same period. As the CTC installation neared completion and as the R&D project began to show promise, it became clear that the Alabama Division was a logical location for determining how computer aided dispatching could further improve performance.

DEVELOPMENT OF THE SUPPORT SYSTEM

Southern Railway's operations research staff (which is now the Norfolk Southern Corporation's OR staff) has existed since the mid-1960s. Originally oriented toward computer model development, the operations research group by the early 1970s had become a corporate consulting staff providing *applications* support using tested analytical techniques, on one hand, and supporting *research and development* on the other.

The development staff began to investigate computer aid for the train dispatcher in 1975. Information systems for yard and terminal operations were already in place at many locations on the railroad. Extensions to this system requiring chief dispatchers to report realtime status of key trains were already envisioned. No other division-level systems were then being contemplated.

Concurrently, several signal manufacturers started selling turn-key systems to support CTC operations, providing features such as automatic "OS-ing (*On Station* reporting of the time a train passed a key location). Some systems permitted automated record keeping. One system even incorporated a rudimentary planning capability, tracing the routes of two opposing trains to determine when they would meet.

Operations research personnel reviewed a number of these systems and rejected them as being too inflexible. They saw the potential for automating the vast amount of division level information being manually recorded and for integrating this with other information systems. With extensive experience using simulation models to analyze line changes, they also foresaw the real possibility of on-line predictive planning aids for the dispatcher. They proposed that a computerized physical simulator be developed to explore these possibilities. Southern's top management computer usage committee approved the R&D project in late 1976.

The mini-computer based simulator, built and thoroughly tested over a three-year period, emulated a centralized-traffic-control-office environment and permitted designers and dispatchers alike to play and replay real-life scenarios, refining features that could eventually be installed in a division office. The simulator contained a bank of four color CRT's. Two displayed the track layout of the territory being studied. A simulation model was written to emulate movement of trains over the territory and it displayed movement of trains on the two track-layout CRT's based on route decisions interactively keyed by the "dispatcher."

A third CRT served as a work sheet for updating automated train-data files. A specially designed function keyboard permitted screen formats to be displayed which allowed dispatchers to update train sheets, reports of delay, locomotive failures, weather conditions, and many other records, all of which were then kept manually at division offices. The computerized system did not change what was being recorded; it merely changed the manner in which data was being recorded. A fourth CRT was reserved for displaying how trains should be routed—a capability which was being developed at the same time.

The potential for an on-line planning algorithm lay in considering all feasible future train meets throughout the territory and advising the dispatcher of that combination which would minimize total train delay. This "meet/pass plan," as it was labeled, had to account for all realistic operating conditions: travel times between sidings based on power and tonnage, speed limits, speed restrictions, train length compared with siding length, the ability of a train to start once stopped in a siding, train adherence to schedule, special cargo requiring special handling, work locations, and so forth. It also had to respond to dynamically changing conditions and display its latest recommended plan of action to the dispatcher in a manner he could readily comprehend.

The time-distance graph shown in Figure 24.2 is a standard method for displaying train meeting points and associated delay. Even in this simplified example involving five sidings and four eastbound and five westbound trains, there are thousands of meet combinations that could occur. The meet-pass plan was designed to reevaluate the combination at any time conditions changed and to display this new plan starting at the current time (8:30 am in the Figure 24.2 example) and projecting six to eight hours into the future.

Also incorporated was the ability for the dispatcher to override the plan by stating specific meet locations, by taking track out of service and by forcing trains in one direction to be stopped in sidings prior to the arrival of an opposing train. This permitted dispatcher experience and judgment to be reflected in the plan. It also formed the basis for a "what if" planning capability!

The first attempt to model the process evaluated feasible train routes with a decomposition approach incorporating a shortest path algorithm and a linear programming formulation. Although optimal solutions were obtainable, more often than not, convergence time was excessive and suboptimal solutions resulted. This method was subsequently replaced with a branch-and-bound technique enumerating all feasible meet locations and this approach did insure optimal results in a highly responsive fashion.

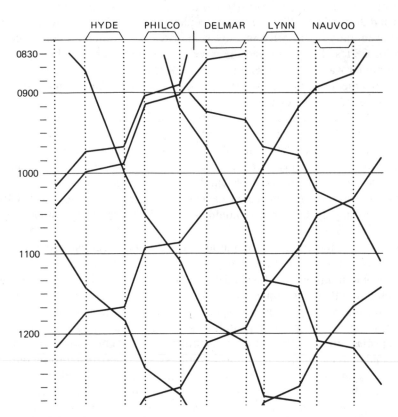

FIGURE 24.2 A time-distance graph displaying train movement through a five siding network in a four and one-half hour time frame. Four eastbound trains move diagonally from left to right meeting five westbound trains where the lines intersect.

The meet/pass plan was integrated into the simulator, and its use for on-line tactical planning was evaluated in detail. Possibly its most significant use was predicting the impact of the system operating in a real environment. During a periodic review of the project's status, the computer usage committee directed the operations research group to evaluate the potential of the system on the North Alabama District.

Operation was simulated both with and without computer-aided planning, and the impact on resulting train delay was measured. Train sheets for the North Alabama line were reviewed, and a typically heavy, yet normal, day of operation was selected. Train-meet delay for the first eight-hour shift on that day had amounted to 457 minutes. An Alabama Division dispatcher operated that same shift of operation in the simulator. The session began with train locations shown and information available concerning oncoming trains. The dispatcher worked the entire shift with no planning assistance, and the delay recorded at the conclusion of the session amounted to 455 minutes—a two minute difference.

The dispatcher then replayed the shift, this time following meets recommended by the plan. The resulting delay, 300 minutes, reflected a reduction of 34 percent. Reductions in other scenarios subsequently simulated ranged from 22 to 38 percent. When the OR group presented these findings, the committee, perceiving that if even half of these benefits could be realized they would create a significant performance impact, immediately approved the project. The North Alabama pilot project was underway.

IMPLEMENTATION AND ITS IMPACT

Interfacing the mini-computers and the CTC system was the only significant task involved in converting from a simulated to an on-line environment. CRTs were added to the North Alabama dispatcher's work station to complement the CTC display board: two "work" CRT's were installed to provide flexibility and backup, and a third CRT was installed solely for meet/pass plan display.

Installation and parallel testing of the North Alabama system began in January 1980. On September 15, 1980, the system was placed in production and the dispatcher's manual train sheets were removed. Six weeks later, instructions were issued to dispatchers to utilize the computer-generated plan.

Earlier in 1980, groundwork had been laid for installing a second, independent system to support the East End Alabama Division dispatcher. In the meantime, Data General Corporation, the mini computer system manufacturer, announced an advanced operating system that would permit a *single* minicomputer, with additional internal memory, to support a large number of users and work stations simultaneously. The desirability of such a single system that could support two or more dispatchers and any others needing access to the system was evident.

Conversion of the system started in mid-1981, with East End operations added to the dispatching system in March 1982. A final system supporting all territories on the Alabama Division became a reality in September. What had begun as a system to support a single train dispatcher had now evolved into one supporting all division operations.

Auditing operating performance as the system gained acceptance and comparing it with prior performance experience was a vital step in measuring the impact of computer-aided dispatching. The improvement predicted in the simulator experiment now had to be verified. For two full years since implementation, performance statistics have been compiled daily reflecting the total numbers of trains operating, train meets, and the total delay caused by these meets. Reviewing manual train sheets for a full year of operation starting in September, 1979, provided similar data for pre-implementation comparison.

Forty weeks of operations in each of these periods were then selected for a comparison study (a choice made necessary to compensate for a ten-week coal strike in 1981). Corresponding weeks were used for the year before implementation (the base period) and the year after. In the second year of operation, the first 40 contiguous weeks, beginning September 15, 1981 were used, thereby eliminating from consideration a period when business took a sharp downturn during the latter half of 1982.

Stringent guidelines were developed for analyzing delay reports to insure consistent measurement across periods:

1. Only delay within the limits controlled by the dispatcher was included.
2. Only delay that the dispatcher's planning would influence was considered.
3. Days reflecting highly abnormal operation, such as during a derailment, were excluded and replaced with an average for the same day in the four previous weeks. The operating statistics for the three measured periods are summarized in Table 24.1.

Comparing the first year of implementation with the previous year, traffic increased nearly nine percent, yet delay per train operated and delay per meet were down more than twelve percent. Traffic in the second year of operation returned to pre-implementation levels. The average number of trains operating weekly is nearly identical in the two periods, yet delay is more than 25 percent less in the 1981–1982 period.

Of the two measures, delay/train and delay/meet, the latter is more meaningful because division personnel have some control in scheduling trains to avoid meets but have little control over the numbers of trains operating. This ability to plan and control meets is evident in the figures for the second year of operation when delay per meet was reduced 18.8 percent. Overall, combining the 80 weeks of measured operation since computer-aided dispatching was placed on line, delay per meet has improved 15.5 percent. In addition, as

TABLE 24.1 North Alabama District Operating Statistics for the Three-Year Period Starting September 15, 1979

	PERIOD A	PERIOD B	PERIOD C
	Year Prior to Implementation	First Year since Implementation	Second Year since Implementation
Average Weekly Meet Delay (Minutes)	8893	8290 (–6.8%)	6645 (–25.3%)
Trains Operated (Weekly)	147.4	156.9 (+8.5%)	147.7 (+0.2%)
Train Meets (Weekly)	245.9	262.1 (+6.6%)	226.3 (–8.0%)
Meets Per Train Operated	1.67	1.67	1.53
Delay Per Train (Minutes)	60.3	52.8 (–12.4%)	45.0 (–25.4%)
Delay Per Meet (Minutes)	36.2	31.6 (–12.7%)	29.4 (–18.8%)

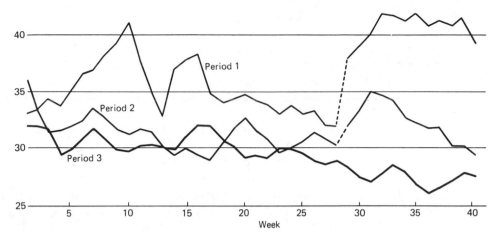

FIGURE 24.3 Minutes of Delay per Meet, a Three-Week Moving Average

Figure 24.3 shows, the operation is more consistent. In the year prior to implementation delay per meet ranged from 31.0 to 44.4 minutes. In the first year after implementation, it ranged from 26.6 to 40.2 and in the second, from 26.2 to 33.7 minutes.

Optimal planning together with information availability has improved performance significantly, and the resulting operation is a more consistent one. Several of the reasons are:

1. *A cleaner, neater, more professional operation.* Information is mechanically and electronically recorded, replacing hand-scrawled and often altered massive documents.

2. *A readily accessible information base.* Information recorded by the dispatcher is readily available and functional in inquiry form to all division personnel. Train information can also be transferred from one dispatcher's territory to another, reducing manual recording.

3. *An optimal plan clearly reflecting management policy.* The meet/pass plan considers management directives regarding key priorities for dispatching trains. The continually updated nature of the plan ensures compliance with this policy under dynamic conditions.

4. *An equitable attitude toward dispatcher responsibility and action.* As should be expected, dispatchers are severely criticized for delays caused by poor planning or inattention, for example if a high-priority train is delayed because a low-priority opposing train blocks its movement. A common dispatching solution had been to clear the low-priority train into a siding far in advance to minimize possibility of delaying the hot train. Computer aided dispatching has virtually eliminated this waste. Dispatchers are encouraged to use the plan and are not hauled on the carpet if they follow it, even should a delay occur.

In addition to freeing the dispatcher from complex, diversionary, time-consuming calculations and risks, this computerized system has ancillary benefits. For instance, train crews now make their runs in consistently less time, giving them more time at home and substantially improving morale. By the same token, locomotive fuel and equipment requirements are cut, thereby effecting a measurable reduction in mechanical costs.

Reduction in train delay translates directly to cost savings. One hour of train operation equates to more than $240 using a formula which considers fuel consumption, crew costs, locomotive availability and utilization, freight car ownership costs, revenue producing potential, and a variety of other factors. The more than 15 percent reduction in delay experienced in the 80 measured weeks of performance directly reflects savings of $316,000 in each of the first two years of operation.

What are the anticipated division wide savings now that the system does in fact support all operating districts on the division? It is reasonable to expect similar percentage savings on the East End CTC line between Atlanta and Birmingham. On the non-CTC portion of the division, some lesser improvement will occur from better planning and train scheduling. On this basis, future savings for the Alabama Division, when traffic returns to pre-1982 levels, are estimated at $675,000 annually. In addition, a proposed new passing siding on the North Alabama line, at a cost of $1,500,000, has been postponed indefinitely as a direct result of the greater dispatching efficiency.

Another monetary saving which cannot be easily quantified is additional track time for various types of maintenance crews. The dispatcher can now more quickly and efficiently allocate working time, because he can adjust the locations of train delays to accommodate these crews. Using the meet/pass plan's "what-if" capability, he can determine the best times to allocate, maximizing on-track working time yet minimizing train delay.

BEYOND THE BASIC SYSTEM

On the same basis that expected division wide savings were estimated for the Alabama Division, implementation of the computer-aided dispatching system on all Southern Railway divisions will produce cost savings of $3,000,000 annually in train delay reduction alone.

On September 27, 1982, a memo sent to the Executive Vice President for Administration, Norfolk Southern, from the President of the Southern Railway read in part:

> ...I am very much interested in extending this system to other divisions. I feel the results on the Alabama Division have been even better than we anticipated, and I believe we should move now to the north end of the Georgia Division between Chattanooga and Atlanta...

Computer hardware to support the Georgia Division operation was delivered in the last week of December. Starting in early January, operations research analysts, working with Georgia Division personnel, "defined" the division, using interactive file definition programs. On January 27, the Georgia Division support system was put on-line to begin dispatcher training and no computer program changes were required to transfer the existing Alabama Division support system to the Georgia Division.

Training continued through February, and on March 18 manual train sheets for the north end of the Georgia Division, Atlanta to Chattanooga, were removed. The total conversion effort required less than six operations-research man weeks, and less than three Georgia Division man weeks, including system support and training.

Systems for three additional Southern Railway divisions are budgeted for the remainder of 1983. In January of 1983, the President of Southern Railway convened a task force representing transportation, engineering, operations research, and data processing to produce an implementation plan that considers real installation costs matched against previously derived benefits. At the present time, it is expected that total installation cost at each division, except for one that requires new building facilities, will be less than $300,000.

The system described to this point is in operation and results have been demonstrated. The need for some new features became evident in working with the implemented system and they will be implemented soon.

First is formal planning assistance for the chief dispatcher. Improved efficiency in his duties has already been achieved through the information processing capabilities of the system. The meet/pass plans now used by the train dispatchers are tactical plans that consider trains now on the territory and trains whose arrival is imminent. In a new approach, appropriately dubbed "SUPERPLAN," the individual meet/pass plans for each dispatching territory will provide input to a division-wide planning process and allow the chief dispatcher to adjust train schedules and work assignments to avoid unnecessary train meets and traffic congestion.

A second innovation provides information transfer among division offices. This step ties together each of the divisions through Southern Railway's central computer complex in Atlanta. This feature, first of all, eases the chief dispatcher's clerical effort in reporting key train movements. More important, it provides the basis for "SUPER-PLAN-II"—optimal planning among divisions. The ultimate capability, now a potential reality, is vastly improved planning among divisions, at the general manager level and at the system control and coordination level. What was once a blue-sky dream of optimizing system-wide operation is now within reach because the basic building block, the division-level computer-aided dispatching system, works!

SUMMARY

Today the working computer-aided dispatching system continues to demonstrate significant dollar impact. Direction to expand the application to other territories testifies to the faith management has in the future benefits of the system. From a management scientist's viewpoint, the dispatching system is a marriage of information processing and management science. It is a distributed system and a decision support system. Proven management science optimization techniques form the basis of the system which around the clock provides dispatchers and managers alike the real time key to improving productivity and expanding profitability.

QUESTIONS

1. Describe the responsibilities of a train dispatcher.
2. Describe the development approach for the train-dispatching DSS at Southern Railway.
3. Does Southern Railway's train-dispatching DSS support or automate decision making? Discuss.
4. Discuss the benefits that have resulted from the implementation of Southern Railway's train-dispatching DSS.

25

FINANCIAL PLANNING IN ACTION

Ronald L. Olson,
Ralph H. Sprague, Jr.

In the fall of 1973, the Louisiana National Bank in Baton Rouge was faced with decreasing profits and an increasing level of short-term borrowed funds. The situation was not responding to traditional management practices, and the underlying reasons were not obvious.

Since the early 1960s, the bank has made innovation its unofficial trademark. It was first in the city to offer credit cards and automatic teller machines (ATMs). It developed a sophisticated computerized financial accounting system and an advanced transaction cost accounting system.

While innovation was significant in marketing and operations, the bank held to traditional management policies in asset/liability management until 1973. Lending officers granted loans to credit worthy customers at the prevailing interest rates. Public deposits were actively sought. In short, the bank accepted all deposits offered and gave loans to anyone who met credit standards.

Reprinted from *The Magazine of Bank Administration* (February 1981) with the permission of Bank Administration Institute.

Against this background, in mid-1973 the bank found itself in trouble. Daily operations were characterized by excessive short-term borrowing to support the expanding loan portfolio and bank examiners were indicating displeasure with the bank's liquidity position. In the words of the chief financial officer, "We suddenly discovered that we were not making money. More seriously, we did not know why."

THE FINANCIAL PLANNING SYSTEM

To tackle the problem, the bank decided to implement a set of tools that would meet the challenge of the situation. The statement of management needs was straightforward: Something to help manage the bank at the top level, especially in the areas of profit planning and liquidity analysis. The need was not phrased in terms of technology or information required, but in terms of final results.

The specific task evolved as the development and implementation of a system that would provide reporting, analysis and forecasting. The resulting system extracts data from primary management information systems and presents it in summary reports; forecasts the coming 12 months and five years on a "constant horizon" basis; and analyzes the historical data and emphasizes key asset/liability management issues such as resource allocations, interest rates, liquidity, growth and capital.

Over the past six years, the system has grown and evolved with management's use. It has changed as the bank and its environment have changed.

BENEFITS

The top management team is unanimous in its praise of the system; indeed the most important benefit is that it has helped make the bank more profitable. LNB's profit had fallen from $3.4 million in 1972 to $2.5 million in 1973 and $2.1 million in 1974. In 1975, LNB's profits rebounded to $3.9 million, an increase of 92% over the previous year. The chairman of the board attributed the profit turn-around to "...management's creative use of the Financial Planning System. The system enabled us to identify ways to restructure our asset and liability relationships and allowed us to test alternative action plans."

The decisions that led to the profit turnaround radically revised the financial structure of the bank. These decisions were the result of an intensive series of meetings in which the bank was analyzed in ways that had never been attempted. The new analytical information helped formulate decisions and evaluate the impact of those decisions. The most notable example of this analysis was the segmentation of the bank's business and an analysis of profitability of each segment. Management discovered that some areas thought to be profitable were not. For example, with its location in the state capital, LNB has always carried a large portfolio of time deposit accounts, termed "public funds." State law required these deposits to be matched by liquid government securities. Because of the relative rates of interest on the deposits and securities, the public fund sector of the bank was unprofitable. Although it was not feasible to eliminate public funds, the bank decided to reduce their relative impact, as the bank grew, by not soliciting any more such funds.

Through similar analyses, management decided to curtail installment loan growth until additional sources of retail funds were found and to sell a sizable portion of the real estate and construction loan portfolios. These strategies may have seemed sensible to an objective observer, but they were diametrically opposed to the bank's traditional policies as a retail bank in the state capital. As the president said, "The biggest benefit was to enable us to establish a solid base from which to run a profitable bank." The long-range test of that statement has been the continued growth and profitability of the bank.

HOW THE SYSTEM IS USED

The planning system (FPS) is used in three general ways: At the beginning of each month to report the previous month's activity; during the month to explore special issues or prepare strategic plans; and in the fall of each year to facilitate the budgeting process.

FPS produces the primary input to the planning committee meeting on the first Tuesday of each month. The committee is comprised of the chairman and CEO, the president, the chief financial officer, and the vice presidents in charge of each major market segment of the bank. The vice president of corporate planning uses FPS to prepare the reports and graphs and serves as the resource for questions about the information. The general purpose of this meeting is to review the previous month's performance, examine the newly prepared 12-month forecast and discuss anticipated changes or pending issues.

There are frequently questions and possibilities which need to be explored further with additional runs of FPS and considered at the next meeting. The committee currently meets twice a month, but in periods of rapid change or when a major set of strategies is under consideration, it meets weekly. The system is frequently used to prepare forecasts which test alternative strategies. Every officer has become interested in the bankwide impact of decisions because they all know their recommendations and actions will be examined in this context.

Special runs are also done to investigate the impact of pending changes in money market rates, banking regulations, market trends and internal policy changes.

Although completely separate, the financial planning system facilitates the budgeting process in the fall of the year. The budget is a detailed accounting budget, part of the automated financial control system which includes a cost accounting module, the general ledger and the budgeting system. A "grass roots" budget, as it is called, is composed of about 9,000 data items—one for each budget line item, for each of the cost centers, for each of the 12 months of the coming year.

The data are initially gathered from the cost center managers and entered into the budgeting system. Summaries are then extracted and entered into FPS in the same way that actual data are transferred after the end of each month. The tentative budget summary is then analyzed using FPS to assess the combined impact of the budget estimates, examine the reasonableness of the estimates compared to top management's judgment and search for any inconsistencies in interrelated areas. If necessary, adjustments are made through negotiation between top management and cost center managers, and the budget is approved by mid-December. The detailed budget is then carried in the automated accounting system, which produces monthly budget variance reports for each cost center during the year. The summary form of the budget is also stored in FPS for use in summary reports and comparative analyses.

It is important to note that the bank considered and rejected a combined budgeting/planning system. Management found that there are major differences in the purpose, procedure, and format of budgeting versus planning. The budget mechanism is primarily a motivation and control device that requires fine levels of detail. Such detail tends to become "quicksand" for planning. Effective planning on concise data can reveal rather than obscure trends and underlying relationships. Plans must also be subject to change and extend across fiscal year reporting boundaries. For these reasons, FPS was designed to be separate from the budgeting segment of the automated accounting system.

A DECISION SUPPORT SYSTEM

The evolution of information technology has seen major developments, successes, failures and shifts in thinking. The concept of large-scale, all encompassing "management information systems" was recognized in the early 1970s. More recently, however, the concept of top management, modeling-based, summary-level "decision support systems," has become recognized as a logical approach for strategic analysis, planning and decision making. The financial planning system at Louisiana National Bank is a good illustration of a decision support system. The system is a summary model of the bank's automated financial control system; operates in an on-line computer environment which gives managerial access at any time rather than on a fixed processing schedule; permits experimental forecasting to test alternative assumptions and strategies; uses its own independent data base; and permits rapid redesign to accommodate changing circumstances.

SYSTEMS COMPONENTS

Data

At the end of each month, summary accounting data are extracted from the general ledger system. The process of reformatting and data entry requires about two hours of clerical effort. No adjustments or modifications are made to the data, that is, the summary statements produced by FPS will agree precisely with those produced by general ledger. As we shall see, this is a critical point.

Each month, the data are added to the historical data base which maintains up to three years of monthly figures and up to 7.5 years of quarterly figures. In addition, 12 periods of future data in the same format are maintained. These data are developed from the forecasting and simulation capability.

Reports and Analysis

Each month the system produces a full set of summary financial statements, including the balance sheet, income statement and standard operating ratio reports. The current monthly actual data are compared with the forecast, budget, and actual for the previous year. The system also produces a series of special reports which analyze critical areas of the bank. Of particular importance is the interest rate-volume-mix analysis, and an analysis of product lines. The latter portrays the sources and uses of funds for three major segments of the bank—retail or consumer sector, public sector and commercial sector. Figure 25.1 illustrates the key ratio report, Figure 25.2 illustrates the interest variance report and Figure 25.3 illustrates the funds allocation report.

Forecasts

The reports outlined above are also available for each of the coming 12 months which are forecast by the system. Independent variables may be entered by management or generated by statistical techniques with management override capability. A built-in

	1/75-12/75 ACTUAL	1/74-12/74 ACTUAL	DIFF	PRCT
PER SHARE:				
NOEAT ($)	2.65	1.35	1.30	95.99
NET INCOME ($)	2.53	1.36	1.17	86.16
BOOK VALUE ($)	16.83	15.49	1.34	8.67
EARNING POWER:				
RETURN ON EQUITY (%)	15.01	8.76	6.25	71.31
NET RET ON ASSETS (%)	0.97	0.54	0.43	80.19
GROSS RET ON ASSETS(TE%)	9.07	9.25	-0.19	-2.02
OPER PROFIT MARGIN (TE%)	10.72	5.83	4.89	83.90
EARNING ASSET MIX (%)	85.86	86.10	-0.25	-0.29
NET INTEREST SPREAD(TE%)	3.81	2.32	1.49	64.13
YIELD ON E.A. (TE%)	9.75	10.00	-0.25	-2.50
OVERHEAD TO NET INC (%)	327.85	519.80	-191.95	-36.93
LIQUIDITY POSITION:				
TIME TO TOTAL DEP (%)	63.67	64.16	-0.49	-0.76
LOANS TO DEPOSITS (%)	70.67	75.38	-4.71	-6.25
LOANS TO AVAIL DEP (%)	117.03	133.67	-16.64	-12.45
TOT SEC TO PLDG REQ (%)	98.67	99.04	-0.36	-0.37
BOR FDS TO CASH+FFS (%)	34.67	82.47	-47.80	-57.95
NET FEDERAL FUNDS ($)	-9324.	-31125.	21801.	70.04
CAPITAL ADEQUACY:				
ASSETS TO CAPITAL	12.11	12.70	-0.59	-4.65
DEPOSITS TO CAPITAL	9.50	9.14	0.36	3.93
LOANS TO CAPITAL	6.72	6.89	-0.18	-2.56
RISK ASSETS TO CAPITAL	9.31	10.11	-0.79	-7.85
LOAN LOSS RESERVE (%)	1.15	0.97	0.18	18.41
LOAN LOSS PROVISION (%)	0.65	0.51	0.14	27.73
LEVERAGE RATIO (%)	1545.22	1625.31	-80.09	-4.93
GROWTH/CHANGE:				
INTEREST MARGIN ($T.E.)	20080.	14736.	5343.	36.26
NON-INTEREST INCOME ($)	3034.	2696.	338.	12.54
NON-INTEREST EXPENSE ($)	15475.	12917.	2558.	19.81
NOEBT ($)	5538.	2249.	3289.	146.24
NOEAT ($)	4438.	2249.	2189.	97.33
NET INCOME ($)	4238.	2261.	1977.	87.44
TOTAL DEPOSITS ($)	342229.	301835.	40394.	13.38
TOTAL LOANS ($)	241860.	227528.	14331.	6.30
TOTAL ASSETS ($)	436141.	419276.	16865.	4.02

FIGURE 25.1 Louisiana National Bank Key Ratio Report

ASSETS/INCOME CHANGE DUE TO:	ACTUAL 1/75-12/75 VOLUME TOTAL	ACTUAL 1/74-12/74 RATE	TOTAL CHANGE
SECURITIES:			
GOVERNMENTS	616.	-42.	573.
OTHER SECURITIES	-622.	217.	-405.
TAX EXEMPTS	-113.	-82.	-195.
TAX EXEMPTS T.E.	-210.	-152.	-362.
SECURITIES INC CHANGE	-120.	93.	-28.
SECURITIES INC CHG T.E	-217.	23.	-194.
LOANS:			
COMMERCIAL LOANS	745.	-577.	169.
CONSTRUCTION LOANS	150.	-449.	-299.
REAL ESTATE LOANS	210.	97.	306.
INSTALLMENT LOANS	4.	329.	333.
CREDIT CARD LOANS	376.	68.	444.
LOAN INCOME CHANGE	1484.	-532.	953.
FUNDS SOLD:			
FEDERAL FUNDS SOLD	327.	-92.	235.
SEC. PUR. URA	-262.	-324.	-586.
TEMP. FUNDS SOLD	65.	-416.	-351.
INTEREST INC CHANGE	1429.	-855.	575.
INTEREST INC CHG T.E.	1333.	-925.	408.
LIABILITIES/EXPENSE CHANGE DUE TO:	VOLUME TOTAL	RATE	TOTAL CHANGE
TIME DEPOSITS:			
REGULAR SAVINGS	304.	6.	310.
GOLDEN SAVINGS	34.	-12.	22.
TIME CD'S	847.	-849.	-2.
PUBLIC FUND CD'S	252.	-909.	-657.
TIME DEP EXP CHANGE	1437.	-1763.	-326.
BORROWED FUNDS:			
SEC. SOLD URA	-487.	-1265.	-1752.
FED. FUNDS PURCHASED	-960.	-1645.	-2605.
FUNDS BORROWED	-135.	0.	-135.
LOAN PART. SOLD	47.	-34.	13.
TEMP. FUNDS SOLD	-1534.	-2945.	-4479.
CAPITAL NOTES	-0.	-130.	-130.
COST OF FUNDS CHANGE	-97.	-4838.	-4935.
NET CHANGE	1527.	3983.	5510.
NET CHANGE T.E.	1430.	3913.	5343.

FIGURE 25.2 Louisiana National Bank Interest Variance Analysis Summary Report

optimization model is available when needed. The forecast is a "rolling" or "constant horizon" forecast, always covering the next 12 periods, and is recast at the beginning of each new month. In addition, the bank may expand the horizon as far into the future as it desires on a monthly or quarterly basis.

CONTINUING BENEFITS

The continued growth and profitability of the bank is paralleled by a set of interacting benefits involving the planning system that facilitate management of the bank. Some of these contributing benefits include the following:

- Establishing a mechanism for managing the balance sheet over time. Two important parts of this mechanism are liquidity management and the capital analysis that monitors the bank's most critical constraints.
- Providing a framework and structured discipline around which to organize and coordinate the decision making of the top management team. Such a system gets everyone focused on the same issues and working toward the same organizational goals.

	1/75-12/75 ACTUAL	1/74-12/74 ACTUAL	DIFF	PRCT

FIGURE 25.3 Louisiana National Bank Funds Allocation Report

RETAIL BANKING

	1/75-12/75 ACTUAL	1/74-12/74 ACTUAL	DIFF	PRCT
SOURCES OF FUNDS:				
INDIVIDUAL DDA	32196.	29272.	2923.	9.99
REGULAR SAVINGS	53419.	46679.	6740.	14.44
GOLDEN SAVINGS	21877.	21243.	633.	2.98
TIME CDS(PERSONAL)	11300.	3968.	7332.	184.78
GROSS SOURCES	118791.	101163.	17628.	17.43
LESS CASH RES & FLOAT	9302.	8284.	1018.	12.29
NET SOURCES	109489.	92879.	16610.	17.88
USES OF FUNDS:				
REAL ESTATE LOANS	34595.	31946.	2648.	8.29
BANKAMERICARD(NET PART.)	19500.	17889.	1610.	9.00
INSTALLMENT LOANS	45847.	45818.	30.	0.06
TOTAL USES	99941.	95653.	4288.	4.48
NET SOURCES(-USES)	9547.	-2775.	12322.	444.06

COMMERCIAL BANKING

	1/75-12/75 ACTUAL	1/74-12/74 ACTUAL	DIFF	PRCT
SOURCES OF FUNDS:				
COMMERCIAL DDA(NET T&O)	50871.	42915.	7956.	18.54
DUE TO BANKS	20177.	14747.	5430.	36.82
OTHER DDA (NET US DDA)	2000.	2000.	0.	0.
TIME CDS	49088.	45143.	3945.	8.74
GROSS SOURCES	122137.	104806.	17331.	16.54
LESS CASH RES & FLOAT	17922.	14835.	3088.	20.81
NET SOURCES	104214.	89971.	14243.	15.83
USES OF FUNDS:				
COMMERCIAL LOANS	103872.	96246.	7626.	7.92
CONSTRUCTION LOANS	33580.	32218.	1362.	4.23
TOTAL USES	137452.	128463.	8988.	7.00
NET SOURCES(-USES)	-33237.	-38492.	5255.	13.65

INVESTMENTS & PUBLIC BANKING

	1/75-12/75 ACTUAL	1/74-12/74 ACTUAL	DIFF	PRCT
SOURCES OF FUNDS:				
US GOVERNMENT DDA	1851.	2476.	-625.	-25.26
PUBLIC FUNDS	10475.	10751.	-276.	-2.57
PUBLIC FUND CD'S	66274.	62368.	3906.	6.26
TRUST DDA	4395.	4171.	224.	5.37
TRUST CDS	15945.	14258.	1687.	11.83
SEC. SOLD URA	34617.	43120.	-8503.	-19.72
GROSS SOURCES	133557.	137145.	-3588.	-2.62
LESS CASH RES & FLOAT	5567.	5569.	-2.	-0.04
NET SOURCES	127990.	131575.	-3585.	-2.72
USES OF FUNDS:				
GOVERNMENTS	51950.	43350.	8601.	19.84
OTHER SECURITIES	18619.	26800.	-8181.	-30.53
TAX EXEMPTS	49199.	51463.	-2264.	-4.40
SEC. PUR. URA	7608.	11692.	-4084.	-34.93
TOTAL USES	127376.	133305.	-5929.	-4.45
NET SOURCES(-USES)	614.	-1730.	2344.	135.47

FUNDS RECONCILIATION

	1/75-12/75 ACTUAL	1/74-12/74 ACTUAL	DIFF	PRCT
SOURCES OF FUNDS:				
NET RETAIL	9547.	0.	9547.	0.
NET COMMERCIAL	0.	0.	0.	0.
NET INVESTMENTS & PUBLIC	614.	0.	614.	0.
CAPITAL NOTES	5000.	5000.	0.	0.
FUNDS BORROWED	0.	1710.	-1710.	-100.00
CAPITAL(NET OA,OL & FA)	17149.	16719.	430.	2.57
NET FEDERAL FUNDS PURCH	9324.	31125.	-21801.	-70.04
TOTAL SOURCES	41633.	54553.	-12920.	-23.68
USES OF FUNDS:				
NET RETAIL	0.	2775.	-2775.	-100.00
NET COMMERCIAL	33237.	38492.	-5255.	-13.65
NET INVESTMENTS & PUBLIC	0.	1730.	-1730.	-100.00
DUE FROM BKS/EXCESS CASH	8396.	11556.	-3160.	-27.35
NET FEDERAL FUNDS SOLD	0.	0.	0.	0.
TOTAL USES	41633.	54553.	-12920.	-23.68

- Providing a mechanism for satisfying the bank examiners' reporting requirements, and giving management a tool for communicating its analyses to the examiners.
- Enabling the top management team to anticipate and respond to changes in regulations, market opportunities and internal operations.
- Reducing the clerical cost, time and effort of preparing required periodic reports for management, regulators and others.

In the following section, some of the benefits cited above are followed by brief accounts of events which illustrate them.

ASSET/LIABILITY MANAGEMENT

1. The best example is the market sector analysis, which revealed the serious imbalance in assets and liabilities. After the initial analysis in 1974, this report has been used regularly to maintain a profitable balance. It enables the bank to accommodate change in the demand structure of the marketplace.
2. In 1975, regulators authorized consumer certificates of deposits in small denominations with four- and six-year maturities. Most banks could see only the possibility that savers would shift from regular savings to CDs, with a consequent increase in total interest expense on the same money. By using FPS, LNB realized that the "consumer CDs" were precisely what they needed—long-term, fixed-rate funds—on which to build an expansion of their consumer loan portfolio. Heavy promotion of the CDs resulted in increased profitability of the retail segment.
3. A similar analysis led to a major change in the pricing of installment loans based on maturity rather than type. The bank now uses a sliding-rate scale for an installment loan based on the length of time it will be outstanding. An analysis using FPS helped produce appropriate rates and schedules.

FRAMEWORK, STRUCTURE AND DISCIPLINE FOR UNIFIED DECISION MAKING

A recent analysis revealed a growth in credit card loans beyond the ability of the retail sector to support them. A decision was made to sell off a large portion of credit card loans. With the bank's history as the regional lender in credit cards, this move would have been strongly opposed by several managers without the convincing analysis generated through the use of the FPS.

RESPONSE TO CHANGES

1. After several years of liquidity shortages, LNB's management was in a "state of euphoria" in March 1978 with excess liquidity. FPS runs, however, indicated that loan growth and deposit shrinkage would generate another shortage of liquidity by early fall. In June, the planning committee cut back on installment loan expansion, set

maximum growth goals for all departments and sold participations in some of the larger loans with good customers. In October it was clear that LNB had averted a major liquidity crisis because of the early warning.

2. A key determinant in profitability is control of "overhead" expenses. At LNB growth in staff levels and salaries has generally kept pace with the growth of the bank, but total overhead expenses have never exceeded 55% of interest margin, management's upper control limit. Forecasts for 1979 showed the ratio moving to 56% and higher late in the year. The bank instituted a hiring control program so that the number of employees actually decreased through attrition, and overhead expenses remained within the guideline.

3. The bank is currently studying several anticipated changes in regulation. Interest on checking accounts will soon be allowed; Louisiana is considering bank holding company legislation; higher interest on saving deposits seems certain. The planning committee is using FPS to assess the impact of these changes and evaluate potential management decisions.

QUESTIONS

1. Describe the situation that led to the creation of the financial planning system at the Louisiana National Bank.
2. What benefits have been derived from the financial planning system at the Louisiana National Bank?
3. How is the Louisiana National Bank's financial planning system used?
4. Describe the components of the financial planning system at the Louisiana National Bank.

26

PLANETS: A MODELING SYSTEM FOR BUSINESS PLANNING

Robert L. Breitman,
John M. Lucas

Multinational planning is complex. In the automotive sector alone, this involves the manufacture and distribution of thousands of products supported by hundreds of facilities worldwide. In order to guarantee timely delivery at competitive prices, these facilities have to be properly designed, tooled, and situated. Lead times for tooling and facility changes can be three years or more and routinely involve capital expenditures in the tens or hundreds of million dollars. Errors in implementing and changing facilities can be costly. The planning departments are continually evaluating new alternatives.

While the business planning organizations of most large multinational corporations are well organized and structured, the actual planning processes are unstructured and multipurposed. Some planning may be unstructured in that complete overhauls of all or part of a business plan can occur at any time that competitive pressure dictates. Ad hoc management studies of product mix, site selection, or divestiture can occur at

Reprinted by permission of Robert L. Breitman and John M. Lucas, "PLANETS: A Modeling System for Business Planning," *Interfaces,* Volume 17, Number 1, January–February 1987. Copyright 1987, The Institute of Management Sciences.

any time. In addition, routine planning tasks must be satisfied, including quarterly business plans, annual budgets, and five-year business plans. The planning horizon varies from study to study and can range from months to years.

Planning is multipurposed since both corporate and divisional objectives must be satisfied and can involve any of the functional areas of business (engineering, finance, logistics, management, manufacturing, marketing, and purchasing). The scope of an analysis frequently depends upon how and where in the organization the study originates.

THE TECHNOLOGY NEED EVOLVES—*PLANETS* IS BORN

In late 1973, General Motors decided that it needed a system of mathematical models to assist management in determining the best strategies for placing facilities to support new products in new overseas markets. Responsibility for this effort was assigned to a corporate management science support staff. In evaluating the type of decision support system required (for example, simulation, optimization, or spreadsheet scenario), this group compiled a list of over 300 probable decision variables and factors (labor availability, flexible capacity, local content regulations, and so forth) which might have to be considered by a model. A survey of GM managers worldwide was conducted to solicit their input and to order these factors by priority. Involving the managers in this survey turned out to be crucial for the ultimate acceptance of PLANETS by corporate and divisional management.

During the survey, the scope of the requested modeling capabilities expanded substantially as the economy changed. Management now wanted to evaluate whether to

- Buy or build new facilities (location and timing to be determined);
- Expand capacity at existing plants, (when, where, and how);
- Use a nonallied manufacturing source (when, who, how much);
- Reallocate products among existing plants (when, where, how, what volume); and
- Introduce a new product (go/no-go, when, where, how).

Furthermore, senior management wanted the modeling capability to use standard business terminology to facilitate expression of business scenarios to the system. They also wanted the system to be available for use by managers worldwide.

Not all managers wanted to trust an optimization model. Some wanted only a tool that would quickly evaluate the financial, production, or marketing impact of specific scenarios. As with prior manual studies, these managers would set all variable values and use the model as a big calculator. Others, who already trusted the concept of optimization, wanted the capability to have every business factor float to satisfy some paramount objective.

The possible objectives included

- Maximize profit,
- Maximize market penetration,

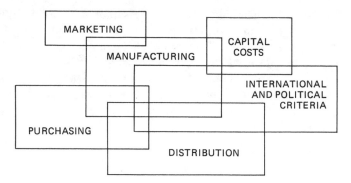

FIGURE 26.1 Production Location Analysis NETwork System

- Maximize facility utilization,
- Maximize exports,
- Maximize production,
- Maximize sales,
- Minimize costs,
- Minimize losses,
- Minimize investment, and
- Minimize imports.

The management science group realized that traditional approaches to mathematical model building would not adequately support, on an ongoing basis and in a timely manner, the quantity and variety of scenarios to be evaluated. Skilled management science resources were not available in sufficient quantities. Conventional model development was too slow. Models did not use business terminology and did not include enough real-world interactions. Therefore, what resulted was not just a system or collection of mathematical models specific to some proportion of the automotive business, but rather, PLANETS: a sophisticated, yet easy to use, flexible model-building system applicable to any industry (Figure 26.1).

AN OVERVIEW OF *PLANETS'* CAPABILITIES

The basic premise of PLANETS was that if people could be taught how to evaluate a business problem and reformat it into a mathematical program, then a computer system could be "taught" to do the same, only faster. Long before *expert systems* became a widely used term, the first version of PLANETS (1974) provided business planners with a comprehensive network of computer programs to facilitate the following tasks, which had previously required the direct involvement of management science model builders:

1. *Define a Business Environment.* PLANETS provides a structure with which a business planner can communicate conversationally to develop a working outline

POLICIES/OBJECTIVES

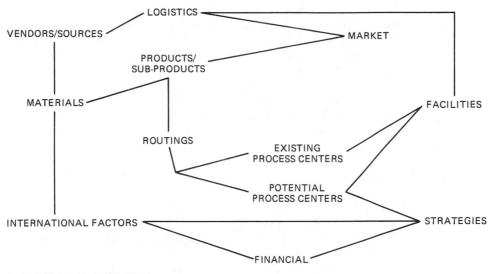

TIMING/PLANNING HORIZONS

FIGURE 26.2 PLANETS Building Block Framework. Most business situations can be structured by using combinations of the available PLANETS building block categories, which act as either sources and/or sinks in the business flow process. Underlying this problem network are quantifiable management objectives and policies that can be imposed over some definable planning horizon.

of various business situations using standard business terminology and data estimates. The PLANETS building blocks that form the basis for this structure are shown in Figure 26.2. In addition to providing a structured approach to defining business problems, PLANETS handles all file manipulation so that the planner needs only to specify new, changed, or deleted data. PLANETS will then update the data structures accordingly and provide a review of the information.

2. *Define Specific Business Analysis Assumptions.* Through user friendly dialogue, the business planner can design specific what-if scenarios. These scenarios are a hybrid of the data provided and the business analysis assumptions and options. PLANETS combines all this information to build a model specific to the problem at hand. Using PLANETS, the business planner can quickly and efficiently define an unlimited number of scenarios from a single set of base data.

3. *Automatic Feasibility Check of Any Potential Scenario.* PLANETS automatically analyzes each scenario or "English model" to be evaluated or optimized for inherent mathematical and logical structure, data completeness and integrity, and then performs a premodel feasibility check.

4. *Automatic Mathematical Model Generation and Solution.* PLANETS interprets the problem database and model specifications for each business scenario and builds a mixed-integer programming model to solve that scenario. PLANETS creates input files for commercially available solution tools like MPSX and

SCICONIC. A typical problem has in excess of 10,000 variables, including over 100 integer variables. Formulating and generating the input deck for MPSX or SCICONIC takes approximately one to two minutes. The same task done manually would typically take weeks and would require an operations research analyst. PLANETS automatically generates a job deck and then submits a job that will run the solution tool (MPSX or SCICONIC), which then solves the problem.

5. *Automatic Mathematical Model Interpretation and Business Report Generation.* After the problem is solved, PLANETS interprets the MPSX or SCICONIC output of the model run and integrates this information with the problem data and modeling options to generate business reports. The business planner can select from a menu of standard business reports similar to those listed below.

THE BASIC REPORTS

The Process Center Utilization Report identifies by facility each process center, its activity, variable cost, fixed cost, total cost, and utilization percent by timestage.

The Process Center Graphical Report is a histogram of capacity utilization for each process center by timestage.

The Strategy Implementation Report identifies which strategies were implemented by the model. Strategy costs are represented by facility, asset category, and pre-tax investment.

The Material Usage Report identifies the materials used by facility including transfer products. Specific detail for timestage, volume, material cost, inbound freight, and tariffs are included along with a total cost.

The Product Cost Allocation Report identifies for each product which routings were used by timestage. The process centers associated with the routings are shown with volume, unit cost, and total cost by timestage.

The Product-Shipment-by-Facility Report enumerates each product and the market that it is shipped to by timestage. Volume, price, total revenue, freight, and tariffs are included with each market and timestage combination.

THE FINANCIAL REPORTS

The Investment Summary Report shows investments by asset type, facility, and timestage, as well as an investment grand total.

The Revenue Summary Report shows revenue by product and by facility for each timestage as well as a total for all timestages.

The Expense Summary Report shows facility, freight, and tariff costs by timestage. Facility costs are broken into variable and fixed, direct and indirect. The freight costs are enumerated by type of freight (that is, inbound and outbound).

The Facility-Revenue-and-Cost Report shows sales by product and costs by process center for each facility. Information is shown by number of units and value by timestages.

The Facility-Income-and-Cash-Flow Report shows for each facility an income statement consolidating the information from the facility revenue and cost report.

The Consolidated-Income-and-Cash-Flow Report provides a summary of all the facility income-and-cash-flow reports.

The Investment Detail Report provides investment data by asset type showing pre-tax cost and depreciation by timestage.

The Infeasibility Report is used to help the analyst determine why a feasible solution could not be found.

The Sensitivity Report provides information as to the amount that a variable in either the objective function or the RHS may vary before the solution will change.

The PLANET system does not simply take input data and fill in data matrices for a canned linear program. It is not a model but a highly elastic model-building system that can automatically generate unique mathematical models to support large and small, simple or complex business scenarios. Because actual problem formulation and data input are facilitated by PLANETS through the use of standardized "building block" terminology, PLANETS has been referred to as an open-end scenario and model building language for business planners. It keeps track of which business information is mandatory for any valid or feasible scenario description; in addition to this mandatory information, the user can include other optional business descriptors. There are 11 basic building block categories; each has its own specific attribute data, which are maintained via conversational dialogue and full-screen editors.

The first of these, *Timestage,* is a mandatory building block that defines the financial and productive planning horizon as well as permissible periods during which decision activity can take place. *Timestages* can correspond to calendar or budgetary time periods (for example, individual months or years) but more often represent decision periods which can be multiples of calendar time.

The *Facility* building block is also mandatory and represents geographic location and the availability of resources that are location dependent (for example, labor skills, floor space types, public utilities, and default area efficiency and work environment). *Facilities* are commonly used to represent plant shells. The attribute productive capacity is never applied to *Facilities*. Buildings or locations (*Facilities*) have no capacity; however, things that go into buildings (*Process Centers*) do have capacity.

The mandatory building block *Process Center* represents people, equipment, or any other resources that can have productive capacity. *Process Centers* must be assigned to a *Facility* with a status of either existing or potential. *Process Centers* represent resource requirements (for example, labor skills, and floor space type) and resource dependent fixed and variable costs as well as efficiency.

Strategy building blocks are optional and represent potential investment alternatives that can add, modify, combine, or remove *Process Centers*. Within any business problem, *Strategies* can interact and be mutually exclusive, dependent, contingent, or additive. This building block incorporates the details of financial amortization schemes and the timing options of expenditures. In the resulting mixed-integer mathematical formulation, *Strategies* are represented by integer variables.

The optional *Materials* building block represents purchasable commodities required by *Product-Routing* combinations. (For example, *Product* A produced via *Routing* 1 may require five pounds of *Material* X, a plastic compound; however, if *Product* A is produced via *Routing* 2 then three units of *Material* Z, a metallic alloy, would be required since the *Process Centers* referenced by this *Routing* 2 use totally different processing.) The *Material* building block also incorporates *Vendor* purchase plan availability and pricing options.

The *Vendor* building block of PLANETS must be referenced if the *Material* building block category is utilized. *Vendors* typically represent external sources for *Material* having a sourcing location. This building block can also be used to define inventories in scheduling models.

Market is an optional building block that represents potential external demand locations for a *Product*.

Product is the mandatory keystone building block that ties everything in the "English model" together. *Products* represent the marketable output of the business process being modeled. *Products* specify *Market* demand at various pricing levels for a given *Timestage;* this demand can have lower and upper range values, either of which may be forced into the solution by the user. The *Product* building block also defines *Product-Routing* combinations specifying permissible production options, *Material* requirements, and any internally produced material needed. (*Transfer Product*).

The mandatory *Routing* building block represents alternative operating plans for producing a *Product*. *Routings* contain a sequence of existing or potential *Process Center* references with specific capacity attributes. Typically, more than one *Routing* is specified for a *Product* (otherwise no process selection is performed by the resulting model). *Routings* can also be mutually exclusive, dependent, or directly tied to a specific *Market* demand.

The *Freight* building block is optional and represents inbound, interplant, intraplant, and outbound logistic planning options, including cost and mode of transport.

The *International/Geopolitical* building block category is a collage of policy options. These can represent constraints dependent on country or economic community that concern tariffs, local content, balance of trade, trade complementation, or other specific policy. This category specifies volume or monetary limits, penalties, ratios, and exclusions. In addition, inflation and exchange rate can be specified by country and *Timestage*.

PLANETS can be used by management to evaluate the following questions, either independently or simultaneously:

- What to make,
- When to make it,
- Which markets to satisfy,
- How to make it,
- Whether to make or buy,
- Where to ship,
- Where to make, and
- How to purchase.

While the capability exists in PLANETS to evaluate all the preceding what-if questions simultaneously, not all problems or scenarios will be set up in this manner. For example, raw material and vendor selection are often not factors, or perhaps the

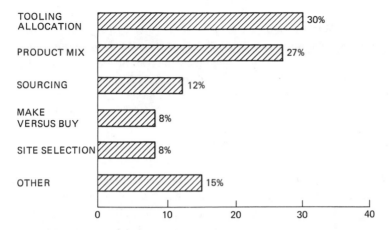

FIGURE 26.3 A Breakdown of 80 Major PLANETS Studies by Type

processing sequence is already fixed and only logistics variables need to be evaluated. Any of the preceding criteria or sets of variables can be included or eliminated.

The direct financial benefits from the PLANETS model-building process are the reduction in procurement, manufacturing, and distribution costs achieved by taking advantage of the following:

- Differences in direct labor and fixed and variable burden rates,
- Increased equipment utilization,
- Optimal volume production,
- Best use of capital expenditure options,
- Higher volume purchasing and vendor pricing schedules,
- Reduced transportation costs,
- Elimination of low-profit and capacity-inefficient products,
- Optional market pricing/volume considerations, and
- Difference in currency exchange rates.

Since 1974, PLANETS has been used for over 80 major corporate studies as well as numerous divisional and plant studies. Figure 26.3 provides a percentage breakdown of the problem types that have been addressed using the PLANETS technology. Most of these modeling applications were performed by planning analysts who had little or no prior background in operations research.

PLANETS IN ACTION—A CASE STUDY

We will now describe a representative case study that demonstrates many of the types of planning issues that can be evaluated with PLANETS. Most of the 80 major studies (Figure 26.3) were of the size and complexity of this case study. This example demonstrates that PLANETS models can be used for ad hoc and recurring applications.

This case study also provides a glimpse of the PLANETS philosophy or discipline that we suggest for each major study (Figure 26.4). We have found that at least 50 percent of the effort of the planning analyst should be devoted to working with management to properly define the scope of the problem in business terms.

In this particular study, management and the analyst jointly defined the following problematic situation:

- A new vehicle is planned for introduction in the marketplace in four years.
- Totally new major components will be required.
- Existing facilities do not have the capability to manufacture these components.
- New tooling, and possibly new facilities, will have to be procured.
- Tooling purchase and installation often require lead times of two to three years.
- New facility construction, if required, could involve more than three years effort.

FIGURE 26.4   PLANETS Discipline. The initial 50 percent of a typical project effort utilizes PLANETS problem structuring philosophy and terminology without actually accessing any PLANETS software. This involves defining overall business problem scope, planning horizons, and objectives. In the second stage, the user begins accessing the Planet System software to construct a database outline of the business problem. The completion of the project effort (final 25 percent) involves interacting with the system to perform automatic model generation and analysis.

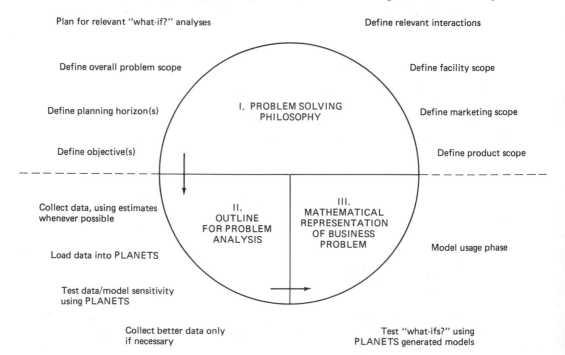

The actual study involved 14 major automotive components. However, for simplicity we will focus on engines and transmissions only.

The issues that management wanted to optimize were

- How many facilities are required?
- What is the ultimate size of each facility?
- Which engine and transmission design or designs should be selected for each market?
- What is the best sourcing and distribution pattern for each component, in each year?

These issues had to be optimized for the following management objectives:

- Minimize the 10-year corporate cost;
- Adhere to export/import requirements; and
- Satisfy management's noneconomic constraints.

The planning horizon criteria are embodied in the PLANETS *Timestage* building block. While a standard 10-year financial analysis was needed, the actual decision timestages representing the planning horizon are four and add up to 12 years. The first *Timestage* represented three calendar years spanning the actual investment timing and the initial start of production. The next two *Timestages* represented the next two years of the plant capacity acceleration and modification. The final timestage represented seven business years, during which no tooling decisions were planned (Figure 26.5).

There were two engineering designs for both engines and transmissions that could be marketed, each represented by a PLANETS *Product* building block. The locations where these components could end up on finished vehicles were worldwide and would be represented by the *Market* building block.

Eight locations were possible for new engine facilities and almost as many for the transmission facilities. The *Facility* building block contains information pertinent to location, such as floor space and the availability of public utilities.

The final size of each new facility was also a variable. Historically, tooling to manufacture the components was purchased and installed in modules with finite economies of scale. One-half a module may have one-half the capacity of a full module at two-thirds the cost. One-half, one, or two modules could be combined to create facilities of several different sizes at each potential location. Each module representation conformed to a *Process Center* building block specification. These *Process Center* building blocks are utilized by *Product Routing* building blocks.

In this study, six weeks elapsed as we defined the problem scope, issues, timing, and objectives with management using the PLANETS building block specifics and terminology. Once this information was in hand, the PLANET system was accessed, and the second half of the study effort began (Figure 26.4).

The types of data used in this study are listed in Table 26.1. This information was supplied by the user through a conversational dialogue specific to each PLANETS building block. Given this input, PLANETS generated the relevant interactions, and the stage was then set for the final what-if phase of the study (Figure 26.4).

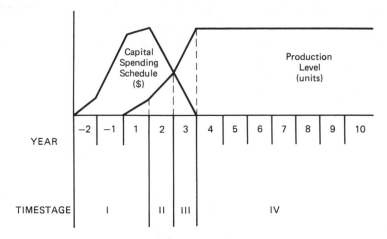

FIGURE 26.5   The Case Study Planning Horizon of 12 Years. The entire business planning horizon is predefined by using the *Timestage* building block category. Each *Timestage* segregates binary decision points. For example, each potential increase in production capacity levels is a decision point that would be represented by its own *Timestage* designation. The four production levels, while spanning 12 years, can be represented by four *Timestages.* Capital spending schedules of one or more years do not have to be represented by single *Timestages* since each *Timestage* can have a variable planning horizon length associated with it and any financial discounting would be handled accordingly.

In addition to "free run," (nonpolicy-constrained) economic optimizations, over 40 what-if management prerogatives were also modeled. Of these scenarios, only 10 were originally planned; the remaining 39 were the result of ideas spawned by management after reviewing the scenario output as it progressed, and they led directly to concepts which avoided projected costs of hundreds of millions of dollars.

Had the PLANETS study not been performed, management would have proceeded with capital appropriation requests derived by traditional manual analysis methods. The reduced expenditure projections provided by PLANETS were readily compared to this baseline.

The output determined the number of new facilities required, their locations, the size and tooling requirements of each facility, facility start-up timing, and specific product volume allocation and distribution patterns. This entire study effort, including the non-PLANETS portions, took approximately three months.

Further proof of the acceptance of this PLANETS analysis approach by management was the fact that these optimization results were fully implemented. In addition, this specific application did not end with the completion of this ad hoc study; it led directly to further usage. Three years after the site location study and once the facilities had been built, a PLANETS model focusing on engine variants only was used regularly to optimize the purchase and allocation of tooling sets to optimize shipping schedules and to optimize product mix allocations.

TABLE 26.1   Case Study Information

Problem Scope

14 Potential Products
2   Engineering designs per product
7   Market areas
11 Potential facility locations
66 Basic tooling options per product
40 Economic scenarios

Data

- Inbound, interplant, and outbound freight costs and modes
- Variable cost, capacity and efficiency per tooling option
- Fixed and variable burden cost
- Effect of shift differentials and overtime
- Fixed expenses for facilities and tooling
- Investment timing, options, schedules and amortization schedules
- Engineering compatibility of component designs
- Flexible capacity interference losses
- Local content requirements
- International trade complementation options
- Minimum export level requirements
- Balance of trade factors
- Vendor material availability and material costs
- 10-year product forecast by market
- Product transfer pricing options by market
- Penalties for lost sales

While many different variables were included, the resulting models were not sensitive to all the data. Whenever possible, easily collectible range estimates (with some plus or minus variance) were input as opposed to difficult-to-collect, highly accurate point values. This study was typical in that 85 percent of the original data range estimates remained valid, while only 15 percent of the data needed refinement (greater accuracy).

As this case demonstrates, planners have used PLANETS to determine what products to make, when to make or introduce a product, and where to base production. They used it to decide which markets to satisfy, where and how to ship, whether to make a product instead of purchasing it, how to make or process a product, and which vendors and purchasing strategies to use. No mandatory policy requires the use of PLANETS; planners have used and continue to use PLANETS because they want to. By using PLANETS, they are able to evaluate these issues simultaneously, whereas in the past they could not.

WHAT WE HAVE LEARNED—12 YEARS OF *PLANETS* EXPERIENCE

In the course of applying PLANETS technology worldwide, a number of lessons have been learned that have caused General Motors and EDS to adapt their game plan for implementing MS/OR technology to the changing environment. Here is what the past 12 years of implementing PLANETS have taught us.

Managers as Direct System Users

PLANETS was designed to capture the quantitative MS/OR expertise required to formulate, model, and solve complex business-planning problems. The original objectives of the PLANETS development and implementation effort were to minimize end-user dependence on MS/OR practitioners and to maximize the benefits of transferring mathematical modeling technology to business planners. We originally intended PLANETS as a decision support tool that management would use directly; we learned early on that analysts, not management, would be the hands-on users.

Management works through the analyst, and all the expert systems and user friendliness that we could possibly design into the system will not appreciably change that. Senior management prefers to concentrate on managing the enterprise and to delegate hands-on analysis to analysts.

The Importance of Optimality

Experience has also demonstrated that managers frequently do not require optimal solutions. They have used the quantitative optimal results less than 10 percent of the time. The rest of the time they choose a less than optimal solution that satisfies qualitative criteria not incorporated in the model. PLANETS calculates the quantitative impact of these qualitative decisions. For example, management may override the PLANETS investment options in favor of their preference, while using PLANETS to optimize the remaining logistics and product-mix alternatives. Because optimization capability is guaranteed behind the scenes, management can now establish benchmarks for decisions. PLANETS is a form of decision makers' insurance. One divisional general manager said that he liked the PLANETS approach because he now knew the cost of going with a decision based on his "qualitative feel," compared to the quantitative or economic optimum. Because of such use, since 1974, we have added many more scenario evaluation and direct management controls to PLANETS.

Faster Algorithms versus Scenario Manipulation

Since most of the recurring planning models are generated only three or four times a year or as needed to support ad hoc studies, such as facility site selections, turnaround times of one hour to one day are entirely satisfactory. Therefore, the mathematical solution algorithms currently available commercially are more than adequate to satisfy users. Further substantial improvement of the solution turnaround would generally provide minimal benefit to the business planner. Our assessment is based upon the content of requests for the development or enhancement of user-specified systems. Repeatedly, such qualities as solution integrity and input/output understandability rank higher than faster solution turnaround.

We have learned that the capabilities to evaluate and optimize specific scenarios must co-exist. A blend of solid MS/OR and simple scenario evaluation gives the planning analyst a sense of control and comfort. PLANETS has made a quantum leap in applied management science capability; problem formulations that used to take weeks or months now take days; models and matrices that would have taken days or weeks to generate even using commercial mathematical programming packages now take a couple of minutes; and mathematically optimized solutions are only minutes or hours away. In accomplishing this, MS/OR expertise has been leveraged, and in many cases replaced, by MBA skills.

Supporting PLANETS

As is often the case, unexpected side effects accompanying a new technology over-shadow the original objectives. While PLANETS helped us solve most of the quantitative puzzle, its ease of use created new organizational problems.

- How does management prevent the tool from being misused?
- How will the MS/OR activity adapt to user demands for training?
- How can competent PLANETS use be maintained when the successful business planners get promoted elsewhere?

In order to better support the development and implementation of PLANETS and other MS/OR technologies, the various management science and applications support staff functions involved were consolidated into what is now the Decision Technologies Division of EDS.

A blend of MS/OR practitioners, MBAs and explanners provides the nucleus of expertise that promotes PLANETS' use. This strategic analysis services group also provides professionally developed training programs at a variety of levels. A management appreciation course exposes financial and planning managers to business situations that would be good candidates for PLANETS applications. The PLANETS course for planning analysts is designed to accomplish true technology transfer and end-user independence.

Supporting this formal classroom instruction are professional documentation materials such as capabilities guides, user guides, and an overview of the system mechanics and mathematics.

BENEFITS—THE VALUE OF *PLANETS*

The benefits of using PLANETS have involved projections of significant monetary cost avoidance. A handful of the 80 major PLANETS applications are projected to have resulted in over $1 billion in documented cost avoidance. While the remaining studies were not fully documented or had no cost projection benchmarks, we estimate that PLANETS use results in at least two to three percent savings in overall capital expenditures.

Another effect of PLANETS is that more scenarios can now be generated and analyzed reliably. This has both tangible and intangible benefits; more scenarios analyzed should guarantee that less expense or more profitability are likely; as more scenarios are evaluated, the risk associated with scenario selection decreases.

Because PLANETS is ideal for evaluating scenarios with little more than estimated variables, less time is now required for each analysis. Even though PLANETS can review more variables simultaneously, less overall study time is typically required.

Finally, one of the best benefits of all is the satisfaction of knowing that PLANETS has successfully transferred MS/OR technology to planning analysis.

PLANETS has provided a means of taming the dynamic elements of the planning process. Electronic Data Systems Corporation is proud to provide professional planning technologies like PLANETS, which complement the overall planning procedures encountered in business.

ACKNOWLEDGMENTS

PLANETS has benefited from many contributors in its 12-year history. We especially thank and recognize the following individuals for their dedication, support, and insights: Z. Barlach, W. Carr, M. Carter, D. E. Hackworth, G. Herrin, B. Hittner, S. Hoffman, M. Kerr, C. Lustenberger, K. Markle, S. Marney, C. Medley, R. L. Miller, M. L. Moore, G. Oberg, J. Pechenik, B. Popko, J. Shanker, L. W. Rearick, R. Vander-Hooning, and A. F. Welch.

QUESTIONS

1. What were the key design considerations associated with PLANETS?
2. Describe how PLANETS was developed?
3. Summarize what has been learned from the 12 years of PLANETS experience.

University Support Programs Offered by Vendors of DSS Generators

A number of companies have developed and marketed DSS generators. Some of these vendors have university support programs that allow universities to use their products for instructional purposes at a significantly reduced price. It is also common for them to offer instructional materials, training programs, and hot-line services under favorable terms. Their motivations for offering university support programs include the following: (1) to improve information systems education, (2) to influence future sales of their products, and (3) to expand the number and range of their product applications. The end result is that universities can now offer state-of-the-art training on many of the leading selling DSS generators at an affordable price.

The following pages list much of the information needed to select and contact vendors of DSS generators that have strong and active university support programs. This list is not all-inclusive and the information is subject to rapid change. It should provide a good starting point, however, for obtaining a DSS generator for your university.

DSS Generator:	EXPRESS
Vendor:	Information Resources, Inc. 200 Fifth Avenue Waltham, MA 02254
Contact:	Gary Farner or Paul Murray (617) 890-1100
Installations:	Commercial: 400 University: 15
Cost(s)	Commercial: Mainframe is $40,000–$125,000 PC version is $1,495/copy University: Negotiable
Compatible Systems:	IBM mainframes running under VM or MVS, DEC VAX, Prime PRIMOS, HP, PC/AT compatibles
User Support:	Hot lines during business hours; training materials used with hot-line personnel available; introductory course online for self-study; intensive introductory and advanced courses
Capabilities:	yes — English-like yes — Nonprocedural: and procedural using an embedded programming language yes — Forecasting: regression, trend analysis, Box-Jenkins yes — Statistical analysis yes — Financial analysis yes — Optimization: linear programming yes — Goal seeking yes — What-if yes — Monte Carlo yes — Consolidations yes — Database management yes — Report generator yes — Graphical display yes — Security system: available to individual cell level
Other Features:	Specific applications using Express are also available

DSS Generator:	FCS
Vendor:	Thorn/EMI Computer Software 400 Perimeter Center Terrace, Suite 650 Atlanta, GA 30346
Contact:	Jim Ward (404) 393-1903

Installations: Commercial: 2,000 total, 90% in-house
                University: 15–20

Cost(s)   Commercial: In-house versions $14,000–$150,000 depending on CPU type and options and 15% annual maintenance
       University: Micro—$500–$1,200 depending on quantities, 50% discount off list price

Compatible Systems: IBM, DEC, Univac, Wang, Honeywell, HP, DG, Prime, Micro-subset, IBM compatible (not stand-alone) WANG, IBM PC, WANG PC, 14 time-sharing systems

User Support: 800 number hot line

Capabilities:
   yes — English-like, user guide, primers, introductory class, advanced class, videocassettes, consulting
   yes — Nonprocedural: but procedural programming options for advanced procedures
   yes — Forecasting: correlation curve fitting, multiple linear regression
   yes — Statistical analysis
   yes — Financial analysis
   yes — Optimization: limited
   yes — Goal seeking: "TARGET" option
   yes — What-if
   yes — Monte Carlo
   yes — Consolidations: multidimensional
   yes — Database management; relational database only; interface with IDS DBMS, IDMS, ADABAS, FOCUS & SQL ACCESS to DB2 & SQL/DS
   yes — Report generator
   yes — Graphical display (discrete plotting and continuous line multicolor, felt pen plotter support, screen painting, form handling)
   yes — Security system: limited

DSS Generator:	IFPS/PLUS, Release 11
Vendor:	Execucom Systems Corporation P.O. Box 9758 Austin, TX 78766
Contact:	Donna Carter (512) 346-4980
Installations:	Commercial: 1,400 University: 260
Cost(s)	Commercial: $100,000 plus maintenance University: $3,200 use limited to instruction, research, internal university planning, not for consulting
Compatible Systems:	Burroughs, DEC, Honeywell, HP, IBM, Prime, UNIVAC, Sun, Apollo, IFPS mini on WANG, Apollo, Sun, micro version available on IBM PC and Macintosh
User Support:	Hot line, case materials developed in-house and by university users, on-site presentations, text available (McGraw-Hill), placement activities, student guide for IFPS, student guide for IFPS/Personal (includes software)
Capabilities:	yes — English-like yes — Nonprocedural yes — Forecasting: linear regression, smoothing yes — Statistical analysis: many common procedures yes — Financial analysis: depreciation subroutines, multiple rates of return, mortgages, amortization yes — Optimization: linear, nonlinear, integer, mixed integer yes — Goal seeking: multiple variables yes — What-if yes — Monte Carlo yes — Consolidations: universal capability, hierarchical, allocations yes — Database management yes — Report generator yes — Graphical display: color graphics available yes — Security system: limited internal security; password, file encription
Other Features:	Explain (AI) capability, full screen forms, system building commands, full screen data editor (PLUS), "easy to use" features; i.e., synonyms and entity recall

DSS Generator:	SIMPLAN
Vendor:	Simplan Systems, Inc. 300 Eastowne Drive Chapel Hill, NC 27514
Contact:	Robert C. Verboon, President (919) 493-2495

Installations:

Commercial:	150 in-house; time-sharing networks
University:	5 currently (University of California, Berkeley, Penn State, New Mexico, Georgetown, ITESM)

Cost(s)

Commercial:	$60,000–$80,000 depending upon configuration and options or annual fee of $10,000
University:	$1,500 annually; includes most options, SIMPLAN must be fully integrated into one course per semester—no administrative use

Compatible Systems: IBM and lookalikes (OS/CMS); Prime. Micro version

User Support: 1 seat in workshop, 2 hours consulting per month, and 1 speaker per year. University assumes travel and expenses, comprehensive materials include case examples

Capabilities:

yes — English-like
yes — Nonprocedural
yes — Forecasting
yes — Statistical analysis: many statistical routines
yes — Financial analysis
no — Optimization: under development
yes — Goal seeking
yes — What-if
yes — Monte Carlo
yes — Consolidations
yes — Database management
yes — Report generator
yes — Graphical display
yes — Security system

DSS Generator:	SYSTEM W DSS
Vendor:	COMSHARE, Inc. 3001 South State Street Ann Arbor, MI 48108
Contact:	Chris Kelly (800) 922-7979 in Michigan (313) 994-4800)
Installations:	Commercial: 400 University: 12
Cost(s):	Commercial: IBM: $47,000–$221,000. DEC: $36,800–$131,900, depending on machine size and options chosen; 15% annual maintenance includes regular product enhancements and hot-line telephone support University: license fee and program maintenance are waived providing product is used solely in pursuit of education
Compatible Systems:	Hardware: IBM: 9370 series and above (370 and 370/XA architecture) or compatibles. DEC: Micro VAX II, Micro VAX 3000 series, VAX 11/780 and above, including 8000 series
Operating systems:	IBM: MVS/TSO VS2 3.8, SP 1.0 or higher, or XA 2.1 or higher; or VM/CMS version VM/SP 2.0 or higher, or VM/SP/HPO 3.0 or higher. DEC: VMS version 4.5 and above
User Support:	16 U.S. offices, 14 international offices, 14 international sales agents and licensees; product enhancements, maintenance, hot-line telephone support, on-site presentations and training, corporate visits, systems design, analysis, and implementation
Capabilities:	yes — English-like yes — Nonprocedural yes — Forecasting yes — Statistical analysis yes — Financial analysis yes — Optimization: heuristic yes — Goal seeking yes — What-if no — Monte Carlo yes — Consolidations: multidimensional yes — Database management: relational, multidimensional, pipeline software to other DBMS yes — Report generator yes — Graphical display yes — Security system: dependent upon operating system

DSS Bibliography

A large body of DSS writings has been published in books, articles, conference proceedings, trade publications, and the like. This diversity can be seen in the varied sources of materials included in this book of readings. To help you find other materials of interest, the following DSS bibliography is provided. While it contains references to what the authors feel are the most important, interesting, and accessible materials on DSS, it includes only a small percentage of what has been written. There are many other excellent DSS writings, with more appearing daily. This bibliography should provide assistance, however, as you strive to learn more about DSS.

This bibliography includes books and articles. The articles have been categorized by their major topic(s): (1) general overview; (2) relationship with OR/MS and MIS; (3) DSS framework; (4) planning for DSS; (5) development process; (6) software interface; (7) model subsystem; (8) database subsystem; (9) integrating the software interface, models and data; (10) integrating DSS into the organization; (11) evaluation of DSS; (12) applications of DSS; (13) executive information systems; (14) expert systems; (15) group decision support systems; and (16) future of DSS. Many of these categories are divided into subcategories. The numbers shown for each category or subcategory reference the numbered articles in the bibliography.

BOOKS

1. ALTER, STEVEN L. *Decision Support Systems: Current Practices and Continuing Challenges.* Reading, Mass.: Addison-Wesley, 1980.

2. BENNETT, JOHN L., ed. *Building Decision Support Systems.* Reading, Mass.: Addison-Wesley, 1983.

3. BONCZEK, ROBERT, CLYDE HOLSAPPLE, AND ANDREW WHINSTON *Foundations of Decision Support Systems.* New York: Academic Press, 1981.

4. FICK, GLORIA, AND RALPH H. SPRAGUE, JR., eds. *Decision Support Systems: Issues and Challenges.* London: Pergamon Press, 1980.

5. KEEN, PETER G. W., AND MICHAEL S. SCOTT MORTON *Decision Support Systems: An Organizational Perspective.* Reading, Mass.: Addison-Wesley, 1978.

6. MCCOSH, ANDREW, AND MICHAEL S. SCOTT MORTON *Management Decision Support Systems.* New York: John Wiley, 1978.

7. SCOTT MORTON, MICHAEL S. *Management Decision Systems: Computer Support for Decision Making.* Boston: Harvard University Press, 1971.

8. SPRAGUE, RALPH H., AND ERIC D. CARLSON *Building Effective Decision Support Systems.* Englewood Cliffs, N.J.: Prentice-Hall, 1982.

9. THIERAUF, ROBERT J. *Decision Support Systems for Effective Planning and Control: A Case Study Approach.* Englewood Cliffs, N.J.: Prentice-Hall, 1982.

10. THIERAUF, ROBERT J. *User-Oriented Decision Support Systems: Accent on Problem Finding.* Englewood Cliffs, N.J.: Prentice-Hall, 1988.

11. TURBAN, EFRAIM *Decision Support and Expert Systems.* New York: Macmillan, 1988.

ARTICLES

1. ABDOLMOHANNADI, M. J. "Decision Support and Expert Systems in Auditing: A Review and Research Directions," *Accounting and Business Research,* 17, no. 3 (Spring 1987), 173–85.

2. ADELMAN, L. "Involving Users in the Development of Decision-Analytic Aids: The Principal Factor in Successful Implementation," *Journal of the Operational Research Society,* 33, no. 4 (April 1982), 333–42.

3. ADELMAN, L. "Real-Time Computer Support for Decision Analysis in a Group Setting: Another Class of Decision Support Systems," *Interfaces,* 14, no. 2 (March–April 1982), 75–83.

4. AKOKA, J. "A Framework for Decision Support System Evaluation," *Information and Management,* 4 (July 1981), 133–41.

5. ALAVI, M., AND J. C. HENDERSON "Evolutionary Strategy for Implementing a Decision Support System," *Management Science,* 27, no. 11 (November 1981), 1309–23.

6. ALTER, S. L. "Development Patterns for Decision Support Systems," *MIS Quarterly,* 2, no. 3 (September 1978), 33–42.

7. ALTER, S. L. "Why Is Man-Computer Interaction Important for Decision Support Systems?" *Interfaces*, 7, no. 2 (February 1977), 109–15.

8. ALTER, S. L. "A Taxonomy of Decision Support Systems," *Sloan Management Review*, 19, no. 1 (Fall 1977), 39–56.

9. AVRAMOVICH, D., T. M. COOK, G. D. LANGSTON, AND F. SUTHERLAND "Decision Support System for Fleet Management: A Linear Programming Approach," *Interfaces*, 12, no. 6 (June 1982), 1–9.

10. BAHL, H. C., AND R. G. HUNT "A Framework for Systems Analysis for Decision Support Systems," *Information and Management*, 7 (June 1984), 121–31.

11. BAHL, H. C., AND R. G. HUNT "Decision Making Theory and DSS Design," *Data Base*, 15, no. 4 (Summer 1984), 12–19.

12. BAKER, D. W., S. C. CHOW, M. T. HENNEN, T. P. LUKEN, G. J. ROBINSON, AND H. L. SCHEURMAN "An Integrated Decision Support and Manufacturing Control System," *Interfaces*, 14, no. 5 (September–October 1984), 44–52.

13. BALACHANDRAN, B. V., AND A. A. ZOLTNES "Interactive Audit-Staff Scheduling Decision Support System," *Accounting Review*, 56 (October 1981), 801–12.

14. BARBOSA, L. C., AND R. G. HERKO "Integration of Algorithmic Aids into Decision Support Systems," *MIS Quarterly*, 4, no. 1 (March 1980), 1–12.

15. BELARDO, S., K. R. KARWAN, AND W. A. WALLACE "Managing the Response to Disasters Using Microcomputers," *Interfaces*, 14, no. 2 (March–April 1984), 29–39.

16. BENBASAT, I., AND A. S. DEXTER "Individual Differences in the Use of Decision Support Aids," *Journal of Accounting Research*, 20 (Spring 1982), 1–11.

17. BENBASAT, I., AND R. N. TAYLOR "The Impact of Cognitive Styles on Information Systems Design," *MIS Quarterly*, 2, no. 2 (June 1978), 43–54.

18. BERRISFORD, T., AND J. WETHERBE "Heuristic Development: A Redesign of Systems Design," *MIS Quarterly*, 3, no. 1 (March 1979), 11–19.

19. BLANNING, R. W. "What Is Happening in DSS?" *Interfaces*, 13, no. 5 (October 1983), 71–80.

20. BONCZEK, R. H., C. W. HOLSAPPLE, AND A. B. WHINSTON "Computer Based Support of Organizational Decision-Making," *Decision Sciences*, 10, no. 2 (April 1979), 268–91.

21. BONCZEK, R. H., C. W. HOLSAPPLE, AND A. B. WHINSTON "The Evolving Roles of Models in Decision Support Systems," *Decision Sciences*, 11, no. 2 (April 1980), 337–56.

22. BONCZEK, R. H., C. W. HOLSAPPLE, AND A. B. WHINSTON "Future Directions for Developing Decision Support Systems," *Decision Sciences*, 11, no. 4 (October 1980), 616–31.

23. BONCZEK, R. H., AND OTHERS "Generalized Decision Support System Using Predicate Calculus and Network Data Base Management," *Operations Research*, 29 (March–April 1981), 263–81.

24. BRENNAN, J. J., AND J. J. ELAM "Understanding and Validating Results in Model-Based Decision Support Systems," *Decision Support Systems*, 2 (1986), 49–54.

25. BRIGHTMAN, H. "Differences in Ill-Structured Problem Solving Along the Organizational Hierarchy," *Decision Sciences*, 9, no. 1 (January 1978), 1–18.

26. BUNEMAN, O. P., AND OTHERS "Display Facilities for DSS Support: The DAISY Approach," *Data Base*, 8, no. 3 (Winter 1977), 46–50.

27. CANNING, R. G. "APL and Decision Support Systems," *EDP Analyzer*, 14, no. 5 (May 1976), 1–12.

28. CANNING, R. G. "What's Happening with DSS," *EDP Analyzer*, 22, no. 7 (July 1984), 1–12.

29. CANNING, R. G. "Interesting Decision Support Systems," *EDP Analyzer,* 20, no. 3 (March 1984), 1–12.

30. CARLIS, J. V., G. W. DICKSON, AND S. T. MARCH "Physical Database Design: A DSS Approach," *Information and Management,* 6 (August 1983), 211–24.

31. CARLSON, E. "Decision Support Systems: Personal Computing Services for Managers," *Management Review,* 66, no. 1 (January 1977), 4–11.

32. CARLSON, E. D., B. F. GRACE, AND J. A. SUTTON "Case Studies of End User Requirements for Interactive Problem Solving Systems," *MIS Quarterly,* 1, no. 1 (March 1977), 51–63.

33. CONHAGEN, A. E., AND OTHERS "Decision Support Systems in Banking," *Bankers Magazine,* 165 (May–June 1982), 79–84.

34. COOPER, D. O., L. B. DAVIDSON, AND W. K. DENISON "A Tool for More Effective Financial Analysis," *Interfaces,* February 1975, 91–103.

35. CRESCENZI, A. D., AND G. K. GULDEN "Decision Support for Manufacturing Management," *Information and Management,* 6 (April 1983), 91–95.

36. CULLUM, R. L. "Iterative Development," *Datamation,* 31 (February 1985), 92–98.

37. CURLEY, K. F., AND L. L. GREMILLION "The Role of the Champion in DSS Implementation," *Information and Management,* 6 (August 1983), 203–209.

38. DAFT, R. L., AND N. B. MACINTOSH "New Approach to Design and Use of Management Information," *California Management Review,* 21, no. 1 (Fall 1978), 82–92.

39. DAVIS, R. "A DSS for Diagnosis and Therapy," *Data Base,* 8, no. 3 (Winter 1977), 58–72.

40. DE, P., AND A. SEN "Logical Data Base Design in Decision Support Systems," *Journal of Systems Management,* 32 (May 1981), 28–33.

41. DESANCTIS, G., AND B. GALLUPE "A Foundation for the Study of Group Decision Support Systems," *Management Science,* 33, no. 5 (May 1987), 589–609.

42. DICKSON, G. W., AND M. A. JANSON "The Failure of a DSS for Energy Conservation: A Technical Perspective," *Systems, Objectives, Solutions,* 4, no. 2 (April 1984), 69–80.

43. DOKTOR, R. H., AND W. F. HAMILTON "Cognitive Style and the Acceptance of Management Science Recommendations," *Management Science,* 19, no. 8 (April 1973), 884–94.

44. DONOVAN, J., AND S. MADNICK "Institutional and Ad Hoc DSS and Their Effective Use," *Data Base,* 8, no. 3 (Winter 1977), 79–88.

45. DYER, J. S., AND J. M. MULVEY "An Integrated Information/Optimization System for Academic Planning," *Management Science,* 22, no. 12 (August 1976), 1332–41.

46. EASON, K. D. "Understanding the Naive Computer User," *Computer Journal,* 19, no. 1 (February 1976), 3–7.

47. EBENSTEIN, M., AND L. I. KRAUS "Strategic Planning for Information Resource Management," *Management Review,* 7 (June 1981), 21–26.

48. EDEN, C., AND D. SIMS "Subjectivity in Problem Identification," *Interfaces,* 11, no. 1 (February 1981), 68–74.

49. ELAM, J. J., AND J. C. HENDERSON "Knowledge Engineering Concepts for Decision Support Design and Implementation," *Information and Management,* 6 (April 1983), 109–14.

50. EL SARVY, O. A. "Personal Information Systems for Strategic Scanning in Turbulent Environments: Can the CEO Go On-Line?" *MIS Quarterly,* 2, no. 1 (March 1985), 53–60.

51. ERBE, R., AND OTHERS "Integrated Data Analysis and Management for the Problem Solving Environment," *Information Systems,* 5 (1980), 273–85.

52. ERICKSEN, D. C. "A Synopsis of Present Day Practices concerning Decision Support Systems," *Information and Management,* 7 (October 1984), 243–52.

53. ETGAR, M., S. LICHT, AND P. SHRIVASTA "A Decision Support System for Strategic Marketing Decisions," *Systems, Objectives, Solutions,* 4, no. 3 (August 1984), 131–40.

54. FARWELL, D. C., AND T. FARWELL "Decision Support System for Ski Area Design," *Journal of Systems Management,* 33, no. 3 (March 1982), 32–37.

55. FERGUSON, R. L., AND C. H. JONES "A Computer Aided Decision System," *Management Science,* June 1969, B550–61.

56. FLAM, P. G. "User-Defined Information System Quality," *Journal of Systems Management,* 30, no. 8 (August 1979), 30–33.

57. FRANZ, L. S., S. M. LEE, AND J. C. VAN HORN "An Adaptive Decision Support System for Academic Resource Planning," *Decision Sciences,* 12, no. 2 (April 1981), 276–93.

58. FRIEND, DAVID "Executive Information Systems: Successes and Failures, Insights and Misconceptions," *Journal of Information Systems Management,* 3 (Fall 1986), 31–36.

59. FUERST, W. L., AND P. H. CHENEY "Factors Affecting the Perceived Utilization of Computer-Based Decision Support Systems in the Oil Industry," *Decision Sciences,* 13, no. 4 (October 1982), 554–69.

60. GERRITY, T. P. "Design of Man-Machine Decision Systems: An Application to Portfolio Management," *Sloan Management Review,* 12, no. 2 (Winter 1971), 59–75.

61. GINZBERG, M. J. "Finding an Adequate Measure of OR/MS Effectiveness," *Interfaces,* 8, no. 4 (August 1978), 59–62.

62. GINZBERG, M. J. "Redesign of Managerial Tasks: A Requisite for Successful Support Systems," *MIS Quarterly,* 2, no. 1 (March 1978), 39–52.

63. GORRY, G. A., AND M. S. SCOTT MORTON "A Framework for Management Information Systems," *Sloan Management Review,* 13, no. 1 (Fall 1971), 55–70.

64. GRACE, B. F. "Training Users of a Decision Support System," *Data Base,* 8, no. 3 (Winter 1977), 30–36.

65. GREER, W. J., JR. "Value Added Criterion for Decision Support System Development," *Journal of Systems Management,* 31 (May 1980), 15–19.

66. GRINDLAY, A. "Decision Support Systems," *Business Quarterly,* 45 (Summer 1980), 76–79.

67. HACKATHORN, R. D., AND P. G. W. KEEN "Organizational Strategies for Personal Computing in Decision Support Systems," *MIS Quarterly,* 5, no. 3 (September 1981), 21–26.

68. HAMILTON, W. F., AND M. A. MOSES "A Computer-Based Corporate Planning System," *Management Science,* 21, no. 2 (October 1974), 148–59.

69. HAMMOND, J. S., III "The Roles of the Manager and Management Scientists in Successful Implementation," *Sloan Management Review,* 15, no. 2 (Winter 1974), 1–24.

70. HASEMAN, W. D. "GPLAN: An Operational DSS," *Data Base,* 8, no. 3 (Winter 1977), 73–78.

71. HEHNEM, M. T., ET AL. "An Integrated Decision Support and Manufacturing Control System," *Interfaces,* 14, no. 5 (September–October 1984).

72. HENDERSON, J. C., AND P. C. NUTT "Influence of Decision Style on Decision Making Behavior," *Management Science,* 26, no. 4 (April 1980), 371–86.

73. HENDERSON, J. C., AND P. C. NUTT "On the Design of Planning Information Systems," *Academy of Management Review,* 3, No. 3 (October 1978), 774–85.

74. HOGUE, J. T., AND H. J. WATSON "Managements' Role in the Approval and Administration of Decision Support Systems," *MIS Quarterly,* 7, no. 2 (June 1983), 15–26.

75. HUBER, G. P. "The Nature of Organizational Decision Making and the Design of Decision Support Systems," *MIS Quarterly,* 5, no. 2 (June 1981), 1–10.

76. HUBER, G. P. "Cognitive Style as a Basis for MIS and DSS Designs: Much Ado about Nothing?" *Management Science,* 29, no. 5 (May 1983), 567–79.

77. HUBER, G. P. "Issues in the Design of Group Decision Support Systems," *MIS Quarterly,* 8, no. 3 (September 1984), 195–204.

78. HUFF, S. L. "DSS Development: Promise and Practice," *Journal of Information Systems Management,* 3 (Fall 1986), 8–15.

79. KEEN, P. G. W. "Adaptive Design for Decision Support Systems," *Data Base,* 12, nos. 1 and 2 (Fall 1980), 15–25.

80. KEEN, P. G. W. "Computer-Based Decision Aids: The Evaluation Problem," *Sloan Management Review,* 16, no. 3 (Spring 1975), 17–29.

81. KEEN, P. G. W. "Decision Support Systems: The Next Decade," *Decision Support Systems,* 3 (1987), 253–65.

82. KEEN, P. G. W. "Decision Support Systems: Translating Analytic Techniques into Useful Tools," *Sloan Management Review,* 21, no. 3 (Spring 1980), 33–44.

83. KEEN, P. G. W. "Interactive Computer Systems for Managers: A Modest Proposal," *Sloan Management Review,* 18, no. 1 (Fall 1976), 1–17.

84. KEEN, P. G. W. "Value Analysis: Justifying Decision Support Systems," *MIS Quarterly,* 5, no. 1 (March 1980), 1–16.

85. KEEN, P. G. W., AND G. R. WAGNER "DSS: An Executive Mind-Support System," *Datamation,* 25, no. 12 (November 1979), 117–22.

86. KING, W. R., AND D. I. CLELLAND "Decision and Information Systems for Strategic Planning," *Business Horizons,* April 1973, 29–36.

87. KING, W. R., AND J. I. RODRIQUEZ "Participative Design of Strategic Decision Support Systems," *Management Science,* 27, no. 6 (June 1981), 717–26.

88. KINGSTON, P. L. "Generic Decision Support Systems," *Managerial Planning,* 29 (March–April 1981), 7–11.

89. KLAAS, R. L. "A DSS for Airline Management," *Data Base,* 8, No. 3 (Winter 1977), 3–8.

90. KLING, R. "The Organizational Context of User-Centered Software Designs," *MIS Quarterly,* 1, no. 4 (December 1977), 41–52.

91. KOESTER, R., AND F. LUTHANS "The Impact of the Computer on the Choice Activity of Decision Makers: A Replication with Actual Users of Computerized MIS," *Academy of Management Journal,* 22, no. 2 (June 1979), 416–22.

92. KOSAKA, T., AND T. HIROUCHI "An Effective Architecture for Decision Support Systems," *Information and Management,* 5 (March 1982), 7–17.

93. LARRECHE, J., AND V. SRINIVASAN "STRATPORT: A Decision Support System for Strategic Planning," *Journal of Marketing,* 45 (Fall 1981), 39–52.

94. LEIGHTON, R. T. "Decision Support System," *Journal of Systems Management,* 32 (February 1981), 40–41.

95. LITTLE, J. D. C. "Decision Support Systems for Marketing Managers," *Journal of Marketing,* 43 (Summer 1979), 9–26.

96. LOCANDER, W. B., A. NAPIER, AND R. SCAMELL "A Team Approach to Managing the Development of a Decision Support System," *MIS Quarterly,* 3, no. 1 (March 1979), 53–63.

97. LUCAS, H. C., JR. "Experimental Investigation of the Use of Computer Based Graphics in Decision Making," *Management Science,* 27, no. 7 (July 1981), 757–68.

98. LUCAS, H. C., JR. "Empirical Evidence for a Description Model of Implementation," *MIS Quarterly,* 2, no. 2 (June 1978), 27–42.

99. LUCAS, H. C., JR. "The Evolution of an Information System: From Key-Man to Every Person," *Sloan Management Review,* 19, no. 2 (Winter 1980), 39–52.

100. MACINTOSH, NORMAN B., AND RICHARD L. DAFT "User Department Technology and Information Design," *Information and Management,* 1 (1978), 123–31.

101. MCCLEAN, E. R. "End Users as Application Developers," *MIS Quarterly,* 3, no. 4 (December 1979), 37–46.

102. MCCLEAN, E. R., AND T. F. RIESING "MAPP: A DSS for Financial Planning," *Data Base,* 3, no. 3 (Winter 1977), 9–14.

103. MCKENNEY, J. L., AND P. G. W. KEEN "How Managers' Minds Work," *Harvard Business Review,* May–June 1974, 79–90.

104. MEADOR, C. L., AND D. N. NESS "Decision Support Systems: An Application to Corporate Planning," *Sloan Management Review,* 16, no. 2 (Winter 1974), 51–68.

105. METHLIE, L. "Data Management for Decision Support Systems," *Data Base,* 12, nos. 1 and 2 (Fall 1980), 40–46.

106. MINTZBERG, H. "Managerial Work: Analysis from Observation," *Management Science,* 18, no. 2 (October 1971), B97–110.

107. MINTZBERG, H., D. RAISINGHANI, AND A. THEORET "The Structure of 'Unstructured' Decision Processes," *Administrative Science Quarterly,* 21, no. 2 (June 1976), 246–75.

108. MOSES, M. A. "Implementation of Analytical Planning Systems," *Management Science,* 21, no. 10 (June 1975), 1133–43.

109. NAYLOR, T. H. "Effective Use of Strategic Planning, Forecasting, and Modeling in the Executive Suite," *Managerial Planning,* 30, no. 4 (January–February 1982), 4–11.

110. NAYLOR, THOMAS H. "Decision Support Systems or Whatever Happened to M.I.S.?" *Interfaces,* 12, no. 4 (August 1982), 92–97.

111. NESS, D. N., AND C. R. SPRAGUE "An Interactive Media Decision Support System," *Sloan Management Review,* 14, no. 1 (Fall 1972), 51–61.

112. NEUMANN, S., AND M. HADASS "Decision Support Systems and Strategic Decisions," *California Management Review,* 22, no. 2 (Spring 1980), 77–84.

113. NUNAMAKER, J. F., L. M. APPLEGATE, AND B. R. KONSYNSKI "Facilitating Group Creativity: Experience with a Group Decision Support System," *Journal of Management Information Systems,* 3, no. 4 (Spring 1987), 5–19.

114. NYWEIDE, J. O. "Decision Support through Automated Human Resource Systems," *Magazine of Bank Administration,* 62, no. 5 (November 1986), 60–62.

115. PARTOW-NAVID, P. "Misuse and Disuse of DSS Models," *Journal of Systems Management,* 38, no. 4 (April 1987), 38–40.

116. PRASTACOS, G. P., AND E. BRODHEIM "PBDS: A Decision Support System for Regional Blood Management," *Management Science,* 26, no. 5 (May 1980), 451–63.

117. RECK, R. H., AND J. R. HALL "Executive Information Systems: An Overview of Development," *Journal of Information Systems Management,* 3 (Fall 1986), 25–30.

118. REMUS, W. E., AND J. KOTTERMAN "Toward Intelligent Decision Support Systems: An Artificially Intelligent Statistician," *MIS Quarterly,* 10, no. 4 (December 1986).

119. RICHMAN, L. S. "Software Catches the Team Spirit," *Fortune,* September 1985, 125–36.

120. ROBEY, D., AND D. FARROW "User Involvement in Information System Development," *Management Science,* 28, no. 1 (January 1982), 73–85.

121. ROBEY, D., AND W. TAGGART "Human Information Processing in Information and Decision Support Systems," *MIS Quarterly,* 6, no. 2 (June 1982), 61–73.

122. ROBEY, D., AND W. TAGGART "Measuring Managers' Minds: The Assessment of Style in Human Information Processing," *Academy of Management Review,* 6, no. 2 (July 1981), 375–83.

123. ROCKART, J. F., AND M. E. TREACY "The CEO Goes On-Line," *Harvard Business Review,* 60, no. 1 (January–February 1982), 32–38.

124. ROLAND, R. "A Model of Organizational Variables for DSS," *Data·Base,* 12, nos. 1 and 2 (Fall 1980), 63–72.

125. ROY, A., A. DeFALOMIR, AND L. LASDON "An Optimization Based Decision Support System for a Product Mix Problem," *Interfaces,* 12, no. 2 (April 1982), 26–33.

126. RUCKS, A. C., AND P. M. GINTER "Strategic MIS: Promises Unfulfilled," *Journal of Systems Management,* 33 (March 1982), 16–19.

127. SANDERS, L. C., J. F. COURTNEY, AND S. L. LOY "The Impact of DSS on Organizational Communication," *Information and Management,* 7 (June 1984), 141–48.

128. SEABURG, R. A., AND C. SEABURG "Computer-Based Decision Systems in Xerox Corporate Planning," *Management Science,* 20, no. 4 (December 1973), 575–84.

129. SHORE, B., AND T. J. WHARTON "Analysis of Microcomputer DSS Projects," *Journal of Systems Management,* 37, no. 6 (June 1986), 25–31.

130. SPRAGUE, R. H., JR. "Conceptual Description of a Financial Planning Model for Commercial Banks," *Decision Sciences,* 2, no. 1 (January 1971), 66–80.

131. SPRAGUE, R. H., JR. "The Financial Planning System at the Louisiana National Bank," *MIS Quarterly,* 3, no. 3 (September 1979), 1–11.

132. SPRAGUE, R. H., JR. "Systems Support for a Financial Planning Model," *Management Accounting,* 53, no. 6 (June 1972), 29–34.

133. SPRAGUE, R. H., JR., AND H. J. WATSON "Bit by Bit: Toward Decision Support Systems," *California Management Review,* 22, no. 1 (Fall 1979), 60–68.

134. SPRAGUE, R. H., JR., AND H. J. WATSON "A Decision Support System for Banks," *Omega: The International Journal of Management Science,* 4, no. 6 (1976), 657–71.

135. SPRAGUE, R. H., JR., AND H. J. WATSON "MIS Concepts: Part I," *Journal of Systems Management,* 26, no. 1 (January 1975), 34–37.

136. SPRAGUE, R. H., JR., AND H. J. WATSON "MIS Concepts: Part II," *Journal of Systems Management,* 26, no. 2 (February 1975), 35–40.

137. STEFIK, M., ET AL. "Beyond the Chalkboard: Computer Support for Collaboration and Problem Solving in Meetings," *Communications of the ACM,* 30, no. 1 (January 1987), 32–47.

138. STOTT, K. L., JR., AND B. W. DOUGLAS "A Model-Based Decision Support System for Planning and Scheduling Ocean Borne Transportation," *Interfaces,* 11, no. 4 (August 1981), 1–10.

139. SUSSMAN, P. N. "Evaluating Decision Support Software," *Datamation,* 30 (October 1984), 171–72.

140. TURBAN, E., AND P. R. WATKINS "Integrating Expert Systems and Decision Support Systems," *MIS Quarterly,* 10, no. 2 (June 1986), 121–36.

141. VAZSONYI, A. "Decision Support Systems: The New Technology of Decision Making?" *Interfaces,* 9, no. 1 (November 1978), 72–77.

142. VAZSONYI, A. "Decision Support Systems, Computer Literacy, and Electronic Models," *Interfaces,* 12, no. 1 (February 1982), 74–78.

143. VIERCK, R. K. "Decision Support Systems: An MIS Manager's Perspective," *MIS Quarterly,* 5, no. 4 (December 1981), 35–48.

144. WAGNER, G. R. "Decision Support Systems: Computerized Mind Support for Executive Problems," *Managerial Planning,* 30, no. 2 (September–October 1981), 9–16.

145. WAGNER, G. R. "DSS: Dealing with Executive Assumptions in the Office of the Future," *Managerial Planning,* 30, no. 5 (March–April 1982), 4–10.

146. WAGNER, G. R. "Decision Support Systems: The Real Substance," *Interfaces,* 11, no. 2 (April 1981), 77–86.

147. WATKINS, P. R. "Perceived Information Structure: Implications for Decision Support System Design," *Decision Sciences,* 13, no. 1 (January 1982), 38–59.

148. WATKINS, P. R. "Preference Mapping of Perceived Information Structure: Implications for Decision Support Systems Design," *Decision Sciences,* 15, no. 1 (Winter 1984), 92–106.

149. WATSON, H. J., AND M. M. HILL "Decision Support Systems or What Didn't Happen with MIS," *Interfaces,* 13, no. 5 (October 1983), 81–88.

150. WATSON, H. J., AND R. I. MANN "Expert Systems: Past, Present, and Future," *Journal of Information Systems Management,* 5 (Fall 1988).

151. WHITE, K. B. "Dynamic Decision Support Teams," *Journal of Systems Management,* 36, no. 6 (June 1984), 26–31.

152. WILL, H. J. "MIS—Mirage or Mirror Image?" *Journal of Systems Management,* September 1973, 24–31.

153. WYNNE, B. "Decision Support Systems—A New Plateau of Opportunity or More Emperor's New-Clothing?" *Interfaces,* 12, no. 1 (February 1982), 88–91.

154. WYNNE, B., AND G. W. DICKSON "Experienced Managers' Performance in Experimental Man-Machine Decision System Simulation," *Academy of Management Journal,* 18, no. 1 (March 1975), 25–40.

155. WYNNE, B. "A Domination Sequence—MS/OR, DSS, and the Fifth Generation," *Interfaces,* 14, no. 3 (May–June 1984), 51–58.

156. YOUNG, L. F. "Another Look at Man-Computer Interaction," *Interfaces,* 8, no. 2 (February 1978), 67–69.

157. ZALUD, B. "Decision Support Systems—Push End User in Design/Build Stage," *Data Management,* 19, no. 1 (January 1981), 20–22.

CATEGORIES OF DSS ARTICLES

GENERAL OVERVIEW

32, 66, 85, 88, 94, 111, 127, 134, 136, 138, 143, 144, 145, 146, 147, 154

RELATIONSHIP WITH O*R/MS* AND *MIS*

19, 21, 94, 136, 138, 142, 114, 151, 153, 156

DSS FRAMEWORK

8, 44, 56, 63, 78, 134

PLANNING FOR *DSS* (JUSTIFICATION FOR DEVELOPMENT)

52, 65, 74, 84, 115, 122, 129

DEVELOPMENT PROCESS

Design (adaptive, iterative, evolutionary, etc.): 10, 18, 36, 49, 79, 100, 120
User involvement: 2, 6, 56, 62, 87, 90, 96, 101, 121, 157
Organizational variables: 25, 38, 72, 75, 90, 100, 106, 125
Others: 6, 22, 78, 96

SOFTWARE INTERFACE

Impact of cognitive style: 17, 43, 72, 76, 124
Impact on decision making: 16, 91, 97, 122
Others: 26, 27, 83, 90, 134, 138

MODEL SUBSYSTEM

Modeling of decision making: 11, 20, 25, 48, 103, 107
Human information processing: 122, 148, 149
Others: 14, 21, 24, 27, 92, 110, 134, 136, 138, 146

DATABASE SUBSYSTEM

21, 23, 30, 40, 51, 92, 110, 134, 136, 138

INTEGRATING THE SOFTWARE INTERFACE, MODELS, AND DATA

92, 136, 138

INTEGRATING *DSS* INTO THE ORGANIZATION

Implementation: 2, 5, 6, 37, 46, 59, 61, 69, 82, 98, 108, 109, 155
Training: 62, 64
Relationship with management: 47, 82, 96, 116, 157
Use of intermediaries: 7, 83, 152, 157

EVALUATION OF *DSS*

4, 61, 80, 98, 99, 122, 141

APPLICATIONS OF *DSS*

Banking: 33, 131, 132, 135
Transportation/distribution: 3, 9, 89, 139
Financial planning: 34, 102, 131, 132, 133, 145
Corporate and strategic planning: 68, 73, 86, 93, 104, 110, 116, 130
Marketing: 53, 95, 124
Academia: 45, 57
Manufacturing: 12, 35, 71
Others: 13, 15, 28, 29, 32, 35, 39, 42, 47, 54, 55, 60, 70, 85, 112, 120

EXECUTIVE INFORMATION SYSTEMS

50, 58, 117, 123

EXPERT SYSTEMS

2, 118, 140, 150

GROUP DECISION SUPPORT SYSTEMS

41, 77, 113, 119, 137

FUTURE OF *DSS*

19, 22, 28, 143

Index